Advances in Database Programming Languages

ACM PRESS

Editor-in-Chief:

Peter Wegner, *Brown University*

ACM Press books represent a collaboration between the Association for Computing Machinery (ACM) and Addison-Wesley Publishing Company to develop and publish a broad range of new works. These works generally fall into one of four series.

Frontier Series. Books focused on novel and exploratory material at the leading edge of computer science and practice.

Anthology Series. Collected works of general interest to computer professionals and/or society at large.

Tutorial Series. Introductory books to help nonspecialists quickly grasp either the general concepts or the needed details of some specific topic.

History Series. Books documenting past developments in the field and linking them to the present.

In addition, ACM Press books include selected conference and workshop proceedings.

Advances in Database Programming Languages

Edited by

François Bancilhon

Altaïr

Peter Buneman

University of Pennsylvania

ACM PRESS
New York, New York

Addison-Wesley Publishing Company

Reading, Massachusetts · Menlo Park, California · New York
Don Mills, Ontario · Wokingham, England · Amsterdam · Bonn
Sydney · Singapore · Tokyo · Madrid · San Juan

Chapter 18: Copyright, 1987, Incremental Systems Corporation. This work was supported in part by the Department of Defense, Defense Advanced Research Projects Agency, Order No. 5057, monitored by the Department of the Navy, Space and Naval Warfare Systems Command, under contract No. N00039-85-C-0126. Approved for Public Release, Distribution Unlimited.

Many of the designations used by manufacturers and sellers to distinguish their products are claimed as trademarks. Where those designations appear in this book, and Addison-Wesley was aware of a trademark claim, the designations have been printed in caps or initial caps.

The programs and applications presented in this book have been included for their instructional value. They have been tested with care, but are not guaranteed for any particular purpose. The publisher does not offer any warranties or representations, nor does it accept any liabilities with respect to the programs or applications.

Library of Congress Cataloging-in-Publication Data

Advances in database programming languages / edited by François
   Bancilhon, Peter Buneman.
        p.   cm. — (Frontier series)
     Includes bibliographical references.
     ISBN 0-201-50257-7
     1. Data base management.   I. Bancilhon, François.   II. Buneman,
Peter, 1943– .   III. Series: Frontier series (New York, N.Y.)
   QA76.9.D3A348   1990
   005.74—dc20   89–37181
                                                            CIP

ACM Press Frontier Series
Instrumentation for Future Parallel Computer Systems

First printed 1990

Copyright © 1990 by the ACM Press, A Division of the Association for Computing Machinery, Inc. (ACM).

ABCDEFGHIJ-MA-943210

CONTRIBUTORS

Serge Abiteboul
INRIA
Le Chesnay, France

Peter M. G. Apers
University of Twente
The Netherlands

Guy Argo
Glasgow University
Glasgow, Scotland

Malcolm Atkinson
Department of Computing Science
University of Glasgow
Glasgow, Scotland

Paolo Atzeni
Dipartimento di Informatica
  e Sistemistica
Universita degli studi di Napoli
Napoli, Italy

Deborah A. Baker
Incremental Systems Corporation
Pittsburgh, PA

David Beech
Hewlett-Packard Laboratories
Palo Alto, CA

Kim B. Bruce
Department of Computer Science
Williams College
Williamstown, MA

Michael Caruso
Computer Science Department
Boston University
Boston, MA

Michelle Connolly
Department of Computer Science
Queen's University of Belfast
Belfast, Ireland

Jon Fairbairn
Glasgow University
Glasgow, Scotland

David A. Fisher
Incremental Systems Corporation
Pittsburgh, PA

Stéphane Grumbach
INRIA
Le Chesnay, France

Maurice A. W. Houtsma
University of Twente
The Netherlands

J. G. Hughes
Department of Computer Science
Queen's University of Belfast
Belfast, Ireland

John Hughes
Glasgow University
Glasgow, Scotland

Richard Hull
Computer Science Department
University of Southern California
Los Angeles, CA

Dean Jacobs
Computer Science Department
University of Southern California
Los Angeles, CA

Paris Kanellakis
Department of Computer Science
Brown University
Providence, RI

Setrag Khoshafian
Microelectronics and Computer
   Technology Corporation
Austin, Texas

Ravi Krishnamurthy
MCC
Austin, Texas

M. Lacroix
Philips Research Laboratory
Brussels, Belgium

John Launchbury
Glasgow University
Glasgow, Scotland

Christophe Lecluse
Altaïr
INRIA
Le Chesnay, France

Maurizio Lenzerini
Dipartimento di Informatica
   e Sistemistica
Universita degli Studi di Roma
   "La Sapienza"
Roma, Italy

David Maier
Oregon Graduate Center
Beaverton, OR

David C. J. Matthews
Computer Laboratory
Cambridge University
Cambridge, England

Ronald Morrison
Department of Computational
   Science
University of St. Andrews
St. Andrews, Scotland

J. Eliot B. Moss
Department of Computer and
   Information Science
University of Massachusetts
Amherst, MA

John Mylopoulos
Department of Computer Science
University of Toronto
Toronto, Canada

Shamim Naqvi
Bellcore
Morristown, NJ

Rishiyur S. Nikhil
MIT Laboratory for Computer
   Science
Cambridge, MA

Brian Nixon
Department of Computer Science
University of Toronto
Toronto, Canada

Atsushi Ohori
Department of Computer Science
University of Glasgow
Glasgow, Scotland

D. Stott Parker Jr.
Computer Science Department
UCLA
Los Angeles, CA

Peter Z. Revesz
Department of Computer Science
Brown University
Providence, RI

Philippe Richard
Altaïr
INRIA
Le Chesnay, France

Edward Sciore
Computer Science Department
Boston University
Boston, MA

Tim Sheard
Department of Computer and
   Information Science
University of Massachusetts
Amherst, MA

Jonathan C. Shultis
Incremental Systems Corporation
Pittsburgh, PA

David Stemple
Department of Computer and
   Information Science
University of Massachusetts
Amherst, MA

Philip Trinder
Glasgow University
Glasgow, Scotland

Patrick Valduriez
Microelectronics and Computer
   Technology Corporation
Austin, Texas

M. Vanhoedenaghe
Philips Research Laboratory
Brussels, Belgium

Fernando Velez
Altaïr
INRIA
Le Chesnay, France

Peter Wegner
Department of Computer Science
Brown University
Providence, RI

Carlo Zaniolo
MCC
Austin, TX

Stanley B. Zdonik
Department of Computer Science
Brown University
Providence, RI

CONTENTS

II IMPLEMENTATION ISSUES

III OBJECT-ORIENTED SYSTEMS AND PERSISTENCE

FOREWORD

Recent research in database programming languages will, we believe, be of interest not only to the academic community but also to any software development group that is contemplating the use of a new language or database system. Although much further development is needed to achieve an ideal language (and, of course, opinions differ about the nature of this ideal) there is a growing number of commercial products that are intended as database programming languages. Several of the papers may help to provide an understanding of the power of these new systems and how they compare to the traditional multilingual and multisystem approach to database applications.

In September 1987 a meeting was held in Roscoff, France, to bring together a number of researchers and implementors who have a practical interest in database programming. This collection of papers is based on the presentations that were originally given at that meeting. One of the results of this meeting was the emergence of common interests among researchers in several areas of computer science: databases, programming languages, software engineering, and logic programming. While the subject of database programming languages is still in its infancy we hope that this collection conveys these common interests.

PREFACE

The need for a uniform database programming environment for database applications will be well appreciated by anyone who has had to write large database applications using the techniques that are currently available. Programming tasks that cannot be expressed in a simple query language generally require the programmer to be bi- or trilingual, requiring knowledge of a host language, an embedded query language, and possibly a data definition language. Moreover, traffic between the host language and the database generally consists of sequentially controlled transfer of a large number of small pieces of data such as integers or strings. Transfer at any higher level is generally impossible because the larger structures available in the database cannot be made to match any structure available in the language. The idea in database programming languages is to solve this problem by making database management an integral part of the programming language. This requires that persistent database structures should appear as structures that can be directly manipulated in the language, which in turn may require an extension of the types or classes available in the programming language to accommodate these persistent structures. In addition one would want the database issues of concurrency and transaction processing to be addressed by the language. General surveys of database programming languages and object-oriented databases are to be found in Atkinson [1987] and Bancilhon [1988].

Although research in database programming languages has recently intensified, the subject has a history which, when measured against that of computer science, is quite extensive. Credit for the realization of a programming language with integrated database management must surely go to Pascal/R [Schmidt, 1977], which was developed in the mid 1970s. This language demonstrated a simple extension to Pascal which allowed the manipulation of relations together with the appropriate mechanisms to support persistence and efficiency. One of the important lessons of this language was that the type system of a language could be cleanly extended to accommodate the relational data model; thus the definition of the database schema is simply a type declaration in Pascal/R.

A second important step was the demonstration, in PS-algol [Atkinson, et al., 1983], that it is possible to design a programming language with uniform *persistence*. In PS-algol, data of any type may persist: the persistent structures are not limited to being files or relations; moreover the programmer does not explicitly control data movement between, say, primary and secondary storage—a value persists whenever it has a persistent label or is a part of some structure with a persistent label. With a general form of persistence it is possible to maintain databases that contain a variety of different data structures such as large bitmaps or complicated pointer structures that are typically used in "nonstandard" engineering databases.

At the same time various research groups started to think about languages that might incorporate more sophisticated data models. The idea of *inheritance*, which has been widely discussed in artificial intelligence, databases, and programming languages, was an ingredient of various prototype languages [Albano, 1985; Mylopoulos, 1980]. Not long after, with the simple expedient of adding persistence to object-oriented languages [Copeland and Maier, 1984], another approach to a database programming language that supported inheritance emerged that gave rise to the name "object-oriented" databases.

During this period, a more theoretical component of the database community was investigating the connection between logic and databases. From this emerged a number of interesting languages based on logic programming. It is still an open question as to whether these languages have either the expressive power or an implementation efficiency that will allow them to be of widespread practical use. However some implementations are beginning to emerge, and it is well worth comparing these new languages with existing languages both for expressive power and for efficiency.

From the history of the subject, it is apparent that one of the main issues involved in the integration of databases and programming languages is the representation of a database schema within the type system of the language. This is the subject of the first section, *Types and Inheritance*, of this collection. It emerges from these papers that inheritance is used in different ways for different purposes. In particular, in object-oriented languages inheritance is a mechanism used to specify code sharing, while in databases it is a structural property of data models and may require a sophisticated type system or some system of constraints to capture.

Notably in the field of object-oriented databases, a number of commercial products and several prototype languages have recently been developed. In the part *Implementation Issues* there are contributions both from implementors and from language designers that indicate some of the practical issues and the principles that govern implementation of a successful language. In particular, this section includes a number of different paradigms (functional, object-oriented, etc.) for database programming.

Several of the papers in *Object-Oriented Systems and Persistence* deal with issues that arise when persistence is added to a language. For example, at the top level a database is usually a collection of named structures, and it is such a collection—a namespace—that is the usual form of persistent structure. What operations should be available on namespaces, and how do they interact with the type system of the language? If there is dynamic manipulation of namespaces, does this call for dynamic type checking? From an object-oriented standpoint it appears that something more than persistent objects are called for in database work; we need to have some way of capturing "extents" or sets of objects associated with some class.

As we have already noted there has been extensive activity in trying to bring the elegant formulation of deductive databases—pure Datalog—to a point where it can be used as a practical language. Among other things, we need to represent updates, sets, and functions within the language. The papers in the *Logic* part are all connected with these issues and come from groups where there is a practical implementation effort underway.

Finally the *raison d'être* of the Roscoff workshop was that database programming languages are essential for the future of database applications. But is it possible that by trying to achieve this high level of system integration, we are losing the simplicity, efficiency, or reliability that the various components of traditional database programming environments give us? In the final part on *Database Programming Languages* some papers present alternative views on the subject. Others also indicate how database programming might relate to other areas programming languages and software engineering. After all, what is a software environment but a database of programs?

We would like to acknowledge the help of Dawn Griesbach and Glenda Kent in typesetting this book. We would also like to thank Peter Wegner, Helen Goldstein, and Peter Gordon for their advice.

Bibliography

Albano, A., Cardelli, L., and Orsini, R., (1985). "Galileo: A strongly typed interactive conceptual language," *ACM Transactions on Database Systems*, Vol. 10, No. 2, March.

Atkinson, M. P., Bailey, P. J., Chisholm, K. J., Cockshott, W. P., and Morrison, R., (1983). "An approach to persistent programming," *Computer Journal*, Vol. 26, No. 4, November.

Atkinson, M. P., and Buneman, O. P., (1987). "Types and Persistence in Database Programming Languages," *ACM Computer Surveys*, June.

Bancilhon, F., (1988). "Object-oriented database systems," *PODS*, March.

Copeland, G., and Maier, D., (1984). "Making Smalltalk a database system," *Proceedings of SIGMOD 84*, Vol. 14, No. 2, June, pp. 316–325.

Mylopoulos, J., Bernstein, P. A., and Wong, H. K. T., (1980). "A language facility for designing database intensive applications," *ACM Transactions on Database Systems*, Vol. 5, No. 2, June.

Schmidt, J. W., (1977). "Some high level language constructs for data of type relation," *ACM Transactions on Database Systems*, Vol. 2, No. 3, September, pp. 247–281.

François Bancilhon
Altaïr

Peter Buneman
University of Pennsylvania

PART I

TYPES AND INHERITANCE

CHAPTER 1

CONSTRUCTION AND CALCULUS OF TYPES FOR DATABASE SYSTEMS

David Stemple
Tim Sheard

1.1 INTRODUCTION

Database systems should allow the construction of types for the kinds of complex objects used in modern applications such as design systems and artificial intelligence applications. In addition to complex structures, the type system should incorporate encapsulation and inheritance features appropriate to such applications. Furthermore, arbitrary constraint specification should be a feature of such a type system in order to bind the systems to the semantics of the occasion. Incorporating these features in a database system specification language must be done very carefully in order to produce a facility that

1. Can be used effectively by database system designers.
2. Can be implemented efficiently.
3. Supports the kinds of mechanical reasoning required to satisfy 1 and 2.

The ADABTPL system under development at the University of Massachusetts represents an attempt to provide the features and meet the requirements just listed. The following aspects of ADABTPL are designed to make the system usable by database designers:

1. Schema and transaction program model of system specification
2. Database in the name space of transaction programs (no I/O)
3. Relational model a subset of the data model
4. Robust feedback on design of transactions in the presence of constraints
5. Rapid prototype capability

The mechanical reasoning required to verify that transactions obey all integrity constraints and to provide robust feedback to designers is facilitated by

1. Basing the formal semantics of the schema structures on a few abstract data types—tuples, lists, finite sets, and natural numbers—that are predefined axiomatically.
2. Using computational logic along with the recursive function semantics of the the ADABTPL language to build a usable theory of constraints and updates of complex objects.
3. Using higher order theory and polymorphic types to make theorem proving more efficient.

The ADABTPL type system is an essential element in the support of both mechanical reasoning and usability, and it contains the following features:

☐ A type construction approach with embedded constraints
☐ Parametric polymorphic types = user-defined type constructor functions
☐ Encapsulated abstract data types
☐ Multiple inheritance
☐ Constraints specifiable on function input and checked at compile time (verified) on all calls
☐ Type conditions specifiable on type parameters

In this paper we present features of the ADABTPL type specification language and discuss the criteria used to choose and form those features. We will take care to motivate the limitations we have placed on certain sophisticated features such as recursive types and inheritance.

A database system is specified in ADABTPL by defining the type of the database object and writing transactions to define the operations allowable on the database object. Transactions are written in the ADABTPL procedural language which is a high-level, set-oriented language whose namespace comprises the components of the database object and the transaction input variables. The database type is specified in the ADABTPL schema language, which is a type definition language that includes a predicate language for defining constraints on any type, including the types of all constituents of the database as well as the database type itself. Both procedural and schema languages include a function definition language for defining predicate and object functions. In the rest of the paper we will describe the salient features of the type definition.

1.2 CONSTRUCTION OF STRUCTURAL TYPES

The basic type constructors of ADABTPL can be used to specify types for "simple" objects such as tuples, finite sets, and lists. The first two of these constructors allow the specification of first normal form relation types. For example, the following defines a simple employee relation.

EmpTuple = [EmpNo: Integer, EmpName: String, EmpDept: Integer];
EmpRel = Set(EmpTuple)

The definition of EmpTuple uses the brackets to form a tuple type and then that type is used as input to the finite set type constructor written as a prefix function. Of course, the tuple type could have been left anonymous as in

EmpRel = Set([EmpNo: Integer, EmpName: String, EmpDept:
          Integer])

A tuple type may not contain a component that is either of the tuple type itself or depend in any way on it, except in the recursive union type described as follows.

Constraints are specified in where clauses of type defining equations. They may be specified in any definition. For example, to constrain a range for employee numbers (EmpNo) and to constrain the employee relation to be keyed on EmpNo, we write

EmpTuple = [EmpNo: Integer, EmpName: String, EmpDept: Integer]
    where EmpNo < 10000;

EmpRel = Set(EmpTuple) where Key(EmpRel, EmpNo)

These definitions illustrate two features of constraints. The first is that component names in tuple types can be used as variables in where clauses, for example, in the EmpTuple definition. Our semantic capture of component names is as axiomatized functions on the elements of the tuple type. A tuple type definition also creates an axiomatized constructor function for elements of the type. This function can have its name supplied by the user, but has been left as the default, MakeEmpTuple, in the example. The main axioms specifying the behavior of the constructor and selector functions are similar to the following for MakeEmpTuple and EmpNo.

$$EmpNo(MakeEmpTuple(e, n, d)) = n$$

where e, n, and d are variables universally quantified over their appropriate types. Thus, the constraint on the EmpTuple type corresponds to the axiom

$$EmpNo(t) < 10000$$

for t universally quantified over the EmpTuple type.

The Key constraint on EmpRel uses another naming convention that allows the type name to stand for an element of the type in a where clause. Key is a predicate function that takes a set of tuples and a list of component names (selector functions) and returns true if the component names determine unique values over the set. Other functions, including user-defined functions, may be used in where clauses. Thus, the constraint language is open-ended. (It must be noted that the ability to reason effectively about constraints, though open, is at any time limited by the theory that has been developed by that time. The system reasons from lemmas that are kept in its knowledge base and is limited by this extendable resource (see [Sheard and Stemple, 1986]).

In order to specify interrelational constraints in a relational database, a where clause is added to the database type definition that must end any ADABTPL schema. For example, to define referential integrity for the department number in EmpRel, the following would be written.

```
EmpTuple = [EmpNo: Integer, EmpName: String, EmpDept: Integer]
    where EmpNo < 10000;

EmpRel = Set(EmpTuple) where Key(EmpRel, EmpNo)

DeptRel = Set([DeptNum: Integer, DeptName: String, NumberOfEmps:
            Integer]);

Database EmployeeDB: [Emps: EmpRel, Depts: DeptRel]
    where Contains(Depts.DeptNum, Emps.EmpDept) and
        For all d in Depts:
            d.NumberOfEmps = Count(All e in Emps
                where e.EmpDept = d.DeptNum)
```

The second constraint requires the NumberOfEmps component of all Depts tuples to be the count of Emps tuples matching in the department number components. In this we see an example of the ADABTPL predicate language including universal quantification over a set (For all), projection (denoted by the dot folowing a variable that ranges over a relation), and selection (denoted by the All phrase). Note that EmployeeDB constitutes the only identifier that plays the role of a programming language variable. In the transaction specifications that complete the database system definition, the component names of the database tuple are used as variables much as in the where clauses of tuple type definitions.

The discussion so far has given a brief view of how a simple database schema can be written in ADABTPL. The following should be observed. Declaring a tuple type does not declare a type for a collection of tuple instances. Even a declaration of a relation type does not declare that one relation of that type will be maintained in the database. The constitution of the database is declared in the database declaration that completes a schema. It is only at this point that relations and their tuples are declared to be maintained as instances. There are a number of reasons for this. The main two are a desire to maintain independence of particular semantic data models (ADABTPL is a generic data model in that it can model a large number of different semantic data models) and the desire to keep everything explicit and directly translatable into axiomatic, functional semantics. One result of this is that non–first normal form relations as well as nonrelational database components are simple to specify. The following example demonstrates the ease with which non–first normal form relations and nonrelational data is accommodated.

```
Task = [RequestDate: date, RequestTime: time, Requester: String,
        TaskDescr: String]

TaskQueue = Set([Priority: Integer, TaskList: List(Task)])
   where Key(TaskQueue, Priority) and
      not (TaskList = NIL)

EmpTuple = [EmpNo: Integer, EmpName: String, EmpDept: Integer,
            Tasks: TaskQueue]
   where EmpNo < 10000;

EmpRel = Set(EmpTuple) where Key(EmpRel, EmpNo)

Database EmpTaskDB: [Emps: EmpsRel, TotalTasks: Integer]
```

Note that Emps is no longer a first normal form relation and that Total-Tasks is not even a relation. TaskQueue defines the structure for a priority queue object containing non-empty lists of task descriptions paired with unique priorities. The design could be refined further to constrain operations on TaskQueue objects to obey queue protocol and to guarantee that the TotalTasks component of the database always reflects the total number of tasks queued for all employees(see [Stemple, et al., 1986]). These examples, though limited, give the essential flavor of the basic ADABTPL features for specifying the structure of databases along with integrity constraints. Advanced features of the language include refined, parametric, union, recursive, and encapsulated types, most of which are used to achieve and control inheritance. We now turn to the ADABTPL means of dealing with inheritance.

1.3 INHERITANCE

Inheritance is one type's acquisition of a property by virtue of its being a subtype of another type. The fundamental property involved in inheritance is the eligibility of instances of types to be passed as arguments to functions. Other uses of inheritance are extant, for example, as an implementation aid (allowing reusable generic code) and as part of a logic programming computational paradigm [Ait-Kaci, 1984]. The subtype relationship among types can be based on the inclusion relationship among the types' value sets or among the operations allowed by the types. Each of these bases for subtyping has its use, and both are supplied by ADABTPL type constructors.

The simplest subtyping in ADABTPL is based on subsets of value sets and is accomplished by using the where constructor. For example,

   Person = [Name: String; Age: Number; Gender: (male, female)];
   OldPerson = Person where Age > 80;

creates a subtype relationship making OldPerson a subtype of Person.

Subranges create the same kind of subtype relationship that the where clause does. For example,

   SmallNumber = 1..9

makes SmallNumber a subtype of Number. Note that any SmallNumber can be used as input to any function requiring a Number, but the closure properties of functions may not be preserved. For example, although SmallNumbers can be added, the results may not be SmallNumbers.

While value set subsetting is a convenient and useful method of subtyping, it is not sufficient for building robust, well-controlled systems. For this we need to control inheritance in ways that speak more to the behavior of types than to the set of legitimate instances. In order to illustrate the means for controlling inheritance in ADABTPL, we now turn to a lattice capture of the subtyping achievable in ADABTPL and enumerate the type constructors and their effects on the type lattice.

1.4 THE TYPE LATTICE AND ITS CONSTRUCTION

It is useful to place types in a lattice based on the subtype relation, where the LUB of the structure is called UNIVERSE (the type on which almost no functions operate, but which, when thought of as a set, contains all objects); and where the GLB of the structure is called EMPTY, (the type on which all functions operate, but which, when thought of as a set, contains no objects). If x is a subtype of y then x is "lower" in the structure than y. For example, the OldPerson and Person types as previously defined yield the following lattice.

```
UNIVERSE
    *
    *
Person
    *
    *
OldPerson
    *
    *
EMPTY
```

Thus, in general, as one moves down the structure the types have more and more functions defined on them, but the sets defined by the types have fewer and fewer elements.

Equivalent types appear as types with horizontal arcs in the lattice. For example,

Age = Number

causes

```
UNIVERSE
    * *
    *  *
    *   *
Number *** Age
    *   *
    *  *
    * *
EMPTY
```

We will now go through the type defining constructs of ADABTPL and show their effects on the type lattice.

1.4.1 With

The With clause explicitly creates subtypes by adding new components to preexisting types. Thus the value set of a subtype created by a With has no overlap with its supertype. (Though the obvious projection on the subtype value set is equal to the supertype.) However, the semantics of the With construct is to allow all functions defined on the base type to be defined on the new type in addition to the new component names (which are selector functions). As an example of a subtype created using With, a Student type can be constucted from Person as follows:

Person = [Name: String; Age: Number; Gender: (male, female)];
Student = Person With [GPA: Number];

The type following the With keyword must be a tuple type. In this example it specifies a new function, GPA from Student to Number. It also declares that Student is a subtype of Person. The following type, though structurally equivalent to Student, is not considered a subtype of Person in ADABTPL.

Student2 = [Name: String; Age: Number; Gender: (male, female);
            GPA: Number];

We reason that if the user wants two tuple types with nested component structure to be related by the subtype relation, he or she will use the With clause, otherwise two similar types are not subtypes.

```
          UNIVERSE
             * * *
           *   *   *
          *    *    *
         *     *     *
        *            *
    Person...Student2
       *           *
       *     *     *
       *     *     *
    Student *      *
       *    *      *
        *   *     *
         *   *   *
          * * *
          EMPTY
```

1.4.2 Parametric Types

A parametric type is a new type constructor which takes types as input and returns a new type. A parametric type is to types as functions are to objects

[Cardelli and Wegner, 1985]. In ADABTPL, parametric types are defined using a parenthesized parameter notation. We can identify a parametric type with the union of all types that can be produced by all substitutions for the type parameters, and place the parametric type above any type produced by supplying a concrete type for any of the type parameters. For example,

WeightedObject(Alpha) = [Object: Alpha; Weight: Number]

defines a parametric type with parameter Alpha. Alpha is a type variable and stands for any type. When it is instantiated then the expression stands for a concrete type. For example,

WeightedBoolean = WeightedObject(Boolean)

stands for

WeightedBoolean = [Object: Boolean; Weight: Number]

In addition to user-defined parametric types there are some system-defined parametric types as well. The List, Set, and Array types are in this class. The List and Set types take the element type as input, while the Array type takes two types as input, an index type and an element type. List and Set types were illustrated in the preceding section on structural types. Array types are unremarkable in ADABTPL and are declared as in

Percentile = Array [0..99] of Number;

In the type lattice an instantiated type is a subtype of its parametric parent. For example,

```
                    UNIVERSE
                      *    *
                   *           *
                *                 *
             *                       *
    WeightedObject(Alpha)    Array[0..99] OF Alpha
             *                       *
             *                       *
             *                       *
       WeightedBoolean         Array[0..99] OF Number
             *                       *
           *                           *
         *                               *
           *    *
            EMPTY
```

1.4.3　Union

The discriminated union constructor is a case of disjunctive aggregation and creates a new supertype. All the components of the union become subtypes of the newly created type. In ADABTPL the Union type is written much like the Tuple type, except that the colon is replaced with a right arrow. The colon stands for conjunctive aggregation, and the right arrow for disjunctive aggregation.

Atom = Union [n –> Number; s –> String; b –> Boolean];

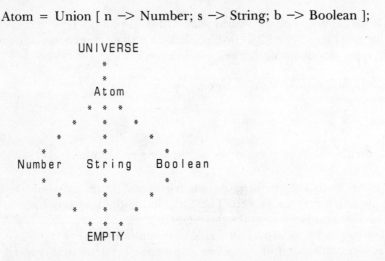

Of course, any subtype of Number is also a subtype of Atom. The labels n, s, and b may only appear in case expressions where they are used to determine the type of an instance of a Union type. For example, the following expression evaluates to a character string reflecting the base type of variable x of type Atom.

Case x of
    n –> "x is a number";
    s –> "x is a string";
    b –> "x is a boolean"
end;

1.4.4　Inherits

The Inherits type forms a conjunctive aggregation with inheritance (unlike tuple types which do not support inheritance). An Inherits type is the same as a tuple type except that it is also a subtype of its components' types. This means that an Inherits tuple can be used to stand for one of its components whenever that is unambiguous. As in tupling we use the colon (:) syntax to indicate conjunction.

GradStudent = Inherits [t: Teacher; s: Student];

GradStudent now inherits all the functionality of both teachers and students. GradStudent also becomes a subtype of both Teacher and Student.

```
                    UNIVERSE
                      *     *
                   *           *
                *                 *
             *                       *
          Teacher               Student
             *                       *
                *                 *
                   *           *
                      *     *
                   GradStudent
                        *
                        *
                     EMPTY
```

The component labels can be used to disambiguate expressions. Suppose both Teacher and Student types have a function called F, and that X is of type GradStudent. The compiler could not disambiguate the expression F(x). By adding .t to x we cause the compiler to use the F which is defined on teachers. That is, F(x.t) uses the Teacher function F, and F(x.s) uses the Student function F.

1.4.5 Abstract Type

More active control of inheritance can be gained with the Abstract Type construct with its transparent (and implicit opaque) clause along with the type condition option.

When a type is defined it automatically inherits all of the operations of its defining type. Sometimes we would like the new type not to have these operations defined (for reasons such as we do not want the users of the type to see its implementation, or we would like to construct our own operations on the type, or rename the inherited ones.) For example, we may implement a Queue type as a list with newly defined operations Add and Remove. We would not want the users of the type to be able to Cons elements onto a queue, since that is not a queue operation.

Queue(Alpha) = Abstract Type

Structure List(Alpha);

Function Add(a:Alpha; s:Queue(Alpha)):Queue(Alpha);
Function Remove(s:Queue(Alpha)):Queue(Alpha);

Export Add, Remove;
end;

When the Abstract Type constructor is used the structure of the type is "opaque" and cannot be seen by the user. Only the functions defined in the body and functions renamed or exported can be used. Thus the type lattice Queue(Alpha) and List(Alpha) previously defined would appear as two mutually separate types, neither being a subtype of the other even though they share the same structure.

```
                    UNIVERSE
                     *   *
                  *       *
               *          *
            *             *
   Queue(Alpha)    List(Alpha)
         *              *
           *            *
             *          *
               *    *
                EMPTY
```

1.4.6 Transparent

If the user wishes the structure of an abstract type to be seen he or she may use the Transparent Structure clause. This causes the new type to inherit the functions of its basic structure. Of course, new operations can be defined as well. One might consider defining an ordered list as a list with some new operations such as Sort. For example,

OrderedList(Alpha) = Abstract Type

Transparent Structure List(Alpha);

Function Sort(s:List(Alpha)):OrderedList(Alpha);

end;

Here all the operations on lists are available on OrderedLists as well. In addition, the new function, Sort, sorts an ordinary list into an ordered one. When the transparent structure is used then the new type becomes a subtype of the old type.

```
              UNIVERSE
                 *
                 *
                 *
             List(Alpha)
                 *
                 *
                 *
        OrderedList(Alpha)
                 *
                 *
                 *
               EMPTY
```

1.4.7 Type Conditions

Of course, the above type definition for OrderedLists assumes that the element type in the list, Alpha, can be ordered, which may not be the case. Thus,
we must modify the type definition somewhat to restrict OrderedLists to only
those element types which can be ordered. We restrict a type by using a type
condition.

    Type Condition Orderable(Alpha; before:function(Alpha, Alpha):
      Boolean);

    Universal x,y:Alpha;
    not before(x,x);
    before(x,y) and before(y,z) => before(x,z);
    before(x,y) => not before(y,x)
    end;

A type condition is a predicate on types, the conjunct of the statement
predicates after Universal in the example. Type conditions are used in the
definition of abstract types. When used, any instantiations of the abstract
type must have arguments that pass the type condition to be accepted by the
compiler. If the following parametric Abstract Type declaration is present,

    OrderableList(Alpha,less: function(Alpha,Alpha) -> Boolean) =
      Abstract Type

    Type Condition Orderable(Alpha,less)

    Transparent Structure List(Alpha);

    Function Sort(s:List(Alpha)):OrderedList(Alpha);

        Export Sort;
        end;

then declaring

        NumbersList = OrderableList(Number,<)

causes the compiler to check several things: first, that the (infix) less than
function has the correct type, that is, is a function from Number X Number to
Boolean, and second, that it meets the three conditions of the type condition,
namely that it is nonreflexive, transitive, and antisymmetric. Type conditions
are similar in effect and use to Goguen's theories [Burstall and Goguen,
1977].

1.4.8 Abstract Type and the Inherits type

The Structure clause in an Abstract Type declaration can be an Inherits type.
It is the means by which we can gain some control over multiple inheritance.
Inside the Abstract Type body the type defined is a type that has all the
functions of all its parent types defined on it. These functions can then be
exported or renamed to make a new type with only those functions the user
wants being visible. For example, consider a graphics terminal system. One
of the types might be a box drawn on the screen. The second may be some
sort of sequential file. One might define a Window as a type that has both the
properties of a SequentialFile(character) and a box. That is, one could read
or write from or to it as well as move it about on the screen.

        Window = Abstract Type
        Structure Inherits [b: Box; f: SequentialFile(Character)]

        Function1 . . .

        Function2 . . .

        Exports close.f as CloseWindow, ...
        end;

    The functions defined on Windows must be exported since the Inherits
clause is opaque. If both Window and SequentialFile have a function with
the same name, we disambiguate the function by using the labels in Inherits
clause. Thus close.f means the "close" function on files, while close.w is the
Window "close" function.
    If the Structure clause is Transparent then all functions of both types are
seen by the system as valid functions on the new type. Sometimes we wish to
combine several types and add a few new features as well. This can be done
by using an Inherits type and a With clause.

Window1 = Abstract Type
Transparent Structure Inherits [b: Box; f: SequentialFile(character)]
   With [visible: Boolean];

Exports f.close as CloseWindow, w.close as EraseWindow;
end;

In this example, Window1 is both a box and a SequentialFile. All the operations are available, as well as a new function called "visible." The two functions named Close are renamed so as to remove all ambiguity.

In Abstract Types only the Transparent clause creates subtypes. In the case of the first Window type from before, only those functions specifically exported are available.

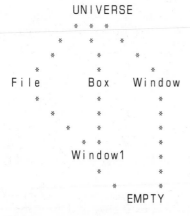

1.4.9 Recursive Union

Theoretically there is no problem with a type definition referencing the type being defined. Properly constructed recursive types have well-defined semantics and are useful in specifying types that have as substructures elements of the same type as themselves. Lists and sets are examples of nonproblematic recursive types. From a practical point of view, recursive definitions, which reference themselves through a long chain of mutually recursive types, can be hard to type check and reason about. For this reason ADABTPL allows only one kind of recursive type, the recursive union. The recursive union is a disjunctive aggregation with recursion. Its syntax is similar to the normal union type, except the types of the discriminants can involve expressions involving the type being defined or the type Bottom, that is, the type consisting of constants and the equality relation (used especially for the unconstructable elements of types, such as nil and empty set). In ADABTPL if the discriminant has type Bottom, then the discriminant also names a nullary (constant) function that returns the (unique) element of the union with the bottom discriminant. A recursive union defines a new type that is not a subtype of any other type other than UNIVERSE. The classical example is the list that could be defined structurally by

    List(Alpha) = Recursive Union [nil -> Bottom;
      dtpr -> Cons [Car:Alpha;
        Cdr:List(Alpha)]];

This uses the named tuple constructor option, Cons, mentioned in the earlier discussion of tuple types. Typing a discriminant with Bottom is a shorthand for typing it as a componentless tuple with the discriminant as the constructor function. For example, nil could be defined by

    nil -> nil []

using the same way of introducing the constructor function as was used for Cons, that is, preceding the left bracket. Note that this defines nil as a nullary function (constant) and we can write x = nil rather than the more cumbersome

    Case x of nil -> true ; dtpr -> false end

to test if one has reached the "bottom" of a recursive structure.

1.5 SUBTLE POINTS ABOUT FUNCTION AND ARRAY TYPES

ADABTPL subtyping has two subtle points not obvious to the casual observer. They involve types created with the Array constructor and function types. Consider the two (false) subtype assertions where it is known that Gamma and Delta are subrange types and Gamma is a subtype of Delta.

    F = Function(Gamma) -> Beta is a subtype of G = Function(Delta)
      -> Beta

    Array[Gamma] of Alpha is a subtype of Array[Delta] of Alpha

These two subtype expressions are false because the types they compare do not meet the semantics of subtyping. Roughly speaking, if A is a subtype of B, then anywhere in a program an object of type B is expected, an object of type A could be used without causing an error. In the preceding example we should be able to use a function of type F wherever we can use a function of type G, if F is a subtype of G. But since the domain type of F (as a set of objects) has fewer objects than G, there may be some objects in the domain type of G on which F is not defined. Thus for two functions to be subtypes of each other, the normal subtyping order of the domain types is reversed (while it remains the same for the range type).

Function(Delta) –> Alpha is a subtype of Function(Gamma) –> Beta

if and only if

Gamma is a subtype of Delta and Alpha is a subtype of Beta

If F is a Subtype of G, then F must be defined everywhere G is (and possibly more places), but return only a subset (perhaps the same set) of objects G does.

A similar thing happens with the index parameter type of arrays. The index parameter (which has to be a number or enumerated type or a subrange of one of these) does not participate in the normal subtyping order either. In other words,

Array[Delta] of Alpha is a subtype of Array[Gamma] of Beta

if and only if

Gamma is a subtype of Delta and Alpha is a subtype of Beta

For example,

Array[1..100] of Alpha is a subtype of Array[20..50] of Alpha

This is because the array access function for the array with indexes from 1..100 is defined everywhere over the array with indexes from 20..50. Thus an access to the smaller array (in terms of the range of the index) can be used anywhere an access to the larger array can be used.

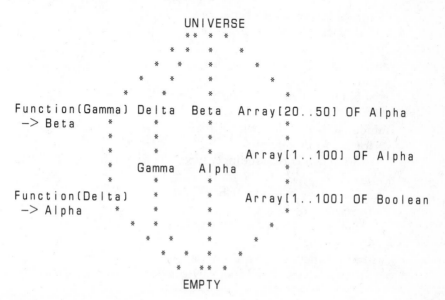

1.6 THE SUBTYPING ALGORITHM

We now give a very rough outline of our subtype algorithm. In this version Subtype is a predicate of x and y that returns either true or false, True if x is a subtype of y and False otherwise. This algorithm is for the simple case where all parameterized types are fullly instantiated. If x and y are allowed to contain type variables, then the algorithm must return a unifier binding the type variables to concrete types. It cannot be a simple predicate.

```
Function Subtype(x,y:types):Boolean;
begin

If (y = top) or (x = bottom)          – The Primitive Cases
  then true
  else if (x = top) or (y = bottom)
    then false
else if HasTheSameStructure(x,y)      – Both have the same
                                        STRUCTURE
  then case x.structure
    Function: Subtype(y.inputType,x.inputType) and
      Subtype(x.outputType,y.outputType);

  NumericSubrange: (x.low >= y.low) and (x.high <= y.high);

EnumeratedSubrange: sameEnumeration(x,y) and
      (x.low >= y.low) and (x.high <= y.high);

    array: Subtype(y.indexType, x.indexType) and
      Subtype(x.elementType, y.elementType);

    tuple: match(x.names,y.names) and
      for each t in x.types
        Subtype(t,coresponding(y.types));

    union: subset(x.labels,y.labels) and
      for each t in x.types
        Subtype(t,coresponding(y.types));

    inherits: subset(y.labels,x.labels) and
      for each t in y.types
        Subtype(t,coresponding(x.types));

    with: Subtype(x.baseType, y.baseType) and
      Subtype(x.extensionType, y.extensionType);
```

```
        where: Subtype(x.baseType, y.baseType) and
            (x.whereClause) => (y.whereClause)
            end;
        - The RECURSIVE CASES
    else if x.type = where then Subtype(x.baseType,y)
    else if y.type = where then Subtype(x, y.baseType)
    else if x.type = with then Subtype(x.baseType,y)
    else if y.type = union then for some t in y.types Subtype(x,t)
    else if x.type = inherits then for some t in x.types Subtype(t,y)
    else if x.type = NumericSubrange then Subtype(Number,y)
    else if x.type = EnumeratedSubrange then Subtype(enumeration(x),y)

    else if (x.type = userDefined) and (x.visiblity = transparent)
        - IF USER DEFINED, USE DEFINITION IF TRANSPARENT
        then Subtype(expand(x), y)
        else if (y.type = userDefined) and (y.visiblity = transparent)
        then Subtype(x,expand(y))
        else false
end
```

1.7 SUMMARY

We have presented the type construction facilities of the ADABTPL system being developed at the University of Massachusetts. We have concentrated on the effects of the type constructors on the lattice formed by the subtype relation produced by use of the constructors. The contribution of this work is to integrate in a usable manner sophisticated inheritance and encapsulation mechanisms with a robust structural definition facility that is a felicitous evolution of the database schema paradigm.

ACKNOWLEDGMENTS

This research was supported by NSF grants DCR-8503613 and IST-8606424 and by the Office of Naval Research University Research Initiative contract number N00014-86-K-0764.

REFERENCES

Ait-Kaci, H., (1984). *A Lattice-Theoretic Approach to Computation Based on on a Calculus of Partially Ordered Type Structures*, Ph. D. Thesis, University of Pennsylvania.

Burstall, R. M., and Goguen, J. A., (1977). "Putting Theories Together to Make Specifications," *Fifth International Joint Conference on Artificial Intelligence*, Cambridge, Mass., August, pp. 1045–1058.

Cardelli, L., and Wegner, P., (1985). "On Understanding Types, Data Abstraction, and Polymorphism," *ACM Computing Surveys*, Vol. 17, No. 4, December, pp. 471–572.

Sheard, T., and Stemple, D., "Automatic Verification of Database Transaction Safety," *University of Massachusetts Computer and Information Science Technical Report 86-30* (submitted for publication).

Stemple, D., Sheard, T., and Bunker, B., (1986), "Abstract Data Types in Databases: Specification, Manipulation and Access," *Proceedings of the IEEE Second International Conference on Data Engineering*, Los Angeles, California, February, pp. 590–597.

CHAPTER 2

ON THE RELATIONSHIP OF CONGRUENCE CLOSURE AND UNIFICATION

Paris C. Kanellakis
Peter Z. Revesz

2.1 INTRODUCTION

Congruence closure and unification are fundamental notions in symbolic computation. The unification of terms is the basic operation for most logic programming languages [Lloyd, 1984] and the congruence closure of equalities among terms is a central pattern-matching task in all systems which compute with equations [Huet & Oppen, 1980; Nelson & Oppen, 1980; Oppen, 1980]. In this paper we clarify the relationship between these two notions.

All problems we examine here have polynomial time sequential algorithms, (i.e., they are in the complexity class *PTIME*). Our analysis and comparisons are based on the theory of parallel algorithms and complexity. Let us briefly mention the few but central concepts that we use from this theory. *The complexity class NC* [Pippenger, 1979] contains those problems solvable on a *PRAM* [Fortune, 1978] in polylogarithmic parallel time using a polynomial number of processors. Intuitively, *NC* consists of those problems whose solution can be significantly sped up using a multiprocessor. It has been shown that $NC \subseteq PTIME$ and it is strongly conjectured that this containment is proper. A problem is *log-space complete for PTIME* if it is in *PTIME* and every problem in *PTIME* is reducible to it using only logarithmic auxiliary space. Any log-space reduction can be computed in *NC* and hence (unless the unlikely fact *PTIME* $\subseteq$ *NC* is true) problems log-space complete for *PTIME* do not have *NC* algorithms. Intuitively, problems that are log-space complete for *PTIME* are inherently sequential. A prototypical such problem is the *circuit value problem* [Ladner, 1975]. The class NC^2 is the subclass of *NC* restricted to log-squared parallel time.

In formalizing the notions of "congruence" and "unification" we follow Downey et al. [1980]. The two definitions we use exhibit a certain directional duality on the same inputs, namely, congruence closure is defined bottom-up and unification closure top-down.

Let $G = (V, A)$ be a directed graph such that for each vertex v in G, the successors of v are ordered. Let C be any equivalence relation on V. The *congruence closure CC* and the *unification closure*[1] *UC* of C are the finest equivalence relations on V that contain C and satisfy the following properties for all vertices v and w in G:

Let v and w have successors $v_1, v_2, \ldots, v_k$ and $w_1, w_2, \ldots, w_l$, respectively. If $k = l \geq 1$ and $(v_i, w_i) \in CC$ for $1 \leq i \leq i \leq k$, then $(v, w) \in CC$.

Let v and w have successors $v_1, v_2, \ldots, v_k$ and $w_1, w_2, \ldots, w_l$, respectively. If $k = l \geq 1$ and $(v, w) \in UC$, then $(v_i, w_i) \in UC$ for $1 \leq i \leq k$.

Congruence closure is common in decision procedures for formal theories, where it is necessary to determine equivalent expressions. An important use is in solving the following expression equivalence problem, which is called the *uniform word problem for finitely presented algebras*:

"determine whether an equality $t_1 = t_2$ logically follows from a set of equalities $S = \{t_{11} = t_{12}, t_{21} = t_{22}, \ldots, t_{k1} = t_{k2}\}$, where the t's are ground terms constructed from constant and function symbols."

For this application the directed graph G is a representation of the t's and therefore an acyclic graph.

If the set of equalities S is empty, we have the well-known *common subexpression elimination* problem, which occurs often in compiling. If the set of equalities S contains only a *single equality*, we have a problem that is relevant to our exposition and that arises in verifying a class of array assignment pro-

---

[1]Congruence closure is the terminology used in Downey *et al.* [1980]. Unification closure is slightly different from "unifier" defined in Downey *et al.* [1980] and is terminology introduced here to emphasize the directional duality.

grams in Downey & Sethi [1978]. If the set of equalities S is fixed and there-fore not part of the input, we have the (nonuniform) *word problem for finitely presented algebra S*. As shown in Kozen [1977], the uniform word problem for finitely presented algebras is log-space complete for *PTIME*, even when there is only a unique constant and a unique *binary* function symbol in the input terms.

Several authors have suggested algorithms for congruence closure. Downey et al. [1980] have the fastest known sequential algorithms for various cases of congruence closure. Their algorithm for the general case requires $O(N log N)$ time, where N is the input size. They also provide $O(N)$ and there-fore optimal sequential time algorithms for two cases that are of interest to us here: (1) congruence closure when G is a directed acyclic graph and C contains a single pair of distinct vertices, and (2) congruence closure when we get an acylic graph from G if we contract the equivalence classes of CC.

Unification closure is the directional dual of congruence closure and has a number of important applications. It can be used in testing equivalence of finite automata [Hopcroft & Karp, 1971] and in determining a most general set of substitutions (i.e., a most general unifier) to make two terms equal [Martelli & Montanari, 1982; Paterson & Wegman, 1978; Robinson, 1965]. The technique of Hopcroft & Karp [1971] combined with the fast *UNION-FIND* method of Tarjan [1975] provides an $O(N\alpha(N))$ time algorithm for unifi-cation closure, where $\alpha(N)$ is a functional inverse of Ackermann's function. Huet [1976] and Robinson [1975] independently provided similar bounds for computing most general unifiers. Paterson & Wegman [1978] have given an $O(N)$ time algorithm for the case where we get an acyclic graph G if we contrast the equivalence classes of UC; the acyclicity condition here is critical for the linear-time behavior.

Let us briefly comment on the relationship of computing unification closures and computing most general unifiers. Given two terms constructed out of variables, constants, and function symbols, the problem of computing the *most general unifier, mgu is*: "finding a most general substitution, if it exists, which makes the two terms equal." One way to compute the mgu is to first compute a unification closure and then test it for two conditions, called homogeneity and acyclicity in Paterson & Wegman [1978]. If the acyclicity test is omitted then we have a most general unifier that permits infinite terms as substitutions (mgu^∞). Both homogeneity and acyclicity are testable in *NC* and determine if the mgu exists. Therefore from a parallel complexity point of view the unification closure is the operation of greater interest.

Computing unification closure is shown to be log-space complete in *PTIME* in Dwork et al. [1984] and Yasuura [1983]. This lower bound is strengthened in Dwork et al. [1988]. Parallel algorithms for unification clo-sure and a number of its NC^2 subcases are examined in Auger [1985], Dwork et al. [1988], Ramesh et al. [1987], and Vitter & Simons [1986].

The main contribution of this paper is in clarifying the directional duality between congruence closure and unification closure (Theorems 2.1 and 2.2). Based on this duality we extend the class of unification problems known to be in NC (Theorem 2.3). We also clarify the relationship of unification closure and deterministic finite automata equivalence (Theorem 2.4).

We first log-space reduce unification closure to congruence closure. Given that both problems are known to be log-space complete in $PTIME$, such a reduction is in principle possible. The particular reduction that we use, however, has some nice properties that accurately capture the directional duality. In Theorem 1.1 we reduce computing the mgu^x of two terms to the uniform word problem for *monadic* finitely presented algebras. Multiple occurences of variables in the terms are transformed into algebra axioms. If $k =$ (number of occurences of variables in the terms) − (number of distinct variables in the terms), then the uniform word problem has $1 + k$ axioms. This reduction and the lower bounds in Dwork et al. [1984, 1988] extend the log-space completeness results of Kozen [1977] to uniform word problems for terms constructed out of one constant and two monadic function symbols. This is syntactically tight because we also show that for terms constructed out of any number of constants and one monadic function symbol the uniform word problem is in NC. This can be shown to follow from the proofs in Auger [1985]. We simplify these proofs to a large degree and extend them from the *mgu* to the *mgu^x* cases (Proposition 2.5). If the uniformity condition is removed we also have word problems in NC (Proposition 2.6). This is based on the theory of finite tree automata of Thatcher & Wright [1968] and also follows from the properties of context-free languages [Ruzzo, 1980].

We next restrict our attention to inputs consisting of a directed acyclic graph G and an equivalence relation C defined by k pairs of distinct vertices. Let us call these restricted problems *dag-CC [k axioms]* and *dag-UC [k axioms]* respectively. As noted there is a practical application for *dag-CC [1 axiom]* Downey & Sethi, [1978]. In Theorem 2.2 we show that the problem *dag-CC [1 axiom]* in NC^2, whereas it is known that *dag-UC [1 axiom]* is log-space complete for $PTIME$. This demonstrates that a straightforward view of the directional duality may be misleading and that the transformation of multiple occurrences of variables into axioms from Theorem 2.1 provides a better view of this duality. In Theorem 2.2 we also show (by a simple modification of the proof in Kozen [1977]) that *dag-CC [3 axioms]* is log-space for $PTIME$. The status of *dag-CC [2 axioms]* is an interesting open question. As part of the proof of Theorem 2.2 we show that when C is the trivial equivalence relation, that is, each distinct vertex is an equivalence class, then congruence closure is in NC^2. The tricky issue here is the possible existence of cycles in G in the general case. The acyclic G case was already known to be in NC^2 via common subexpression elimination for directed acyclic graphs.

Having investigated the relationship of congruence closure and unification closure we then proceed to examine the acyclicity condition that is often added to these computations. We say that G is acyclic under the equivalence relation C' if the directed graph we get by contracting the vertices in each equivalence class of C' is still acyclic. Acyclic congruence closure returns the congruence closure for instances where G is acyclic under CC and the message "has cycle" otherwise. In Theorem 2.3 we show that acyclic congruence closure is in NC^2 if C has fixed number of nontrivial equivalence classes, i.e., classes with more than a single vertex. Together with Theorem 2.1 this leads to a new class of instances where computing the mgu of two terms is in NC^2. These instances consist of two terms with a fixed number of distinct variables that occur more than once in the instance. The use of the acyclicity condition is important for this proof and we do not know how to remove it. There is an analog here with the use of acyclicity made in the linear time algorithms for acyclic congruence and unification closure in Downey et al. [1980] and Paterson & Wegman [1978].

Our final contribution is in clarifying the relationship of unification with the testing of two deterministic finite automata for equivalence. Let G be a graph with vertices having outdegree 0 or 2 and let us call outdegree 0 vertices *leaves* and outdegree 2 vertices *internal nodes*. There is no loss of generality from the point of view of parallel complexity if we thus restrict G. In Theorem 2.4 we show that if G has a fixed number of leaves, then computing the unification closure is NC^2. Note that for the deterministic finite automata application there are no leaves. This result also extends the circuit bounds of Yasuura [1983] on unification of terms with a fixed number of variables, because the graph G can have cycles and is thus more general than the acyclic representation of terms.

In Section 2.2 we give brief but formal definitions of the problems examined in this paper; Section 2.3 contains our duality theorem; Section 2.4 the analysis of *dag-CC* with a fixed number of axioms; Section 2.5 the analysis of acyclicity; and Section 2.6 the relationship of unification closure and deterministic finite automata equivalence. In Section 2.7 we have our conclusions (shown graphically in Figure 2.5) and open questions.

2.2 THE PROBLEMS

A *term* is a finite string that is either a *variable* symbol, or a *constant* symbol, or a string $f(t_1, \ldots, t_a)$, where f is a *function* symbol of *arity* $a \geq 1$ and $t_1, \ldots, t_a$ are terms. A *ground term* is a term that does not contain any occurences of variables.

A set of terms is naturally represented as a *simple directed acyclic graph* (*sdag*). Sdags are directed acyclic graphs, where only the leaves (outdegree

0 vertices) can have indegree larger than one [Dwork et al., 1984], i.e., the graph looks like a forest except at the leaves.

If a term is a variable or a constant symbol it is denoted by a tree of one vertex labeled by that symbol. If a term is $f(t_1, \ldots, t_a)$ it is denoted by a tree, whose root is a vertex labeled by symbol f and such that the root has as a ordered successors the trees denoting $t_1, \ldots, t_a$. Given a set of terms we represent them by the sdag that results from the trees denoting the terms, if we merge all vertices labeled by the same variable or constant symbol into one such vertex. For example, Figure 2.1a is the sdag representation of the set of terms $\{f(f(a,y),x), f(x,(f(y,b)))\}$.

UWORD. The *uniform word problem for finitely presented algebras* is defined as follows. Given ground terms $t_{11}, \ldots, t_{n1}, t_{12}, \ldots, t_{n2}, \ldots, t_1, t_2$ decide whether the implication $S \models \{t_1 = t_2\}$ is true, where $S = \{t_{11} = t_{12}, \ldots, t_{n1} = t_{n2}\}$.

If S is a fixed set of equalities we have the problem *S-WORD* (the word problem for finitely presented algebra S). If S has k equalities we use the notation *UWORD[k axioms]*. If the function symbols in all the input ground terms are monadic, then we have the problem *mon-UWORD*. We use *mon-UWORD[k functions]* if the input has only k distinct function symbols.

MGU. The problem of computing the *most general unifier (mgu)* is defined as follows. Given terms t_1, t_2, find the most general substitution of terms for variables in t_1 and t_2 that makes them equal or report that there is no such substitution.

Note that if there is such a substitution there is a most general one [Robinson, 1965]. For example, the mgu for the terms $f(x,x)$ and $f(g(y), g(g(z)))$ consists of substituting $g(z)$ for y and $g(g(z))$ for x. The terms $f(x,x)$ and $g(x)$ are not unifiable and neither are the terms $g(x)$ and x.

MGU^x. This is an extension of the mgu of two terms where we allow substitutions of infinite terms for variables in t_1, t_2. For example, we say that the terms $g(x)$ and x are *unrestricted unifiable* by substituting $g(g(g(\ldots)))$ for x (see Dwork et al., 1984; Paterson & Wegman, 1978 for the technical definitions).

If the input terms have at most k distinct variables, we have the problems *MGU[k vars]* and *MGU^x[k vars]*. A variable is *repeated* if it occurs more than once in the input, (i.e., it occurs in both t_1 and t_2, or it occurs twice in t_1 or t_2). If the input terms have at most k repeated variables we have the problems *MGU[k repeated vars]* and *MGU^x[k repeated vars]*. Clearly if we have *[k vars]* we have *[k repeated vars]* but not inversely. If one of the two terms contains no repeated variables we have the problems *linear-MGU* and *linear-MGU^x* [Dwork et al., 1988]. Finally, if we are given a *set* of input pairs $\{t_{11}, t_{12}\}, \ldots, \{t_{k1}, t_{k2}\}$, where all the function symbols have arity 1, and we want the most general substitution that simultaneously makes t_{11} equal to $t_{12}, \ldots, t_{k1}$ equal to t_{k2}, then we have the problems *mon-MGU* and *mon-MGU^x*.

EDFA. This is the problem of determining whether two given deterministic finite automata accept the same language.

The preceding problems represent a wide spectrum of applications which will now reduce to two combinatorial problems.

CC. Let $G = (V, A)$ be a directed graph such that each vertex $v \in V$ has 0 or 2 ordered successors. Let C be any equivalence relation on V. The *congruence closure* $\approx$ of C is the finest equivalence relation on V that contains C such that for all vertices v and w with corresponding successors v_1, w_1 and v_2, w_2 we have:

$$v_1 \approx w_1, v_2 \approx w_2 \Rightarrow v \approx w$$

UC. Let $G = (V, A)$ be a directed graph such that each vertex $v \in V$ has 0 or 2 ordered successors. Let C be any equivalence relation on V. The *unification closure* $\sim$ of C is the finest equivalence relation on V that contains C such that for all vertices v and w with corresponding successors v_1, w_1 and v_2, w_2 we have:

$$v_1 \sim w_1, v_2 \sim w_2 \Leftarrow v \sim w$$

We distinguish among several cases of congruence closure and unification closure depending on the structure of G and C. We use the notation *[k axioms]* when C is the reflexive, symmetric, and transitive closure of k *pairs of distinct vertices*. We use the notation *[k classes]* when C has at most k *nonsingleton equivalence classes*. We use the notation *[k leaves]* when G has at most k *leaves*. *(s)dag-CC* and *(s)dag-UC* refer to cases where the input graph is a (simple) directed acyclic graph.

Remark on outdegree. In the introduction, *CC* and *UC* are presented without any restrictions on the outdegrees of vertices in G. In our formalization we restrict the outdegrees to 0 or 2. This makes the combinatorial problems easier to state and simplifies the notation in our proofs. It is used for the same purposes in Downey et al. [1980]. More importantly, using the techniques of Downey et al. [1980] one can easily show that both for sequential algorithms and for *NC* algorithms the restriction can be made without any loss of generality. For example, vertex labels in the sdag representation of terms can be eliminated without loss of generality, using sdags with vertex outdegrees 0 or 2.

Many applications of unification closure and congruence closure require that the graph formed from the input graph by contracting the equivalence classes of the closures be acyclic. We define *ACC* and *AUC* to have the same inputs as *CC* and *UC*. They return the closure (if the graph formed by the input graph by contracting the closure's equivalence classes is acyclic) or the message "has cycle" (otherwise).

We state four propositions from the literature, which relate the applications *UWORD, MGU, MGU^x*, and *EDFA* to the combinatorial problems *CC* and *UC*. Two problems are log-space equivalent if each one is log-space reducible to the other. All the reductions in Propositions 2.1 to 2.4 involve simple and straightforward manipulations of the representations commonly used for terms and for finite automata. Hence, for each one of these cases we will use the combinatorial problems to reason about the application problems.

Proposition 2.1. *UWORD[k axioms]* is log-space equivalent to *sdag-CC[k axioms]*.

Kozen [1977] reduces *UWORD[k axioms]* to the more general version of *sdag-CC[k axioms]*, where the vertices in the input graph may have other than 0 or 2 successors. This is done based on straightforward representation of terms via sdags. Downey et al. [1980] reduce this more general case to *sdag-CC[k axioms]* where the vertices in the input graph have 0 or 2 successors.

Proposition 2.2. *MGU* is log-space equivalent to *sdag-AUC[1 axiom]*.

Proposition 2.3. *MGU^x* is log-space equivalent to *sdag-UC[1 axiom]*.
The reductions follow from Paterson & Wegman [1978].

Proposition 2.4. *EDFA* is log-space equivalent to *UC[0 leaves]*.
This reduction follows from Hopcroft & Karp (1971).

We close this section with algorithms for solving *CC* and *UC*. Let G and C be as in the preceding definitions of *CC* and *UC* and let u and v be vertices of G. We define symmetric and reflexive relations E and F on pairs of vertices of G. These relations are represented by undirected edges added to G and labeled E or F. For each two vertices u and v that are in the same equivalence class of C we *add* undirected edges uEv and uFv to the graph. Also,

Add undirected edge uEv if it is not present and either:

1. u_1Ev_1 and u_2Ev_2 are present, where u_1, u_2 and v_1, v_2 are the ordered successors of u, v. In this case u and v are distinct vertices. This is called *up-propagation step uPv*.
2. uEw and wEv are present, where w is some vertex in G. In this case u and v are distinct vertices. This is called *transitivity step uTv*.

Add undirected edge uFv if it is not present and either:

1. $u'Fv'$ is present, where u and v are corresponding successors of u', v'. In this case u and v are distinct vertices. This is called down-propagation step $uP'v$.
2. uFw and wFv are present, where w is some vertex in G. In this case u and v are distinct vertices. This is called *transitivity step uTv*.

From Kozen [1977] and Paterson & Wegman [1978] we have the following characterization of the congruence closure relation ($\approx$) and the unification closure relation ($\sim$).

Proposition 2.5. $u \approx v(u \sim v)$ "iff" undirected edge $uEv\,(uFv)$ is added after some finite sequence of up(down)-propagation and transitivity steps.

2.3 UNIFICATION CLOSURE REDUCES TO CONGRUENCE CLOSURE

Let I be an instance of UC and u, v be two vertices in I. In this section we will transform the question whether the pair (u, v) is in the unification closure of I (i.e., $u \sim v$) into a uniform word problem for monadic finitely presented algebras. This together with Proposition 2.1 reduces unification closure to congruence closure.

Given I, u, v as stated we now produce a set of equations $S(I)$, an equation $s(I)$, and an instance of CC we call *dual(I)* as follows:

1. For each vertex x_1 in I with indegree $i > 1$, do the following modification. If $(z_1, x_1), \ldots, (z_i, x_1)$ are the arcs coming into x_1, with arc labels 1 or 2, then replace $(z_2, x_1), \ldots, (z_i, x_1)$, by $(z_2, x_2), \ldots, (z_i, x_i)$, with the same arc labels, where $x_2, \ldots, x_i$ are *new* vertices. Add *new* axioms $x_1 \sim x_2, \ldots, x_1 \sim x_i$.

2. The graph resulting from step 1 is a forest, thus there is at most one arc coming into each vertex. Add vertex labels using the following procedure. If vertex x has incoming arc (z, x) with arc label 1 (2), then label x with monadic function symbol $h(g)$. If vertex x has no incoming arc then label x with a unique constant symbol.

3. In the graph resulting from step 2, reverse the directions of the arcs and change all arc labels to 1. The resulting graph is the sdag representation of a set of monadic ground terms. These monadic ground terms are constructed from constants and the symbols h and g. In this sdag every vertex x denotes a monadic ground term t_x.

4. $S(I)$ is $\{t_x = t_y|$ where $x \sim y$ is an axiom of I or a new axiom from step 1}; $s(I)$ is $t_u = t_v$.

5. The instance of $CCdual(I)$ consists of a graph G' and an equivalence relation C'. The graph G' is the directed graph with arc labels resulting from step 3 with the following modification. Add two new vertices h and g and make new vertex $h(g)$ the second successor of each vertex labeled by symbol $h(g)$. The equivalence relation C' is the one defined by axioms of I and the new axioms from step 1.

Figure 2.1 illustrates this method of reduction. The *sdag-UC[1 axiom]* instance in Fig. 2.1*a* (ignore vertex labels) is transformed into Fig. 2.1*b*. This

FIGURE 2.1
Example of reduction from sdag-UC to mon-UWORD

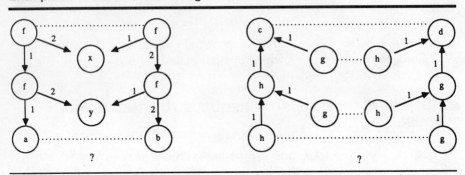

in turn is the sdag representation for the *mon-UWORD* instance $\{g(h(c)) = h(g(d)), g(c) = h(d), c = d\} \models \{h(h(c)) = g(g(d))\}$. Compare this sdag with the sdag in Fig. 2.3*a* which can be used for computing the unification closure of terms $f(f(a,y),x))$ and $f(x,f(y,b))$. The implication in the word problem holds. In the unification closure of the two terms the vertices labeled a and b are in the same class; this leads to a failure of the homogeneity test of Paterson & Wegman [1978] for mgu's.

THEOREM 2.1.   Let I be an instance of *UC* and u,v be two vertices in
I. Let $S(I)$ be a set of equations, $s(I)$ an equation, and *dual(I)* an instance of *CC* defined as before. Then the following are equivalent:

   a. $u \sim v$ is in the unification closure of I.
   b. $S(I) \models s(I)$.
   c. $u \approx v$ is in the congruence closure of *dual(I)*.

Proof.   The equivalence of (b) and (c) follows from Kozen's algorithm for the uniform word problem for finitely presented algebras in Kozen [1977].
Consider the instance I' of *UC* that we get right after step 1 of the preceding reduction, that is, after the addition of the x vertices and the new axioms. It is easy to see that $u \sim v$ is in the unification closure of I "iff" $u \sim v$ is in the unification closure of I'. The arc label changes if steps 2, 3, and 5 are such that every down-propagation step on I' corresponds to an up-propagation step in *dual(I)* and vice versa. The same is true for the transitivity steps on I' and *dual(I)*. Thus by Proposition 2.5, (a) and (b) are equivalent.
As we described in Proposition 2.2, computing MGU^x is intimately related to computing the unification closure of *sdag-UC[1 axiom]* instances. The additional homogeneity test can be performed in *NC*. Based on the preceding reduction we have:

FIGURE 2.2
Example of *dag-CC[1 axiom]*

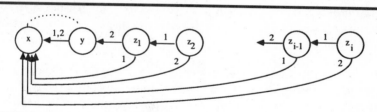

Corollary 2.1. Let I be an instance of *sdag-UC[1 axiom]* and u, v be two vertices in I. Let $k = \sum_x [indegree(x) - 1]$, where x is a leaf in I of *indegree* ≥ 1. The $S(I), s(I)$ defined previously are an instance of *mon-UWORD[1 + k axioms]*, such that, $u \sim v$ "iff" $S(I) \models s(I)$.

Consider the MGU^x instance t_1, t_2. If represented in sdag form then there are leaves denoting both variable and constant symbols. One can replace each occurrence of a constant with a unique new variable and use the unification closure on the sdag of the new terms t_1', t_2'. This closure can be used to find the mgu^x of t_1, t_2, because constants can only be unified with themselves. Therefore for the MGU^x application the k used in Corollary 2.1 is $k =$ (number of occurrences of variables in t_1, t_2) − (number of distinct variables in t_1, t_2).

Using the reduction of Theorem 1.1 and reductions from Dwork et al. [1984, 1988] one can show that:

Corollary 2.2. *mon-UWORD[2 functions]* is log-space complete in *PTIME*.

One constant and two monadic function symbols suffice for the proof of Corollary 2.2. However, for one monadic function symbol we have the following.

Proposition 2.5. *mon-UWORD[1 function]* is in NC^2.

Proof. Consider a directed graph $G = (V, A)$ such that each vertex $v \in V$ has 0 or 1 successor. Let C be an equivalence relation on V. The closure of C is the finest equivalence relation C^* such that for all vertices v, w with successors v', w' we have: $(v, w) \in C^* \Rightarrow (v', w') \in C^*$.

Computing C^* is the monadic outdegree version of UC. By reversing the direction of the arcs it is easy to see that computing C^* in NC^2 would suffice to prove this theorem.

Each *component* of graph G is either a tree directed toward the root or a single directed cycle onto whose vertices such trees are rooted. The NC^2 algorithm consists of two parts. In the first part components are *merged*. In the second part the computation is performed on *separate* components.

Merge. If an axiom (v, w) of C has vertices in two components, we merge these components into one component. This merge operation is performed by merging descendants of v and w that have the same distance from v and w. One merge operation can be performed in $O(logN)$ parallel time. Merges can be performed so that after $O(logN)$ phases there are no axioms between components.

Separate. We have reduced the computation of C^* to subcomputations where G is one component. Each one of these subcomponents is a special case of UC, namely, $UC[0\ leaves]$ or $UC[1\ leaf]$. These can be performed in NC^2. We will give a more general proof for $UC[k\ leaves]$ k fixed in Theorem 2.4.

Using the proof of this theorem we have, (as in Auger [1985] for *mon-MGU*):

Corollary 2.3. *mon-MGU$^\times$ is in NC^2.*

Let us close this section by noting that the uniformity of the word problem is important for the log-space completeness. The following proposition can also be shown to follow from Ruzzo [1980], so we only provide a sketch of the proof.

Proposition 2.6. *$S - WORD$ is in NC^2 for any fixed S.*

Proof. (Sketch) For a fixed S we can produce in constant time a tree automaton presentation of the algebra of Thatcher & Wright [1968]. To check for an equality $t_1 = t_2$ in the algebra all we have to do is run this automaton on t_1 and t_2. This can be performed in NC^2.

2.4 CONGRUENCE CLOSURE WITH A FIXED NUMBER OF AXIOMS

In this section we show that there is a distinction between UC and CC. Namely, we show that $dag\text{-}CC[1\ axiom]$ is in NC^2 whereas it is known that $sdag\text{-}UC[1\ axiom]$ is log-space complete for *PTIME*.

THEOREM 2.2. $CC[0\ axioms]$ and $dag - CC[1\ axiom]$ are in NC^2. $CC[k\ axioms]$ and $dag - CC[k + 1\ axioms]$ are log-space complete in *PTIME* for each fixed $k \geq 2$.

We first prove two lemmas. In this section by propagation steps we mean up-propagation steps, and by a (congruence) proof we mean any valid sequence of up-propagation and transitivity steps.

LEMMA 2.1. $CC[0\ axioms]$ is in NC^2.

Proof. The lemma follows from two observations: (1) C has no axioms, so all proofs containing some transitivity steps can be replaced by proofs

FIGURE 2.3
Example of *dag-CC[3 axioms]*

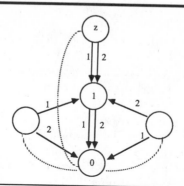

containing only propagation steps, and (2) sequences of propagation steps can be done in NC^2.

To show (1) we apply repeatedly the following claim for any proof, always replacing the rightmost transitivity step until none remains.

Claim: When C has no axioms, any transitivity step preceded by propagation steps only can be replaced by a sequence of propagations.

Let vTw be a counterexample to the claim, such that, it is preceded by the fewest number of propagation steps. Without loss of generality the sequence must look as follows:

$$P_1, vPu, P_2, uPw, P_3, vTw$$

where P_1, P_2 and P_3 are (possibly empty) sequences of propagation steps.

Since C has no axioms, $v \approx u$ and $u \approx w$ were proven by propagation and all of v, u, w have exactly two children, say v_1, v_2, u_1, u_2, and w_1, w_2, respectively. Note that either v_1 is u_1 or $v_1 P u_1$ must precede vPu, and either u_1 is w_1 or $u_1 P w_1$ must precede uPw. Therefore, either v_1 is w_1 or we can replace the end of the original sequence to get

$$P_1, vPu, P_2, v_1 T w_1$$

Since $v_1 T w_1$ is preceded by fewer propagation steps than vTw, it cannot be a counterexample. Hence $v_1 T w_1$ can be replaced by a sequence of propagations, showing that $v_1 \approx w_1$ can be proven by propagations only. Reasoning similarly, $v_2 \approx w_2$ can also be proven by propagations only. Therefore $v \approx w$ also has a propagation proof, which is a contradiction to the counterexample vTw. This completes (1).

To show (2) we reduce $CC[0\ axioms]$ with $G = (V, A)$ to transitive closure of the directed graph $G' = (V', A')$, where $V' = \{(v, w) : v, w \in V\} \cup \{x\}$ where x is a new node, and A' is as follows:

For all $v \in V$ let (v,v) have successor x in G'. For all $v,w \in V$ with successors v_1, v_2 and w_1, w_2 in G, respectively, let (v,w) have successors (v_1, w_1) and (v_2, w_2) in G'.

Then for all $v,w \in V$, $v \approx w$ if and only if the following conditions both hold:

Each descendant of (v,w) has x as a descendant (except for x itself). The descendants of (v,w) form an acyclic graph.

The correctness of this reduction can be easily proven by induction on the length of propagation sequences. This completes (2) and the lemma.

The single pair congruence closure problem seems harder than congruence closure with no axioms. Given a directed acyclic graph like that in Fig. 2.4, we need transitivity steps to show, for example, that $x \approx z_1$. Moreover, to show that $x \approx z_i$, we need i alternations in propagation and transitivity steps. However, since x does not have any children, in this case we could *merge* it with y and then perform propagation and transitivity steps. In this way the problem reduces to the no axioms case, and only propagation steps are needed. The next theorem shows that this can be done in general.

Lemma 2.2. *dag-CC[k + 1 axioms]* log-space reduces to *CC[k axioms]*, $k \geq 0$.

Proof. Let us first give the proof for $k = 0$.

Let $G = (V, A)$ be any dag with $x \approx y$ an axiom in C, where x and y are two *distinct* vertices in V, and let T be an arbitrary topological ordering of the vertices. Without loss of generality, $T(y) > T(x)$. Let us assume that there are no common subexpressions, that is, we performed congruence closure with 0 axioms. This is because this computation can be done in NC^2 by Lemma 2.1. Now we prove the following claim.

Claim: When G is acyclic and $T(y) > T(x)$, if $u \approx v$ holds, then $T(u)$, $T(v) \geq T(x)$. The claim is shown by induction on the length of the proof for $u \approx v$.

FIGURE 2.4
Example of *CC[2 axioms]*

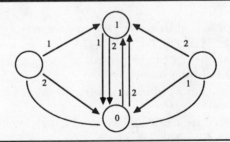

Base: Suppose $u \approx v$ has a proof of length 1. Then it must be a propagation proof. Let u_1 and u_2 be the successors of u, and v_1 and v_2 be the successors of v. Since $u \not\approx v$ when C has no axioms (because of common subexpression elimination), the proof must depend on $x \approx y$. Then without loss of generality $(u_1, v_1) = (x, y)$. Therefore, $T(u), T(v) > T(x)$, and the claim holds for proofs of length 1.

Induction hypothesis: "If $u \approx v$ has a proof of length $i \geq 1$, then $T(u)$, $T(v) \geq T(x)$." Then suppose $u \approx v$ has a proof of length $i + 1$. There are two cases:

1. The last step was transitivity of the form: $uEw, wEv \Rightarrow uTv$. Then $u \approx w$ and $w \approx v$ have proofs shorter than $i + 1$, hence by the induction hypothesis, $T(u), T(v), T(w) \geq T(x)$. Hence $T(u), T(v) \geq T(x)$.
2. The last step was propagation. Then $u_1 \approx v_1$ and $u_2 \approx v_2$ have proofs shorter than $i + 1$, hence by the induction hypothesis, $T(u_1)$, $T(u_2)$, $T(v_1)$, $T(v_2) \geq T(x)$. Since the graph is acyclic, $T(u), T(v) \geq T(x)$ also holds.

Since nodes that are greater than x cannot use the descendants of x, by the preceding claim, we can make the successors of x be the same as the successors of y. This modification of G will not change the computation of the congruence closure but will allow us to merge vertices x and y and still get a directed graph with outdegrees 0 or 2. Then the problem reduces to congruence closure with no axioms, which by Lemma 2.1 is in NC^2. Note that this reduces *dag-CC* to *CC* and not to *dag-CC*.

Finally if $k \geq 0$ the same technique can be used to eliminate one equality by starting from the vertex with the lowest number in the topological order. This completes the lemma.

Proof of Theorem 2.2.   The theorem follows for $k = 0$ by Lemmas 2.1 and 2.2 and for $k \geq 2$ by a reduction from the circuit value problem (CVP) which was proven log space complete for *PTIME* by Ladner [1975]. The circuit value problem is a sequence $g_1, g_2, \ldots, g_n$, where each g_i is either (*i*) a Boolean variable, which is assigned true or false, or (*ii*) $NOR(j, k)$, with $j, k < i$. The circuit value problem operation is: for a given circuit and an assignment to the variables, find the output of the circuit.

To do the reduction, we introduce two special vertices 1 and 0. Every Boolean variable g_i that is assigned true is assigned to 1, and every Boolean variable g_i that is assigned false is assigned to 0. In addition, for each g_i that is not a variable we create a vertex with first successor g_j and second successor g_k. We can encode into the congruence closure problem the function of a NOR gate by adding three congruences in Fig. 2.3. Out of these the congruence $0 \approx z$ can be eliminated by merging the vertices 0 and z (see Fig. 2.4).

Now it is easy to prove by induction that the CVP is true if and only if the node g_n will be congruent to 1. Hence the CVP problem can be reduced to dag congruence closure with three axioms and to congruence closure with two axioms. The cases for $k > 2$ are also immediately implied.

Note that the complexity of $CC[1\ axiom]$ and $dag\text{-}CC[2\ axioms]$ is open. $dag\text{-}CC[2\ axioms]$ reduces to $CC[1\ axiom]$ by Lemma 2.1. Finally, the large number of paths in a dag was important in the proof of Theorem 2.2. The complexity of $sdag\text{-}CC[k\ axioms]$ for fixed $k \geq 2$ is open.

2.5 ACYCLIC CONGRUENCE CLOSURE

In this section we show that there is a further distinction between UC and CC.

THEOREM 2.3. $ACC[k\ classes]$ is in NC^2 for each fixed $k \geq 0$.

Proof.   Suppose that we have an input graph with k classes. If the input graph is cyclic, then return a "has cycle" message, else eliminate common subexpressions. Then take the graph G formed from the input graph by contracting the equivalence classes in C. If G is cyclic, then return a "has cycle" message, else pick an arbitrary topological ordering of the vertices in G. Find the vertex in some nontrivial equivalence class, such that this vertex has the least topological number. Similarly to Lemma 2.2 we can show that the descendants of this merged vertex are not needed. By acyclicity this is true for the other vertices in its class. Hence we can take the input graph and merge only these vertices whose descendants are not needed and discard their descendants. Since the merged vertices correspond to one nontrivial equivalence class in C, this yields a new graph with $k - 1$ classes. The new graph is also acyclic. Since this reduction is in NC^2, we can repeat it k times, and the theorem must hold.

Based on this theorem and on Proposition 2.2 we can show the following.

Corollary 2.4.   *MGU[k repeated vars]* is in NC^2 for each fixed $k \geq 0$.

As after Corollary 2.1, there is only one fine point. Consider the *MGU* instance t_1, t_2. If represented in sdag form then there are leaves denoting both variable and constant symbols. One can replace each occurrence of a constant with a unique new variable and use the unification closure on the sdag of the new terms t_1', t_2'. This closure can be used to find the *mgu* of t_1, t_2, because constants can only be unified with themselves.

In Corollary 2.4 we have a new class of term unification problems that is shown to be in NC^2. The previously known cases were *linear-MGU* [Dwork et al., 1988], *mon-MGU* [Auger, 1985], and *MGU[k vars]* [Yasuura, 1983] for each fixed $k \geq 0$.

2.6 ON DETERMINISTIC FINITE AUTOMATA EQUIVALENCE

THEOREM 2.4.   *UC[k leaves]* is in NC^2 for each fixed $k \geq 0$.

Proof.   Let us implement the procedure of Proposition 2.5 as the following algorithm *NU* (for naïve unification).

1. On the graph G add the axioms of C as undirected edges uFv, as well as all self-loops uFu.
2. Perform as many down-propagation steps as possible.
3. Perform as many transitivity steps as possible.
4. If a leaf is connected via an undirected edge to another, then merge it with that vertex.
5. If any new propagation is possible then go to step 2, else terminate.

By Proposition 2.5 this algorithm will produce the closure, provided we keep track of which vertices the leaves are merged with. Steps 2 and 3 can be performed in *NC*. The problem with this algorithm as a general parallel algorithm is that steps 2 and 3 might have to alternate $O(N)$ times [Dwork et al., 1984].

Let us first examine the $k = 0$ case; (by Proposition 2.4 this is log-space equivalent to *EDFA*). In this case we can argue that executing steps 2 and 3 once suffices. Suppose it does not. Then some new propagation step is enabled, that is, at step 3 we have shown some $x_1 Fx_i$ and y_1, y_i are corresponding successors of x_1, x_i for which we have not discovered $y_1 Fx_i$ and y_1, y_i are corresponding successors of x_1, x_i for which we have not discovered $y_1 Fy_i$. Now in order to show $x_1 Fx_i$ we have found a (perhaps empty) sequence of vertices $x_2, \ldots, x_{i-1}$ such that $x_1 Fx_2, \ldots, x_{i-1} Fx_i$. Because there are no leaves and all outdegrees are 2 there exist $y_2, \ldots, y_{i-1}$, which are the corresponding successors of $x_2, \ldots x_{i-1}$. In Steps 2 and 3 we would have already discovered $y_1 Fy_2, \ldots, y_{i-1} Fy_i$ and therefore $y_1 Fy_i$. This is the desired contradiction.

For the $k \geq 0$ case all we have to note is that in step 4 at every iteration one leaf is eliminated at least. Since k is fixed we reduce to the $k = 0$ case after a fixed number of NC^2 computations. This completes the proof of the theorem.

An immediate Corollary of this theorem is that $MGU^x[kvars]$ for fixed k is in NC^2. Since the mgu^x has only k variables, by counting the number of possible substitutions (i.e., $O(N^k)$) we could reach a similar conclusion. However, the proof of Theorem 2.4 gives a more structured way of building NC^2 circuits for mgu^x. A more involved construction for $MGU[kvars]$ is contained in Yasuura [1983].

Corollary 2.1. $MGU^x[kvars]$ is in NC^2 for each fixed $k \geq 0$.

FIGURE 2.5
The reduction map, ○ in *NC*, ● is P-complete

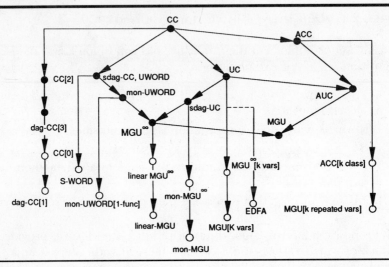

2.7 OPEN PROBLEMS

In Fig. 2.5 we summarize the known results about subcases of congruence closure and unification. The edges (P, Q) between problems can be read as "Q reduces to P."

There are a few problems whose complexity is open. These are *CC[1 axiom]*, *dag-CC[2 axioms]*, *sdag-CC[k axioms]*, and *MGU^x[k repeated vars]*, where $k \geq 2$ and is fixed. We conjecture that these problems are in *NC*.

REFERENCES

Auger, I. E., and Krishnamoorthy, M. S. (1985). "A Parallel Algorithm for the Monadic Unification Problem," *BIT*, Vol. 25, pp. 302–306.

Downey, P. J., and Sethi, R. (1978). "Assignment Commands with Array References," *Journal ACM*, Vol. 25, No. 4, 652–666.

Downey, P. J., Sethi, R., and Tarjan, R. E. (1980). "Variations on the Common Subexpression Problem," *Journal ACM*, Vol. 27, No. 6, pp. 758–771.

Dwork, C., Kanellakis, P., and Mitchell, J. (1984). "On the Sequential Nature of Unification," *Journal of Logic Programming*, Vol. 1, No. 1, pp. 35–50.

Dwork, C., Kanellakis, P., and Stockmeyer, L. (1988). "Parallel Algorithms for Term Matching," *IBM Research Report*, RJ 5328 (to appear in the *SIAM Journal of Computing*).

Fortune, S., and Wyllie, J. (1978). "Parallelism in Random Access Machines," *Proceedings of the 10th ACM STOC*, pp. 114–118.

Hopcroft, J. E., and Karp, R. M. (1971). "An Algorithm for Testing the Equivalence of Finite Automata," *Technical Report 71–114,* Computer Science Dept. Cornell Univ., Ithaca, N.Y.

Huet, G. (1976). "Résolution d'equations dans les langages d'ordre $1, 2, \ldots, \omega$," Thè se d'état de l'Université de Paris 7.

Huet, G., and Oppen, D. (1980). "Equations and Rewrite Rules: A Survey," In *Formal Languages: Perspectives and Open Problems*, Book, R. (ed.), New York: Academic Press, pp. 349–403.

Kozen, D. (1977). "Complexity of Finitely Presented Algebras," *Proceedings of the 9th ACM STOC,* pp. 164–177.

Ladner, R. (1975). "The Circuit Value Problem is Log Space Complete for P," *SIGACT News,* Vol. 7, No. 1, pp. 18–20.

Lloyd, J. W. (1984). *Foundations of Logic Programming,* Berlin: Springer-Verlag.

Martelli, A., and Montanari, U. (1982). "An Efficient Unification Algorithm," *ACM Transactions on Programming Languages and Systems* Vol. 4, No. 2, pp. 258–282.

Nelson, G., and Oppen, D. (1980. "Fast Decision Procedures Based on Congruence Closure," *Journal ACM,* Vol. 27, No. 2, pp. 356–364.

Oppen, D. (1980). "Reasoning about Recursively Defined Data Structures," *Journal ACM,* Vol. 27, No. 3, pp. 403–411.

Paterson, M. S., and Wegman, M. N. (1978). "Linear Unification," *JCSS,* Vol. 16, pp. 158–167.

Pippenger, N. (1979). "On Simultaneous Resource Bounds," *Proceedings of 20th IEEE FOCS,* pp. 307–311.

Ramesh, R., Verma, R. M., Krishnaprasad, T., and Ramakrishnan, I. V. (1987). "Term Matching on Parallel Computers," *ICALP '87.* In *Springer-Verlag Lecture Notes on Computer Science 267,* pp. 336–346.

Robinson, J. A. (1965). "A Machine-Oriented Logic Based on the Resolution Principle," *Journal ACM* Vol. 12, No. 1, pp. 23–41.

Robinson, J. A. (1965). Private Communication in Paterson & Wegman [1978].

Ruzzo, W. L. (1980) "Tree-size Bounded Alternation," *JCSS,* Vol. 21, No. 2, pp. 218–235.

Tarjan, R. E. (1975). "Efficiency of a Good but not Linear Set Union Algorithm," *Journal ACM,* Vol. 22, pp. 215–225.

Thatcher, J. W., and Wright, J. B. (1968). "Generalized Finite Automata Theory with an Application to a Decision Problem of Second Order Logic." *Math. Syst. Th. 2.*

Vitter, J. S., and Simons, R. (1986). "New Classes for Parallel Complexity: A Study of Unification and Other Complete Problems," for *P. IEEE Transactions on Computers C-35,* No. 5, pp. 406–418.

Yasuura, H. (1983). "On the Parallel Computational Complexity of Unification." ER 83-01, Yajima Lab.

CHAPTER 3

CLASS HIERARCHIES AND THEIR COMPLEXITY

Maurizio Lenzerini

3.1 INTRODUCTION

A fundamental feature of an object-oriented database system is to provide modeling primitives for establishing relationships among objects. One of them is classification, which allows objects to be grouped into classes. A *class* represents a set of objects with common properties, called its instances. The set of instances of a class is referred to as its extension. *Membership relationship* is the relationship holding between an object α and any class whose extension includes α. Various kinds of relationships can be established among classes. An important role is played by the so-called *interdependency relationships* [Israel, 84], which allow asserting that a certain set relation holds among the extensions of a collection of classes. For example, disjointness is the interdependency relationship holding between two or more classes having no common instances.

In object-oriented systems, a class is also defined in terms of behavioral properties, as well as aggregations with other classes; however, these aspects are not dealt with in this paper.

Database languages and models include many types of interdependency relationships, such as the *is-a* relationship (see Buneman [1986] and Albano [1985]), which is used to specify inclusion between the extensions of two classes. Several recent works (see Atzeni [1986], Atzeni [1987], Lenzerini [1987], Arisawa [1986], and McAllester [1986]) have considered more complex interdependencies, with the main goal of devising sound and complete rules for their inference.

In Atzeni [1986] a set of inference rules, with correponding algorithms, is presented for is-a and binary disjointness relationships between classes. The work is extended in Atzeni [1987], where negative statements, asserting that a given binary interdependency relationship does not hold, and class complementation, allowing the definition of a class as the complement of another class, are taken into account.

In Lenzerini [1987], relationships among classes and holding when a class is a subset of the union of other classes are considered, and an algorithm for covering relationship inference is provided. Also, the interaction with disjointness relationships is analyzed.

In Arisawa [1986], two interdependency relationships, called intersection extended generalization and union extended generalization, are introduced. The first one allows one to define is-a relationships in which intersections of classes are involved. The second one allows the union of classes to be explicitly referenced in the is-a relationships. For both of these classes, a set of sound and complete inference rules is presented. In the same paper a further type of constraint, expressing that a given disjointness constraint does not hold, is considered, and its interaction with both intersection and union extended generalization is studied.

In McAllester [1986] the usual notion of class is extended to take into account classes that are Boolean combinations of other classes. Interdependency relationships can be expressed in the form $(C$ implies $B)$, where C is a primitive class, and B is a Boolean class expression. Such a relationship specifies that every instance of C is also an instance of B. Membership relationships between objects and primitive classes are also considered. A primitive class C is said to inherit from a class expression E under a set of interdependency relationships S, if $(C$ implies $E)$ is a logical consequences of S. The major goal of the paper is to propose a method for computing inheritance.

In this paper we present a classification of class interdependencies, together with a complexity analysis of reasoning (i.e., performing inferences) about them. To this end, we define the concept of *class hierarchy scheme (CHS)*, which is intended to represent a set of membership and interdependency relationships in an object-oriented system. Typical inferences performed on a CHS T include:

1. *Membership inference*: Is the object α an instance of the class C in T?
2. *Interdependency inference*: Does the interdependency Σ hold in T?

In Section 3.2 we present the syntax and the semantics of a general language for class hierarchy scheme specification. Similar to the work described in McAllester [1986], the language allows one to use not only primitive classes, but also expressions denoting classes obtained from other classes by means of set operations. It is important to note that such a language allows one to specify both that a given relationship (membership or interdependency) holds and that a given relationship *does not* hold in a class hierarchy scheme. As previously mentioned, the same approach is taken in Atzeni [1987], for the case of is-a and disjointness relationships. In the same section we show how a class hierarchy scheme can be expressed in first-order logic. In particular, it is shown that there is a strong correspondence between class hierarchy schemes and monadic first-order theories (i.e., logical theories whose predicates have a single argument).

Using this correspondence, we present in Section 3.3 a classification of class interdependencies, based on the syntactic form of the logical formulas that can be expressed in monadic theories. We also provide a complexity analysis of the inference problem for different types of class hierarchy schemes.

Finally, in Section 3.4 we consider a subclass of CHSs, namely the Horn CHSs, presenting efficient algorithms for membership and interdependency inference in such a subclass.

3.2   A LANGUAGE FOR CLASS HIERARCHY SPECIFICATION

In this section we present a general language, called L_{CH}, for specifying class hierarchy schemes. Such a language allows one to denote not only primitive classes, but also classes whose extensions are obtained as intersection, union, or complement of the extensions of other classes. Class expressions are then used in the specification of interdependency and membership relationships holding among classes.

The description of the syntax of L_{CH} follows.

```
<class expression> ::= <and class> | <or class> |
                       <class literal>

<and class> ::= <class literal> and <class literal> |
                <class literal> and <and class>

<or class> ::= <class literal> or <class literal> |
               <class literal> or <or class>

<class literal> ::= <class symbol> |
                    non <class symbol> |
                    Everything  |  Nothing

<interdependency assertion> ::= [ not ]
                                <class expression> is
                                <class expression>

<membership assertion> ::= [not] <object symbol>
                           is-instance-of
                           <class expression>
```

```
<assertion>  ::=  <interdependency assertion>  |
                     <membership assertion>
```

In the following, we call positive (negative) assertion any interdependency or membership assertion that does not include (includes) the symbol *not*. A class literal, or simply a literal, is called negative if it has the form (*non* < class symbol>), positive otherwise. If C is a positive literal, then (*non C*) is called its complement. Conversely, C is the complement of the negative literal (*non C*).

A *class hierarchy scheme* is a finite set of assertions expressed in L_{CH}.

Turning our attention to the semantics of L_{CH}, we define an interpretation for a class hierarchy scheme T as a triple $<D,O,P>$, where D is a finite set of objects, O is a mapping associating to each object symbol of T an element of D, and P is a mapping associating to each class symbol of T a subset of D, with the constraints: $P(\text{Everything}) = D$, and $P(\text{Nothing}) = \varnothing$.

EXAMPLE 3.1.

Let α be an object symbol, and let A, B, C, D, E, and F be class symbols. Then the following is a class hierarchy scheme expressed in L_{CH}:

> $T = \{ F$ *and* B *is* Nothing
> 　　　A *is* B *or* C
> 　　　*not* (D *and* C *is non* F *or* E)
> 　　　α *is-instance-of* A *and non* $B\}$

The triple $J = <\{a,b\}, O, P>$, where $O(\alpha) = a$, $P(A) = \{a\}$, $P(B) = \varnothing$, $P(C) = \{a,b\}$, $P(D) = \{b\}$, $P(E) = \{a\}$, $P(F) = \{b\}$, is an interpretation for T.

If $I = <D,O,P>$ is an interpretation and C is a class expression, then the *extension* of C with respect to I, denoted by $EXT(C,I)$, is determined by the following rules:

☐　If C is a positive class literal L, then $EXT(C,I) = P(L)$.
☐　If C is negative class literal (*non L*), then $EXT(C,I) = D - EXT(L,I)$.
☐　If C is an And class (L_1 *and* ... *and* L_n), then $EXT(C,I) = \cap_i EXT(L_i,I)$.
☐　If C is an Or class (L_1 *or* ... *or* L_n), then $EXT(C,I) = \cup_i EXT(L_i,I)$.

An interpretation I *satisfies* the positive interdependency assertion

S *is* D

if and only if the extension of S with respect to I is a subset of the extension of D with respect to I. Moreover, I satisfies the positive membership assertion

a *is-instance-of* D

if and only if $O(a)$ is an element of the extension of D with respect to I. An interpretation I satisfies the negative assertion

   not Σ

just in case it does not satisfy the positive assertion Σ.

A *model* for T is an interpretation that satisfies every assertion in T. A class hierarchy specification T is *satisfiable* if there exists at least one model for T, *unsatisfiable* otherwise. *Class hierarchy satisfiability (unsatisfiability)* is the problem of checking if a class hierarchy specification is satisfiable (unsatisfiable).

An assertion Σ *logically follows* from T (alternatively, T *logically implies* Σ) if every model of T satisfies Σ. In this case we write

   $T| = \Sigma$

It can be easily verified that if Σ is a positive assertion, then $T| = \Sigma$ if and only if $T \cup \{$ *not* $(\Sigma)\}$ is unsatisfiable. Conversely, if Σ has the form *not* (Σ), then $T| = \Sigma$ if and only if $T \cup \{\Sigma\}$ is unsatisfiable.

If T' is a set of assertions, then T' logically follows from T (written $T| = T'$) if, for each element t' of T', it holds that

   $T| = t'$

Two sets of assertions T and T' are *equivalent* if $T| = T'$ and $T'| = T$.

Let T be a CHS, and let σ be an assertion; σ is said to be consistent (inconsistent) with T if $T \cup \{\sigma\}$ is satisfiable (unsatisfiable).

A class hierarchy specification T is said to be in *normal form* if the following conditions hold:

1. Every positive interdependency assertion of T is of the form

   S is D

   where S is either a positive literal or an And class composed by positive literals, and D is either a positive literal or an Or class composed by positive literals.

2. Every membership assertion is of the form

   α *is-instance-of D*

   where D is a class expression in which neither Everything nor Nothing appears.

3. No And class or Or class in T contains Everything or Nothing; moreover, no assertion contains Nothing in the left-hand side or Everything in the right-hand side.

Every class hierarchy scheme T can be transformed into an equivalent scheme T' that is in normal form. The following algorithm can be used to perform such a transformation.

Algorithm NORMAL FORM TRANSFORMATION
Input Class Hierarchy Scheme T
Output Class Hierarchy Scheme in normal form T' equivalent to T
begin

1. Replace every assertion of the form

   A_1 *or* . . . *or* A_n *is* D (with $n > 1$)

   with the following n assertions:

   A_i *is* D $(i \in \{1, \ldots, n\})$

2. Replace every assertion of the form

   S *is* A_1 *and* . . . *and* A_n (with $n > 1$)

   with the following n assertions:

   S *is* A_i $(i \in \{1, \ldots, n\})$

3. For each assertion of the form

   S *is* D

   delete any negative literal from S (from D), and add its complement to the Or class D (to the And class S). After all such deletions, replace the empty left-hand side (right-hand side) of any assertion with Everything (Nothing).

4. Replace every membership assertion of the form

   not α *is-instance-of* D

   with the assertion

   α *is-instance-of* D'

   where D' is determined as follows: if D is a literal, then D' is the corresponding complement; if D is an Or class (And class), then D' is the And class (Or class) constitued by the complements of the literals of D.

5. For each assertion Σ, remove Nothing (Everything) from any Or class (And class) appearing in Σ, and replace any And class (Or class) that includes Nothing (Everything), with Nothing (Everything).

end

In the rest of this section we concentrate our attention on the relationship between class hierarchies and first-order logic. In particular, we show how a class hierarchy scheme can be expressed in terms of a first order monadic theory, that is, a first-order theory whose predicate symbols have just one argument. To this end, we describe a mapping MON, which allows any class hierarchy scheme T in normal form to be transformed into a monadic theory MON(T), such that the set of models of MON(T) is in one-to-one correspondence with the set of models of T.

Let T be a class hierarchy specification T in normal form. MON(T) is defined as follows:

☐ The constant symbols of MON(T) are in one-to-one correspondence with the object symbols of T; the predicate symbols of MON(T) have one argument, and are in one-to-one correspondence with the class symbols of T; moreover, MON(T) contains two further unary predicate symbols, namely Everything and Nothing, corresponding to the symbol Everything and Nothing of T; finally, MON(T) includes one variable symbol x.

☐ The axioms of MON(T) are established by the following rules:

  —MON(T) includes the two axioms: ($\forall x$ Everything(x)) and ($\forall x \neg$ Nothing(x)).

  —For each positive interdependency assertion

  S_1 and . . . and S_n is D_1 or . . . or D_m

  of T, MON(T) includes an axiom of the form

  $\forall x(\neg S_1(x) \vee \ldots \vee \neg S_n(x) \vee D_1(x) \vee \ldots \vee D_m(x))$

  —For each negative interdependency assertion

  not S is D

  of T, MON(T) includes an axiom of the form

  $\exists x(\text{MON\_TRANSF}(S,x) \wedge \neg \text{MON\_TRANSF}(D,x))$

where MON_TRANSF(E,z) denotes the logical formula obtained
from the class expression E by transforming respectively *not* into
$\neg$, *and* into $\wedge$, *or* into $\vee$, and every class symbol C of E into the
atomic formula $C(z)$.

—For each membership assertion

α *is-instance-of* D

of T, MON(T) includes an axiom of the form MON_TRANSF(D, α).

EXAMPLE 3.2.

If T is the class hierarchy scheme shown in Example 3.1, then MON(T) is the
monadic theory with constant symbol α, variable symbol x, predicate symbols
A, B, C, D, E, and F, and the following axioms:

$\forall x\,\text{Everything}(x)$
$\forall x\,\neg\,\text{Nothing}(x)$
$\forall x(\,\neg\,F(x)\vee \neg B(x)\vee\,\text{Nothing}(x))$
$\forall x(\,\neg\,A(x)\vee\,B(x)\vee\,C(x))$
$\exists x(D(x)\wedge C(x)\wedge F(x)\wedge\,\neg\,E(x))$
$A(\alpha)\wedge\,\neg\,B(\alpha)$

It is easy to verify that the set of models MON(T) is in one-to-one correspondence with the models of T. In particular, given a model $I = <D, O, P>$
for T, we can construct a model $I' = <D', O', P'>$ for MON(T) as follows:

- D' is the same as D.
- For each constant symbol c of MON(T), $O'(c) = O(a)$, where a is the
  object symbol of T corresponding to c.
- For each predicate symbol U of MON(T), $P'(U) = P(C)$, where C is
  the class symbol of T corresponding to U.

An analogous method can be used to construct a model of T from a model
for MON(T).

Notice that the axioms of a monadic theory obtained from a class hierarchy scheme by the mapping MON are "single-argument formulas," that
is, formulas in which all the predicates have the same argument (either a
variable or a constant).

It is well known that any first-order theory M can be transformed into a
set of clauses (i.e., disjunctions of literals) which is satisfiable if and only if M is
satisfiable. It follows that, for any class hierarchy scheme T, one can construct
a set of clauses (denoted by CLAUSES(T)) which is satisfiable if and only if T
is satisfiable. Notice that CLAUSE(T) may include additional constant symbols

(usually called Skolem constant symbols, as opposed to ordinary constant symbols) with respect to MON(T), due to the elimination of the existential quantifiers.

EXAMPLE 3.3.

We have shown in Example 3.2 the monadic theory MON(T) corresponding to the class hierarchy specification T of Example 3.1. From MON(T) one can easily obtain the following set of clauses CLAUSE(T):

Everything(x)
$\neg$ Nothing(x)
$\neg F(x) \vee \neg B(x) \vee$ Nothing(x)
$\neg A(x) \vee B(x) \vee C(x)$
$D(z), C(z), F(z), \neg E(z), A(\alpha), \neg B(\alpha)$

Notice that z is a Skolem constant symbol, α is an ordinary constant symbol.

3.3 COMPLEXITY ANALYSIS OF CLASS HIERARCHIES

In the first part of this section we present a classification of the basic membership and interdependency relationships expressible in a class hierarchy scheme. We have shown in Section 3.2 that for any class hierarchy scheme, we can construct a set of clauses which is satisfiable if and only if the original class hierarchy scheme is satisfiable. Starting from this observation, we base our classification on the syntactic form of the possible clauses expressible in monadic first order logic. In Figure 3.1 we show such a classification in the form of a diagram.

The formula

$$\forall x \, (A(x) \vee B(x) \vee C(x))$$

is an example of disjunctive positive assertion; it specifies that every object is an instance of at least one of the classes A, B, and C. This corresponds to the interdependency assertion

Everything *is A or B or C*

in the language L_{CH}. When applied to a particular object, these assertions specify that an object is an instance of at least one set of classes. For example, the fact that c is an instance of A or B can be represented by the disjunctive positive assertion

FIGURE 3.1

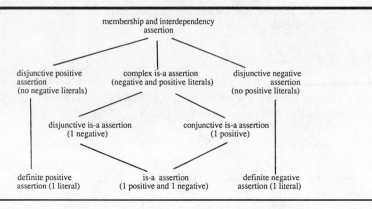

$$\neg A(c) \vee \neg B(c)$$

which corresponds to the negative membership assertion

not c is-instance-of A and B

in L_{CH}.

The formula

$A(c)$

is an example of definite positive assertion, which states that c is an instance of A. In L_{CH}, it corresponds to

c is-instance-of A

Complex is-a assertions allow stating that the extension of an And class is contained in the extension of an Or class. The formula

$$\forall x(\neg A(x) \vee \neg B(x) \vee C(x) \vee D(x))$$

is an example of this kind of assertion, corresponding to

A and B is C or D

in L_{CH}. Complex is-a assertions with a single positive literal on the left-hand side are called disjunctive is-a assertions, whereas complex is-a assertions with a single positive literal on the right-hand side are called conjunctive is-a assertions.

Disjunctive negative assertions allow stating that a set of classes are mutually disjoint. For example, the formula

$$\forall x \, (\neg A(x) \vee \neg B(x))$$

which corresponds to

A and B is Nothing

expresses disjointness between *A* and *B*. When applied to a particular object, these assertions specify that an object is not an instance of a set of classes simultaneously. For example, the fact that *c* is not an instance of both *A* and *B* can be represented by the assertion

$$\neg A(c) \vee \; \neg B(c)$$

which corresponds to the negative membership assertion

not c is-instance-of A and B

in L_{CH}. Finally, a definite negative assertion specifies either the fact that a class has no instances ($\forall x \, \neg A(x)$), or the fact that an object is not an instance of a class ($\neg A(c)$).

It is easy to verify that in Atzeni [1987] the membership and interdependency relationships taken into account are is-a assertions, disjunctive negative assertions involving at most two literals, and positive and negative definite assertions. In Lenzerini [1987], disjunctive is-a assertions together with binary disjunctive negative assertions are considered. The intersection (union) extended generalizations introduced in Arisawa [1986] are simply sets of conjunctive (disjunctive) is-a assertions. Finally, the context in which inheritance is studied in McAllester [1986] is the one of a language including complex is-a assertions and definite positive membership assertions.

The preceding taxonomy provides the basis of our investigation on the computational complexity of the inference problem for class hierarchy schemes. In particular, we now consider in turn different subclasses of class hierarchy schemes, characterized by different types of assertions.

We shall start from the observation that the problem of checking a class hierarchy scheme for satisfiability is in general NP-complete. In fact, the following proposition can be easily verified by considering the relationship between propositional satisfiability and class hierarchy satisfiability (see, for example, Lenzerini [1987]).

Proposition 3.1. Class hierarchy satisfiability is NP-Complete.

The first subclass of CHSs that we consider includes conjunctive is-a assertions and binary disjunctive positive assertions (i.e., disjunctive positive assertions with two literals). The following result shows that the membership inference problem in such a subclass is at least as complex as propositional satisfiability. It is easy to see that the same problem is hard also for the "dual" subclass, that is, the subclass consisting of disjunctive is-a assertions and binary disjunctive negative assertions.

Proposition 3.2. Let T be a CHS with conjunctive is-a assertions and binary disjunctive positive assertions. Let A be a class symbol of T. Then determining if $(T| = \alpha$ *is-instance-of* $A)$ is NP-hard.

Proof. Let PROP be a propositional formula in conjunctive normal form with variables $v_1, \ldots, v_p$. Define a class hierarchy scheme $\Phi(\text{PROP})$ such that

- ☐ for each variable v_i in PROP, there are two class symbols in $\Phi(\text{PROP})$, V_i and V_i'; moreover, $\Phi(\text{PROP})$ includes a distinguished class symbol R.

- ☐ for each variable v_i in PROP, $\Phi(\text{PROP})$ includes an axiom of the form

  (Everything *is* V_i *or* V_i')

- ☐ for each clause

  $$\neg\, v_1 \lor \ldots \lor \neg\, v_n \lor v_{n+1} \lor \ldots \lor v_{n+m}$$

  in PROP, $\Phi(\text{PROP})$ includes an axiom of the form

  (V_1' *and* $\ldots$ *and* V_n' *and* V_{n+1} *and* $\ldots$ *and* V_{n+m} *is* R)

Notice that $\Phi(\text{PROP})$ includes only conjunctive is-a assertions and binary disjunctive positive assertions.

We claim that PROP is unsatisfiable if and only if $(\Phi(\text{PROP}) | = \alpha$ *is-instance-of* $R)$. Assume that $(\Phi(\text{PROP}) | = \alpha$ *is-instance-of* $R)$, and suppose that J is a model for PROP. Define an interpretation $I = <\{\alpha\}, C, P>$ for $\Phi(\text{PROP})$ such that

- ☐ if $J(v_i) = 0$, then $P(V_i') = \varnothing$ and $P(V_i) = \{\alpha\}$.
- ☐ if $J(v_i) = 1$, then $P(V_i) = \Phi$ and $P(V_i') = \{\alpha\}$.
- ☐ $P(R) = \varnothing$.

It is easy to see that I is a model for $\Phi(\text{PROP}) \cup \{not\ \alpha\ is\text{-}instance\text{-}of\ R\}$, which contradicts the hypothesis that $(\Phi(\text{PROP}) | = \alpha\ is\text{-}instance\text{-}of\ R)$.

On the other hand, assume that $\Phi(\text{PROP}) \cup \{not \ \alpha \ \text{is-instance-of} \ R\}$ is satisfiable and let $I = \ <\{\alpha\}, C, P>$ be one of its models. Define an interpretation J for PROP such that

- ☐ if it is not the case that $\alpha \in P(V_i')$, then $J(v_i) = 0$.
- ☐ if it is not the case that $\alpha \in P(V_i)$, then $J(v_i) = 1$.
- ☐ if $\alpha \in P(V_i')$ and $\alpha \in P(V_i)$, then $J(v_i) = 1$.

It is easy to see that I is a model for PROP.

We now consider the class hierarchy schemes in which only complex is-a assertions and definite positive assertions can be expressed, and show that membership inference is NP-hard also for this type of class hierarchy schemes.

Proposition 3.3. Let T be a CHS with complex is-a assertions and definite positive membership assertions. Let A be a class symbol of T. Then, determining if $(T| = \alpha \ \text{is-instance-of} \ A)$ is NP-hard.

Proof. Let PROP be a propositional formula in conjunctive normal form with variables $v_1, \ldots, v_p$. Define a class hierarchy scheme $\Phi(\text{PROP})$ such that

- ☐ for each variable v_i in PROP, there is a class symbol V_i in $\Phi(\text{PROP})$; moreover, $\Phi(\text{PROP})$ includes two distinguished class symbols, Y and N.
- ☐ $\Phi(\text{PROP})$ includes the axiom $(\alpha \ \text{is-instance-of} \ Y)$.
- ☐ for each clause

  $$\neg v_1 \vee \ldots \vee \neg v_n \vee v_{n+1} \vee \ldots \vee v_{n+m} \text{ (with } n > 0 \text{ and } m > 0)$$

  in PROP, $\Phi(\text{PROP})$ includes an axiom of the form

  $$(V_1' \ and \ldots and \ V_n' \ is \ V_{n+1} \ or \ldots or \ V_{n+m})$$

- ☐ for each clause

  $$v_1 \vee \ldots \vee v_n$$

  in PROP, $\Phi(\text{PROP})$ includes an axiom of the form

  $$Y \ is \ V_1 \ or \ldots or \ V_n$$

☐ for each clause

$$\neg v_1 \vee \ldots \vee \neg v_n$$

in PROP, Φ(PROP) includes an axiom of the form

$(V_1 \text{ and} \ldots \text{and } V_n \text{ is } N)$

Notice that Φ(PROP) includes only complex is-a assertions and definite positive assertions.

We claim that PROP is unsatisfiable if and only if (Φ(PROP) $| = \alpha$ *is-instance-of N*). Assume that (Φ(PROP) $| = \alpha$ *is-instance-of N*), and suppose that J is a model for PROP. Define an interpretation $I = <\{\alpha\}, C, P>$ for Φ(PROP) such that $P(Y) = \{\alpha\}$, $P(N) = \varnothing$; moreover, if $J(v_i) = 1$, then $P(V_i) = \{a\}$, else $P(V_i) = \varnothing$. It is easy to see that I is a model for Φ(PROP) $\cup$ {*not α is-instance-of N*}, which contradicts the hypothesis that (Φ(PROP) $| = \alpha$ *is-instance-of R*).

On the other hand, assume that Φ(PROP) $\cup$ {*not α is-instance-of R*} is satisfiable and let $I = <\{\alpha\}, C, P>$ be one of its models. Define an interpretation J for PROP such that if $\alpha \in P(V_i)$, then $J(v_i) = 1$, else $J(v_i) = 0$. It is easy to see that I is a model for PROP.

Finally, we analyze the membership inference problem for class hierarchy schemes with disjunctive positive assertions and disjunctive negative assertions.

Proposition 3.4. Let T be a CHS with disjunctive positive assertions and disjunctive negative assertions. Let A be a class symbol of T. Then, determining if ($T| = \alpha$ *is-instance-of A*) is NP-hard.

Proof. Let PROP be a propositional formula in conjunctive normal form with variables $v_1, \ldots, v_p$. Define a class hierarchy scheme Φ(PROP) such that

☐ for each variable v_i in PROP, there are two class symbols in Φ(PROP), V_i and V_i'; moreover, Φ(PROP) includes a distinguished class symbol R.

☐ for each variable v_i in PROP, Φ(PROP) includes an axiom of the form $(V_i \text{ and } V_i' \text{ is Nothing})$.

☐ for each clause

$$\neg v_1 \vee \ldots \vee \neg v_n \vee v_{n+1} \vee \ldots \vee v_{n+m}$$

in PROP, Φ(PROP) includes an axiom of the form

$(\text{Everything } is \text{ } V_1' \text{ or } \ldots \text{ or } V_n' \text{ or } V_{n+1} \text{ or } \ldots \text{ or } V_{n+m} \text{ or } R)$

Notice that $\Phi(\text{PROP})$ includes only disjunctive positive assertions and disjunctive negative assertions.

We claim that PROP is unsatisfiable if and only if $(\Phi(\text{PROP}) \mid = \alpha$ *is-instance-of* $R)$. Assume that $(\Phi(\text{PROP}) \mid = \alpha$ *is-instance-of* $R)$, and suppose that J is a model for PROP. Define an interpretation $I = <\{\alpha\}, C, P>$ for $\Phi(\text{PROP})$ such that

- □ if $J(v_i) = 0$, then $P(V_i) = \varnothing$ and $P(V_i') = \{\alpha\}$.
- □ if $J(v_i) = 1$, then $P(V_i') = \varnothing$ and $P(V_i) = \{\alpha\}$.
- □ $P(R) = \varnothing$.

It is easy to see that I is a model for $\Phi(\text{PROP}) \cup \{not\ \alpha\ \text{is-instance-of}\ R\}$, which contradicts the hypothesis that $(\Phi(\text{PROP}) \mid = \alpha$ *is-instance-of* $R)$.

On the other hand, assume that $\Phi(\text{PROP}) \cup \{not\ \alpha\ \text{is-instance-of}\ R\}$ is satisfiable and let $I = <\{\alpha\}, C, P>$ be one of its models. Define an interpretation J for PROP such that:

- □ if $\alpha \in P(V_i)$, then $J(v_i) = 1$.
- □ if $\alpha \in P(V_i')$, then $J(v_i) = 0$.

It is easy to see that I is a model for PROP.

Keeping the assumption of classifying hierarchies on the basis on the syntactic form of the expressible membership and interdependency assertions, there are basically three classes that have not been shown to be intractable by the preceding analysis, namely:

- □ Class hierarchy schemes including conjunctive is-a assertions, disjunctive negative assertions, and definite positive assertions.
- □ Class hierarchy schemes including disjunctive is-a assertions, disjunctive positive assertions, and definite negative assertions.
- □ Class hierarchy schemes including is-a assertions, and binary disjunctive assertions (both positive and negative).

The next section is devoted to the first of these classes. Notice that all the considerations presented below can be easily applied to the second class too, for it represents the dual case of the first one.

3.4 HORN CLASS HIERARCHY SCHEMES

In this section we describe a method for performing inferences in a subclass of CHSs, namely the Horn CHSs.

A *Horn CHS (HCHS)* is a class hierarchy scheme such that its normal form satisfies the following conditions:

1. Every positive assertion has a class literal on the right-hand side.
2. For each negative interdependency assertion

   not S is D

   if S is an Or class, then it contains at most one positive literal; if D is an And class, then it contains at most one negative literal.
3. For each membership assertion

   α *is-instance-of D*

   if D is an Or class, then it contains at most one positive literal.

It is easy to see that HCHSs are precisely those class hierarchy schemes whose corresponding sets of clauses are Horn sets.

Our method for performing inferences in HCHSs requires an HCHS to be represented by means of a graph.

Let T be an HCHS. The associated graph G^T is a directed graph $<V, R>$, where

☐ V is the set of nodes, which is partitioned into sets, the P-nodes and the A-nodes. There is one P-node for each class symbol of T, and there is one A-node for each clause of CLAUSE(T) containing two or more negative literals. Moreover, the set of P-nodes includes two distinguished nodes, namely E and N. In the following we denote a P-node of G^T by the name of the associated predicate.

☐ R is the set of arcs, labeled with the constant and variable symbols of CLAUSE(T). For each clause of the form

$Q(w)$

in CLAUSE(T), where Q is different from Everything, there is an arc $<E, Q>$ labeled with w in R. For each clause of the form

$\neg\ Q(w)$

in CLAUSE(T), where Q is different from Nothing, there is an arc $<Q, N>$ labeled with w in R. For each clause of the form

$$\neg\ Q(w) \vee\ P(w)$$

in CLAUSE(T), there is an arc $<Q,P>$ labeled with w in R. For each clause of the form

$$\neg\ Q_1(w) \vee\ \ldots\ \vee \neg\ Q_n(w) \vee P(w)$$

in CLAUSE(T) associated with the A-node A, there are the arcs $<Q_1,A>, \ldots, <Q_n,A>, <A,P>$ labeled with w in R. For each clause of the form:

$$\neg\ Q_1(w) \vee\ \ldots\ \vee \neg\ Q_n(w)$$

in CLAUSE(T) associated with the A-node A, there are the arcs $<Q_1,A>, \ldots, <Q_n,A>, <A,N>$ labeled with w in R.

In the following, we call an *H-graph* any graph associated with a HCHS. If T is a HCHS, and G^T is the associated graph, we say that G^T is also the graph associated with CLAUSE(T). The label of an arc e of a H-graph will be denoted by label(e).

EXAMPLE 3.4.

The following is an HCHS:

$T =$ {*F and B is* Nothing
        A is B
        not (D and C is non F or L)
        C and L is G
        α is-instance-of M and non B
        β is-instance-of non G
        β is-instance-of non M or L)

whose corresponding set of clauses is

CLAUSE(T) = {Everything(x), $\neg$ Nothing(x), $\neg$ $F(x) \vee \neg$ $B(x) \vee$ Nothing(x)
        $D(z), Cz, Fz, \neg$ $L(z), \neg$ $C(x) \vee \neg$ $L(x) \vee G(x)$,
        $M(\alpha), \neg$ $B(\alpha), \neg$ $G(\beta), \neg$ $M(\beta) \vee L(\beta)$}

The H-graph G^T associated with T is shown in Figure 3.2. The A-nodes $A1$ and $A2$ are associated with the third and fifth preceding clauses, respectively.

Let G be an H-graph, and let $Q_1, \ldots, Q_n, P$ be P-nodes of G. A subgraph G' of G is a *c-hyperpath* of G from $\{Q_1, \ldots, Q_n\}$ to P if one of the following conditions holds

FIGURE 3.2

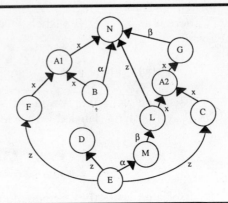

1. $P \in \{Q_1, \ldots, Q_n\}$.
2. There is an A-node A and arcs $<P_1, A>, \ldots, <P_m, A>, <A, P>$ labeled with c or x in G' such that
   - ☐ $P_1, \ldots, P_m$ are all the predecessors of A in G.
   - ☐ For each $i \in \{1, \ldots, m\}$, there is a c-hyperpath of G from $\{Q_1, \ldots, Q_n\}$ to P_i in G'.
3. There is a P-node P_1, and an arc $<P_1, P>$ labeled with c or x in G', and there is a c-hyperpath of G from $\{Q_1, \ldots, Q_n\}$ to P_1 in G'.

Proposition 3.5. An HCHS T is unsatisfiable if and only if there is a c-hyperpath from $\{E\}$ to N in G^T, for some constant or variable symbol c of CLAUSE(T).

Proof. (Sketch) The proof is based on the fact that unit resolution is a sound and complete inference rule for Horn clauses. It is shown that there is a c-hyperpath from $\{E\}$ to N in G^T, for some constant or variable symbol c of CLAUSE(T), if and only if there is a unit refutation of CLAUSE(T).

We now present an algorithm for checking for the existence of a w-hyperpath in an H-graph. The algorithm makes use of a Boolean value mark(P) associated with each node P of the graph. We use unify(a, b) to mean a relation holding when either a and b are the same constant symbol, or one of a and b is a variable. Finally, ground(a, b) is defined as follows: if both a and b are variables, then ground(a, b) = a; otherwise, if a is a constant, then ground(a, b) = a, else ground(a, b) = b.

Algorithm HYPERPATH(G, w, Q)
Input H-graph G, label w, node Q of G, Boolean value mark(P) for each node P of G

Output Boolean value mark(N), which is true if only if there is a w-hyperpath from $\{Q, Q_1, \ldots, Q_m\}$ to N, where $Q_1, \ldots, Q_n$ are the nodes of G such that the initial value of mark(Q_i) is true

```
begin
     if not mark(Q)
     then if Q is a P-node
          then set mark(Q) to true;
               if Q=N then return;
               for each outgoing arc e=<Q,M> of Q
                  such that unify(label(e),w)
               do HYPERPATH(G, ground(label(e),w), M)
               enddo
          else if for each predecessor M of Q,
             mark(M)=true
               then set mark(Q) to true;
                    HYPERPATH(G,w, P), where P is the
                       successor of Q in G
               endif
          endif
     endif
end
```

It is easy to see that there is a c-hyperpath from $\{Q_1, \ldots, Q_m\}$ to N in G if and only if, after the execution of

for each node P of G **do** set mark(P) to false **enddo**;
for each $i \in \{1, \ldots, m\}$ **do** HYPERPATH(G^T, c, Q_i) **enddo**

the value of mark(N) is true. Therefore, the algorithm HYPERPATH can be used for checking an HCHS T for unsatisfiability as follows (we can assume, without loss of generality, that T contains at least one constant symbol):

Algorithm UNSATISFIABLE(T)
Input HCHS T
Output true, if T is satisfiable, false otherwise

begin
    for each constant symbol c (either ordinary or Skolem) of
        CLAUSE(T)
    do for each node P of G^T **do** set mark(P) to false **enddo**;
        HYPERPATH(G^T, c, E);
        if mark(N) = true **then return**(true)
    enddo;
    return(false)
end

If n is the number of constant symbols of CLAUSE(T), which corresponds to the number of objects and negative interdependency assertions of T, and m is the size of CLAUSE(T), then the preceding method can be implemented in $O(nm)$ time. Notice that a method similar to the one used in the algorithm HYPERPATH was presented in Dowling [1984] for the simpler case of propositional satisfiability.

When T is built incrementally, the efficiency of the method can be improved. Suppose we want to construct an HCHS in such a way that new assertions are accepted if and only if the resulting class hierarchy scheme is satisfiable.

Let T be a satisfiable HCHS, and let mark(P) = false for each node P of G^T. We want to add an assertion A to T, obtaining a new HCHS which logically implies A and is satisfiable. Three cases have to be taken into account, depending on the type of assertion to be added to T.

1. If we want to add an interdependency assertion Σ to T, we perform the following operations: first, we check if $S = T \cup \{\Sigma\}$ is an HCHS; if so, we execute

   HYPERPATH(G^S, x, E)

   It can be easily verified that S is satisfiable if and only if, after such an execution, mark(N) = false. In this case, S is the resulting HCHS.

2. Analogously, when we add a membership assertion σ of the form

   α *is-instance-of* D

   to T, we check if $S = T \cup \{\sigma\}$ is an HCHS and, if so, we execute

   HYPERPATH(G^S, α, E)

   S is satisfiable if and only if, after such an execution, the value of mark(N) is false.

3. Finally, when we add a negative interdependency assertion Σ' of the form

   not Σ

   to T, we first check if $S = T \cup \{\Sigma'\}$ is an HCHS and, if so, we execute

   HYPERPATH(G^S, z, E)

   where z is the Skolem constant symbol of CLAUSE(S) which is associated with Σ'. The resulting HCHS S is satisfiable if and only if, after such an execution, mark(N) = false.

These considerations show that the cost of adding an assertion to T is $O(m)$, where m is the size of the resulting HCHS S.

Using the preceding framework, we can efficiently solve the inference problem in HCHSs. In the following, T denotes an HCHS.

Suppose we want to check if a positive interdependency assertion Σ logically follows from T. Let $\{\sigma_1, \ldots, \sigma_n\}$ be the set of assertions obtained by transforming Σ into normal form. Since $(T| = \Sigma)$ if and only if, for each i, $(T| = \sigma_i)$, we can reduce the problem of checking if $(T| = \Sigma)$ to the problem of checking each $(T \cup \{\,not\ \sigma_i\})$ for unsatisfiability. Notice that each $(T \cup \{\,not\ \sigma_i\})$ is an HCHS and, therefore, we can proceed as in case 3 above.

With regard to the membership assertions, notice, first of all, that a negative membership assertion can be transformed into an equivalent positive one. Hence, we deal only with positive assertions in the following. In particular, we distinguish between two cases. If the membership assertion σ has the form:

α *is-instance-of* L_1 *and* $\ldots$ *and* L_p

then $(T| = \sigma)$ if and only if, for each i, $(T| = \alpha$ *is-instance-of* $L_i)$, that is, if and only if for each i $(T \cup \{\alpha$ *is-instance-of* $L_i'\})$ is unsatisfiable, where L_i' is the complement of L_i. Notice that $(T \cup \{\alpha$ *is-instance-of* $L_i'\})$ is an HCHS (see preceding case 2). On the other hand, if σ has the form

α *is-instance-of* L_1 *or* $\ldots$ *or* L_p

then $(T| = \sigma)$ if and only if $S = T \cup \{\alpha$ *is-instance-of* L_1' *and* $\ldots$ *and* $L_p'\}$ is unsatisfiable. Since S is an HCHS, the problem of checking if $(T| = \sigma)$ can be solved by executing

HYPERPATH(G^S, α, E)

and checking if, after such an execution, the value of mark(N) is true.

Finally, with regard to negative interdependency assertions, notice that $(T| = not\ S\ is\ D)$ if and only if there exists a constant symbol α (either ordinary or Skolem constant symbol) of CLAUSE(T) such that $(T| = \alpha$ *is-instance-of* $S)$ and $(T| = not\ \alpha$ *is-instance-of* $D)$. Therefore, we can reduce our original problem to the one of checking if two membership assertions are logically implied by T, for each constant symbol of CLAUSE(T).

An interesting application of membership inference allows us to avoid adding membership assertions that are logically implied by the original class hierarchy scheme. In fact, when we add a membership assertion σ to T, we can not only check if $(T \cup \{\sigma\})$ is satisfiable, as specified by the preceding case 2, but also check if $(T| = \sigma)$; σ will be added to T if and only if it is consistent with T (i.e., $T \cup \{\sigma\}$ is satisfiable) and it is not logically implied by T (i.e., $T| = \sigma$ does not hold).

In order to illustrate how this can be accomplished, let us consider the case in which we want to add a membership assertion σ of the form

α *is-instance-of* Q

to T, where Q is a class literal. The following procedure specifies a method for efficiently deal with this case:

> for **each** node P of G^T do set mark(P) to false **enddo**;
> HYPERPATH(G^T, α, E);
> **if** mark(Q) = true
> **then return**("σ is logically implied by T")
> **else let** S be $T \cup \{\sigma\}$
>   **in** HYPERPATH(G^S, α, P)
>   **if** mark(N) = true
>   **then return**("σ is inconsistent with T")
>   **else return**("S is the resulting CHS")
>   **endif**
> **endif**

It can be shown that with this procedure σ is added to T if and only if it is consistent with T and it is not logically implied by T. Notice that this method is particularly important for CHSs with a large number of membership assertions, as in database applications.

3.5 CONCLUSIONS

Many recent works in object-oriented databases and languages deal with the problem of performing inference on membership and interdependency relationships. In order to provide a common framework for these works, we have presented a taxonomy of such relationships, based on a correspondence between class hierarchy schemes and first-order monadic theories. We have also studied the computational complexity of the inference problem for class hierarchy schemes. Finally, we have considered a subclass of CHSs, namely the Horn class hierarchy schemes, and we have presented efficient methods for performing inference in such a subclass.

In the future, we aim at extending our method to more expressive class hierarchy schemes. For example, one may wonder if there is any method to deal with complex is-a assertions in HCHSs, without falling into the intractability cliff. We believe that one possibility for meeting this requirement is to treat complex is-a assertions differently from the other assertions, namely as integrity constraints. Let T be a CHS in normal form constituted by two disjoint parts: a Horn CHS T_H, and a set T_I of (nonbinary) complex is-a assertions. Say that T is *concrete* if, for each object α of T, and for each complex is-a assertion of the form

S *is* D_1 *or* ... *or* D_p (with $p > 1$)

in T_I, $(T_H| = \alpha$ *is-instance-of* S) implies that there is at least one D_i such that $(T_H| = \alpha$ *is-instance-of* D_i). It turns out that in concrete CHSs, membership inference can be efficiently performed. In fact, it can be shown that if T is a concrete CHS, and σ is a membership assertion of the form (α *is-instance-of* C), where C is a class symbol, then $(T| = \sigma)$ if and only if $(T_H| = \sigma)$. Obviously, a sound and efficient method is needed for incrementally building a CHS in such a way that the resulting scheme be concrete. We shall deal with this and other aspects in future works.

References

Albano, A., Cardelli, L., and Orsini, R., (1985). "Galileo: A Strongly Typed Interactive Conceptual Language," *ACM Transactions on Database Systems*, Vol. 10, No. 2, March.

Arisawa, H., and Miura, T., (1986). "On the Properties of Extended Inclusion Dependencies," *Proceedings of the Twelfth VLDB Conference*, Kyoto.

Atzeni, P., and Stott Parker, D., (1986). "Formal Properties of Net-based Knowledge Representation Schemes," *Proceedings of the 2nd IEEE International Conference on Data Engineering*, Los Angeles, February.

Atzeni P., and Stott Parker, D., (1987). "Set Containment Inference," *Proceedings of the International Conference on Database Theory, Lecture Notes in Computer Science, N.243*, New York: Springer-Verlag.

Buneman, P., and Atkinson, M., (1986). "Inheritance and Persistency in Database Programming Languages," *Proceedings of ACM SIGMOD International Conference on the Management of Data*, Washington, D.C.

Dowling, W. P., and Gallier, J. H., (1984). "Linear-Time Algorithms for Testing the Satisfiability of Propositional Horn Formulae," *Journal of Logic Programming*, Vol. 1, No. 3.

Israel, D. J., and Brachman, R. J., (1984). "Some Remarks on the Semantics of Representation Languages," in Broadie, M. L., et al. (eds.), *On Conceptual Modelling*, New York: Springer-Verlag.

Lenzerini, M., (1987). "Covering and Disjointness Constraints in Type Networks," *Proceedings of the 3rd IEEE International Conference on Data Engineering*, Los Angeles, February.

McAllester, D., and Zabih, R., (1986). "Boolean Classes," *Proceedings of ACM OOPSLA Conference*.

CHAPTER 4

STATIC AND DYNAMIC TYPE CHECKING

David C. J. Matthews

4.1 TYPE CHECKING

Type checking is an effective way of reducing programming errors. Its function is to identify those values to which an operation can be "sensibly" applied. The definition of "sensible" depends on the type system, but usually an operation like adding together two functions is not regarded as sensible, while adding two numbers is.

4.1.1 Static and Dynamic Checking

One way of doing the type checking is to tag each value with a few bits that describe its type. Each operation checks the tag bits and gives some sort of failure if the values have the wrong type. *Dynamic* type checking will prevent some of the more obscure errors but has the disadvantage that the failure is only generated when the program is run.

A better method involves placing some restrictions on the programs that can be written so that the compiler can decide *statically* whether a program could possibly generate type failures when it is run. If the program can be shown to be type correct there is no need for the tags, and we know before the program is ever run that type errors will not occur.

4.1.2 Binding

Related to this method is the question of binding. Declarations bind names to values and so have types. When an identifier is looked up, the value with its type is returned. If there are several identifiers with the same name there must be rules for deciding which one is meant in a particular context.

One of the restrictions for static type checking to be possible is that the compiler must know the type of all the identifiers in the program. This requires *static binding* to identifiers, that is, the identifiers are matched up with their declarations when the program is compiled and does not depend on the execution paths.

It is possible to have *dynamic binding* where an identifier is looked up when the program is run, but static type checking is possible only if all the identifiers with the same name have the same type. General dynamic binding requires dynamic type checking.

4.2 STATIC TYPE CHECKING

Testing a program to try and find errors is difficult, and can never guarantee correctness. The ideal programming language would be one that imposed no restrictions but where the compiler could decide whether the program was correct. Unfortunately that is impossible, so we must accept some restrictions, and even then we only have a limited form of correctness. Type correctness is sufficiently useful that paying the penalty in terms of accepting some restrictions is reasonable, however. Recent developments in the design of type systems, particularly polymorphism, have extended the range of static type checking into areas where traditionally dynamic type checking was thought necessary.

At the lowest level a type must describe the structure of its values in terms of type constructors such as records and unions and the primitive types of the language, in order that the primitive operations can be type checked. In one form of type checking, if a type can be given a name it is treated as an abbreviation for the structure and two values are treated as the same type if they describe the same structure. This is *structural type equivalence* used, for example, in Algol 68.

An alternative is to define that two values have the same type only if they have the same type name. If the type names are different the types are incompatible even if the structures of the types are the same. *Name equivalence* does not mean that the structure of the type is not visible, only that it is not used for type equivalence. *Abstract types* are a variation of name equivalence where the association between a type name, the *abstraction*, and its structure, the *implementation*, is only visible within the abstract type definition. Outside that it has no structure and name equivalence is used. When types can be returned as a result of functions, name equivalence or a variation of it is needed to ensure that type checking is decidable.

4.3 DYNAMIC BINDING AND TYPE CHECKING

Static type checking is useful when a program is being produced to be executed later. If the program is to be executed immediately, and particularly if it just consists of a single command, there is really very little difference between static and dynamic type checking. Command line interpreters, or "shells," are an example. The command

```
edit afile
```

typed to a command interpreter would probably involve a search for the files `edit` and `afile` and checks that `edit` is an executable file and `afile` is a text file. The search and type checking for `afile` might well be done from within the `edit` program. There is no advantage in treating type checking separately from execution.

If several commands are put together in a command script, however, it starts to look more like writing a program. Because the individual commands are dynamically bound and type checked, it is not possible to statically type check the completed script even though it resembles a programming language procedure. Apart from command interpreters the Mentor programming environment is another example where structure editing commands in the Mentol language can be put together into procedures.

Apart from the fact that there is no advantage in statically checking a command that is to be executed immediately, there are other reasons why dynamic type checking is used. Programs often create file names, for instance, by appending standard suffixes unto a name to make a set of related file names. Since the files are dynamically bound they must be dynamically type checked.

Dynamic binding may not only be by name but by other mechanisms as well. In a structure editor a user may select an item by pointing to it with a mouse. Different parts of the structure will have different types so that changes to the structure are constrained, but the function that returns a selected value must be able to return a value of any type. Dynamic type checking must be used if this value is to be copied somewhere else in the structure.

4.4 COMBINING THE TWO

Static type checking is needed for programs that are to be executed in the future, but dynamic type checking is needed for interactive operations. If we have a system where both of these activities can occur we really need both mechanisms.

The obvious way to do this is to take a static type system and add some additional syntax and a new type *dynamic*.

Dynamic *x*

constructs a value of type *dynamic* by packaging up the value with information
describing its type. The inverse operation

coerce *d* **to** *t*

checks that *d* is a dynamic value with the type information appropriate to the
type *t* and returns the original or raises an exception. The syntax is taken
from Amber. Dynamic binding can be done by returning values of *dynamic*
type and then coercing them to the appropriate type.

A dynamic value contains a value and a representation of the type. The
type representation must contain enough information for the **coerce** operation to do the same kind of checking at run-time as the compiler would do
at compile-time. We do not want the dynamic type mechanism to subvert
the static type system. This may be more complicated than it appears. The
rules for static type equivalence, which are applied at compile-time, may not
be reproducible at run-time. To see how the static type system influences
the dynamic typing some static type systems will be examined, both from
languages that have dynamic types and those that do not.

4.4.1 Structure Equivalence

The simplest type systems for this purpose are those, such as Amber, that
have a fixed number of primitive types and use structural equality between
types. Each primitive type can be assigned a unique identifier and data structures used to describe the structured types. Because names for types are
just synonyms for the structure we can always use a representation of the
structure for the type representation. Although the name may be declared
locally the structure representation is valid anywhere so dynamic type checking is safe. Type inheritance in Amber does not have any serious effect on
this.

4.4.2 Polymorphism

If the language allows polymorphic operations, as in ML, dynamic type checking has to be arranged more carefully. Consider the following two functions.

fun *get_dynamic d* = **coerce** *d* **to** α;
fun *make_dynamic x* = **dynamic** *x*;

get_dynamic takes a dynamic value and coerces it to the type variable α.
If the dynamic type matching rules follow the static type rules these should
match for any type since unification of a type variable with any type would
succeed. Clearly this would allow the type system to be broken because

we could make a dynamic value out of, say, an integer value, pass it into *get_dynamic*, and treat the result as a string.

make_dynamic will take any value and make a dynamic value from it. This again could break the type system. A solution to both of these problems is simply to forbid polymorphic types in **coerce** or **dynamic** operations.

4.4.3 Abstract Types

If the static system allows the user to create abstract types we have to produce a unique identifier for each abstract type and use those in type representations. A dynamic value created from the abstract type will contain different type information than a dynamic value created from the representation. This may be difficult if the dynamic value is created inside the abstract type package since there the distinction between the values of the abstract type and the implementation type is blurred.

4.4.4 Parameterized Types

Parameterized abstract types created another problem. If we have a type that can be parameterized by other types or values we need to ensure that any dynamic values created from values of the result type or the argument types have the correct type representation. If the parameterization simply involves macro-expansion this is relatively easy, but if it is done at run-time the type representations will have to be passed as run-time values. The type identifier for the resultant type may have to be created dynamically when the parameterization is done.

For example, we may define a type *tree*, which is a binary tree parameterized by the type of the leaves. Inside the type definition we write an operation to walk over the tree in response to commands from the user and return either a leaf or a piece of tree as a dynamic type.

```
abstype α tree  =  Leaf of α  |Tree of α tree * α tree
with
    fun move "value" (Leaf l) = dynamic l (* Return the leaf *)
     |  move "value" (Tree t) = dynamic t (* Return the tree *)
     |  move "left" (Tree (l, _)) =
            move (nextcommand()) l (* Move left *)
     |  move "right" (Tree (_, r)) =
            move (nextcommand()) r (* Move right *)
     |  move __= raise bad_command (* Anything else *)
end
```

In this example Standard ML has been used with the addition of the operation to create dynamic types. The **dynamic** operations have been applied to polytypes, which would allow the type system to be broken, so clearly this cannot be allowed as it stands. In any case it is difficult to see how it would achieve what is wanted, which is for leaves of *int* trees to be returned as dynamic values coercible to values of type *int*.

If we treat the parameterized type more like a function so that the parameterized type is always used in its parameterized form we can safely allow dynamically typed values to be created and probably get the required behavior. In Standard ML this could be done using a parameterized module, called in ML a *functor*.

> **functor** = *Tree* (*Elem:* **sig type** *t* **end**) =
>   **struct**
>   **datatype** *tree* = *Leaf* **of** *Elem.t* |*Tree* **of** *tree* * *tree;*
>   **fun** *move* = ... (* As before *)
>   **end**

The type *tree* is only available when the functor *Tree* has been applied to a module, in ML a *structure*, containing a type. Other rules in ML ensure that this is a monotype.

> **structure** *IntTree* = *Tree*(**struct type** *t* =*int* **end**);

This creates a tree whose leaves are integers. In order to get the effect we want, the type representation for *int* must have been passed into the functor so that the dynamically typed values returned from leaves are recognizably integers. The tree type *IntTree.tree* itself is a new atomic type so the representation for the type can be created dynamically when the functor is applied.

In CLU, which has parameterized clusters and dynamic types, this is rather more difficult. A cluster parameterized by the same parameter values denotes the same type wherever it appears in a program. Since the type may appear in different segments the CLU linker must examine all the types, construct unique identifiers for each different type, and then pass the identifier to be used for the result of each parameterized type into the type as an additional argument.

4.4.5 Types as Values

In languages such as Russell and Poly types can be treated as first-class values. A type and operations associated with it are packaged together and treated as a run-time value. To ensure decidability, name equivalence has to be used. An expression such as

> **Let** *atype* = = **if** ... **then** *type1* **else** *type2;*

declares *atype* to be a type that is not the same as either *type1* or *type2*, since it is in general not decidable which is actually being returned.

This causes problems if we try to use the dynamic type scheme suggested previously for ML. Suppose *type1* and *type2* are different implementations of trees as in the ML example. They both have *move* functions which return dynamically typed values. If we make a tree of type *type1* we expect the dynamically typed values to be coercible to *type1* but not to *type2* or to *atype*. Similarly, values from *atype* should not be compatible with either *type1* or *type2*. Unfortunately if the type representation is put into the dynamic values inside the abstract type declaration the dynamic values returned from *atype* trees will be either *type1* or *type2*, depending on the actual type returned by the **if**. There seems to be no way to avoid the dynamic type checking behaving differently to the static type checking.

4.5 CONCLUSIONS

Certain applications require dynamic type checking in an otherwise statically typed language. For some type systems this is relatively easy to arrange, but others require considerable thought if the security of the static type system is not to be undermined.

REFERENCES

Cardelli, L., (1984). *Amber*, AT&T Bell Labs, Technical Report.

Demers, A., and Donahue, J., (1979). *Revised Report on Russell*, TR 79-389, Department of Computer Science, Cornell University.

Gordon, M., et al., (1978). "A Metalanguage for Interactive Proof in LCF," *Fifth Annual Symposium on Principles of Programming Languages,* Tucson.

Liskov, B., et al., (1981). *CLU Reference Manual*, Berlin: Springer-Verlag.

MacQueen, D. B., (1985). *Modules for Standard ML*, AT&T Bell Labs, Technical Report.

Matthews, D. C. J., (1985). *Poly Manual*, SIGPLAN Notices, Vol. 20, No. 9, September.

Mélèse, B., et al., (1985). *The Mentor–V5 Documentation*, Technical Report 43, INRIA.

Milner, R., (1984). "A Proposal for Standard ML," In *Proceedings of the 1984 ACM Symposium on Lisp and Functional Programming*, Austin, Tex.

van Wijngaarden, A., et al., (1976). *Revised Report on the Algorithmic Language Algol68*, Berlin: Springer-Verlag.

CHAPTER 5

AN ALGEBRAIC MODEL OF SUBTYPE AND INHERITANCE

Kim B. Bruce
Peter Wegner

5.1 INFORMAL INTRODUCTION

5.1.1 Families of Subtypes

In this paper we develop an algebraic model of subtype based on the idea that a type is a form of behavior and a subtype is a behaviorally compatible specialization of the behavior. This specialization occurs in two related ways. A subtype typically describes a more restricted set of elements than the super-type, but may also involve more specialized information on these elements. This notion of subtype is suggested by object-oriented inheritance, but is broad enough to capture other notions of subtype. In particular we examine three notions of subtype known as "subset," "isomorphically embedded," and "object-oriented" subtypes. Examples of these are

1. Subset: **Int(1..10)** is a "subset" subtype of **Int**.
2. Isomorphically embedded: **Int** is an "isomorphically embedded" subtype of **Real**.
3. Object-oriented: **Student** is an "object-oriented" subtype of **Person**.

Our objective is to characterize both the similarities and the differences between these notions of subtype, and to focus on the algebraic characterization of object-oriented subtypes. We begin by examining informal properties of these three kinds of subtypes and consider the motivations that led to inclusion of these notions of subtype in programming languages. In particular in this section we will work only with an informal, intuitive notion of behavioral compatibility, postponing a more formal description to Section 5.2. These motivating remarks will lead to our definitions of "partial" and "complete" subtypes, also in Section 5.2.

Subset Subtypes.   Subset subtypes restrict the domain of the parent type to a subset, without necessarily considering whether operations of the type are closed over the subset. A subtype **Int(1..10)** of **Int** restricts the domain of integers without regard to the closure of operations such as addition, multiplication, or successor on the set $\{1, \dots, 10\}$. If we restrict the domain and range of the successor function in this way, then it becomes a partial function since successor(10) is outside 1..10. This means that the behavior of **Int(1..10)** is only partially compatible with **Int** because the behavior of successor on the argument 10 for the subtype is incompatible with the behavior of successor for this argument in the parent type. However, if we let the permitted range be 2..11 or some superset, such as the full set of integers, then complete behavioral compatibility for the successor function is retained. The subtypes of **Int** of the form **Int(1..10)** may be defined in two alternative ways; namely as "complete" or "partial" subtypes.

Complete subtypes are behaviorally compatible with their parent types, while partial subtypes are only required to be partially behaviorally compatible. While we will be concerned primarily with complete subtypes, we will also consider partial subtypes.

Isomorphically Embedded Subtypes.   Isomorphically embedded subtypes are generally well-behaved algebras in their own right. They are embedded in larger domains to achieve closure under certain operations. For example, Int is a well-behaved algebra under addition and multiplication, but must be extended to the rationals to achieve closure under nonzero division. Pythagoras realized that the rationals were not closed under square root and this led to an extension of the rationals to the algebraic numbers, and later to the reals. Lack of closure of the reals for square roots with negative arguments led to the further extension from the reals to complex numbers.

We note here that in the formal mathematical development of the reals from the integers, while an isomorphic copy of the integers is contained in the reals, the integers themselves are set theoretically much simpler objects. This, of course, is true as well of the computer representations of reals and integers. The integer "2" is not represented the same way as the real number "2," although there is an obvious coercion of the integer representation to the real representation. This may look like nitpicking here, but we will see later that this notion of "coercion" or mapping from a subtype to a supertype is quite important to our development.

In viewing **Int** as a type in relation to the type **Real**, the function "sqrt" is highly partial when looked at as a function from integers to integers, but is defined for all nonnegative integers if the value of the function is allowed to be real. Thus if the range of the function "sqrt" over **Int** is the reals, **Int** will be a complete subtype of **Real** (presuming the other functions inherited from the reals are behaviorally compatible), whereas if the range of "sqrt" over **Int** is the integers, then **Int** could only be a partial subtype of **Real**. If we further wish to view **Int** as a subtype of **Complex** and allow the values to be complex, "sqrt" determines a total function on the integers.

Object-Oriented Subtypes.   Object-oriented subtypes have better closure properties than subset or isomorphically embedded subtypes. Consider the type **Person** with the following operations:

> name : Person → Character String
> age : Person → Integer
> add-a-year : Person → Person

Let the subtype Student have the additional operation gpa (grade-point average).

> gpa : Student → Integer

Operations on the names and ages of students have the same closure properties as for persons. The range of name and age is independent of the parent type, while the operation add-a-year modifies a person by changing its age attribute. Thus if the domain of add-a-year is restricted to students, its values will be students.

Note that subtypes which are defined in terms of the restriction of the range of component operations may cause a breakdown for closure properties. For example, if the class of minors is defined as the class of persons under 21, then functions like "add-a-year" are no longer closed.

When operations have a range dependent on the supertype, closure may again become a problem. Consider adding the following operation to **Person**:

> parent : Person → Person

Specializing the domain and range of the parent operation to students results in closure problems for the partial subtype. The subtype that uses the original range is needed for behavioral compatibility, just as in the case of subset and isomorphically embedded subtypes, since the parent of a student need not be a student. However, object-oriented operations whose range is restricted to traditional types, as well as those which modify the object to which the operation is applied, are generally well-behaved in the sense that they are closed over the partial subtype formed by replacing all occurrences of sorts from the supertype with the corresponding ones in the subtype. Thus the problem of distinguishing between partial subtypes and complete subtypes often does not arise since partial subtypes and complete subtypes are usually equivalent.

5.1.2 Algebraic Framework

Traditional algebras have just a single sort that denotes the values of the algebra and have a collection of operation symbols that denote operations for transforming tuples of arguments into values. For example, the algebra of integers has the sort "Integer" and operation symbols "+" and "*" that denote binary operations on integers.

Programming language types are modeled by many-sorted algebras whose operations may have arguments and values of more than one sort. For example stacks with integer elements have the sorts "Int," "Boolean," and "Stack," and may have the following operations:

"push" which takes arguments of the sorts "Int" and
"Stack" and produces a value of the sort "Stack,"

"empty" which takes an argument of the type "Stack" and
produces a value of the sort "Boolean."

As a first step toward capturing the notion of subtype, we will extend algebras to include an ordering relation " $\leq$ " on sorts. The intuition behind this ordering is that if $s \leq t$ then every element of s can be understood (treated) as an element of t. Goguen and Meseguer [1986] defined " $s \leq t$ " to mean that s is a subset of t and all operations in the parent type involving arguments of the sort t correspond to behaviorally compatible operations in the subsort. We will define $s \leq t$ later (as part of the definition of a generalized order-sorted algebra) by the notion of having a "well-behaved" coercer from elements of s to elements of t. To be "well-behaved," the coercion functions should preserve partial behavioral compatibility of all functions under the coercion.

Generalized order-sorted algebras are more inclusive than order-sorted algebras because they allow many-to-one as well as one-to-one coercion mappings of subsorts into sorts of a supertype. Many-to-one coercers are very useful in modeling object-oriented subtypes, as we illustrate in this paper. However, even one-to-one coercers may be more natural than subsets. For example, the embedding of integers in the reals is more naturally described by a one-to-one coercion mapping than by viewing the integers as a subset of the reals. A similar case can be made for characters and strings. The weakening of the requirement on order-sorted algebras from complete behavioral compatibility to partial behavioral compatibility also will allow us to model natural situations arising in programming languages that would be excluded under the more restrictive condition.

We can use this ordering and its related intuition to define the notion of subtype. If T_1 and T_2 are types, the notion "T_2 is a complete subtype of T_1" may be defined in terms of generalized order-sorted algebras roughly as follows (the more precise definition will be given later):

1. The types T_2 and T_1 must coexist in the same generalized order-sorted algebra.
2. Every sort of T_1 is "$\geq$" a corresponding sort of T_2.
3. T_2 has all the operations of T_1 and they are "behaviorally compatible."

Our definition of complete subtype lifts the ordering relation on sorts to an ordering relation on types. Notice that the definition of $\leq$ on sorts preserves partial behavioral compatibility, whereas that given for subtypes requires (complete) behavioral compatibility. We believe that this distribution of responsibility leads to a more flexible and inclusive modeling of subtypes. We will also define partial subtypes essentially by modifying clause (3) to refer to "partially behaviorally compatible" operations.

Since inheritance is modeled by the presence of overloaded operators, it is quite important to be able to resolve ambiguity introduced by overloaded operators. Goguen and Meseguer [1986] introduced a syntactic constraint on programming languages, called regularity, to resolve ambiguities caused by overloading and inheritance.

Intuitively, the ordering of sorts yields a derived ordering on both overloaded operations and types. Regularity implies that terms that can be assigned a sort have a unique least sort. We show that regularity, combined with our definition of subtype, allows us to resolve potential ambiguities due to overloading. In particular, we prove the following uniqueness theorem for terms of a generalized order-sorted algebra:

THEOREM 5.1   Let $(\Sigma, \leq)$ be a regular signature and A a generalized order-sorted algebra for $(\Sigma, \leq)$. If M can be assigned sort s then all interpretations of M in the carrier of s are identical.

This theorem asserts that even if there is more than one way of assigning a sort s to the term M (due to overloading of operators), all interpretations of M in this carrier are unique. The proof of this theorem is similar to that of the initiality theorem of Goguen and Meseguer [1986], but is given in a more general setting here.

In summary, the contributions of this paper include:

1. A generalization of order-sorted algebras to provide a subtler and more useful notion of ordering on sorts.
2. Algebraic definitions of type and subtype for order-sorted algebras.

3. A classification of subtypes into complete and partial subtypes, based on preserving complete or partial behavioral compatibility.

4. A demonstration that these notions of subtype capture both traditional and object-oriented notions of subtype.

5. A uniqueness theorem for interpreting terms in the presence of overloading.

5.2 ALGEBRAIC MODELS OF TYPE

Algebras can be syntactically specified by their signatures, where a signature specifies the sorts and operations of the algebra. The signature forms the basis for the syntax of a formal language of terms. From a given signature, one may form terms, which will denote individual elements of the algebra. The semantics is given with respect to an algebra and is specified by an interpretation of sort symbols as carrier sets of the algebra and of operations as functions whose domain and range are carrier sets.

5.2.1 Many-Sorted Algebras

A many-sorted algebra consists of a collection of sets and operations on these sets. These algebras can be classified according to the number of sets and kinds of operations included in the algebra. Let S be a collection of symbols, called sorts. An S-sorted set is a collection $A = \{A_s \mid s \in S\}$ of sets. A will consist of the carriers (base sets) of our many-sorted algebras, while S provides names for these sets. In the following we will use w_i to denote an n-tuple of elements from S. The functionality of operations provided in the algebra can be described using a signature. The signature of a many-sorted algebra can be denoted by

$$\Sigma = \ <S; f_1: \ <w_1, s_1>, f_2: \ <w_2, s_2>, \ \ldots >$$

where S is a collection of sorts, each $s_i \in S$, and each w_i is a tuple of elements from S. Each f_i denotes a function whose domain corresponds to w_i and whose codomain corresponds to s_i. An example should make this clearer. A stack of integers is built on the sorts "Int, Stack, and Bool," and has the following signature:

$ST = \ <\{\text{Int, Stack, Bool}\}; \text{push}: \ <<\text{Stack,Int}>, \text{Stack}>, \text{pop}:$
$<<\text{Stack}>, \text{Stack}>, \text{top}: \ <<\text{Stack}>, \text{Int}>, \text{empty}: \ <<\text{Stack}>,$
$\text{Bool}>> \ .$

Note that the signature only provides symbols to be used in describing an algebra. Thus the symbols Int, Stack, Bool, push, pop, top, and empty are all uninterpreted. The many-sorted algebras will provide the meaning or semantics of these symbols by providing a set of elements for each sort and a function with a corresponding domain and range for each function symbol in the signature.

Definition 5.1. Let Σ be a signature with sort set S. A is a **many-sorted algebra** for Σ if A consists of an S-sorted set $\{A_s \mid s \in S\}$, consisting of the carriers of A, and a partial function $A_f : A_w \rightarrow A_s$ for each $f : <w,s>$ in Σ, where $A_w = A_{s1} \times \ldots \times A_{sn}$ when $w = <s_1, \ldots, s_n>$ and A_w is a one-point set when w is empty.

Since a type in a programming language consists of both objects and operations on the objects, we will use many-sorted algebras to model the notion of type. Because a type may contain many carrier sets, it is not immediately apparent how to define the notion of subtype. It will turn out, for instance, that the notion of subalgebra from mathematics is too restrictive to capture the richness of subtype in programming languages. In the next section we explore generalizations of many-sorted algebras which will enable us to also model subtype.

5.2.2 Generalized Order-Sorted Algebras

The notions of subtype and inheritance can be modeled by first defining an ordering relation on the sorts. Goguen and Meseguer [1986] have introduced the notion of an "order-sorted algebra" to model subtypes and inheritance.

Definition 5.2. An **order-sorted signature** is a pair $<\Sigma, \leq>$, where Σ is a many-sorted signature and $\leq$ is a partial ordering on the sorts in Σ. We extend this ordering to ordered tuples of sorts by writing $<s_1, \ldots, s_n> \leq <s_1', \ldots, s_n'>$ if $s_i \leq s_i'$ for $1 \leq i \leq n$. We say that an operation is **overloaded** if it appears in the signature Σ with two different typings. We will say that t is a **subsort** of s if $t \leq s$.

An order-sorted algebra with signature $<\Sigma, \leq>$ is a many-sorted algebra with an ordering relation on the carriers of its sorts, and is given by the following definition.

Definition 5.3. A is an **order-sorted algebra** for order-sorted signature $<\Sigma, \leq>$ if A is a many-sorted algebra for Σ such that:

1. If $s \leq t$ then $A_s \subseteq A_t$.
2. If $f : <w,s>, f : <w',s'>$ with $<w,s> \leq <w',s'>$ then $A_f : A_w \rightarrow A_s$ and $A_f' : A_{w'}' \rightarrow A_{s'}'$ agree on A_w (where $A_f : A_w \rightarrow A_s$ and $A_f' : A_{w'}' \rightarrow A_{s'}'$ are the meanings of the overloaded f).

Conditions (1) and (2) state respectively that the interpretation of a subsort is a subset (although the reverse is not necessarily true), and that corresponding operations on the subsort and supersort must be "behaviorally compatible." A first approximation at a definition of "behavioral compatibility" could be the following: Corresponding operations on a sort and subsort are "behaviorally compatible" if they are defined for exactly the same elements of the subsort, and where defined, they give the same result.

We note that a many-sorted algebra corresponds to a degenerate order-sorted algebra in which each sort is only related to itself.

While the definition of order-sorted algebras implies that interpretation of the subsort relation is subset, different interpretations of subsort will produce somewhat different semantics. In this paper we propose a new interpretation of $\leq$ on the carrier sets which preserves a somewhat weaker form of behavioral compatibility. Our generalized order-sorted algebras will interpret $\leq$ via a set of coercion functions $c_{s,t}$, one for each pair s,t such that $s \leq t$. This generalization to coercers will prove to be most useful in modeling subtypes in real programming languages, especially object-oriented languages.

Definition 5.4. A is a **generalized order-sorted algebra** for order-sorted signature $< \Sigma, \leq >$ if $A = < A, CO >$ where A is a many-sorted algebra for Σ and $CO = \{cs,s' : A_s \to A'_s | s \leq s'\}$ is a collection of functions such that the following conditions hold:

1. For each pair $s \leq s'$ there is a unique $c_{s,s'} : A_s \to A'_s$ in CO.
2. For each sort s, $c_{s,s}$ is the identity on A_s, and if $s \leq t \leq u$ then $c_{s,u} = c_{t,u} \circ c_{s,t}$.
3. Suppose $< w,s > \leq < w',s' >$ and $f : < w,s >$, $f : < w',s' >$, for $w = < s_1, \ldots, s_n >$ and $w' = < s'_1, \ldots, s'_n >$ in the order-sorted signature $< \Sigma, \leq >$, and let $A_f : A_w \to A_s$ and $A'_f : A'_w \to A'_s$ be the meanings of the overloaded f. Then for all $a_1 \in A_{s1}, \ldots, a_n \in A_{sn}$, if $A_f(a_1, \ldots, a_n)$ is defined, then $c_{s,s'}(A'_f(a_1, \ldots, a_n)) = A'_f(c_{s1,s1'}(a_1), \ldots, c_{sn,sn'}(a_n))$.

Thus (1') and (2') of the new definition replace the previous requirement that $\leq$ be set inclusion by the requirement that there be a coercer from the smaller set to the larger. (3') is the equivalent of (2) for this new ordering on carriers, and continues to ensure that if an attribute of a type is redefined in a subsort, then the new definition is consistent with that of the old one. In other words, the coercers behave like homomorphisms.

It is important to note that we do not require the coercers to be injective. This will be quite important when we look at examples of subtypes which arise from object-oriented languages. While if we restrict all coercers to be simply set inclusion maps we get back something close to the original order-sorted algebras, there is another important difference between the two definitions.

In the generalized order-sorted algebras the corresponding functions in the supersort and subsort are only "partially behaviorally compatible" (modulo the coercion function). That is, we require the definitions over the supersort and subsort to correspond (via the coercers) if the function is defined on the subsort. However we do not necessarily require the function on the subsort to have a value if it has a value on the supersort. This weakening of the conditions results in some fairly major differences from the preceding definition of order-sorted algebras. The following example illustrates these differences.

Let $\Sigma_C = \; <\{R,C\}; \; \text{sqrt}: \; << R >, R >, \; \text{sqrt}: \; << C >, C >>$ be a many-sorted signature and let **Comproot** be the many-sorted algebra for Σ_C in which R and C are interpreted as the sets of real and complex numbers, respectively. In this algebra let sqrt: $<< R >, R >$ be interpreted as $\sqrt{R}$, the usual partial square root function on the reals, whose domain is the nonnegative reals. Similarly let $\sqrt{C}$ be a total square root function on the complex numbers which extends $\sqrt{R}$. It is then impossible to make **Comproot** into an order-sorted algebra corresponding to the preceding signature where $R \leq C$, since $\sqrt{R(-1)}$ is undefined, but $\sqrt{C(-1)}$ is defined (typically as i). Note that adding new functions to the signature and algebra will not help since (2) of the definition of order-sorted algebra requires the meanings of all versions of overloaded functions to agree if the domains are related.

Our definition of generalized order-sorted algebra does not suffer from this defect. **Comproot** can easily be made into a generalized order-sorted algebra by adding the coercer $c_{R,C}$, where $c_{R,C}$ is the usual coercer from reals to complex numbers (e.g., $c_{R,C}(r) = r + 0i$). Since $\sqrt{R}$ and $\sqrt{C}$ agree on the nonnegative reals (the domain of $\sqrt{R}$), they satisfy (3') of the definition of generalized order-sorted algebras.

Not surprisingly, this is an example of a general phenomenon. It is quite common in mathematics to start with an algebra with partial functions and extend to a larger algebra in which the partial functions become total. One commonly views the extension from the natural numbers to the integers as a way of obtaining a set that is closed under subtraction; the extension from integers to rationals as a way of closing under nonzero division, the extension from rationals to reals as closing under limits of Cauchy sequences; and the extension from reals to complex numbers as closing under roots of polynomials. We feel it would be unfortunate to bar these original partial functions from coexisting in order-sorted algebras with the corresponding total functions on the extensions.

On the other hand, the generalized order-sorted algebras may be criticized as failing to preserve behavior since the corresponding function defined in the subsort may be highly undefined relative to the function defined on the supersort when restricted to elements of the subsort. We see this as a positive feature that reflects the flexibility of the system. However, when we formalize the notions of complete subtype in what follows, we will place stronger restrictions on overloaded functions which will ensure that there is at least one version of the overloaded function in the subtype which is completely "behaviorally compatible" with that in the supertype. We will also introduce a weaker notion of subtype without this restriction, which we will call "partial subtype."

5.2.3 Types and Subtypes

Generalized order-sorted algebras may be used to model both single types and collections of related types. Collections of types will have a set of sorts that is the union of the sets of sorts associated with types in the collection. A type **T** that is interpreted in a generalized order-sorted algebra A may be defined as follows.

Definition 5.5.   Let A be a generalized order-sorted algebra with signature Σ, and let $\Sigma \supseteq \Sigma_0$. A **type T** with signature Σ_0 in A is a generalized order-sorted algebra with signature Σ_0 such that for each sort s in Σ_0, $T_s = A_s$, and for each f in Σ_0, $T_f = A_f$.

Notice that because **T** itself must be a generalized order-sorted algebra (and thus a many-sorted algebra) with signature Σ_0, all sorts that occur in the range and domain of operations in Σ_0 are in Σ_0, and hence are interpreted in **T**. A special case occurs when the type is the entire order-sorted algebra. The more interesting cases will occur when several types are represented in the same generalized order-sorted algebra. This will be the situation in our definition of subtype.

We note here that it is possible to state our definition of type in a more general way by having each sort of Σ_0 map to a sort of Σ, and having operators f of Σ_0 map to operators definable in Σ. For example, the sort IntStack might be mapped to a sort List(Int), pop might be mapped to a function tail, and so on. While this definition might be more appropriate in discussing implementations of abstract data types, we will retain the preceding definition for simplicity.

Note that there are no conditions on either the order-sorted or generalized order-sorted algebras which require functions definable on a supersort to be inherited by the subsort. Since our motivation for looking at the notion of subtype comes from object-oriented languages, an important part of the definition of subtypes will have to do with inheritance of behaviorally compatible operations. We begin with a definition of partial subtypes. These are weak forms of subtypes in which the inherited operations need only be "partially behaviorally compatible."

Definition 5.6.   Let T_1 and T_2 be types with signatures $<\Sigma_1, \leq_1>$ and $<\Sigma_2, \leq_2>$, respectively, in the same generalized order-sorted algebra A whose signature, $<\Sigma, \leq>$, includes $<\Sigma_1, \leq_1>$ and $<\Sigma_2, \leq_2>$. Then T_1 is a **partial subtype** of T_2 "iff"

1. For every sort t in Σ_2, there is a sort s in Σ_1 such that $s \leq t$.
2. For all operators f, if $f : <w, s>$ in Σ_2 and $w' \leq w$ for w' from Σ_1, then there is an $s' \leq s$ and an $f : <w', s'>$ in Σ_1.

Note that the syntactic conditions (1) and (2) ensure that operators from T_2 are inherited in T_1. The requirement that T_1 and T_2 live in the same generalized order-sorted algebra combines with these syntactic restrictions to ensure that the inherited operations are "partially behaviorally compatible" with the operations in the supertype. That is, if $f : <<s_1, \ldots, s_n>, s>$ and $f : <<t_1, \ldots, t_n>, t>$ with $s \le t$ and $s_i \le t_i$ for $1 \le i \le n$ in Σ, A is an order-sorted algebra for Σ, a_i in A_{si} for $1 \le i \le n$, and $A_f(a_1, \ldots, a_n)$ is defined, then $c_{s,t}(A_f(a_1, \ldots, a_n)) = A_f'(c_{s1,t1}(a_1), \ldots, c_{sn,tn}(a_n))$, where the A_f on the left side of the equation is the interpretation of the f with signature $<<s_1, \ldots, s_n>, s>$ and the A_f' on the right side of the equation is the interpretation of the f with signature $<<t_1, \ldots, t_n>, t>$. Thus, the coercers essentially behave as homomorphisms from the A_{si} to A_{ti} with respect to overlapping function definitions. Note that if $A_f'(c_{s1,t1}(a_1), \ldots, c_{sn,tn}(a_n))$ is defined, we do not insist that $A_f(a_1, \ldots, a_n)$ be defined.

Thus partial subtypes provide "partially behaviorally compatible" inherited functions. A complete subtype will be a partial subtype in which inherited functions are completely "behaviorally compatible."

Definition 5.7. Let T_1 and T_2 be types with signatures $< \Sigma_1, \le_1 >$ and $< \Sigma_2, \le_2 >$, respectively, in the same generalized order-sorted algebra A whose signature, $< \Sigma, \le >$, includes $< \Sigma_1, \le_1 >$ and $< \Sigma_2, \le_2 >$. Then T_1 is a **complete subtype** of T_2 "iff"

1. For every sort t in Σ_2, there is a sort s in Σ_1 such that $s \le t$.
2. For all operators f, if $f : <w, s>$ in Σ_2 and $w' \le w$ for w' in Σ_1, then there is an $s' \le s$ and an $f : <w', s'>$ in Σ_1 (i.e., f is inherited on w') which satisfies the following property: If $A_f : A_w \to A_s$ and $A_f' : A_{w'}' \to A_s'$ are the meanings of the overloaded f, then for all $a_1 \in A_{s1}, \ldots, a_n \in A_{sn}$, if either of $A_f(a_1, \ldots, a_n)$ or $A_f'(c_{s1,s1'}(a_1), \ldots, c_{sn,sn'}(a_n))$ are defined, then they both are.

Note that (2) can be simplified to read "if $A_f'(c_{s1,s1'}(a_1), \ldots, c_{sn,sn'}(a_n))$ is defined, then so is $A_f(a_1, \ldots, a_n)$." The other implication follows from the definition of generalized order-sorted algebra. For clarity, we leave the definition in the preceding form. It then follows from the definitions of generalized order-sorted algebra and complete subtypes that if either of $A_f(a_1, \ldots, a_n)$ or $A_f'(c_{s1,s1'}(a_1), \ldots, c_{sn,sn'}(a_n))$ are defined then they both are, and have corresponding values (via the coercers). Thus a complete subtype is a partial subtype in which the inherited functions are completely, rather than partially, behaviorally compatible.

Several examples will be given in the next section to illustrate how this definition captures the three most important varieties of subtypes in real programming languages. We give a simple example here to illustrate the previous definitions.

According to the previous definitions, the natural many-sorted algebra (described after the definition of generalized order-sorted algebra) corresponding to $< \{R\}; \text{sqrt}: << R >, R >>$ is only a partial subtype of that corresponding to $<\{C\}; \text{sqrt}: <<C>, C>>$, since there is no interpretation of sqrt in the partial subtype which is "as defined" on the reals as the interpretation of sqrt over the complexes. However, if we add a new function with functionality, sqrt: $<<R>, C>$, the natural algebra corresponding to $<\{R\}; \text{sqrt}: <<R>, R>, \text{sqrt}: <<R>, C>>$ is a complete subtype of that for $<\{C\}; \text{sqrt}: <<C>, C>>$, because the interpretation of the second version of sqrt in the subtype is defined on exactly the same reals as that of sqrt in the supertype (i.e., both are total on the reals).

Notice that in a generalized order-sorted algebra, functions defined on supertypes can almost "automatically" be inherited by their subsorts via the following mechanism. Let $<\Sigma, \le >$ be an order-sorted signature that contains $f: <<s_1, \ldots, s_n>, s>$ and sorts $t_1, \ldots, t_n$ such that $t_i \le s_i$ for $1 \le i \le n$. If A is an order-sorted algebra for $<\Sigma, \le >$, then f can be interpreted as a function from $A_{t1} \times \ldots \times A_{tn}$ to A_s as follows. Define $A_f^i: A_{t1} \times \ldots \times A_{tn} \to A_s$ by $A_f^i(a_1, \ldots, a_n) = A_f(c_{t1,s1}(a_1), \ldots, c_{tn,sn}(a_n))$. Of course the result of A_f^i could also be coerced into a greater sort by applying another coercer after the result in A_s is obtained. Similarly if the range of A_f^i is contained in some other A_t in A, for $t \le s$, f could be added with signature $f: <<t_1, \ldots, t_n>, t>$. This is often the case with object-oriented languages.

Note that if **S** is a complete subtype of **T** in A, then the definition of subtype requires that a corresponding f exist in **S**, so we need not go through this procedure to inherit f. On the other hand this process can be used to add a corresponding f to a partial subtype **S** (or even just a type **S** which, with **T**, satisfies (1) of the definition of subtype) in order to make it into a complete subtype.

Notice the similarity between this process and (3′) in the definition of generalized order-sorted algebras. This similarity helps ensure that if f was overloaded then all legal computations involving f which give a result in the same (or consistent) sort would result in the same (or consistent) answer, no matter which of the possible legal values of the overloaded f was used in the computation. This issue will be explored more carefully in Section 5.4.

5.2.4 Sorts versus Types

It may be helpful at this point to clarify the distinction between sorts, types, and subtypes. The interpretation of a sort (the carrier of the sort) is simply a set of objects (with no associated operations). A type is a generalized order-sorted algebra which consists of the carriers of one or more sorts plus operations acting on (and giving results in) the carriers of the sorts. Thus a type has both sets of elements and operations (consisting of interpretations of the symbols in its order-sorted signature). A type **T** is a subtype (either complete or partial) of a type **U**, if **T** and **U** are embedded in the same generalized order-sorted sorted algebra A in such a way that every sort of **U** is a supersort of a sort of **T** and overloaded functions are behaviorally compatible. Thus while types are generalized order-sorted algebras, we can only determine if one type is a subtype of another by looking at a larger generalized order-sorted algebras in which both live. Typically this generalized order-sorted algebra will contain all of the sorts and operations defined in the language (or at least in the particular program under consideration).

Unfortunately there is great confusion in programming languages about the difference between a type and a sort. Most programming languages define types to be what we have referred to here as sorts. This leads to discussions about the types of terms, whereas we would instead refer to the "sorts" of terms. We are not happy with this confusion of terminology, but have adopted the terminology used here since it is consistent with that used by other workers modeling types by algebras. A possible solution to this confusion might be to reserve the name abstract data type (or ADT) for what we have termed types, and use type interchangeably with sort. Since our types are not necessarily very abstract, we have resisted this temptation.

5.3 SUBTYPES AND INHERITANCE IN PROGRAMMING LANGUAGES

Our formal definitions of types and subtypes in terms of generalized order-sorted algebras were carefully constructed to describe notions of subtype that arise in real programming languages. In particular they are intended to capture the following three notions of subtype:

1. Subset: **Int(1..10)** is a "subset" subtype of **Int**.
2. Isomorphic Copy: **Int** is an "isomorphic embedding" subtype of **Real**.
3. Object-oriented: **Student** is an "object-oriented" subtype of **Person**.

Let us examine each of these situations carefully to see how they fit into our definitions. We begin with "subset" subtypes.

5.3.1 "Subset" Subtypes

Let $< \Sigma, \leq >$ be the order-sorted signature $<$ {Smallint, Int}; $+$: $<<$Smallint, Smallint $>$, Smallint $>$, $+$: $<<$Int, Int $>$, Int $>>$ where $\leq$ is defined as the reflexive closure of the relation given by Smallint $\leq$ Int. Let $< \Sigma_1, \leq_1 >$ be the order-sorted signature $<$ {Smallint}: $+$: $<<$ Smallint, Smallint $>$, Smallint $>>$ where $\leq_1$ is the restriction of $\leq$ to {Smallint}, and let $< \Sigma_2, \leq_2 >$ be the order-sorted signature $<$ {Int}: $+$: $<<$ Int, Int $>$, Int $>>$ where $\leq_2$ is the restriction of $\leq$ to {Int}. Note that if we can find a generalized order-sorted algebra for $<\Sigma, \leq >$, the induced types given by the interpretations of $<\Sigma_1, \leq_1>$ and $<\Sigma_2, \leq_2>$ will be partial subtypes since the signatures satisfy (1) and (2) of the definition of partial subtype.

We easily find a generalized order-sorted algebra for $<\Sigma, \leq>$ by interpreting Int as the set of Integers, Smallint as the set $\{1, \ldots, 10\}$, letting + on Integers be integer addition, and letting + on $\{1..10\}$ be the restriction of integer addition on $\{1..10\}$, where the sum of two numbers is undefined if the integer sum is outside of $\{1..10\}$. It is easy to verify that this interpretation really is a generalized order-sorted algebra, since Smallint $\leq$ Int via the coercer which is simply the set inclusion mapping (i.e., for $1 \leq n \leq 10$, $c_{Smallint, Int}(n) = n$). This coercer preserves operations as required in clause (3') of the definition of generalized order-sorted algebras. We name the types inside of this generalized order-sorted algebra corresponding to $<\Sigma_1, \leq_1>$ and $<\Sigma_2, \leq_2>$, **PInt(1..10)** and **Int**, respectively. By the preceding remarks, **PInt(1..10)** is a partial subtype of **Int**.

PInt(1..10) fails to be a complete subtype, since it fails to preserve complete behavioral equivalence with **Int**. In particular, $7 + 7$ is defined in **Int**, but not in **PInt(1..10)**. Notice that this cannot be repaired by taking addition modulo 10, for instance, and defining $7 + 7 = 4$ in **PInt(1..10)**, since $7 + 7 = 14$ in **Int**. Instead the range of the interpretation of + in **PInt(1..10)** must be expanded so that $m + n$, for m, n in $\{1, \ldots, 10\}$, gives the same values as the original integer addition.

There are several ways to do this. One way is to change the signature of + in Σ and Σ_1 as follows. Replace $+:<<$Smallint, Smallint$>$, Smallint$>$ in each of these signatures by $+: <<$ Smallint, Smallint$>$, Int$>$. We can now interpret the new $<\Sigma, \leq>$ in a way similar to that given before, with $+: <<$ Smallint, Smallint$>$, Int$>$ interpreted as the restriction of integer addition to $\{1, \ldots, 10\}$, but with range all of the integers. If we name the new type corresponding to the new $<\Sigma_1, \leq_1>$ **Int(1..10)**, it is easy to verify that **Int(1..10)** is a complete subtype of **Int**. Note that in this case **Int(1..10)** contains two sorts (Smallint and Int), while the supertype **Int** contains only one (**Int**). Of course there are many other ways to create a type **Int(1..10)** that is a complete subtype of **Int**. For example, we could have made the range of + in the subtype be any new sort that contains $\{1, \ldots, 20\}$, since + then could be interpreted in the subtype in such a way that behavioral compatibility is preserved. If this new sort is added as a subsort of Int, the result will be a complete subtype of **Int**. Other methods of creating such a complete subtype by adding a second "+" to the subtype are suggested by the example given after the definition of complete subtype in Section 5.4.

5.3.2 "Isomorphic Embedding" Subtypes

Historically, systems of numbers were extended in order to make partial operations more defined. The natural numbers were extended successively to the integers, rationals, reals, and complex numbers, in order to obtain closure under operations such as subtraction, nonzero division, limits, and the taking of roots. In each of these cases the previous set of numbers can be isomorphically embedded in the original. In fact for most purposes we simply assume this set is contained (rather than isomorphically embedded) in the successor. It is not surprising then, that a totally defined operation, such as addition over the integers, will be behaviorally compatible with the corresponding operation over one of its supersorts, such as the reals. In this case the natural partial subtypes will in fact turn out to be complete subtypes. Of course, if the operation is originally defined only in the supersort (e.g., logarithm over the reals), then the corresponding function with domain and range restricted to the subsort (e.g., the integers) is likely to result only in a partial subtype. In this case, to get a complete subsort, we would typically let the range of the function in the subsort be the original range of the function in the supersort. For example, we would let the version of logarithm defined on the integers have as range the set of reals.

The argument for the Integers being a subtype of the reals is similar to that of **Int(1..10)** for Int. In this case the coercer $c_{Integer, Real}$ simply maps each integer to the corresponding real number. To make the example more interesting (although less natural), let us take type **Real** with signature $< \{R, C\}: + : << R, C >, C >>$ and the type **Int** with signature $< \{Int\}: + :$ $<< Int, Int>, Int>>$ as before, both interpreted in the natural generalized order-sorted algebra, B, whose signature is the union of those given and where Int $\leq R \leq C$. In B, B_{int} is the set of integers, B_R is the set of reals, and B_C is the set of complex numbers. Then the natural isomorphic embeddings of the integers into the reals, and of the reals into the complex numbers, are the coercers for this algebra. It is a generalized order-sorted algebra since the coercers preserve the operation $+$. Since Integer $\leq$ Real and Integer $\leq$ Complex, (1) of the definition of complete subtype is satisfied. Since $+$ is total on **Int** and is consistent with the definition on **Real**, (2) is satisfied, so **Int** will be a complete subtype of **Real**. It is worth noting here that **Int**, the subtype, has *fewer* sorts than the supertype **Real**.

5.3.3 Object-Oriented Subtypes

The object-oriented case is perhaps the most interesting. The sort Person can be thought of as a record type with fields for name, age, and parent, while Student can be represented as a record type with fields for name, age, parent, and grade point average. The types **Student** and **Person** have the following signatures:

$\Sigma_P = <\{$Person, String, Int$\}$; name : $<<$Person$>$, String$>$,
age : $<<$Person$>$, Int$>$, parent : $<<$Person$>$, Person$>$, age-a-year:
$<<$Person$>$, Person$>>$, and

$\Sigma_S = <\{$Student, Person, String, Int, R$\}$: name :
$<<$Student$>$, String$>$, age : $<<$Student$>$, Int$>$, parent :
$<<$Student$>$, Person$>$, age-a-year:
$<<$Student$>$, Student$>$, gpa : $<<$Student$>$, R$>>$.

Let $\Sigma = \Sigma_P \cup \Sigma_S$. Define $\leq$ as the reflexive closure of Student $\leq$ Person. The generalized order-sorted algebra A of signature Σ that we have in mind for this system has A_{String} defined as the set of all finite character strings, A_{Int} is the set of integers, A_R is the set of real numbers, A_{Person} is $A_{String} \times A_{Int} \times A_{Person}$, and $A_{Student}$ is $A_{String} \times A_{Int} \times A_{Person} \times A_R$. $A_{Student} \leq A_{Person}$ by the coercer which takes ordered quadruples from $A_{Student}$ and "forgets" the fourth component. (Note that the coercer here is *not* injective! Requiring an injective coercer would eliminate the possibility of object-oriented subtypes, unless one interprets objects in a rather unusual way.) It is easy to see that this coercer preserves the operations name, parent, age, and age-a-year, satisfying (2) of the definition of complete subtype and (3′) of the definition of generalized order-sorted algebra. Also (1) of the definition of complete subtype is satisfied since Student $\leq$ Person, Integer $\leq$ Integer, and String $\leq$ String. Notice that R in Σ_S need not be paired in the $\leq$ relation to any sort in Σ_P since it does not occur in any of the signatures of the operators that are in both Σ_P and Σ_S. Thus **Student** is a complete subtype of **Person**. We note that in our subtype **Student**, the range of parent remained Person, while the range of age-a-year changed to Student. This latter case is extremely common in object-oriented types with operators which modify the **Student** object. The range of the operator parent did *not* change since it did not modify the **Student** object (in this case it simply reported an attribute).

In summary, we have shown how our definitions of partial subtype and complete subtype relate to the three most common types of subtype definitions, those arising from subset, isomorphic embedding, and object-oriented subtypes. In each of these cases behavioral compatibility (or at least partial behavioral compatibility) was preserved by the coercers mapping subsorts to supersorts. The fact that these coercers did not have to be injective was crucial for the object-oriented case. Also in the object-oriented case we saw by an example that the ranges of corresponding functions in subtypes may remain the same as in the supertype or may be relativized to the sorts of the subtype, depending on the kind of operator. In spite of these variations, the definitions proposed in Section 5.2 captured all of these notions of subtype.

5.4 OVERLOADING, AMBIGUITY, AND THE INTERPRETATION OF TERMS

So far we have discussed the modeling of types and subtypes in generalized order-sorted algebras. We now wish to take this one step further and examine the problem of interpreting first-order terms which represent elements of the types. In traditional programming languages there are few difficulties associated with this. However in the presence of inheritance, especially multiple inheritance, problems arise due to the presence of overloaded operators. In this section we discuss problems that may arise in interpreting terms in generalized order-sorted algebras, and show that under certain syntactic conditions, terms may be interpreted uniquely.

5.4.1 Definition and Sort Checking of Terms

Since we are working in a strongly typed environment, each term of the language can be assigned a sort. In traditional languages, each term typically can be assigned to a unique sort. In the presence of inheritance this is no longer possible. Instead each term may be assigned many sorts. For example, the constant "3" can be assigned the sorts integer, real, complex, et cetera. The following defines both the legal terms and the possible sorts of these terms by defining "sort" checking rules:

Definition 5.8.   Let $< \Sigma, \leq >$ be an order-sorted signature with S the collection of sorts in Σ. Let $\Sigma_{w,s}$ be the collection of operations in Σ with signature $<w,s>$. We let λ denote the empty tuple in $S*$. Thus $c \in \Sigma_{\lambda,s}$ denotes a constant of sort s. We next define a proof system which will allow us to infer which expressions formed from symbols of Σ form terms that can be assigned sorts.

(A1) $<\Sigma, \leq > \vdash c : s$ if $c \in \Sigma_{\lambda,s}$.

$$(R1) \quad \frac{<\Sigma, \leq > \vdash t : s, s \leq s'}{<\Sigma, \leq > \vdash t{:}s'}$$

$$(R2) \quad \frac{f \in \Sigma_{w,s}, <\Sigma, \leq > \vdash t_i : s_i \text{ for } 1 \leq i \leq n}{<\Sigma, \leq > \vdash f(t_1, \ldots, t_n) : s} \quad (\text{for } w = <s_1, \ldots, s_n>)$$

For $s \in S$, let $T_s = \{t \mid <\Sigma, \leq > \vdash t : s\}$, the set of **terms of sort** s, and let $T = U\{T_s \mid s \in S\}$ be the collection of all **"sortable" terms** (i.e., terms that can be assigned sorts).

5.4.2 Overloaded Terms

As stated earlier, an operator in a typed language is said to be overloaded if it has several distinct meanings. In this case the appropriate meaning is selected on the basis of type information within its context of usage. Examples that commonly occur in programming languages are the use of = and assignment (e.g., $:=$) which apply to terms with identical or compatible types, and the use of "+" to denote a binary operation that can be applied to either integers or reals. An important concern with the use of overloading has to do with ensuring that the potential ambiguity can be resolved, and that interpretations of the same term in related sorts will themselves be consistent. In the definitions of order-sorted algebras and generalized order-sorted algebras, conditions were given which ensured that if a function was redefined in a subtype, its meaning was compatible with that given in the supertype. In the rest of this section we show that under certain restrictions on signatures, terms can be interpreted consistently.

Problems may arise that lead to ambiguities in deciding which interpretation of an overloaded operator to apply in some circumstances. This problem may be especially acute under multiple inheritance. A particularly difficult case arises when $w \leq w_1, w_2$, $f : < w_1, s_1 >$ and $f : < w_2, s_2 >$, and there is no relation between the types s_1 and s_2. (Note that this cannot occur if w occurs in a subtype of a type that includes f and one of w_1 or w_2, by our definition of subtype. However this may occur in general in an order-sorted signature for a generalized order-sorted algebra.) In this circumstance it may be impossible to determine which f to apply to an element of w. In Goguen and Meseguer [1986] a restriction on signatures called regularity is introduced to eliminate this possibility by always ensuring that each term has a least sort.

Definition 5.9. An order-sorted signature $<\Sigma, \leq>$ is **regular** if whenever $w_0 \leq w_1$ and $f : < w_1, s_1 >$, there is a least $< w, s >$ such that $w_0 \leq w$ and $f : < w, s >$.

Thus if f is applied to an element d of type w_0 then this minimal f may be applied. The following theorem is from Goguen and Meseguer [1986].

THEOREM 5.2.   If $<\Sigma, \leq>$ is a regular order-sorted signature and $t \in T$, then there is a least sort s such that $t \in T_s$.

The proof is by a straightforward induction on the complexity of terms.

5.4.3 Interpretation of Terms

We are now ready to define the interpretation of terms in a generalized order-sorted algebra. Since we are working with overloaded operators, we must be concerned with ambiguities of interpretation of terms. We will show that under the condition of regularity, if $t \in T_s$ then all possible ways of determining the meaning of that term which correspond to it being assigned to sort s will result in the same element. More generally, we wish to show that if a term has two comparable "sortings" then the meanings associated with those sortings will be consistent (in the sense that the meaning corresponding to the smaller sort can be coerced to the meaning in the greater sort). We begin by defining the meaning of a term relative to the proof that it has a particular sort. We will then prove that the meaning is dependent only on the target sort and not on the particular proof that the term has that sort.

Definition 5.10. Let $t \in T$ and P be a proof that t has sort s. We define the meaning of t in order-sorted algebra A with respect to proof P, $[[t]]_{A,P}$, by induction on the length of P:

1. Suppose the last step of the proof P is the axiom (A1). Then $t \in \Sigma_{\lambda,s}$ and define $[[t]]_{A,P} = A_t$ where A_t is the interpretation of the t with signature $<\lambda, s>$.

2. Suppose the last step of the proof P is the rule (R1). Then $<\Sigma, \leq>$ $\vdash t : s'$ for some $s' \leq s$, by a proof P' of length less than that of P. Then $[[t]]_{A,P} = c_{s,s'}([[t]]_{A,P'})$ where $c_{s,s'}$ is the coercer in A from A_s to $A_{s'}$.

3. Suppose the last step of the proof P is the rule (R2), and thus t is of the form $f(t_1, \ldots, t_n)$. Then $<\Sigma, \leq> \vdash t_i : s_i$ for $1 \leq i \leq n$ via proofs P_i, each of whose lengths is less than that of P, and $f \in \Sigma_{w,s}$. Then $[[t]]_{A,P} = A_f([[t_1]]_{A,P_1}, \ldots, [[t_n]]_{A,P_n})$ where A_f is the interpretation of the f with signature $<w,s>$.

The following theorem establishes that the meaning of terms is independent of the particular proof that a term can be assigned a sort. The proof is a generalization of the proof of a theorem in Goguen and Meseguer [1986] establishing the existence of initial order-sorted algebras.

THEOREM 5.3.   Let $(\Sigma, \leq)$ be a regular signature and A a generalized order-sorted algebra for $(\Sigma, \leq)$.

1. If M can be assigned sort s then all interpretations of M resulting from a proof that M has sort s are identical. Write $[[M]]_{A,s}$ for this unique interpretation.

2. Moreover, if M is a term in Σ which can be assigned sorts s and s' with $s \leq s'$, then $[[M]]_{A,s'} = c_{s,s'}([[M]]_{A,s})$.

Proof.   (2) For simplicity we will sketch the induction case for M built from a unary operator. Let $M = f(t)$ and suppose there are typings of M assigning types of s and s'. Therefore there are signatures $< w,s_0 >$ and $< w',s_0' >$ for f in S, and sortings assigning sorts w_0 and w_0' to t such that $w_0 \leq w$, $w_0' \leq w'$, $s_0 \leq s$, and $s_0' \leq s'$. Let u be the least type of t. Thus $u \leq w_0, w_0'$. Since $u \leq w$, by regularity there is a least $< v,r >$ such that $u \leq v$ and $f : <v,r>$. Thus $<v,r> \leq <w,s_0>, <w',s_0'>$. It follows that

$$[[M]]_{A,s'} = c_{s_0',s'}(f_{w',s_0'}(c_{w_0',w'}([[t]]_{A,w_0'})))$$
$$= c_{s_0',s'}(f_{w',s_0'}(c_{u,w'}([[t]]_{A,u}))),$$
$$\text{since } [[t]]_{A,w_0'} = c_{u,w_0'}([[t]]_{A,u}) \text{ by induction}$$
$$= c_{s_0',s'}(f_{w',s_0'}(c_{v,w'}(c_{u,v}([[t]]_{A,u}))))$$
$$= c_{s_0',s'}(c_{r,s_0'}(f_{v,r}(c_{u,v}([[t]]_{A,u}))))$$
$$\text{by the definition of generalized order-sorted algebra}$$
$$= c_{r,s'}(f_{v,r}([[t]]_{A,v})).$$

Similarly $[[M]]_{A,s} = c_{r,s}(f_{v,r}([[t]]_{A,v}))$. Hence

$$[[M]]_{A,s'} = c_{r,s'}(f_{v,r}([[t]]_{A,v}))$$
$$= c_{s,s'}(c_{r,s}(f_{v,r}([[t]]_{A,v})))$$
$$= c_{s,s'}([[M]]_{A,s})$$

Other languages may have different restrictions on the formation of terms in order to allow them to resolve ambiguities arising from overloading (e.g., see Ada's restrictions on overloading).

5.5 SUMMARY AND RELATION TO PREVIOUS WORK

In this paper we have shown how to model the notions of type, subtype, and inheritance after having provided a definition of generalized order-sorted algebras. We have demonstrated that this ordering of carriers based on (not necessarily injective) coercion operators can be used to model the notions of complete and partial subtype, especially as used in object-oriented languages. We have also proved that under the assumption of regularity, a term constructed from overloaded operators using inheritance does in fact have consistently defined meanings, no matter in which legal sort the term is interpreted. A comparison of this paper with earlier work is given in what follows.

Goguen [1978] introduced order-sorted algebras as a way of handling errors and overloaded operators. In that original paper, the ordering of sorts was represented by (injective) coercion operators, the partial ordering on sorts was a strict lower semilattice, and if an operator f appeared in the signature with typing $<w,s>$ where $w' \leq w$ and $s \leq s'$ then f also appeared with typing $<w',s'>$. Goguen and Meseguer [1986] redefine order-sorted algebras as given in Section 5.2.2 of this paper, eliminating coercion operators. They introduce the notion of regular signatures, which are used to show that each term has a least type and to show that initial algebras exist. The main focus of their paper is to show how to handle errors using subsorts and supersorts, while supporting the inheritance of operators. A comparison of order-sorted algebras and our generalized order-sorted algebras was given at the end of Section 5.2.2. The main differences in the generalized order-sorted algebras lie in requiring only partial behavioral compatibility and allowing noninjective coercion functions rather than simply taking set inclusion as an interpretation of subsort.

Futatsugi, Goguen, Jouannaud, and Meseguer [1985] discuss the functional programming language OBJ2, which is built on the theoretical foundation of order-sorted algebras. In that paper they discuss three methods ("using," "protecting," and "extending") for new modules to import existing modules, but this notion does not seem to be directly comparable to our notion of subtype. The paper by Goguen and Meseguer [1986a] describes the language FOOPS, which uses the notion of subsort described in Goguen and Meseguer [1986]. In that paper $\leq$ also expresses an ordering on classes (types), with a hint that the definition of $\leq$ on classes is similar to that on sorts (via "reflection").

Reynolds [1980] examines the use of implicit conversions and generic (overloaded) operators in programming language from a category-theoretic point of view. He argues that implicit conversions should behave as homomorphisms with respect to generic operators. For example, if c : Int $\rightarrow$ Real is to be an implicit coercer from integers to reals, then $c(x +_{Int} y) = c(x) + _{Real} c(y)$ for x and y integers. Preordered categories (called category-ordered algebras) are used to model types in the language as well as to denote syntactic categories. Reynolds presents several examples to buttress the case that "subsorts are not subsets," and chooses to model the subsort relation with coercers (homomorphisms) which need not be injective. In that paper, each operator is defined on all types, with functional specifications that are monotone in the ordering of the sorts. Reynolds also does not attempt to define type or subtype.

Our earlier paper [Bruce & Wegner, 1986] presented an algebraic model of type and subtype somewhat different than provided here. In that paper, types were simply many-sorted algebras and one type was a subtype of another if there existed suitable coercers which behaved as homomorphisms between the algebras. That paper also contained an extensive discussion of the notion of subtype and why naïve definitions of subtype such as "subalgebra" and "subset" fail to correspond to natural usage in programming languages. The current paper represents a substantial reworking of these notions to provide a much more rigorous foundation for the study of types and subtypes. We also call the readers attention to Wegner [1987], which also contains a discussion of algebraic models of types in object-oriented languages.

In summary, we have shown that the notion of coercion provides a framework for a general and unified notion of subtype, and provides the basis for a useful algebraic semantics of types. We also point out that this model of subtype based on coercion provides a good model for the implementation of object-oriented programming languages. Traditional programming languages use coercers to interpret integers as reals or other subtypes as elements of the supertypes. In object-oriented language, this occurs much more frequently, since types are defined in a top-down fashion by successive refinement, with the intention of inheriting operations in subtypes from supertypes. Much of the time this inheritance is fairly natural, for example if objects are held as pointers to records, but other times, especially with multiple inheritance, the inheritance of operations involves careful translation of the operation on the supertype down to the subtype (or sometimes, careful coercion of the arguments from subsorts to supersorts).

In a related paper [Bruce & Longo, 1988], it is shown that coercion provides a similarly useful semantics of types in providing the **denotational** semantics of object-oriented programming languages. In that paper we provide the semantics of an extension of second-order lambda calculus, bounded second-order FUN, due to Cardelli and Wegner [1986]. This language provides facilities for expressing multiple inheritance as well as explicit parametric polymorphism (i.e., the provision of procedures which can be applied to objects of various types via passing types as parameters). As well as giving a general definition of models of bounded second-order FUN, the so-called p.e.r. models are also shown to provide a very natural model for subtypes with respect to coercers.

The development of the algebraic and denotational semantics of such languages is likely to provide useful information for both the understanding and development of languages with quite complex type structures, complex relations between types, and powerful facilities for supporting polymorphism. In particular the formal specification of the semantics of such languages will often highlight oversights or complexities in a language not foreseen by the language designers.

ACKNOWLEDGMENTS

We would like to thank José Meseguer and David Gries for a stimulating discussion of our earlier paper [Bruce & Wegner, 1986], which contributed to the reshaping of this paper in terms of order-sorted algebras. We also thank Giuseppe Longo for several interesting discussions.

REFERENCES

Bruce, K. B., and Longo, G., (1988). "A modest model of subtypes and inheritance," to appear in *Proceedings of the Third Symposium on Logic in Computer Science*, Edinburgh.

Bruce, K., and Wegner, P., (1986). "An Algebraic Model of Subtypes in Object-Oriented Languages," *SIGPLAN NOTICES*, Vol. 21, No. 10, pp. 163–172.

Cardelli, Luca, and Wegner, Peter, (1985). "On understanding types, data abstraction, and polymorphism," *Computing Surveys*, Vol. 17, pp. 471–522.

Futatsugi, K., Goguen, J., Jouannaud, J.-P., and Meseguer, J., (1985). "Principles of OBJ2," in *Proceedings, Symposium on Principles of Programming Languages*, pp. 52–66.

Goguen, J., and Meseguer, J., (1986). "Order-Sorted Algebra I: Partial and Over-loaded Operators, Errors and Inheritance," draft of 10/22/86.

Goguen, J., and Meseguer, J.,(1986a). "Extensions and Foundations of Object-Oriented Programming," *SRI Technical Report*, December (an earlier version appears in *SIGPLAN NOTICES*, Vol. 21, No. 10, pp. 153–162).

Reynolds, J., (1980). "Using category theory to design implicit conversions and generic operators," *Semantics Directed Compiler Generation*, LNCS 94, New York: Springer-Verlag, pp. 211–258.

Wegner, P., (1987). "The Object-oriented classification paradigm," *Research Directions in Object-Oriented Programming*, Shriver, B., and Wegner, P. (eds.), Cambridge, Mass.: MIT Press, pp. 479–560.

CHAPTER 6

ORDERINGS AND TYPES IN DATABASES

Atsushi Ohori

6.1 INTRODUCTION

There are a number of attempts to generalize the relational data model beyond first normal form relations (Fischer and Thomas, [1983]; Özsoyoglu, and Yuan, [1985]; Roth, Korth, and Silberschatz, [1985]); there are also other data models that can be seen as generalizations of the relational data model (Abiteboul and Bidoit, [1984]; Bancilhon and Khoshafin, [1986]). The motivation of this study is to draw out the connection between these "higher-order" relations and data types in programming languages so that we can develop a strongly typed programming language in which these data structures are directly available as typed expressions.

We regard database objects as *descriptions* of real-world objects. Such descriptions are *ordered* by how well they describe real-world objects. Relations are then regarded as sets of descriptions describing sets of real-world objects. In (Buneman and Ohori, [1987]), it is shown that *natural join* can be characterized as the least upper bound operation in Smyth's power domain of descriptions. Based on this result, we present a simple typed language that supports nonflat records, higher-order relations, and natural join expressions. We then present a denotational semantics of this language.

Expressions of the language are interpreted in a domain containing Smyth's power domain. In order to give semantics to types, we propose a new model of types, a *filter model*. We regard types as sets of values having common structures. In a domain of descriptions, such sets have properties that they are upward closed and they are closed under finite greatest lower bounds. We therefore interpret types as filters in a semantic domain and show the semantic soundness of the type system. The filter model is particularly suitable for types of partial objects. This model can also give precise semantics to *multiple inheritance* studied by Cardelli [1984].

The rest of this paper is organized as follows. In Section 6.2 we introduce nonflat records to represent database objects and define their ordering. We then introduce types of records and define their ordering. In Section 6.3 we extend expressions, types, and the orderings to sets to represent higher-order relations. We then show that natural join expressions can be generalized in typed higher-order relations. In Section 6.4, we give a formal definition of our language. In Section 6.5, we construct a semantic domain of expressions and give semantics to expressions. We then introduce the filter model of types and give semantics to types and show the soundness of the type inference system.

6.2 DATABASE OBJECTS AS RECORDS

We represent database objects as labeled record structures. Records are associations of labels and values. We assume that we are given a countable set L of labels and sets $B_1, \ldots, B_n$ of primitive values such as the set of integers. Expressions for records are then inductively defined as

E1. b is an expression if $b \in B_i$.

E2. $(l_1 \rightarrow e_1, \ldots, l_n \rightarrow e_n)$ is an expression if $e_1, \ldots, e_n$ are expressions and $l_1, \ldots, l_n \in L$, where $l_1, \ldots, l_n$ are all distinct.

The following is an example of an expression:

$(Name \rightarrow 'Joe\ Doe', EmpId \rightarrow 1234, Age \rightarrow 21)$

In database programming it is convenient to have *null* values to represent incomplete information. For example, we want to allow the following expression:

$(Name \rightarrow 'Joe\ Doe', EmpId \rightarrow 1234, Age \rightarrow null_{int})$

when the value of *Age* is unknown. In order to allow these null values we add the following rule:

E3. $null_{B_i}$ is an expression.

One distinguishing property about these database objects is that they are *ordered*. The ordering comes from an assumption—usually unstated because it is so obvious—that they describe some real-world objects. As such descriptions, they are essentially incomplete. These incomplete descriptions are partially ordered by how well they describe real-world objects. In the relational data model this ordering was first observed by Zaniolo [1984] in connection with null values. The following is an example of this ordering:

$$(Name \rightarrow 'Joe\ Doe',\ EmpId \rightarrow 1234)$$

$$\sqsubseteq (Name \rightarrow 'Joe\ Doe',\ EmpId \rightarrow 1234,\ Age \rightarrow null_{int})$$

$$\sqsubseteq (Name \rightarrow 'Joe\ Doe',\ EmpId \rightarrow,\ Age \rightarrow 21)$$

Formally we define:

1. $e \sqsubseteq e$.
2. $null_{B_i} \sqsubseteq b$ for all $b \in B_i$.
3. $(l_1 \rightarrow e_1, \ldots, l_n \rightarrow e_n) \sqsubseteq (l_1 \rightarrow e_1', \ldots, l_n \rightarrow e_m')$ whenever $n \leq m$ and $e_i \sqsubseteq e_i'$ for all $l \leq i \leq n$.

From this definition, it is easily seen that $\sqsubseteq$ is a partial ordering on expressions.

The least upper bound (lub) of this ordering corresponds to the conjunction of descriptions if they are compatible. For example, if

$$(e_1 = Name \rightarrow 'Joe\ Doe',\ EmpId \rightarrow 1234)$$

and

$$e_2 = (EmpId \rightarrow 1234,\ Age \rightarrow 21)$$

then

$$e_1 \sqcup e_2 = (Name \rightarrow 'Joe\ Doe',\ EmpId \rightarrow 1234,\ Age \rightarrow 21)$$

However, $(Name \rightarrow 'Joe\ Doe',\ EmpId \rightarrow 1234) \sqcup (Name \rightarrow 'John\ Smith')$ does not exist. As we shall see in the next section, natural join operation can be regarded as the lub operation extended to a power domain. This lub operation is also known as the *unification* in *unification-based* grammatical formalisms, where data are descriptions of linguistic entities (see Shieber, [1985] for a survey).

Next we define types for these expressions. Since each primitive set of values corresponds to a basic type and each label denotes certain set of values, types for expressions are defined as:

T1. For each primitive set of values B_i there is a constant type τ_i.

T2. $(l_1 : \sigma_1, \ldots, l_n : \sigma_n)$ is a type if $\sigma_1, \ldots, \sigma_n$ are types and $l_1, \ldots, l_n \in L$, where $l_1, \ldots, l_n$ are all distinct.

These types can be regarded as specifications of structures of database objects. Since database objects are partial descriptions, these types should specify partial structures. A value is regarded as having a type if the value has the partial structure specified by the type. This observation leads us to define the following typing rules syntactically similar to the type system proposed by Cardelli [1984]:

R1. $b : \tau_i$ if $b \in B_i$.

R2. $null_{B_i} : \tau_i$.

R3. $(l_i \rightarrow e_1, \ldots, l_n \rightarrow e_n) : (l_1 : \sigma_1, \ldots, l_m : \sigma_m)$ if $m \leq n$ and for all $1 \leq i \leq m, e_i : \sigma_i$.

The following is an example of typing:

$$(Name \rightarrow 'Joe\ Doe', EmpId \rightarrow 1234) : (Name : string, EmpId : int)$$

From the definitions of typing and $\sqsubseteq$ we can show by simple structural induction that

THEOREM 6.1.   If $e : \sigma$ and $e \sqsubseteq e'$ then $e' : \sigma$.

Indeed the following typing is also valid:

$$(Name \rightarrow 'Joe\ Doe', EmpId \rightarrow 1234, Age \rightarrow: 21)$$
$$: (Name : string, EmpId : int)$$

In our type system, types therefore correspond to upward closed sets of values. Intuitively, this corresponds to the fact that if a database object has certain structure then any better-defined objects also have the structure. For example, if a database object has an attribute *Name* with the type *string*, then we expect that all better-defined objects also have this structure.

Now if we regard types as sets of values then the preceding typing rules induce an inclusion ordering on types. We define a syntactic relation $\leqslant$ on types to represent this ordering:

1. $\sigma \leqslant \sigma$.

2. $(l_1 : \sigma_1, \ldots, l_n : \sigma_n) \leqslant (l_i : \sigma'_1, \ldots, l_m : \sigma'_m)$ if $m \leq n$ and for all $l \leq i \leq m$, $\sigma_i \leqslant \sigma'_i$.

It is easy to check that $\leqslant$ is a partial ordering. This ordering is the ordering of the generality of specifications of types. For example,

(Name : string, EmpId : int, Age : int)
≼ *(Name : string, EmpId : int)*

Since more general means less informative, we can see why the definition of ≼ is the inverse of the definition of ⊑.

From the definitions of typing and ≼ we can show by simple structural induction that

THEOREM 6.2. If $e : \sigma$ and $\sigma \preccurlyeq \sigma'$ then $e : \sigma'$.

The next theorem connects ⊑ and ≼:

THEOREM 6.3. If $e : \sigma, e' : \sigma'$ and $e \sqcup e'$ exists then $\sigma \sqcap \sigma'$ exists and $e \sqcup e' : \sigma \sqcap \sigma'$.

Proof. By induction on the structures of e and e'.

For example, we have:

(Name → 'Joe Doe', EmpId → 1234) ⊔ *(EmpId → 1234, Age → 21)*
= *(Name → 'Joe Doe', EmpId → 1234, Age → 21)*

and

(Name : string, EmpId : int) ⊓ *(EmpId : int, Age : int)*
= *(Name : string, EmpId : int, Age : int)*

thus

(Name → 'Joe Doe', EmpId → 1234) ⊔ *(EmpId → 1234, Age → 21)*
: *(Name : string, EmpId : int)* ⊓ *(EmpId : int, Age : int)*

As we shall see in the next section, this property, when extended to sets, provides types for generalized natural join expressions.

6.3 RELATIONS AS SETS OF RECORDS

Relations are sets of database objects and databases are sets of relations. We therefore want to allow sets of expressions themselves as expressions. Figure 6.1 shows a simple example of a relation and its representation as a set of expressions. In this section we extend expressions, types, and their orderings to sets.

FIGURE 6.1

A RELATION AND ITS REPRESENTATION AS A SET OF EXPRESSIONS

Name	Age	EmpId
'JoeDoe'	21	1234
'JohnSmith'	31	5678

$\{$ $(Name \rightarrow \textit{'JoeDoe'}, Age \rightarrow 21, EmpId \rightarrow 1234),$

          $(Name \rightarrow \textit{'JohnSmith'}, Age \rightarrow 31, EmpId \rightarrow 5678)$ $\}$

Since individual expressions correspond to partial descriptions, sets of expressions correspond to sets of partial descriptions and presumably describe sets of real-world objects. We therefore want to treat these sets of descriptions as descriptions of sets of objects and to order them by their goodness of descriptions. If our primary interest in database programming is query processing or information retrieval from given set of data, then an appropriate ordering is

$$A \sqsubseteq_0 B \text{ iff } \forall b \in B \exists a \in A.a \sqsubseteq b$$

known as Smyth's power domain ordering. Intuitively, this is an ordering on sets of descriptions which "overdescribe" real-world sets; a set contains enough descriptions to describe all objects in a real-world set but may contain irrelevant descriptions. $A \sqsubseteq_0 B$ means that B is a less ambiguous and better-defined description to a real-world set. A query processing can then be regarded as a process that takes a set of descriptions D and returns another set of descriptions A such that $D \sqsubseteq_0 A$. Indeed natural join and selection, the two major operations for query processing, have the property that they carry relations higher in this ordering. It should be noted, however, that this ordering is not appropriate for the ordering on databases themselves. If our interests are operations on databases such as database merging then we need other orderings. In (Buneman and Ohori, [1987]) various properties of orderings on database sets, including this ordering, were studied.

For arbitrary sets, however, $\sqsubseteq_0$ is not a partial ordering; it is a preordering and a partial ordering is derived by taking equivalence classes. Define $A \simeq B$ as $A \sqsubseteq_0 B$ and $B \sqsubseteq_0 A$. If $A \simeq B$ then we regard A and B as having the same amount of information. We use this equivalence relation as equality between sets of descriptions and regard a set of descriptions as a representative of the corresponding equivalence class. Then $\sqsubseteq_0$ becomes a partial ordering. Thus we now regard equivalence classes of sets of expressions as descriptions of sets of objects and extend expressions to these equivalence classes. We also extend the ordering $\sqsubseteq$ on expressions to these equivalence classes, that is, if $[A]$ and $[B]$ are equivalence classes of sets of expressions A and B then $[A] \sqsubseteq [B]$ if $A \sqsubseteq_0 B$.

For $\simeq$ we have (Smyth, [1978]):

THEOREM 6.4.   For any A and B, (1) $A \simeq \overline{A}$ and (2) $A \simeq B$ "iff" $\overline{A} = \overline{B}$, where $\overline{A} = e \,|\, \exists a \in A.a \sqsubseteq e$.

If we restrict attentions to finite sets, then this theorem says that a set A is equivalent to the co-chain of the set of minimal elements in A, where a co-chain is a set such that no member in the set is greater than any other member in the set. Thus we can use co-chains as canonical representatives of equivalence classes. Intuitive justification for this equivalence is that if an object x is in an answer to a query then we know that any better-defined object y such that $x \sqsubseteq y$ also satisfies the query. Thus all better-defined objects are redundant and can be eliminated from the answer.

We have seen that sets of expressions can be also regarded as descriptions, and the approximation ordering $\sqsubseteq$ on expressions can be extended to sets of expressions. We can then include sets of expressions in our language and allow records to contain these sets as values. Since now sets are regarded as expressions ordered by $\sqsubseteq$, by applying the same argument, we can further extend our language to allow sets of sets of expressions as expressions. Indeed we can carry this extension process to any depth.

In the syntax of the language this extension can be done by simply adding the rule

E4. $\{e_1, \ldots, e_k\}$ is an expression if $e_1, \ldots, e_k$ are expressions.

where we allow the empty set $\{\}$ as an expression, since the empty set can be regarded as a valid response to a query. We call these expressions as *set expressions*. Set expressions are regarded as representatives of corresponding equivalence classes. The extended language not only allows simple relations such as the example in Fig. 6.1 but also allows sets of relations and "higher-order" relations such as the example in Fig. 6.2.

In the previous section we have seen that the lub of expressions under the ordering $\sqsubseteq$ corresponds to the conjunction of descriptions. About the lub of the extended ordering on set expressions:

FIGURE 6.2
HIGHER-ORDER RELATION

$\{(Pname \to \text{'Nut'}, Supplier \to \{(Sname \to \text{'Smith'}, City \to \text{'London'}),$
$\qquad\qquad\qquad\qquad\quad (Sname \to \text{'Jones'}, City \to \text{'Paris'}),$
$\qquad\qquad\qquad\qquad\quad (Sname \to \text{'Blake'}, City \to \text{'Paris'})\}),$
$\quad (Pname \to \text{'Bolt'}, Supplier \to \{(Sname \to \text{'Blake'}, City \to \text{'Paris'}),$
$\qquad\qquad\qquad\qquad\quad (Sname \to \text{'Clark'}, City \to \text{'Rome'}),$
$\qquad\qquad\qquad\qquad\quad (Sname \to \text{'Adams'}, City \to \text{'Athens'})\})\}$

LEMMA 6.1. $A \sqcup B = \{a \sqcup b \,|\, a \in A, b \in B, a \sqcup b$ exists$\}$ where all sets are regarded as representatives of their equivalence classes.

Proof. It is clear that $\{a \sqcup b \,|\, a \in A, b \in B, a \sqcup b$ exists$\}$ is an upper bound of A and B. Let C be any upper bound of A and B, that is, $A \sqsubseteq_0 C, B \sqsubseteq_0 C$. Then by the definition of $\sqsubseteq_0$, for any $c \in C$ there are $a \in A, b \in B$ such that $a \sqsubseteq c, b \sqsubseteq c$. Then we have $a \sqcup b \sqsubseteq c$. Thus $\{a \sqcup b \,|\, a \in A, b \in B, a \sqcup b$ exists$\} \sqsubseteq_0 C$.

The importance of this lub in connection with relational algebra is stated in the following theorem (Buneman and Ohori, [1987]):

THEOREM 6.5. If A, B are co-chains of flat records then $A \sqcup B$ is the natural join of A and B.

From this connection we can regard the lub operation as a generalized natural join on extended expressions. We write $A \bowtie B$ for $A \sqcup B$ if A, B are set expressions. Note that if A, B are set expressions then $A \bowtie B$ always exists.

This operation can be also used as selection operation. For example, if

$$e = \{(Name \rightarrow \text{'Joe Doe'}, Age \rightarrow 21),$$
$$(Name \rightarrow \text{'John Smith'}, Age \rightarrow 31)\}$$

then

$$e \bowtie \{(Age \rightarrow 21)\} = \{(Name \rightarrow \text{'Joe Doe'}, Age \rightarrow 21)\}$$

We now turn our attentions to types for database sets. As we extended expressions to include set expressions, we extend our type system to include set types by adding the following rule to the syntax of types:

T3. $\{\sigma_1, \ldots, \sigma_n\}$ is a type if $\sigma_1, \ldots, \sigma_n$ are types.

where we also allow $\{\}$ for convenience.

We noted in the previous section that types specify partial structures of objects. For set types, this corresponds to the following typing rule:

R4. $\{e_1, \ldots, e_n\} : \{\sigma_1, \ldots, \sigma_m\}$ if $\forall e \in \{e_1, \ldots, e_n\} \exists \sigma \in \{\sigma_1, \ldots, \sigma_m\}. e : \sigma$.

It is easy to check that this typing rule yields an upward closed set in set expressions under our ordering on sets and the Theorem 6.1 also holds.

This typing rule also induces an inclusion ordering on set types regarded as sets of values (i.e., sets of set expressions). In order to represent this ordering, we first define the following preordering on set types:

$$\sigma \leqslant_0 \sigma' \text{ iff } \forall \iota \in \sigma \exists \iota' \in \sigma'. \iota \leqslant \iota'$$

As before a partial ordering is obtained by defining equivalence relation $\simeq$ as $\sigma \simeq \sigma'$ "iff" $\sigma \leqslant_0 \sigma'$ and $\sigma' \leqslant_0 .\sigma$. Then by the definition of typing, $\sigma \simeq \sigma'$ "iff" for any $e, e:\sigma \Leftrightarrow e:\sigma'$. This equivalence relation exactly corresponds to the equality between types regarded as sets of values. We therefore regard set types as representatives of equivalence classes.

Parallel to Theorem 6.4, we can show

THEOREM 6.6. For any σ, σ', (1) $\sigma \simeq \underline{\sigma}$ and (2) $\sigma \simeq \underline{\sigma}'$ "iff" $\underline{\sigma} = \underline{\sigma}'$, where $\underline{\sigma} = \{\iota \mid \exists \iota' \in \sigma.\iota \leqslant \iota'\}$.

Therefore set types can be also represented by co-chains.

Note that the definition of $\leqslant_0$ is the inverse of the definition of $\sqsubseteq_0$ and the extended ordering $\leqslant$ still corresponds to the generality of specifications. If we replace $\sigma \leqslant \sigma'$ with $\sigma' \sqsubseteq \sigma$ then we get the same definitions and properties for orderings on expressions and types.

We now extend the ordering relation $\leqslant$ on types to set types using the partial ordering $\leqslant_0$ on equivalence classes of sets of types. It can then shown that Theorem 6.2 still holds for the extended types. We write $\sigma \wedge \sigma'$ for $\sigma \sqcap \sigma'$ if σ, σ' are set types. From the duality of $\sqsubseteq$ and $\leqslant$, we can see that $\sigma \wedge \sigma'$ always exists if σ, σ' are set types.

The following theorem connects $\bowtie$ and $\wedge$:

THEOREM 6.7. If A, B are set expressions with $A:\sigma_1, B:\sigma_2$ then $A \bowtie B$: $\sigma_1 \wedge \sigma_2$.

FIGURE 6.3
NATURAL JOIN OF TYPED HIGHER-ORDER RELATIONS

$r_1 = \{(Pname \rightarrow \text{'Nut'}, Supplier \rightarrow \quad \{(Sname \rightarrow \text{'Smith'}, City \rightarrow \text{'London'}),$
$\quad (Sname \rightarrow \text{'Jones'}, City \rightarrow \text{'Paris'}),$
$\quad (Sname \rightarrow \text{'Blake'}, City \rightarrow \text{'Paris'})\}),$
$\quad (Pname \rightarrow \text{'Bolt'}, Supplier \rightarrow \quad \{(Sname \rightarrow \text{'Blake'}, City \rightarrow \text{'Paris'}),$
$\quad (Sname \rightarrow \text{'Clark'}, City \rightarrow \text{'Rome'}),$
$\quad (Sname \rightarrow \text{'Adams'}, City \rightarrow \text{'Athens'})\})\}$
$\quad : \{(Pname : string, Supplier : \quad \{(Sname : string, City : string)\})\}$
$r_2 = \{(Pname \rightarrow \text{'Nut'}, Supplier \rightarrow \quad \{(City \rightarrow \text{'Paris'})\}, Qty \rightarrow 100),$
$\quad (Pname \rightarrow \text{'Bolt'}, Supplier \rightarrow \quad \{(City \rightarrow \text{'Paris'})\}, Qty \rightarrow 200)\}$
$\quad : \{(Pname : string, Supplier : \quad \{(City : string)\}, Qty : int)\}$
$r_1 \bowtie r_2 = \{(Pname \rightarrow \text{'Nut'}, Supplier \rightarrow \quad \{(Sname \rightarrow \text{'Jones'}, City \rightarrow \text{'Paris'}),$
$\quad (Sname \rightarrow \text{'Blake'}, City \rightarrow \text{'Paris'})\},$
$\quad Qty \rightarrow 100),$
$\quad (Pname \rightarrow \text{'Nut'}, Supplier \rightarrow \quad \{(Sname \rightarrow \text{'Blake'}, City \rightarrow \text{'Paris'})\},$
$\quad Qty \rightarrow 200)\}$
$\quad : \{(Pname : string, Supplier : \quad \{(Sname : string, City : string)\}, Qty : int)\}$

Proof. Let $a \sqcup b$ be any element in $A \bowtie B$. Since $A:\sigma_1$ and $B:\sigma_2$, there are $\iota_1 \in \sigma_1$ and $\iota_2 \in \sigma_2$ such that $a:\iota_1$ and $b:\iota_2$. Then by Theorem 6.3, $a \sqcup b:\iota_1 \sqcap \iota_2$. But by definition $\iota_1 \sqsubseteq \iota_2 \in \sigma_1 \wedge \sigma_2$. This shows $A \sqsubseteq B:\sigma_1 \wedge \sigma_2$.

This theorem shows that we have successfully generalized natural join in typed higher-order relations. Figure 6.3 is an example of a natural join of typed higher-order relations.

6.4 DEFINITION OF THE LANGUAGE

In this section we give formal definition of our language supporting records, higher-order relations, and natural joins.

6.4.1 Expressions

We use $l, l_1, \ldots$ for elements of L. The syntax of expressions is given by the following abstract syntax grammar:

$$e :: = b(b \in B_i)|\ null_{B_i}|$$
$$(l_1 \rightarrow e_1, \ldots, l_n \rightarrow e_n)|(\ldots, l \rightarrow e, \ldots).l|$$
$$\{e_1, \ldots, e_m\}\ |\ \{e_1, \ldots, e_n\} \bowtie \{e'_1, \ldots, e'_m\}.$$

Among expressions, various equations should hold. The first axiom of equality is the axiom for dot expressions (field selections from records):

$$(l_1 \rightarrow e_1, \ldots, l_i \rightarrow e_i, \ldots, l_n \rightarrow e_n).l_i = e_i \tag{6.1}$$

In order to define axioms for set expressions and join expressions, (i.e., the expressions of the form $\{e_1, \ldots, e_n\} \bowtie \{e'_1, \ldots, e'_m\}$), we first define the syntactic relation $\sqsubseteq$ on the sublanguage of expressions that do not contain dot expressions and join expressions as subexpressions.

$$e \sqsubseteq e$$

$$null_{B_i} \sqsubseteq b \text{ for all } b \in B_i$$

$$(l_1 \rightarrow e_1, \ldots, l_n \rightarrow e_n) \sqsubseteq (l_1 \rightarrow e'_1, \ldots, l_m \rightarrow e'_m)$$

$$\text{if } n \le m \text{ and } e_i \sqsubseteq e'_i \text{ for all } 1 \le i \le n$$

$$\{e_1, \ldots, e_n\} \sqsubseteq \{e'_1, \ldots, e'_m\} \text{ if } \forall e' \in \{e'_1, \ldots, e'_m\}.$$

$$\exists e \in \{e_1, \ldots, e_n\}.e \sqsubseteq e'$$

The axiom for set expressions is then defined as

$$\{e_1, e_2, e_3, \ldots, e_n\} = \{e_1, e_3, \ldots, e_n\} \text{ if } e_1 \sqsubseteq e_2 \tag{6.2}$$

Note that this rule induces an equivalence relation that makes $\sqsubseteq$ a partial ordering. Let $\sqcup$ be the least upper bound of this partial ordering. The axiom for join expressions is defined as

$$\{e_{i_1}, \ldots, e_{i_n}\} \sqsubseteq \{e_{j_m}\} = \{e'_{i_k} \sqcup e'_{j_l} \mid 1 \le k \le n, 1 \le l \le m, e'_{i_k} \sqcup e'_{j_l} \text{ exists}\} \qquad (6.3)$$

where e'_{i_k}, e'_{j_l} are expressions that are equal to e_{i_k}, e_{j_l} respectively and do not contain dot expressions or join expressions as subexpressions.

These rules also define a reduction process that eliminates dot expressions and join expressions and reduces set expressions to corresponding co-chain representatives.

6.4.2 Types

We assume that there are constant types $\tau_1, \ldots, \tau_n$ associated with $B_1, \ldots, B_n$. Then the syntax of types for expressions is defined by the following abstract syntax grammar:

$$\sigma :: = \tau_i \mid$$
$$(l_1 : \sigma_1, \ldots, l_n : \sigma_n) \mid$$
$$\{\sigma_1, \ldots, \sigma_m\} \mid$$
$$\sigma \wedge \sigma' \text{ (if } \sigma, \sigma' \text{ are of the form } \{\sigma_1, \ldots, \sigma_n\}).$$

In order to define axioms of equality of types, we first define the syntactic relation $\le$ on the sublanguage of types that do not contain meet types (i.e., types of the form $\sigma \wedge \sigma'$):

$$\sigma \le \sigma$$
$$(l_1 : \sigma_1, \ldots, l_n : \sigma_n) \le (l_1 : \sigma'_1, \ldots, l_m : \sigma'_m) \text{ if } m \le n \text{ and}$$
$$\sigma_i \le \sigma'_i \text{ for } 1 \le i \le m$$
$$\{\sigma_1, \ldots, \sigma_n\} \le \{\sigma'_1, \ldots, \sigma'_m\} \text{ if } \forall \sigma \in \{\sigma_1, \ldots, \sigma_n\}.$$
$$\exists \sigma' \in \{\sigma'_1, \ldots, \sigma'_m\}. \sigma \le \sigma'$$

Axiom for set types is then defined as

$$\{\sigma_1, \sigma_2, \sigma_3, \ldots, \sigma_n\} = \{\sigma_1, \sigma_3, \ldots, \sigma_n\} \text{ if } \sigma_2 \le \sigma_1 \qquad (6.4)$$

This equation makes $\le$ a partial ordering. Let $\sqcap$ be the greatest lower bound of this partial ordering. The axiom for meet types is then defined as

$$\{\sigma_1, \ldots, \sigma_n\} \wedge \{\sigma'_1, \ldots, \sigma'_m\} =$$
$$\{\sigma_i \sqcap \sigma'_j \mid 1 \le i \le n, 1 \le i \le m, \sigma_i \sqcap \sigma'_j \text{ exists }\} \qquad (6.5)$$

6.4.3 Rules for Type Inference

Not all expressions are meaningful. One goal of a type system is to identify the set of all syntactically meaningful expressions as the set of *well typed* expressions. We write $\vdash e{:}\sigma$ for e is *well typed* with type σ. Such well typed expressions are systematically determined by a proof system, called a *type inference system*. A type inference system consists of axioms for constant types and inference rules for compound types. Axioms of our type inference system are

$$const \quad \vdash b : \tau_i \quad \text{ for all } b \in B_i$$

$$null \quad \vdash \text{null}_{B_i} : \tau_i \quad \text{ for all } B_i$$

Inference rules of our type inference system are

$$subtype \quad \frac{\vdash e{:}\sigma \qquad \sigma < \sigma'}{\vdash e : \sigma'}$$

$$recors \quad \frac{\vdash e_1 : \sigma_1, \ldots, \vdash e_n : \sigma_n}{\vdash (l_1 \rightarrow e_1, \ldots, l_n \rightarrow e_n) : (l_1 : \sigma_1, \ldots, l_n : \sigma_n)}$$

$$dot \quad \frac{\vdash e : (\ldots, l : \sigma, \ldots)}{\vdash e.l : \sigma}$$

$$set \quad \frac{\vdash e_1 : \sigma_1, \ldots, \vdash e_n : \sigma_n}{\vdash \{e_1, \ldots, e_n\} : \{\sigma_1, \ldots, \sigma_n\}}$$

$$join \quad \frac{\vdash e_1 : \sigma_1 \qquad \vdash e_2 : \sigma_2}{\vdash e_1 \bowtie e_2 : \sigma_1 \wedge \sigma_2} \quad \text{if } \sigma_1 \text{ and } \sigma_2 \text{ are set types}$$

Based on this type inference system, we can define a typechecking function *type* that takes an expression e and returns a type of e if it is well typed, otherwise it returns *error.type*, which is defined inductively as follows:

$$type(b) = \tau_i \ (b \in B_i)$$

$$type(null_{B_i}) = \tau_i$$

$$type((l_1 \rightarrow e_1, \ldots, l_n \rightarrow e_n)) = (l_1{:}type(e_1), \ldots, l_n{:}type(e_n))$$

$$type(e.l) = \text{if } type(e) = (\ldots, l{:}\sigma, \ldots) \text{ then } \sigma$$

$$\text{else error}$$

$$type(\{e_1, \ldots, e_n\}) = \{type(e_1), \ldots, type(e_n)\}$$

$$type(e \bowtie e') = \text{if } type(e), type(e') \text{ are set types}$$

$$\text{then } type(e) \wedge type(e') \text{ else } error$$

This typechecking function is correct with respect to our type inference system, that is, we can prove the following theorem by induction on the structure of e :

THEOREM 6.8. If $type(e) = \sigma$ then $\vdash e : \sigma$ holds.

This type inference system is not complete under the equality between expressions, that is, this system does not have the property that if $\vdash e : \sigma$ and $e = e'$ then $\vdash e' : \sigma$ because of $\bowtie$. Suppose $\vdash e_1 : \sigma_1$ and $\vdash e_2 : \sigma_2$ hold and σ_1, σ_2 are set types. Then by the rule *join*, $\vdash e_1 \bowtie e_2 : \sigma_1 \wedge \sigma_2$ hold. However, $e_1 \bowtie e_2$ may be equal to the empty set, which has any set types. Because of this incompleteness property, the function *type* does not necessarily return the most specific type (smallest type under $\leqslant$) for a given expression e. We nevertheless think that *type* is an appropriate definition for *static* typechecking. To see this consider the following join expression:

e: {(*Name* : *string*, *Age* : *int*)}$\bowtie e'$: {(*Name* : *string*, *EmpId* : *int*)}

Although the result of the join may be empty set, we usually think that the type of the result relation is {(*Name* : *string*, *Age* : *int*, *EmpId* : *int*)}.

6.5 SEMANTICS OF THE LANGUAGE

In this section we define a denotational semantics of the language. We first define a semantic domain for expressions and define a semantics of expressions. We then show that types are modeled by special subsets called filters in a domain and define a semantics of types. Finally we show the correctness of the type inference system with respect to the semantics.

6.5.1 Semantic Domain

A semantic domain for expressions is given by a recursive domain equation containing flat domains $\mathcal{B}_i$ for primitive values, total functions $(L \to \mathcal{D})$ for records, and Smyth's power domain $\mathcal{P}(\mathcal{D})$ for sets of descriptions.

$$\mathcal{D} = \mathcal{B}_1 + \cdots + \mathcal{B}_n + (L \to \mathcal{D}) + \mathcal{P}(\mathcal{D}) + \{w\} \qquad (6.6)$$

where $+$ is the *separated* sum domain constructor, $\mathcal{B}_i = B_i \cup \{\perp_{\mathcal{B}_i}\}$ with ordering $\perp_{\mathcal{B}_i} \sqsubseteq x$ for all $x \in B_i$, and w is used to interpret the *wrong* value. For $\mathcal{P}(\mathcal{D})$ we include $\varnothing$, the empty set.

A solution of the Eq. (6.6) can be found in a particular class of complete partial orders (c.p.o.) called a *bounded complete ω-algebraic* c.p.o., or simply *domain*.

A c.p.o. is a partial order $(D, \sqsubseteq)$ satisfying:

1. D has the minimal element $\bot_D$.
2. Each directed subset $X \subseteq D$ has a least upper bound $\sqcup X$ where a subset X is directed "iff" $\forall x, y \in X \exists z \in X . x \sqsubseteq z, y \sqsubseteq z$.

An *isolated (finite)* element of a c.p.o. $(D, \sqsubseteq)$ is an element $e \in D$ such that for any directed subset $X \subseteq D$ if $e \sqsubseteq \sqcup X$ then there is $x \in X$ such that $e \sqsubseteq x$. We write D^o for the set of isolated elements of D. A c.p.o. is said to be *ω-algebraic* "iff" D^o is countable and for all $x \in D$ we have $x = \sqcup \{e \mid e \in D^o, e \sqsubseteq x\}$. A c.p.o. is said to be *bounded complete (consistently complete)* if any bounded subset of D has a least upper bound, where a subset X is bounded if it has an upper bound in D.

Construction of a recursive domain without containing power domain can be found in many places such as (MacQueen, Plotkin, and Sethi, [1986]; Barendregt, [1984]; Schmidt, [1986]). Smyth [1978] showed that domains are closed under the power domain construction based on the preordering $\sqsubseteq_0$ and that a domain equation like (6.6) can be solved. In what follows we use $\mathcal{D}$ for a domain satisfying (6.6). We also use injections of component domains $\mathcal{B}_1, \ldots, \mathcal{P}(\mathcal{D})$ into $\mathcal{D}$ implicitly and treat them as if they were actual inclusions.

We use the following notations to represent elements in D.

1. $(l_1 \mapsto d_1, \ldots, l_n \mapsto d_n)$ for the function $f \in (L \to \mathcal{D})$ defined as $f(l) =$ if $l = l_i, 1 \le i \le n$ then d_i else $\bot_{\mathcal{D}}$, where we assume that $d_i \ne \bot_{\mathcal{D}}$.
2. $[d_1, \ldots, d_n]$ for the element $d \in \mathcal{P}(\mathcal{D})$ such that $\{d_1, \ldots, d_n\} \in d$, that is, the equivalence class containing $\{d_1, \ldots, d_n\}$.

It should be noted that the domain $\mathcal{D}$ is equipped with the ordering $\sqsubseteq$. This ordering was originally introduced to model computation. However, if we regard values in $\mathcal{D}$ as descriptions then this ordering corresponds to the approximation ordering on descriptions we discussed in Section 6.2. We therefore believe that the domain $\mathcal{D}$ is an appropriate model of our language.

6.5.2 Semantics of Expressions

Let *Expr* be the set of expressions. We define a semantics of expressions by the semantic function

$$\mathcal{E} : Expr \to \mathcal{D}$$

as follows:

$$\mathscr{E}[\![b]\!] = b \text{ for all } b \in B_i$$

$$\mathscr{E}[\![null_{B_i}]\!] = \bot_{B_i}$$

$$\mathscr{E}[\![(l_1 \to e_1, \ldots, l_n \to e_n)]\!] = (l_1 \mapsto \mathscr{E}[\![e_1]\!], \ldots, l_n \mapsto \mathscr{E}[\![e_n]\!])$$

$$\mathscr{E}[\![e \, . \, l]\!] = \text{ if } \mathscr{E}[\![e]\!] = (\ldots, l \mapsto d, \ldots) \text{ then } d \text{ else } w$$

$$\mathscr{E}[\![\{e_1, \ldots, e_m\}]\!] = [\mathscr{E}[\![e_1]\!], \ldots, \mathscr{E}[\![e_m]\!]]$$

$$\mathscr{E}[\![e \bowtie e']\!] = \text{ if } \mathscr{E}[\![e]\!] \sqcup \mathscr{E}[\![e']\!] \text{ exists then } \mathscr{E}[\![e]\!] \sqcup \mathscr{E}[\![e']\!]$$

$$\text{else } w$$

From this definition, we can easily show, by induction on the structures of expressions, the soundness of the ordering relation on expressions:

THEOREM 6.9.

1. If $e \sqsubseteq e'$ then $\mathscr{E}[\![e]\!] \sqsubseteq \mathscr{E}[\![e']\!]$.
2. If $e \sqcup e'$ exists then $\mathscr{E}[\![e \sqcup e']\!] = \mathscr{E}[\![e]\!] \sqcup \mathscr{E}[\![e']\!]$.
3. If $e \sqcap e'$ exists then $\mathscr{E}[\![e \sqcap e']\!] = \mathscr{E}[\![e]\!] \sqcap \mathscr{E}[\![e']\!]$.

The equations (6.1), (6.2), and (6.3) between expressions are also sound with respect to this semantics, that is, the following equations hold:

$$\mathscr{E}[\![(\ldots, l \to e, \ldots) \, . \, l]\!] = \mathscr{E}[\![e]\!] \tag{6.7}$$

$$\mathscr{E}[\![\{e_1, e_2, e_3, \ldots\}]\!] = \mathscr{E}[\![\{e_1, e_3, \ldots\}]\!] \text{ if } e_1 \sqsubseteq e_2 \tag{6.8}$$

$$\mathscr{E}[\![\{e_1, \ldots, e_n\} \bowtie \{e'_1, \ldots, e'_m\}]\!] =$$
$$\mathscr{E}[\![\{e_1 \sqcup e'_j \mid 1 \leq i \leq n, 1 \leq i \leq m, e_i \sqcup e'_j \text{ exists }\}]\!] \tag{6.9}$$

Equation (6.7) is shown by the definition of $\mathscr{E}$. Equations (6.8) and (6.9) are shown by the definition of $\mathscr{E}$ and Theorem 6.9.

6.5.3 Semantics of Types

Types correspond to sets of expressions and expressions denote values in $\mathscr{D}$. Therefore types should be interpreted as subsets of $\mathscr{D}$. In order to give semantics to types, we should first determine what kind of subsets correspond to types. One such model of types was proposed by MacQueen, Plotkin, and Sethi [1986] where types were interpreted as *ideals* in $\mathscr{D}$. Cardelli [1984] used this ideal model to give semantics to a type system supporting records, variants, and subtype relation *inheritance*. However, the ideal model is not suitable for our language; (*i*) it is not suitable for types for partial objects such as partial descriptions and (*ii*) the ordering on ideals does not agree with the ordering on our types.

To see (*i*) consider the expression $e =$ (*Name* $\rightarrow$ '*Joe Doe*', *Age* $\rightarrow$ 21, it EmpId $\rightarrow$ 1234). This expression should have the type $\sigma =$ (*Name*) : *string*, *Age* : *int*, *EmpId* : *int*). If σ corresponds to a downward closed set of values, then an expression such as (*Name* $\rightarrow$ '*Joe Doe*') also has the type σ. Then the type system cannot eliminate expressions like (*Name* $\rightarrow$ '*Joe Doe*').*Age*.

To see (*ii*) consider the two types $\sigma_1 =$ (*Name* : *string*, *Sex* : *string*) and $\sigma_2 =$ (*Name* : *string*, *EmpId* : *int*). The lub of these two is (*Name* : *string*). Then for their semantics we expect the following property should hold:

$$[\![\sigma_1]\!] \sqcup [\![\sigma_2]\!] = [\![\text{(Name: string)}]\!]$$

If we interpret types as ideals then $[\![\sigma_1]\!] \sqcup [\![\sigma_2]\!] = [\![\sigma_1]\!] \cup [\![\sigma_2]\!]$. However, the type (*Name* : *string*) does not correspond to the union of σ_1 and σ_2. For example, (*Name* $\rightarrow$ '*Joe Doe*', *Sex* $\rightarrow$ 1, *EmpId* $\rightarrow$ '*ABC123*') has the type (*Name* : *string*) but has neither the type σ_1 nor σ_2. This problem arises even if a language does not contain partial values such as the language described in (Cardelli, [1984]).

We regard types as subsets of values having common structures. As we have noted in Section 6.2, subsets having common structures are upward closed sets. In addition to this, we also require that common structures are preserved by finite glb's, the intuition being that the glb $d \sqcap d'$ of two descriptions d, d' corresponds to the description common to d and d' and therefore has all structures common to d, d'. These observations lead us to define types as *filters* in $\mathcal{D}$ that do not contain w.

A nonempty subset $F \subseteq \mathcal{D}$ is a filter "iff"

1. F is upward closed; for any $d \in F$, $d \sqsubseteq d'$ implies $d' \in F$.
2. F is closed under pairwise glb; for any $d, d' \in F$, $d \sqcap d' \in F$.

If filter has a minimal element d them it is a *principal* filter and written as $d \uparrow$. Let $\mathcal{F}(\mathcal{D})$ denote the set of all filters in $\mathcal{D}$ that do not contain w. $\mathcal{F}(\mathcal{D})$ is ordered by set inclusion. Lub and glb are defined as

1. $F \sqcup F' = \{d \mid \exists f \in F \exists f' \in F' . f \sqcap f' \sqsubseteq d\}$.
2. $F \sqcap F' = F \cap F'$.

Note that $F \sqcap F'$ does not necessarily exist.

In order to interpret types in $\mathcal{F}(\mathcal{D})$, we define filter constructors corresponding to type constructors.

1. *Records*
   Let $F_1, \ldots, F_n$ be filters in $\mathcal{D}$. Define $(l_1 \Rightarrow F_1, \ldots, l_n \Rightarrow F_n) = \{(l_1 \mapsto f_1, \ldots, l_m \mapsto f_m) \mid n \leq m, f_i \in F_i, 1 \leq i \leq n\}$.

PROPOSITION 6.1. $(l_1 \Rightarrow F_1, \ldots, l_n \Rightarrow F_n)$ is a filter in $(L \rightarrow \mathcal{D})$.

Proof. It is clear that $(l_1 \Rightarrow F_1, \ldots, l_n \Rightarrow F_n)$ is upward closed. To see that this set is closed under pairwise glb, we note that glb in $(L \to \mathcal{D})$ is pointwise.

From the definition, we have

PROPOSITION 6.2. $(l_1 \Rightarrow F_1, \ldots, l_n \Rightarrow F_n) \sqsubseteq (l_1 \Rightarrow F'_1, \ldots, l_m \Rightarrow F'_m)$ if $m \leq n, F_i \sqsubseteq F'_i, 1 \leq i \leq m$.

2. *Sets*

Let $F_1, \ldots, F_m$ be filters in $\mathcal{D}$. Define $[F_1, \ldots, F_m] = \{[f_1, \ldots, f_k] \,|\, \forall f \in \{f_1, \ldots, f_k\} \exists F \in \{F_1, \ldots, F_m\} . f \in F\}$.

PROPOSITION 6.3. $[F_1, \ldots, F_m]$ is a filter in $\mathscr{P}(\mathcal{D})$.

Proof. It is clear that $[F_1, \ldots, F_m]$ is upward closed. Let $[f_1, \ldots, f_k]$, $[f'_1, \ldots, f'_l] \in [F_1, \ldots, F_m]$. Since $[f_1, \ldots, f_k] \sqcap [f'_1, \ldots, f'_l] = [f_1, \ldots, f_k, f'_1, \ldots, f'_l]$ and $[f_1, \ldots, f_k, f'_1, \ldots, f'_l] \in [F_1, \ldots, F_m]$, $[F_1, \ldots, F_m]$ is closed under pairwise glb.

From the definition, we have:

PROPOSITION 6.4.
   a. $[F_1, \ldots F_n] \sqsubseteq [F'_1, \ldots, F'_m]$ if $\forall F \in \{F_1, \ldots, F_n\} \exists F' \in \{F'_1, \ldots, F'_m\}$. $F \sqsubseteq F'$.
   b. $[F_1, F_2, F_3, \ldots, F_n] = [F_1, F_3, \ldots, F_n]$ if $F_2 \sqsubseteq F_1$.
   c. $[F_1, \ldots, F_n] \sqcap [F'_1, \ldots, F'_m] = [F_i \sqcap F'_j \,|\, 1 \leq i \leq n, 1 \leq j \leq m, F_i \sqcap F_j \text{ exists}]$ where we define $[\,] = \{\varnothing\}$.

We now give semantics to types by the semantic function $\mathcal{T} : Texp \to \mathscr{F}(\mathcal{D})$ where *Texp* is the set of types defined in the previous section:

$$\mathcal{T}[\![\tau_i]\!] = \mathscr{B}_i$$
$$\mathcal{T}[\![(l_1 : \sigma_1, \ldots, l_n : \sigma_n)]\!] = (l_1 \Rightarrow \mathcal{T}[\![\sigma_1]\!], \ldots, l_n \Rightarrow \mathcal{T}[\![\sigma_n]\!])$$
$$\mathcal{T}[\![\{\sigma_1, \ldots, \sigma_m\}]\!] = [\mathcal{T}[\![\sigma_1]\!], \ldots, \mathcal{T}[\![\sigma_m]\!]]$$
$$\mathcal{T}[\![\sigma \wedge \sigma']\!] = \mathcal{T}[\![\sigma]\!] \sqcap \mathcal{T}[\![\sigma']\!]$$

Since we interpret the domain constructor $+$ as the separated sum domain constructor, $\mathscr{B}_i = (\bot_{\mathscr{B}_i}) \uparrow$ and is a filter in $\mathcal{D}$ not containing w. Then by Propositions 6.1 and 6.3 it is immediately seen that $\mathcal{T}$ is well defined. Proposition 6.4 shows that equations between types are sound with respect to this semantics. Using Propositions 6.2 and 6.4, we can show the soundness of ordering on types by induction on the structure of types:

THEOREM 6.10.

1. If $\sigma \leqslant \sigma'$ then $\mathcal{T}[\![\sigma]\!] \subseteq \mathcal{T}[\![\sigma']\!]$.
2. If $\sigma \sqcup \sigma'$ exists then $\mathcal{T}[\![\sigma \sqcup \sigma']\!] = \mathcal{T}[\![\sigma]\!] \sqcup \mathcal{T}[\![\sigma']\!]$.
3. If $\sigma \sqcap \sigma'$ exists then $\mathcal{T}[\![\sigma \sqcap \sigma']\!] = \mathcal{T}[\![\sigma]\!] \sqcap \mathcal{T}[\![\sigma']\!]$.

From this theorem, we see that the filter model is an appropriate model for our type system. It should also be noted that the filter model can give precise semantics to multiple inheritance. The problem of join types we have mentioned in the beginning of Section 6.5 does not arise in this model.

Based on the semantics of types, we show that the type inference system is correct.

THEOREM 6.11. $\vdash e : \sigma$ implies $\mathcal{E}[\![e]\!] \in \mathcal{T}[\![\sigma]\!]$.

Proof.   By induction on the light of the proof tree for $\vdash e : \sigma$.

Since our type checking function is syntactically sound (Theorem 6.8) with respect to the type inference system, we also get:

COROLLARY 6.1.   If e is well typed expression $(type(e) \neq error)$ then $\mathcal{E}[\![e]\!] \neq \omega$.

6.6   CONCLUSION AND FUTURE WORK

By interpreting database objects as descriptions of real-world objects ordered by the goodness of descriptions, we have shown that nonflat records, higher-order relations, and natural joins can be represented as typed expressions in programming languages. We have then defined a simple typed language supporting these data structures and have presented a denotational semantics of the language. In order to give semantics to types, we have proposed a filter model of types. Using this model we have shown that the type system of the language is sound.

In order to develop a practical programming language based on this study, we need to extend the language to include function expressions. One simple way to do this extension is to define a new language using our language. Let e, σ denote expressions and types defined in the previous section. Then a syntax of the extended expressions (ranged over by E) can be given as

$$E ::= x \; (variable) \; | e | \lambda x : \Sigma . E \; | \; EE$$

with the extended types

$$\mathcal{E} ::= \sigma \; | \; \Sigma \rightarrow \Sigma.$$

The extended expressions can be interpreted in a domain satisfying

$$\mathcal{V} = \mathcal{D} + (\mathcal{V} \rightarrow \mathcal{V})$$

where $\mathcal{D}$ is a domain satisfying (6.6) and $\rightarrow$ is the continuous function space constructor. Since the space of filters of a domain is closed under the following function type constructor,

$$F \Rightarrow F' = \{f \in (\mathcal{D} \rightarrow \mathcal{D}) \mid \forall x \in F . f(x) \in F'\}$$

a semantics of the extended types can be also given.

We hope that this study provides a basis to implement typed programming languages for partial objects, including languages for databases, knowledge representations, and natural language processing.

REFERENCES

Abiteboul, S., and Bidoit, N., (1984). "Non-first normal form relations to represent hierarchically organized data," *Proceedings of the Third ACM PODS*, Waterloo, Ontario, Canada.

Bancilhon, F., and Khoshafin, S., (1986). "A calculus for complex objects," *Proceedings of the ACM Conference on Principles of Database Systems.*

Barendregt, H. P., (1984). *The Lambda Calculus*, Vol. 103, *Studies in Logic and the Foundations of Mathematics*, rev. ed., North-Holland.

Buneman, P., and Ohori, A., (1986). "A domain theoretic approach to higher-order relations," *International Conference on Database Theory, Lecture Notes in Computer Science 243*, New York: Springer-Verlag.

Buneman, P., and Ohori, A., (1987). "Using powerdomains to generalize relational databases," to appear in *Theoretical Computer Science*, also available as a technical report, Department of Computer and Information Science, University of Pennsylvania.

Cardelli, L., (1984). "A semantics of multiple inheritance," *Semantics of DataTypes, Lecture Notes in Computer Science 173*, New York: Springer-Verlag.

Fischer, P. C., and Thomas, S. J., (1983). "Operators for non-first-normal-form relations," *Proceedings of IEEE COMPSAC.*

MacQueen, D. B., Plotkin, G. D., and R. Sethi, (1986). "An ideal model for recursive polymorphic types," *Information and Control*, Vol. 71, No. 1/2, pp. 95–130.

Özsoyoğlu, Z., and Yuan, L., (1985). "A normal form for nested relations," *Proceedings of the ACM SIGACT-SIGMOD Symposium on Principles of Database Systems*, Portland, pp. 251–260.

Roth, A. M., Korth, H. F., and Silberschatz, A., (1984). "Extended algebra and calculus for $\neg$ 1NF relational databases," *Technical Report TR-84-36*, Department of Computer Science, The University of Texas at Austin, revised 1985.

Schmidt, D. A., (1986). *Denotational Semantics: A Methodology for Language Development.* Allyn and Bacon.

Shieber, S. M., (1985). "An introduction to unification-based approaches to grammar," *Proceedings of the 23rd Annual Meeting of the Association for Computational Linguistics.*

Smyth, M. B., (1978). "Power domains," *JCSS*, Vol. 16, No. 1, pp. 23–26.

Zaniolo, C., (1984). "Database relation with null values," *JCSS*, Vol. 28, No. 1, pp. 142–166.

CHAPTER 7

ALGORITHMS FOR SET CONTAINMENT INFERENCE

Paolo Atzeni
D. Stott Parker Jr.

7.1 INTRODUCTION

Recently, a number of papers have been published concerning formal studies of set-theoretic properties of type hierarchies, in the context of databases and knowledge bases. These include work of Atzeni and Parker [1986, 1986a, 1988] on containment, disjointness, and intersection constraints; of Lenzerini [1987] on covering and disjointness constraints; and of Arisawa and Miura [1986] on variations of containment constraints. Other related work was published by Schubert, et al. [1983], Attardi and Simi [1981], and Spyratos and Lecluse [1987].

We show how some of these results can be incorporated into a system capable of handling queries of constraints between types. We consider a system that allows the representation of types (i.e., sets of elements of a given universe), and binary containment (*isa*) constraints.[1] An important point is that negation is allowed, as in Atzeni and Parker [1986a], in two ways:

---

[1] Obviously, any knowledge representation system would provide more general kinds of relationships among types than just containment and its negation. Here, we consider only the implementation of the subsystem dealing with type containment inference.

1. It is possible to represent *complements of types*; for example, we can express the fact that the set of the *Students* is a subset of the complement of the set of *Professors*. (As an aside, this is equivalent to saying that the sets *Students* and *Professors* are disjoint).

2. It is possible to express negative statements; for example, we can state that it is not the case that the *Instructors* are a subset of the *Professors*.

Essentially, we have *positive constraints*, which express containment between types or their negations, and *negative constraints*, which negate containment, and therefore specify nonempty intersection: if the set *Instructors* is not a subset of the set *Professors*, then the set *Instructors* intersects the complement of the set *Professors*.

In Atzeni and Parker [1986a], we have shown that the inference problem for this kind of constraint is solvable, by means of inference rules essentially equivalent to Aristotle's syllogisms, in polynomial time. In this paper, we discuss two ways of implementing the queries on the constraints, based on the results in Atzeni and Parker [1986a]. The paper is organized as follows. In Section 7.2 we set up the framework. In Section 7.3 we review the results on inference rules from Atzeni and Parker [1986a]. In Section 7.4 we show how these constraints can be easily represented by means of graphs, with two kinds of edges, one representing containment, closed under transitivity, and the other representing intersection constraints, which are symmetric and are affected by the other edges. The inference rules from Atzeni and Parker [1986a] and their properties [Atzeni & Parker, 1988] allow us to prove a number of results on these graphs. Finally, in Section 7.5 we show how efficient algorithms can be based on small models of the schemes.

7.2 THE FRAMEWORK

We differentiate between a containment *scheme*, and its *interpretations* or *models*. The scheme specifies the structure of the universe of discourse, whereas interpretations of the scheme give instances of objects in the types in the scheme.

A *type scheme* T/U is a collection of *type symbols* $\{U, T_1, \ldots, T_n\}$. The type symbol U is a special symbol and is called the *universe* of the type scheme. Each type symbol T_i will denote a subset of the set denoted by U. The universe symbol U is needed in order to define complements **non**(T_i) of types.

A *type term* X of a type scheme T/U is either

☐ a type symbol T_i or U.
☐ **non**(Y), where Y is a type term.

An *interpretation* I of a type scheme T/U is a map associating with each type term of T/U a (possibly empty) subset of a countable *domain* D, subject to the following restrictions:

1. $I(X) \subseteq I(U)$.
2. $I(\mathbf{non}(\mathbf{non}(X))) = I(X)$.
3. $I(\mathbf{non}(X)) = I(U) - I(X)$.

In other words, with an interpretation, the type term $\mathbf{non}(X)$ denotes the complement under U of the set denoted by X.

From condition 2 above, it follows that for every type term X,

$$I(X) = I(\mathbf{non}(\mathbf{non}(X))) = I(\mathbf{non}(\mathbf{non}(\mathbf{non}(\mathbf{non}(X))))) = \cdots$$

Therefore, it is possible to introduce the notion of *type descriptor* of the type scheme T/U, as an equivalence class of type terms,

$$\{X, \mathbf{non}(\mathbf{non}(X)), \mathbf{non}(\mathbf{non}(\mathbf{non}(\mathbf{non}(X)))), \ldots\}$$

where X is a type term of the form S or $\mathbf{non}(S)$, and S is a type symbol in U; a type descriptor is designated by any element of the class, but usually by X. Therefore, the type scheme $T/U = \{U, T_1, \ldots, T_n\}$ has the type descriptors U, $\mathbf{non}(U)$, T_1, $\mathbf{non}(T_1)$, $\ldots, T_n$, $\mathbf{non}(T_n)$.

The interpretation I is *trivial* if $I(U) = \varnothing$, and so $I(X) = \varnothing$, for each type term X.

A *positive (binary) constraint* p has the form $p : X$ *isa* Y, where X and Y are type descriptors. The constraint p is *satisfied* by the interpretation I if $I(X) \subseteq I(Y)$. A *negative constraint* has the form $\mathbf{not}(p)$, where p is a positive constraint. It is satisfied if p is not.

Note that the positive constraint p is satisfied by I if and only if $I(\mathbf{non}(X)) \cup I(Y) = I(U)$, or, equivalently, if and only if $I(\mathbf{non}(X)) \cap I(Y) = \varnothing$. Therefore, the negative constraint $\mathbf{not}(p)$ is satisfied if and only if $I(X) \cap I(\mathbf{non}(Y)) \neq \varnothing$. In other words, positive constraints make assertions about *inclusions* between types, while negative constraints make assertions about *intersections* between types. Therefore, in order to improve expressiveness, we will write X *int* $\mathbf{non}(Y)$, instead of $\mathbf{not}(X$ *isa* $Y)$.

A *containment scheme* is a pair $S = (T/U, C)$, where T/U is a type scheme and C is a set of containment constraints on type descriptors of T/U. A *model* of a containment scheme $(T/U, C)$ is an interpretation I of T/U that satisfies all constraints in C.

Containment schemes can be 'degenerate.' Consider the following constraints: (1) X *isa* $\mathbf{non}(X)$; (2) $\mathbf{non}(X)$ *isa* X; (3) X *int* $\mathbf{non}(X)$. The first constraint is satisfied only if $I(X) = \varnothing$. Similarly, the second is satisfied only if $I(\mathbf{non}(X)) = \varnothing$, and so X denotes the same set as U. The first two constraints together can be satisfied only if $I(X) = I(\mathbf{non}(X)) = \varnothing$. In other words, any scheme with the first two constraints has only one model: the trivial interpretation. The third constraint is the negation of X *isa* X, which is satisfied by any interpretation; therefore, any scheme with the third constraint has no model.

A type descriptor X is *trivial* in a scheme S if $I(X) = \varnothing$ in every model I of S. A containment scheme is *unsatisfiable* if it has no model; otherwise it is *satisfiable*. A satisfiable scheme is *trivial* if the universe U is trivial in every model (and so all the type descriptors are trivial).

7.3 INFERENCE RULES FOR SET CONTAINMENT

Inference rules have been widely used in database theory to study implication of constraints [Maier, 1983; Ullman, 1982]. We remind the reader that classes of constraints studied in database theory do not involve negation, for the most part. That is, collections of data dependencies (functional dependencies, join dependencies, etc.) do not imply that a specific data dependency *does not* hold, but only that one *does* hold. These systems are always satisfiable. Unsatisfiability can occur with containment, as we have already seen. Therefore, the inference problem here is somewhat different than for data dependencies.

If we are given a set of constraints, we are frequently interested in deducing whether other constraints must also hold. A constraint c is *implied* by a set of constraints C ($C \vDash c$) of a scheme $S = (T/U, C)$ if it holds in all models of S. Given C and c, the *inference problem* is to tell whether C implies c. Algorithms for the solution of the inference problem (called *inference algorithms*) have correctness proofs that are usually based on sound and complete sets of inference rules. An *inference rule* $C \vdash c$ is a rule asserting that the constraint c holds whenever the set of constraints C holds. For example, the rule

$$X \ \textit{isa} \ Y, Y \ \textit{isa} \ Z \vdash X \ \textit{isa} \ Z$$

asserts that the inclusion predicate *isa* is transitive.

Relative to a specific set of inference rules, we write $C \vdash c$ if c can be derived from C using application of the rules.

The basic requirement for each inference rule is to be *sound*, that is, that it derive from C only constraints c such that $C \vDash c$. Moreover, it is important to have sets of inference rules that are *complete*, that is, that allow the derivation of *all* the constraints c such that $C \vDash c$. Thus, a set of rules is sound and complete when $\vdash$ is equivalent to $\vDash$.

Recently, we have shown that the following set of inference rules is sound and complete for containment constraints [Atzeni & Parker, 1986a, 1988]. (X, Y, Z represent arbitrary type descriptors.)

INT0. $X \ \textit{int} \ Y \vdash X \ \textit{int} \ X$

INT1. $X \ \textit{int} \ Y \vdash Y \ \textit{int} \ X$

INT2. $X \ \textit{int} \ Y, Y \textit{isa} \ Z \vdash X \ \textit{int} \ Z$

INC0. $X \ \textit{int}\textbf{non}(X) \vdash Y \textit{isa} \ Z$

INC1. $X \textit{int} \ \textbf{non}(X) \vdash Y \textit{int} \ Z$

ISA0. $\vdash X \ \textit{isa} \ U$

ISA1. $\vdash X$ *isa* X

ISA2. $X isa$ Y, Y *isa* $Z \vdash X$ *isa* Z

ISA3. $X isa$ $Y \vdash \textbf{non}(Y)$ *isa* $\textbf{non}(X)$

TRIV0. $X isa$ $\textbf{non}(X) \vdash X isa$ Y

7.4 GRAPHS FOR SET CONTAINMENT INFERENCE

In Atzeni and Parker [1988], as preliminary steps toward proving completeness of the rules, we proved a number of results on the structures of the derivations of constraints.

FACT 7.1. [Atzeni & Parker, 1988, Lemma 3] The constraint X *isa* Y is derivable from C without using rules INC0, INC1, TRIV0 if and only if there exist type descriptors $Z_0, Z_1, \ldots, Z_n$ such that $X = Z_0, Y = Z_n$, and, for each $i \in \{1, \ldots, n\}$, C contains at least one of $(Z_{i-1}$ *isa* $Z_i)$ and $\textbf{non}(Z_i)$ *isa* $\textbf{non}(Z_{i-1}))$.

FACT 7.2. [Atzeni and Parker, 1988, Lemma 4] X *int* Y is derivable from C without using rules INC0, INC1, TRIV0 if and only if there exist type descriptors W_1 and W_2 such that W_1 *int* W_2 is in C or is derivable from C using only INT0 and INT1, and W_1 *isa* X and W_2 *isa* Y are derivable from C without using INC0, INC1, TRIV0.

Facts 1 and 2 suggest the possibility of associating graphs with containment schemes, as follows. Given a containment scheme $S = (T/U, C)$, we define a graph G, whose nodes correspond to the type descriptors of S, and with two type of edges, representing *isa* and *int* constraints, respectively. Specifically, the graph contains

- ☐ the black edges $(X, X), (X, U)$, and $(\textbf{non}(U), \textbf{non}(X))$, for each type descriptor X of T/U
- ☐ the black edges (X, Y) and $(\textbf{non}(Y), \textbf{non}(X))$, for each X *isa* Y in C
- ☐ the blue edges $(X, Y), (Y, X), (X, X)$, and (Y, Y), for each X *int* Y in C.

It should be noted that the graph contains more edges than a straightforward construction would produce; these additional edges reflect the basic properties of *isa* and *int*, as expressed by some of the inference rules (INT0, INT1, ISA0, ISA1, ISA3). A number of properties follow from the construction of the graph. An immediate fact is that the black graph is reflexive and the blue graph is symmetric. As a consequence, we can consider *undirected* blue edges, corresponding to each pair of directed edges: the edges (X, Y) and (Y, X) will be replaced by the edge $\{X, Y\}$.

THEOREM 7.1. Let S be a satisfiable, nontrivial containment scheme. If the type X is not trivial, then C implies X *isa* Y if and only if there is a black path from the node (corresponding to the type) X to the node Y.

Proof. Follows directly from Fact 1 and the definition of the graph: the presence of the "dual" edge for each *isa* in C is the counterpart to the double possibility $((Z_{i-1}\ isa\ Z_i) \in C$ or $(Z_i\ isa\ Z_{i-1}) \in C)$ provided by Fact 1.

THEOREM 7.2. Let S be a satisfiable, nontrivial containment scheme. The type X is trivial if and only if there is a black path from the node X to the node **non**(X).

Sketch of the proof. It can be easily shown that X is trivial if and only if X *isa* **non**(X) can be derived by means of the inference rules. Therefore it suffices to show that X *isa* **non**(X) can be derived if and only if there is a black path from X to **non**(X). The *if* part is easy, so we concentrate on the *only if* part. If X *isa* **non**(X) can be derived without making use of rule TRIV0, then we can reason as in the proof of the previous theorem. Otherwise, proceeding by induction, we can show that the derivation always involves a constraint Y *isa* **non**(Y) (with a shorter derivation; so the path from Y to **non**(Y) is in the graph) such that X *isa* Y can be derived without making use of TRIV0. Therefore, by the previous theorem, the graph contains a path from X to Y and (due to the duality in the construction of the graph) a path from **non**(Y) to **non**(X), and so the graph contains a path from X to **non**(X).

THEOREM 7.3. Let S be a satisfiable containment scheme. The constraints in C imply X *int* Y if and only if there exist W_1 and W_2 such that the graph contains the blue edge $\{W_1, W_2\}$ and two black paths from W_1 to X, and from W_2 to Y, respectively.

Proof. It follows directly from Fact 2, Theorem 7.1, and the definition of the graph: the various edges corresponding to each *int* correspond to the application of rules INT0 and INT1.

THEOREM 7.4. The containment scheme S is unsatisfiable if and only if there are three type descriptors X, W_1, and W_2 such that the graph contains the blue edge $\{W_1, W_2\}$ and two black paths from W_1 to X, and from W_2 to **non**(X), respectively.

Proof. If the scheme is unsatisfiable, then any constraint is derivable, by INC0 and INC1. Consider any derivation containing steps where either of these rules is used; let the constraint X *int* **non**(X) be used as a premise in the first of these steps: clearly, X *int* **non**(X) is derived without making use of INC0, INC1, and so the claim follows from the previous theorem.

The previous results show that the main queries on a type containment scheme can be implemented by means of algorithms on graphs.

7.5 SMALL MODELS FOR ANSWERING QUERIES

Another way of answering queries of the form "Is constraint c implied by the containment scheme S?" could be based on the following idea: given the scheme, build a model, as small as possible, that satisfies exactly the constraints implied by the scheme. Then, representing the model by means of its characteristic vector, the queries could be efficiently implemented as Boolean operations, in "theoretically" constant time on bit-parallel machines. This approach was followed by Aït-Kaci, et al. [1985, 1987] for positive binary containment.

In database theory, these models are called *Armstrong* models [Armstrong, 1974]. Most of the classes of constraints considered in database theory admit an Armstrong model for any set of constraints. The situation is different here, since negation of constraints is allowed, as opposed to what happens in database theory.

FACT 7.3. The existence of Armstrong models is not guaranteed for containment schemes.

Proof. Let S be a containment scheme and c a constraint such that neither c nor its negation **not**(c) is implied by S. Then an Armstrong model should violate both, and this is clearly impossible.

However, it is still possible to follow the idea by using two models (or even just assignments of values to the type descriptors), one for the positive constraints and one for the negative ones. To be more precise, let us consider a satisfiable, nontrivial containment scheme $S = (T/U, C)$, such that $C = P \cup N$, where P is a set of positive constraints and N is a set of negative constraints; also, let C^+ be the set of containment constraints implied by C (the closure of C), and P', N' be the positive and negative constraints, respectively, in C^+. Then, our goal is to have two assignments, $I_{P'}$ and $I_{N'}$, such that the positive constraints satisfied by $I_{P'}$ are exactly those in P' and the negative constraints satisfied by $I_{N'}$ are exactly those in N'.

Note that $I_{P'}$ and $I_{N'}$ need not be models: $I_{P'}(I_{N'})$ could satisfy all the *isa (int)* and violate some of the intersection *(isa)* constraints. In fact, it follows from the inference rules in Section 7.3 that the intersection constraints do not influence the positive constraints: for any consistent scheme with constraints $C = P \cup N$, the positive constraints in C^+ are exactly those implied by P. Therefore, an assignment satisfying exactly the positive constraints in P would be a perfectly suitable $I_{P'}$.

In order to explain gradually how $I_{P'}$ can be built, let us first consider a simpler framework, allowing only the definition of types (with no complement) and positive constraints. In this case there is always an Armstrong model, which can be easily built as follows. Let $T_1, T_2, \ldots, T_n$ be the types in the scheme and P the set of positive constraints. Let us define an assign-

FIGURE 7.1
POSITIVE CONSTRAINTS ONLY

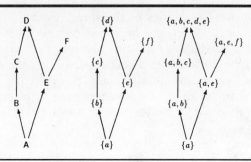

ment I that assigns to each type T_j a distinct singleton set $\{t_j\}$. Obviously, I need not satisfy P; however, it can be forced to do it by means of the following algorithm, a simple variation of the chase algorithm [Aho, Beeri, & Ullman, 1979; Maier, Mendelzon, & Sagiv, 1979] for functional dependencies. The following operation is performed on I, as long as possible: if I violates a constraint T_i *isa* $T_j \in P$, because of an element $t \in (I(T_i) - I(T_j))$, then add t to $I(T_j)$. It can be easily shown that this method always produces an Armstrong model. In Fig. 7.1 we show a scheme, whose positive constraints are represented by directed edges, with the initial assignment and the corresponding chased model.

The model has size proportional to the number n of types; Aït-Kaci, et al. [1987], referring to representation of types by means of characteristic vectors, have shown that in some cases it can be compressed up to a size $\log_2 n$. An example of one of these cases is shown in Fig. 7.2.

The framework adopted in this paper does not allow the use of the preceding algorithm to generate models, because the values in the interpretation of each type descriptor are related to those in its complement: $I(X) = I(U) - I(\textbf{non}(X))$. However, we could still use the assignment produced by the chase to answer queries. In Fig. 7.3, it is shown a containment scheme, with type

FIGURE 7.2
A MODEL WITH LOGARITHMIC SIZE

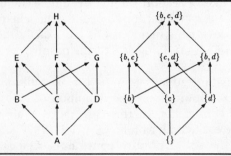

FIGURE 7.3
A SCHEME AND ITS POSITIVE SUBMODEL

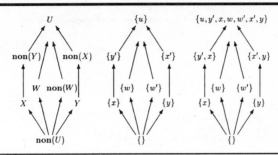

descriptors (that is, types and their complements) and positive constraints, represented again by directed edges (some of the edges corresponding to constraints derivable from others have been omitted). Then, it is shown an initial assignment and the corresponding chased assignment, which is not a model, but satisfies a constraint $p : X$ *isa* Y if and only if S implies p.

With respect to the "negative" interpretation $I_{N'}$, things are more complex, since the negative constraints in N' depend from both the positive and negative constraints in C. The interpretation $I_{N'}$ can be constructed by applying the chase algorithm to an assignment satisfying the intersection constraints in C. The correctness of this method follows from the inference rules in Section 7.3. In Fig. 7.4 is again shown a containment scheme, with *isa* and

FIGURE 7.4
A SCHEME AND ITS NEGATIVE SUBMODEL

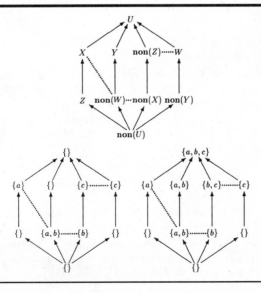

FIGURE 7.5

SCHEMES WITH QUADRATIC NUMBER OF CLIQUES
OF NEGATIVE CONSTRAINTS

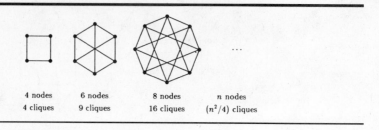

4 nodes	6 nodes	8 nodes	n nodes
4 cliques	9 cliques	16 cliques	$(n^2/4)$ cliques

int constraints (represented by directed solid edges and undirected dotted edges, respectively), an initial assignment, and the interpretation.

The "negative" interpretation described above has a size $O(n^2)$, if n is the number of type symbols in the scheme. Again, the model can be compacted, according to the kind of intersection constraints in C^+.

THEOREM 7.5.   Let $S = (T, C)$ be a containment scheme, and G' be the graph associated with the containment scheme $S' = (T, C^+)$, whose set of constraints is the closure of C; then, the smallest negative model for S has a size proportional to the number of nontrivial blue cliques in G'.

A corollary to Theorem 7.5 is that there is always a negative model with size proportional to n^2, as shown in Fig. 7.5.

REFERENCES

Aho, A. V., Beeri, C., and Ullman, J. D., (1979). "The theory of joins in relational databases," *ACM Trans. on Database Syst.*, Vol. 4, No. 3, pp. 297–314.

Aït-Kaci, H., Boyer, R., and Nasr, R., (1985). *An Encoding Technique for the Efficient Implementation of Type Inheritance.* Technical Report MCC AI-109-85, Microelectronics and Computer Technology Corporation, Austin, Tex.

Aït-Kaci, H., Boyer, R., Lincoln, P., and Nasr, R., (1987). *The Efficient Implementation of Object Inheritance.* Technical Report MCC AI-102-87, Microelectronics and Computer Technology Corporation, Austin, Tex.

Arisawa, H., and Miura, T., (1986). "On the properties of extended inclusion dependencies," In *Twelfth International Conference on Very Large Data Bases*, Kyoto, pp. 449–456.

Armstrong, W. W., (1974). "Dependency structure of database relationships," In *IFIP Congress*, pp. 580–583.

Attardi, G., and Simi, M., (1981). "Consistency and completeness of OMEGA, a logic for knowledge representation," In *Seventh International Joint Conference on Artificial Intelligence (IJCAI)*, Vancouver, pp. 504–510.

Atzeni, P., and Parker, D. S., Jr., (1986). "Formal properties of net-based knowledge representation schemes," In *Second IEEE International Conference on Data Engineering*, Los Angeles, pp. 700–706.

Atzeni, P. and Parker, D. S., Jr., (1986a). "Set containment inference," In *International Conference on Data Base Theory*, Roma, *Lecture Notes in Computer Science 243*, pp. 73–90. New York: Springer-Verlag.

Atzeni, P., and Parker, D. S., Jr., (1988). "Set containment inference and syllogisms," to appear in *Theoretical Computer Science*.

Lenzerini, M., (1987). "Covering and disjointness constraints in type networks," In *Third IEEE International Conference on Data Engineering*, Los Angeles.

Maier, D., (1983). *The Theory of Relational Databases.* Potomac, Md.: Computer Science Press.

Maier, D., Mendelzon, A. O., and Sagiv, Y., (1979). "Testing implications of data dependencies," *ACM Trans. on Database Syst.*, Vol. 4, No. 4, pp. 455–468.

Papalaskaris, M. A., and Schubert, L., (1981). "Parts inference: closed and semi-closed partitioning graphs," In *Seventh International Joint Conference on Artificial Intelligence (IJCAI)*, Vancouver, pp. 304–309.

Schubert, L., (1979). "Problems with parts," In *Sixth International Joint Conference on Artificial Intelligence (IJCAI)*, Tokyo, pp. 778–784.

Schubert, L., Papalaskaris, M. A., and Taugher, J., (1983). "Determining type, part, color, and time relationships," *Computer*, Vol. 16, No. 1, pp. 53–60.

Spyratos, N. and Lecluse, C., (1987). "Incorporating functional dependencies in deductive query answering," In *Third IEEE International Conference on Data Engineering*, Los Angeles, pp. 658–664.

Ullman, J. D., (1982). *Principles of Database Systems*, 2nd ed., Potomac, Md.: Computer Science Press.

PART II

IMPLEMENTATION ISSUES

CHAPTER 8

INTENSIONAL CONCEPTS IN AN OBJECT DATABASE MODEL

David Beech

8.1 INTRODUCTION

One of the main features of database interfaces or sublanguages has been their treatment of large collections of information, with search and retrieval operations applicable to hierarchical structures [Tsichritzis & Lochovsky, 1976], or DBTG sets [CODASYL, 1969], or relations [Codd, 1970], or functional models [Shipman, 1981]. Apart from notable exceptions such as SETL [Schwartz, 1973], Smalltalk [Goldberg & Robson, 1983], and Prolog [Clocksin & Mellish, 1981] in their various ways, programming languages have generally fought shy of providing more than tool kits for dealing with large collections other than arrays.

However, previous database models (and Smalltalk) have emphasized the extensional definition of collections, requiring them to be populated explicitly with their members rather than implicitly by terms which satisfy, or are generated by, some formula. The motivation for wanting a strong intensional model is that much human information is of this kind, employing intensional concepts rather than relying on memory of large extensions, and that different people in any case use different views of the same information. Relational views provide retrieval capability on intensionally defined collections, but are weak in the necessary flexibility of update semantics because of the absence of general operations in the relational model.

The various object models now current in programming languages may be combined with database ideas to provide the answer, since the essence of an object model is that it comprises both the representation and the manipulation of objects. Moreover, object concepts are deeply ingrained in natural language and human thought generally, and find their formal expression in the terms and classes of mathematical logic and in languages such as Prolog.

This paper modifies and develops some ideas originally introduced as part of a comprehensive object database model [Beech, 1987]. A Concept type is introduced to define an intensional concept as either a filter or a generator, depending on whether the defining formula tests whether an object (or n-tuple of objects) exemplifies the concept in the filter case, or produces exemplifying objects iteratively in the generator case. Update operations Assert and Retract are defined on this type, and provide the hooks for dealing with view update by specialized actions where necessary.

The treatment of Concepts may be seen to be in the spirit of Prolog functions, except that formulas are not limited to Horn clauses, negation is given its conventional predicate calculus semantics, and generative definitions are provided. The treatment of generative definitions is most like that of Iterators in CLU [Liskov, et al., 1979]. A kind of duality is exhibited between the filter and generator definitions of Concepts, and may be exploited in providing transparent usage of these objects. Collections such as Sets are then treated as a degenerate (purely extensional) case of Concepts, and Types are treated as a specialization of Sets, having additional properties.

Examples will be given in a higher-level language syntax to illustrate how the underlying primitives can be utilized by extending SQL [ANSI, 1986].

8.1.1 Motivation

Before developing a proposal for the treatment of intensional concepts in an object database model, we will first try to clarify our terminology, and expand on our view of the requirements.

Consider some *concepts* involved in family relationships. There are those like "person," "parent," "grandfather," or "head of family," which correspond to nouns or noun phrases. A given object may be an example of one or more such concepts. Another way of regarding this is that there are corresponding predicates "is-person," and so on, which may be defined to determine whether an object is an example of a given concept. ("It seems suitable to say that a *concept* is a function whose value is always a truth-value." [Frege, 1893, p. 135])

Verbal concepts such as "_ is the grandfather of _," "_ is head of family comprised of _," or "_ loves _," or "_ is child of _ and _," may be regarded as a generalization of the preceding. They may be exemplified by n-tuples of objects, which satisfy corresponding functions of n arguments (usually called "relations" in logic when $n > 1$, although we shall refrain from doing so in order to avoid confusion with database parlance).

When we say that a concept has been given an *extensional* definition, we shall mean that its exemplification is solely determined by a succession of explicit assertions that individual objects (or tuples of objects) are or are not examples of the concept. We will show a first approximation to how this might be expressed:

    Create concept Person (Object o);
    Assert Person(o1), Person(o3), Person(o4);
    Retract Person(o1);
    Assert Person(o9);

    Create concept FatherOf (Person f, Person c);
    Assert FatherOf(o3, o4);

An *intensional* definition of a concept employs some formula or algorithm or rule that enables its exemplification to be determined from other information without requiring direct assertions about this concept. For example,

    Create concept Father (Person p) as
      Exists Person c such that FatherOf(p, c);

    Create concept GrandfatherOf (Person gf, Person gc) as
      Exists Person p such that FatherOf(gf, p) and ParentOf(p, gc);

(Note that the extensional/intensional distinction refers to a particular definition of a concept, not to the concept itself. There may be many ways of defining an interrelated set of concepts with different choices as to what is to be extensional or intensional. Paradoxically, an extensionally defined concept is a rock on which we can build intensional definitions, and at the same time is inherently meaningless. In a way, the choice of something as extensionally defined is a confession of arbitrariness or disinterest or ignorance—we may have to be told explicitly who someone's parents are because we were not present at the birth, and lack other intensional evidence.)

Of course, an intensional definition may use other extensionally defined concepts. It is also often the case in a world of incomplete information that an intensional definition may be indecisive, and yet may be supplemented by direct extensional information about the same concept. For example,

    Assert GrandfatherOf(o1, o9);

We shall say that these are *hybrid* definitions. In this respect, Prolog provides the right structure.

So one major requirement for the kind of database model that we are focusing on is to have a general and convenient means for the representation and manipulation of intensional concepts, well integrated with the treatment of extensional and hybrid ones.

With respect to relational database technology, this calls for major advances in the treatment of "views." First, of course, there must be an object model with a sound entity concept. Then the presence of actions (messages, operations, functions) as a first-class part of an object model makes it possible to define more general views, and especially to specify any desired form of view update. There will also be a shift of emphasis, with the database system depending, like the human mind, much more on knowing how to generate and iterate over examples of concepts when it has to, rather than relying on rote memory.

With respect to artificial intelligence, there is a greater emphasis here on *representation* of information, even where we do not at present know how to automate efficient reasoning with all forms of it. The next generation of database systems will need to evolve to satisfy the requirements of much of the next century. As soon as such systems are available, they can begin collecting information which is intelligible to human users. Initially, these systems will sometimes have to ask users to reformulate questions, just as we do in conversation ourselves, but over the next few decades they will become much smarter and more efficient, and the information they have been amassing for years will be more tractable.

Another major requirement is to be able to get there from here. In this introduction so far, we have tried to suggest a change of perspective, and now we want to balance this by stressing the need to pay attention to existing programming languages and database technology. We shall try to make it clear that our proposals offer the hope of real-world evolution rather than requiring the adoption of completely new languages and systems.

8.2 OBJECT MODEL

We will summarize here as much of a basic object model as needed to introduce the treatment of intensional concepts.

8.2.1 Types

Every object is an instance of one or more types. There is the usual notion of a type semi-lattice, that is, the possibility of multiple inheritance, although we shall not discuss the details of this here. Types may also be added to and removed from objects dynamically, to reflect the need to retain the identity of long-lived objects in a database even while their nature may change considerably. A language interface to this model can look as follows:

```
Create type Person,
        Employee subtype of Person,
        Pilot;

Create Employee instance Smith;

Add type Pilot to Smith;
```

Types are themselves modeled as objects, and like other objects may be alterable and versionable.

8.2.2 Actions

We intend the term "action" to be a neutral way of referring to the general idea of a procedure, operation, function, or message, without implying any of the more specific connotations these terms might have—some of them may deserve to be modeled as subtypes of Action. Actions are also objects, defined to take arguments of certain types and return a result (possibly many-valued) of a certain type. Actions are *applied* to their arguments—"apply" is not itself an action, but is a meta-action of the model. Actions may produce truth values or results of any other type, and may be defined by explicit update or by formulas:

```
Create action name(Person) --------> String;
Assert name(Smith) = 'Z.Y. Smith';
Assert name(Mendoza) = 'Carlos Mendoza';

Create action ManagerName ( Employee e ) --------> String
    as Select name(m)
        for each Employee m
        where m = manager(dept(e));
```

Formulas in the model provide recursive computability. Actions may also be defined by algorithms with side effects, and they may be *foreign actions* written in programming languages provided that their argument and result interfaces are consistent with this model.

8.2.3 Extensional Collections

We treat extensional collections of objects differently from pure sets, and have previously called them *combinations*. A combination is itself an object, and obeys the usual rules for object identity. Objects must be inserted and removed explicitly, and it is thus possible for two combinations to have the same members without being considered identical. This corresponds to the semantic situation in a time-varying world where the objects being modeled are distinct, although at a given level of abstraction and at a given time they cannot be distinguished by their components. Having emphasized this distinction from mathematical sets, we feel it is probably simpler to proceed by calling our combinations Sets in what follows:

```
Create Set S1, S2;
Insert Hecht, Mendoza into S1;
Remove Hecht from S1;

If Empty(S1) or Smith in S2
   Create Set S3;
```

Finite collections that are ordered and may contain duplicate references to the same object are known as *lists*. Lists also are treated as objects. They have Lisp-like actions defined on them as primitives:

```
Create List L1, L2, L3;
L1 := < Smith, Hecht, Mendoza > ;
L2 := tail(L1);
L3 := < head(L1), L2 > ;
```

Iteration is possible over the members of a set or of a list:

```
For each Person p in {Hecht, Mendoza}
      SomeAction(p);
```

8.3 INTENSIONAL CONCEPTS

This section will show how to satisfy the intensional requirements described in the introduction. The main thrust is to determine how the notion of *concept* used in the introductory examples should be expressed in an object model with types, actions, and extensional sets and lists. We will continue to use the original example, with Person and Father respectively as extensional and intensional concepts of one variable, and FatherOf and GrandfatherOf as concepts of two variables.

8.3.1 Actions or Types?

Types in an object model seem to play a classificatory role that equips them to correspond to concepts—yet actions have the greater generality in addressing the different kinds of concept definition that we have discussed.

Extensional concepts of two or more variables may be modeled by actions (e.g., predicates) whose values are explicitly set to determine whether the given arguments exemplify the concept (see Figure 8.1).

FIGURE 8.1
Concepts as Actions or Types

#Args	Extensional	Intensional
1	*Person(o)* Action or Type	*Father(p)* Action
>1	*FatherOf(p1,p2)* Action	*GrandfatherOf(p1,p2)* Action

Intensional concepts of any number of variables may likewise be mod-eled by actions defined procedurally or nonprocedurally in terms of other information.

With an extensional concept of one variable, however, there is a choice between using an action or a type:

```
Create action Person(Object) -------> Boolean;
Create Object instance Smith;
Assert Person(Smith) = True;
```

or

```
Create type Person;
Create Person instance Smith;
```

In the latter case, a corresponding predicate IsPerson may be maintained, but there is more to it than this. A type, in our model at least, can be instan-tiated, whereas setting a predicate True for given arguments does not create a new object—the semantic power of an action to remember such informa-tion is primitive, rather than being modeled in terms of other objects that have some other primitive powers of memory. Moreover, there is another property of types which is very widespread in programming language and data models. This is their use for type checking of parameters and results of actions. The type specified for a parameter or result serves as a constraint, yet is clearly a very partial mechanism, governed usually by the desire for simplicity and as much static checking as possible. Type expressions, and more general constraint expressions, are the subject of important research, but have not yet found their way into general practice. Perhaps we shall see type systems evolve to become richer, or perhaps we shall see the existing limited systems survive as a well-judged engineering trade-off between sim-plicity and power, to be supplemented by more general constraint systems (not limited to argument and result checking) as these become practicable. In any case, the retention of the existing form of types as one way of modeling extensional concepts of one variable appears justified.

But now it is reasonable to pose the question whether *intensional* concepts of one variable should be expressible, not only as actions, but also as types. It would certainly be possible to introduce intensional types into the model, but it would conflict with the current tendency for types to be instantiable. It may be argued that system types like Integer are already not explicitly instantiable, and that in systems that support unbounded integer computation, it may be philosophically uncomfortable to some (the author included) to postulate an infinite set of instances already instantiated. However, this suggests a solution, that new instances of such types may be implicitly created as required, and thereafter remain in existence just like explicitly created instances of a type. This leads to consideration of the second conflict with current usage of types—that the instantiation of types becomes highly dynamic and difficult to check. Worse than this, determination of the types of objects would have to be defined very precisely as to when and in what order it was carried out, in case any of the actions involved had side effects (which are hard to exclude in database systems, which are largely designed to achieve side effects). Then much optimization might be inhibited in case it led to different results, not merely of the computation, but even of the type checking itself.

So for the present, it looks advisable to avoid intensional types. This also helps with the requirement to evolve from the present, without requiring a complete change to a new language. Possible approaches such as the embedding of a data language in a programming language (*à la* SQL), and the sharing of type definitions between languages, are facilitated by adopting a conservative treatment of types.

So we are left with a uniform treatment of the four cases considered, in which extensional or intensional concepts, of one or more variables, may all be modeled by actions. Supplementing this, there is the alternative, in the case of extensional concepts of one variable, of being able to define them as types and to instantiate them explicitly and to have conventional type checking carried out.

8.3.2 Concepts as Actions

The next stage of the inquiry will focus on closer examination of the kinds of actions appropriate for the definition of concepts, and on the relationship between these actions and the collections of objects which exemplify the concepts.

Some actions are essentially filters, whose primary purpose is to determine whether an object exemplifies a certain concept, or whether certain objects are in a specific relationship to each other. In the multiargument case, they may be defined symmetrically on their arguments to return a truth-value, or they may be rearranged into equivalent forms:

```
Create action nameP( Person, String ) ------> Boolean;
Create action name ( Person ) ------> String;
```

We shall want to assert and retract specific propositions involving such actions, and to iterate over the tuples of objects that satisfy them.

Other actions, such as to display a circuit on some class of device, may have a similar interface:

```
Create action display ( Circuit, Device ) ------>
    Integer;
```

The semantics of such an action are essentially directional—given certain input arguments, it will cause certain side effects, and return a result. In this example, the integer result may serve as a return code to indicate error situations such as −1 for a device malfunction. While a syntactic rearrangement into a form returning a Boolean is possible here too, it does not correspond to any semantic symmetry. It will often be the case that the definer of such a function does not want to give any semantics to assertions and retractions and iterations—for example, the assertion that display(c2,d9) = −1 will not be allowed to mean that the device d9 must be caused to malfunction when passed c2.

Thus not all actions are used to model concepts in our sense. Concepts are a specialization of actions, and we therefore introduce the type Concept as a subtype of Action. The meta-action "apply," and certain actions (e.g., to retrieve the action definition) are defined on the Action type, and are applicable to all actions. Other actions such as assertion, retraction, and iteration, are defined on the Concept type, and are available only if an action also has this type.

So in Section 8.2.2, between the creation of the action name and the assertion, we should now have to insert:

```
Add type Concept to name;
```

Better still, if we know in the first place that the action is to be a Concept, we can create it as such, and automatically acquire the supertype Action:

```
Create Concept name(Person) ------> String;
```

Now for the intensional examples, we shall employ an SQL-like syntax, as in Object SQL [Beech, 1988], in order to illustrate the evolutionary possibilities, and the analogies with view definition:

```
Create Concept Father(Person p) as
        Select
        exists Person c
        where FatherOf(p,c);
```

```
Create Concept GrandfatherOf(Person gf, Person gc)  as
      Select
      exists Person p
      where FatherOf(gf,p) and ParentOf(p,gc);
```

Beneath this slightly higher-level language, the underlying object model makes it possible to iterate over instances of a type, or (tuples of) objects satisfying a Concept. Query evaluation strategies must choose between the alternatives in combining the `each` or `for each` clause with the `where` clause. To evaluate

```
Select each Person gf,Person gc where
   GrandfatherOf(gf,gc)
```

it would be possible, for example, to iterate over the Person type and simply apply the `FatherOf` and `ParentOf` Concepts to each p; or to iterate over the `ParentOf` Concept and within that to apply the `FatherOf` Concept. The Iterate primitive in the model passes an Action to be applied to each satisfying tuple, and also an Integer which places an upper bound on the number of iterations if nonnegative.

It is also possible to define `GrandfatherOf` as a hybrid Concept:

```
Create Concept GrandfatherOf(Person gf, Person gc)
   with Set S1  as
         Select
         exists Person p
         where FatherOf(gf,p) and ParentOf(p,gc);
```

The default semantics of querying such a Concept are that the Set object S1 is searched first for an extensional assertion about the given Persons gf and gc, and only if none is found will the intensional formula be evaluated. Other treatments of semantics, such as checking for conflicts between the extension and the intension, can be explicitly specified if desired.

Explicit specification of semantics becomes a much bigger issue for update of intensional or hybrid concepts. The default for Assert or Retract is to make some minimal unique change, if such can be found, to some other extensional information so that the effect is achieved via the intensional part of the concept definition. To override these defaults, the Assert and Retract actions can be defined for specific Concepts:

```
Create Concept GrandfatherOf(Person gf, Person gc)
   with Set S1  as
         Select
         exists Person p
         where FatherOf(gf,p) and ParentOf(p,gc)
```

```
semantics
    Assert: ( GrandfatherOf(gf,gc) : /* no-op ---
    already true */,
            .../* try to change FatherOf, etc. */,
            else add $\langle$gf,gc$\rangle$ to S1;
        );
```

To summarize this intuitive introduction, we list the primitive set of actions defined on Concepts:

Initialize (Concept; Assertions:List of Sets;
Semantics:List of Actions) ————> Concept
GetAssertions (Concept) ————> List of Sets
GetSemantics (Concept) ————> List of Actions
Assert (Concept; Tuple:List; Logical) ————> Concept
Retract (Concept; Tuple:List; Logical) ————> Concept
Iterate (Concept; Action; UpperBound:Integer) ————>
    Concept

The Assertions parameter on Initialize allows for a List of Sets to be provided, so that they may be referenced within the Action part of the combined Action-Concept object. A single set would often suffice, as in the preceding GrandfatherOf example. However, if the definer of the Concept does not want to make the closed world assumption that what is not asserted to be true is false, a separate set may be used for explicit assertions about people known not to be grandfathers (or for those about whom it is unknown, depending on the likely rarity of each case). So an arbitrary number of sets may be provided in the initialization, to be used as desired in the defining Formula for the Action.

The Logical type used in the definition of Assert and Retract is similarly a generalization of Boolean to allow an Unknown truth value, but further discussion of this is beyond the scope of the present paper.

8.3.3 Generative Definition

There is another kind of intensional definition of a concept, where the defining action is not a test of given objects to see whether they exemplify the concept, but is a means of generating successive examples.

Filter and generator definitions have a kind of duality, with similar actions available on the concepts but different relative difficulties of performing them. It is straightforward to use a concept defined as a filter to test given objects, but may be difficult to find an efficient means of generating all examples; whereas for a generatively defined concept, the definition provides a direct means of producing examples, but the method of testing may be difficult to derive, or may even be nonterminating.

We illustrate simple creation of a generative definition and bounded iteration using it:

```
Create concept Fibonacci() ───────────> List of Integer
    generated by sequence (1:) of
        F (Integer n) ───────────> Integer
        ( n < 0: error(),
            n = 0: 1,
            n = 1: 2,
        else F(n−1) + F(n−2) );
```

```
For first 10 Fibonacci() f
    print(f);
```

It is also worth noting that a generative definition, unlike a filter definition, provides for iteration over newly generated as well as preexisting objects, for example, allowing generated objects to be inserted into a collection to materialize the extension of the concept.

8.4 COLLECTIONS AND TYPES REVISITED

It is now instructive to compare the actions defined on concepts with those defined on collections such as sets:

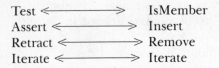

```
Test    <───────────>    IsMember
Assert  <───────────>    Insert
Retract <───────────>    Remove
Iterate <───────────>    Iterate
```

The semantic similarities suggest that corresponding actions be given the same names, and that Collection becomes a subtype of Concept in the type hierarchy—collections are the subset of concepts that are purely extensionally defined. Collections themselves can be classified into a hierarchy according to further constraints and additional actions available, such as the ordering constraint on a list, and an action to reverse the order. We cannot develop this topic fully here, but will indicate the positions of Bag, Set, List, and OrderedSet in our hierarchy (cf. the Smalltalk collection hierarchy, which includes other types, and is also somewhat complicated in structure by the absence of multiple inheritance).

This treatment of collections is in the spirit of data abstraction, where the actions on a collection provide the interface to the collection and make it unnecessary to visualize objects existing inside the collection. It may also ease the philosophical worries as to whether collections exist, at least as regards

FIGURE 8.2
ACTIONS, CONCEPTS, COLLECTIONS, AND TYPES
IN THE TYPE HIERARCHY

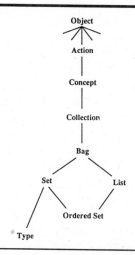

existence in an information model or as mental objects. Thus in *Principia Mathematica* [Whitehead & Russell, 1910, p. 135]:

> "Classes, so far as we introduce them, are merely symbolic or linguistic conveniences, not genuine objects as their members are if they are individuals . . . an extension (which is the same as a class) is an incomplete symbol, whose use always acquires its meaning through a reference to intension."

In our model, we attempt to close the gap by treating extensions as degenerate intensions, whose defining formulas are essentially conjunctions of explicit assertions, of the form

$$\lambda\ (x,y,\dots).\ (x=a \wedge y=b \wedge \dots) \vee \dots$$

Finally, we return to the question of the relationship between a type and an extensional concept of one variable. The actions available on concepts again correspond to actions on types:

Test $\longleftrightarrow$	HasType
Assert $\longleftrightarrow$	AddType
Retract $\longleftrightarrow$	RemoveType
Iterate $\longleftrightarrow$	Iterate

Since the instances of a type do not include duplicates or have a guaranteed ordering, types are analogous to concepts defined as sets. However, they are a special case of sets with additional properties, for example being specifiable for argument and result positions in action definitions, so Type may be placed in the hierarchy as a subtype of Set.

8.5 CONCLUSION

A model of intensional concepts for object databases has been presented at two levels—an intuitive higher level in order to illustrate its potential as an evolutionary continuation of existing programming languages and database languages, and a more primitive level defining the essential semantic actions beneath the syntactic sugar. Semantic similarities between actions, concepts, sets, and types are captured by defining Action to be a supertype of Concept, which is a supertype of Set, which is a supertype of Type.

Something very close to the foundations of this model has been implemented as part of the Iris system [Fishman, et al., 1987]. The extensions previously proposed aim to distinguish updatable from nonupdatable functions, to provide comprehensive view update facilities, to introduce an appropriate treatment of collections such as sets, and to provide a base for more inferential power in the database system, including the use of recursive function definitions and queries.

Much future work will be needed to explore pragmatic issues of how far the default semantics can be carried by the system, how unfruitful searches will be terminated by timing out or other measures, and what new forms of query optimization are called for. The hope is for cumulative progress rather than an immediate breakthrough.

Another major question which arises, as always, is the extent to which the language used to define actions for specifying intensional concepts and their update semantics needs to approach a full-fledged programming language. The conclusion section of a paper is no place to begin that discussion, but, as we have indicated earlier, we make a small extension to give us computability of recursive functions, and provide for this to be supplemented by the use of foreign actions written in other languages.

REFERENCES

American National Standards Institute, (1986). *Database Language SQL*, ANSI X3.135-1986.

Beech, D., (1987). "Groundwork for an Object Database Model," In Shriver, B., and Wegner, P. (eds.), *Research Directions in Object-Oriented Languages*, Cambridge, Mass.: MIT Press.

Beech, D., (1988). "A Foundation for Evolution from Relational to Object Databases," In Schmidt, J. W., Ceri, S., and Missikoff, M. (eds.), *Advances in Database Technology— EDBT '88*. Lecture Notes in Computer Science 303. New York: Springer-Verlag.

Clocksin, W. F. and Mellish, C. S., (1981). *Programming in Prolog*. New York: Springer-Verlag.

Codd, E. F., (1970). "A Relational Model of Data for Large Shared Data Banks," *Comm. ACM*, Vol. 13, No. 6, June, pp. 377–387.

Data Base Task Group of CODASYL Programming Language Committee, (1969). *Report* October.

Fishman, D. H., Beech, D., Cate, H. P., Chow, E. C., Connors, T., Davis, J. W., Derrett, N., Hoch, C. G., Kent, W., Lyngbaek, P., Mahbod, B., Neimat, M. A., Ryan, T. A., and Shan, M. C., (1987). "Iris: An Object-Oriented Database Management System," *ACM Transactions on Office Information Systems*, Vol. 5, No. 1, January, pp. 48–69.

Frege, G., (1893). "Grundgesetze der Arithmetik," In Geach, P., and Black, M., *Translations from the Philosophical Writings of Gottlob Frege*, Oxford: Blackwell.

Goldberg, A. and Robson, D., (1983). *Smalltalk-80: The Language and its Implementation*, Reading, Mass.: Addison-Wesley.

Liskov, B., Atkinson, R., Bloom, T., Moss, E., Schaffert, E., Scheifler, B., and Snyder, A., (1979). *CLU Reference Manual*, MIT/LCS/TR-225.

Schwartz, J. T., (1973). *The SETL Language and Examples of its Use*, Courant Institute, New York University.

Shipman, D. W., (1981). "The Functional Data Model and the Data Language DAPLEX," *ACM Trans. on Database Syst.*, Vol. 6, No. 1, March, pp. 140–173.

Tsichritzis, D. C., and Lochovsky, F. H., (1976). "Hierarchical Database Management Systems," *ACM Computing Surveys*, Vol. 8, No. 1, March.

Whitehead, A. N., and Russell, B., (1910). *Principia Mathematica*, Cambridge, England: Cambridge University Press.

CHAPTER 9

THE VISION OBJECT-ORIENTED DATABASE MANAGEMENT SYSTEM

Michael Caruso
Edward Sciore

9.1 INTRODUCTION

VISION is a computationally complete, object-oriented database system developed at Innovative Systems Techniques. The need for combined database/programming systems has been a recurring theme of academic research. Starting with Pascal/R, there have been numerous proposals for such language systems [Schmidt, 1977; Wasserman, 1979; Sciore & Warren, 1986; Derret, et al., 1985; Maier, et al., 1986; . . .]. Unfortunately, most of them have not reached the commercial marketplace. The VISION system is a response to that need.

Clearly a combined database/programming system should have the storage capabilities of a database system and the expressiveness of a programming language. But how can the necessary features be integrated seamlessly? Are there other capabilities that we would like to have that are not usually provided by either domain? These questions have not been completely answered in previous systems. In this paper we describe the VISION system, and how it addresses these issues.

This paper is organized as follows. Section 9.2 provides the motivation for our approach, and discusses the requirements a database/programming system should have. Section 9.3 is a high-level introduction to the VISION language, and Section 9.4 outlines the architecture on which the language is implemented. In Section 9.5, we conclude by considering the issues that remain to be solved, and how we expect VISION can be extended in the future.

9.2 MODELING COMPLEX APPLICATIONS

9.2.1 The Application Development Process

Traditionally, information-intensive applications have been developed using systems that separate data management facilities from programming environments. Consider Fig. 9.1.

Ideally, the database management system is used to codify the declarative semantics of the application, and the operational semantics of the application is captured in one or more programs. In actuality, however, this separation is not so clean. A database management system only manages the declarative semantics of the shared, persistent data; the application programs must define and manage transient data themselves. Although application programs support the bulk of an application's operational definition, the database's data manipulation language provides some operational capabilities as well. In addition, although application programs can be considered part of a shared, persistent information base, they typically are not managed by the data management system.

This seemingly arbitrary division between the database management system and the programming language makes application development awkward at best. Typically, only the simplest applications—such as traditional record keeping systems—have made good use of these divided database/programming systems. The reason is that simple applications deal with a relatively small set of simple data types, which can be conveniently isolated by the database system from the programs that manipulate them. As applications begin to model fine-grained, real-world entities and systems, they generate large and complex sets of data types. And because a significant component of a complex type's definition is operational, it becomes increasingly difficult to separate the declarative structure of the data from its operational semantics.

The concept of the *Application Development Platform* model is an alternative to this partitioned, dual implementation model. The goal of an application development platform is to provide a single, extensible environment for managing persistent and transient data along with the procedures that access and maintain them. Ideally, it should not be necessary to "step outside the system" to model some key aspect of an application. Conceptually, an

FIGURE 9.1
THE TRADITIONAL APPLICATION DEVELOPMENT MODEL

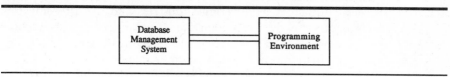

application development platform presents a layered view of itself, as in Fig. 9.1. At its base is a technological foundation that provides a basic model for information organization and system extension. On top of that foundation are built one or more application domain layers. A domain layer captures the general structure and behavior of objects common to some application area. Finally, built on the domain layer are customizations that capture the specific behavior and state of the application required by its users.

Besides being self-contained, an application development platform should be free of sharp discontinuities in functionality and expressive power. Discontinuities introduce modes that partition the capabilities of a system. Such partitioning effectively re-introduces the same problems the application development platform was created to solve in the first place. Thus, the transitions between the technological foundation, application domain, and customization layers of Fig. 9.2 are achieved by incremental refinement and not by an abrupt switch in perspective.

9.2.2 Investment Modeling

The specific modeling, architectural, and engineering requirements imposed on a conceptual framework are determined by its applications. One of VISION's initial commercial applications is investment management decision support. Appearances to the contrary, investment decision support is a nontraditional application. Types of financial instruments are numerous and complex, and are not simply common stocks or corporate bonds. New instrument types are constantly created to meet specific marketplace needs. These instruments typically are complex combinations of components of other securities.

FIGURE 9.2
THE APPLICATION DEVELOPMENT PLATFORM MODEL

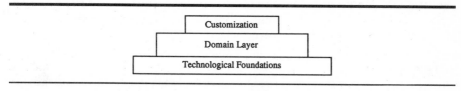

For another example, although all companies appear to have properties like sales, assets, and other key financial variables, there are large differences in behavior between companies in different industries and of different sizes. Moreover, these entities need to be modeled at different levels of abstraction. An application might need to have more detailed information about one aspect of a company than another: either the information is not available, or the users of the application are more interested in some details than others, and are willing to spend more time developing specific parts of the overall model.

Thus investment modeling is a complex application which generates a large number of objects and uses a large quantity of statistical data. Simple, tabular structures like relations do not have the capabilities to model entities at different levels of abstraction. An entity is not just one tuple in a relation; rather, it is several tuples scattered across several relations, which must be related in a specific way.

Time is another important concept that must be captured in order to model investment applications effectively. At least two independent time dimensions exist. A system must be able to capture the history of an object both in the user's world and in the system's model of the world. It must also be possible to discuss various alternative scenarios of what an entity will be like in the future. Time interacts fundamentally with a language's mechanism of update and with a user's view of the database. If an extensible treatment of both is to be provided, an appropriate linguistic home must be found for time.

Database schemas are not static; an application's model of the world must be able to evolve. It is unreasonable to expect a designer to know the complete details of a model when it is created. Consequently, efficient addition, alteration, and deletion of properties applicable to previously existing entities is essential. As types are specialized, it must be possible to selectively refine existing individuals to acquire the behavior of the specializations.

The database required by an investment management decision support system is large. Underlying most applications are several hundred megabytes of statistical data. Iteration over collections of this information is common. Although some iterations are associative, many iterations involve some form of general computation, making them unsuited to traditional "index" based optimizations. Thus the system architecture must be able to handle iteration in nontraditional ways.

The VISION approach is to remove the partition between database management and programming. From the database perspective, we want to eliminate the need for a host language. From the language perspective, we want to add the notion of persistence and sharing. Any capability should be viewable from either perspective. In some cases, such as encapsulating iteration, it is important to take the database perspective. And in other cases, such as encapsulating behavior and execution environments, we want to take advantage of efficient programming language techniques.

9.3 THE VISION LANGUAGE

9.3.1 Language Design Principles

Two principles have guided the design of VISION: the orthogonality of conceptual components, and the encapsulation of iteration over collections. Most modern languages are designed around the premise of orthogonality. The second principle, however, is not common to language design. In fact, most languages treat the concepts of iteration and collection as distinct—some exceptions being programming languages like APL and relational query languages. Aside from its obvious effect on the expressive power of a language, the principal benefit of iteration encapsulation is the opportunity it provides for choosing alternative execution strategies. That benefit is clearly of major importance when managing a large database.

VISION's notion of encapsulation of iteration is not simply a superficial notion of abstract data type encapsulation. Abstract type models of encapsulation allow for different collection types and the optimization of specific operations on those types. However, abstract data types hide critical structural information about a collection from the programs that iterate over it. Consequently, it may not be possible to develop efficient algorithms to encapsulate iteration in the general case. Typically, language designers resort to providing a sublanguage (such as the relational algebra) that restricts the set of operations. Such a restriction weakens the data independence provided by the abstract type, and creates a partition between the database and programming language.

Abstract data types are ultimately dependent on the primitive notions of iteration provided in the core definition of the language. Operations on an abstract collection cannot be more efficient than the primitive operations that they are built from. To compensate for these deficiencies, the notion of encapsulated iteration must be an architectural decision that affects all levels of the system, ranging from the programming language to the object manager.

9.3.2 VISION Basics

In this section, we describe some basic features of the VISION language. Inasmuch as VISION is primarily a database system, these features are very similar to other database languages, in particular functional languages such as DAPLEX. In succeeding sections we will see how these features can be extended to provide a complete programming system.

Central to VISION is the idea of a *collection*. A collection is an assertion about a specified number of distinct objects, which are its *instances*. For example, the collection *employee* might assert that it has 100 instances. Collections are non-information bearing. That is, there is no specification of what these objects are, what values they have, or how they relate to any other objects.

Objects are the constructs that can be named in a VISION program. They do not correspond to real-world entities; in general, an entity might be represented using several objects, each in different collections. Instead, an object denotes a *role* that the entity plays, and the collection it is in describes that role. The objects describing the roles of a single entity are connected to each other using the *super* function, which is described in what follows. The collection *object* contains one instance for every entity modeled by the system.

Some collections, such as *real* and *integer*, are primitive to the language. These collections are thought of by the user as the collection of all real numbers and the collection of all integers. Clearly, these collections do not exist physically, but are simulated by the system. The purpose for this is to remove the need for explicit notions of *class* and *type* in the language. Each collection does define a type for its instances, which specifies the behavior of the instances. However, as we shall see, this concept is transparent to the VISION user. The user can name and manipulate only collections, objects, and relationships between them.

All information about the objects in a collection are embodied in *functions*. A function is simply a mapping from one collection into another. Consider Fig. 9.3. The function *name* maps *person* to *string*, the function *worksIn* maps *employee* to *company*, and so on. Functions are applied to objects using *messages*. VISION uses Smalltalk-like syntax to represent messages. That is, if x is an object in collection c, and f is a function defined in c, then the expression xf applies the function f to the object x, and returns the appropriate object as its value. Parameters are expressed using colons, so that the expression $xp:c$ calls function p with argument c.

Each collection has a special function called *super*. This function maps each object in a collection to the object that it specializes. If *super* maps collection $c1$ to $c2$, then $c1$ is called a *subcollection* of $c2$. In Fig. 9.3, *super* is represented by an unlabeled arrow. Thus *super* maps the collection *employee* to the collection *person*, and the collection *person* to the collection *object*. The function *super* always organizes collections into a generalization tree, whose root is the collection *object*. Note that if collection $c1$ is a subcollection of $c2$,

FIGURE 9.3
SOME COLLECTIONS AND FUNCTIONS

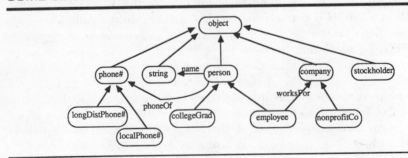

then every object in $c1$ must have an associated object in $c2$. In other words, all (real-world) entities playing the role of c1 must also play the role of $c2$. In particular, every entity plays the role of *object*; thus the instances of *object* correspond exactly to the entities modeled in the system.

The VISION language provides an inheritance mechanism based on the function *super*. If $c1$ is a subcollection of $c2$, then the functions defined in $c2$ are accessible to the instances of $c1$. Consider for example the function *name* in Fig. 9.3, and suppose e is an instance of *employee*. Then the expression e *name* is equivalent to e *super name*. Note that the use of *super* here is different from languages like Smalltalk. In VISION, *super* is a function much like any other; in Smalltalk, *super* is a keyword treated specially in the language.

The function *super* structures individual objects analogously to the way it structures collections. We can define a tree of objects, whose edges are given by the following subobject relationship: x is a subobject of y if y is x *super*. Each object o in the collection *object* is the root of an object tree. Fig. 9.4 provides an example object tree of the employee database. That tree consists of five objects, belonging to the collections *object, person, employee, college Grad*, and *stockholder*.

An object tree represents all possible roles played by a single entity. We define the *superchain* of an object x to be the set $\{x, x\ super, x\ super\ super, \dots \}$. The superchain of x is thus the part of the object tree relevant to x. One can think of the superchain of an object to be all of the different roles that the object must play.

9.3.3 Prototype Objects

Although collections are the fundamental construct in the VISION system, they are less prominent in the user language. Instead, programs name and manipulate the *prototype object* of a collection. A prototype object is the distinguished object that is created when a collection is created, and can be thought of as representing the collection. For example, in the expression *!person ← object specialized*, the name *person* refers to a prototype object for the new collection. In general, the operation *!y ← x specialized* creates a new collection

FIGURE 9.4
AN OBJECT TREE

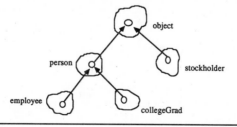

whose prototype object is y, such that y *super* is x. Thus, the collection hierarchy is represented by an object tree of prototypes, with *object* as the root prototype.

Prototype objects are very much like other objects in collections. For example, they have function values, and can be manipulated in VISION expressions. The only difference is that the prototype of a collection does not show up in an enumeration of the collection; the prototype is in a sense the "zeroth" object in a collection.

If y is a prototype, then the expression $!z \leftarrow y$ *new* creates a new object that is *just like y*. That is, it creates a copy of each object in y's superchain. Note that the function values of y act as default values for the collection. This new copy can then be given different values for its functions.

For a concrete example, the following VISION code defines part of the scheme in Fig. 9.3, and creates some instances.

```
!company <-- object specialized;
!person <-- object specialized;
person defineFixedProperty: 'name' .
        defineFixedProperty: 'phoneOf';
!employee <-- person specialized .
        defineFixedProperty: 'worksFor';
!gm <-- company new;
!joe <-- employee new;
joe :worksFor <-- gm;
```

In sum, a user of the VISION language sees and manipulates only collection instances. There is no need to worry about names of collections, or the difference between *instance-of* and *subcollection-of* edges. Of course, the user has to be aware of the collections, since the semantics of the operations is defined in terms of them. But in general, the language is simplified and made more flexible.

The difference that VISION has from the prototypes of [Lieberman, 1986] is that the VISION user, when adding a new object y similar to x, must decide whether it is x *new* or x *specialized*. In the first case, the prototype values are copied; x and y become equals, sharing the same protocol. In the second case, the prototype's values are shared; changing values of the prototype x will change the specialization y. The use of prototypes is also similar to the language SELF [Unger & Smith, 1987]; its main difference is that the VISION system manages collections internally, for the sake of efficiency.

9.3.4 Polymorphic Functions

One way that VISION generalizes traditional database languages is in its treatment of polymorphism. In VISION, a function can map a collection to several collections. Such a function is called *polymorphic*. For example, consider the function *phoneOf* from Fig. 9.3. That function is shown as mapping *person* to *phone#*. Suppose now that we want to treat local phone numbers in a different way than long-distance phone numbers, and that these two types of phone numbers constitute different collections. Then the function *phoneOf* should map some people to the collection *localPhone#* and others to the collection *longDistPhone#*.

Polymorphic functions can be viewed as a way of relaxing the type system. In Fig. 9.3, the function *phoneOf* is declared to map to *phone#*. In a strictly typed language, the result of *p phoneOf* would have to be an object from the collection *phone#*. With polymorphism, the result could be from any subcollection as well. The function *worksFor* in Fig. 9.3 provides another example of polymorphism. It is perfectly reasonable for *p worksFor* to return an object in collection *nonprofitCo* instead of *company*, since a nonprofit company "is" also a company.

If functions can be polymorphic, then in particular so can *super*. This means that the objects in a collection can be nonhomogeneous. For example, consider the collection *stockholder*, and suppose that instances of *stockholder* can be either people or companies. This situation can be modeled by saying that if *x* is an instance of *stockholder*, then *x super* will be an object in either *person* or *company*.

Polymorphic functions are closely related to the concept of alternative generalization in the RM/T database system [Codd, 1979]. Functions can be thought of as ranging from strictly typed to untyped, depending on the collection that they map to. If the function maps to a collection that has no subtypes, then the function is strictly typed; every object in the range of the function must be in that collection. On the other hand, if the function maps to the collection *object*, then the function is effectively untyped. In the current version of VISION, all functions are untyped. In the expression *c defineFixedProperty:A*, there is no specification of the collection that function *A* maps to. Instead, the system assumes that any collection is possible. We currently are considering mechanisms for allowing the user to add a specification of the range of a function.

VISION has two basic mechanisms for creating nonhomogeneous collections. The first is an explicit list-like constructor. For example, the expression *!stockholder ← gm, joe, sue, ibm* creates the collection *stockholder* containing four new objects whose *super* functions point to *gm*, *joe*, *sue*, and *ibm*. The second way is to use the function *extendTo*. The same collection can be created by the following expressions:

```
!stockholder <-- object specialized;
!gm2 <-- gm extendTo:stockholder;
!joe2 <-- joe extendTo:stockholder;
!sue2 <-- sue extendTo:stockholder;
!ibm2 <-- ibm extendTo:stockholder;
```

A difference in this second definition of the collection is that we have given names to each of the objects in it.

In general, the function *x extendTo:y* clones the prototype object *y* and sets the *super* of the new object to be *x*.

9.3.5 Object Specialization

One feature of nonhomogeneous collections is that object trees need not correspond exactly to the collection hierarchy. This property follows from the fact that different objects in the same collection can have different behaviors. Consider the preceding collection *stockholder*. The object trees for this collection appear in Fig. 9.5. Note that there are three different tree structures: the prototype tree, the tree for person stockholders, and the tree for corporate stockholders.

Since prototypes are not much different from other objects, functions such as *new* and *specialized* should be applicable to all objects equally. That is, objects should be able to clone or refine themselves on an individual basis. We call such an ability *object specialization*; to our knowledge, no other language has this feature. For example, if *x* is an object, then the expression *x new* creates a copy of *x* and every object in *x* superchain. This feature is useful when a collection is nonhomogeneous. In the *stockholder* example, we can create new corporate instances by saying *gm2 new*; new individual stockholders are created by saying *joe2 new*. The expression *stockholder new* creates a new *stockholder* object, which is neither a person nor a company.

Another useful consequence of object specialization is that an object can be the *super* of several other objects. This feature is necessary in analyzing future scenarios. Consider for example the object *ford* in class *company*. In order to examine the effect of inflation on the expected future price of the stock, we can create a subclass of *company*, having properties *inflation rate* and *future price*. For each inflation rate we wish to examine, we create a new object in this class, which is a refinement of *ford*. That is, we say

FIGURE 9.5
STOCKHOLDER OBJECT TREES

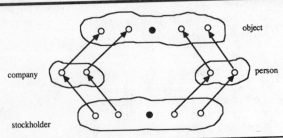

```
!futureCo <-- company specialized;
futureCo defineFixedProperty:'inflationRate'.
          defineFixedProperty:'futurePrice';
!ford1 <-- ford extendTo:futureCo;
!ford2 <-- ford extendTo:futureCo;
```

Note that since the objects *ford1* and *ford2* are refinements of *ford*, they share all of its information. So in particular, if we change the value of some ford function, then this change will be seen by *ford1* and *ford2*.

Yet another feature of object specialization is the ability to represent multiple inheritance elegantly. As we said earlier, inheritance in VISION is performed on object trees; an object inherits all functions defined on its superchain. Thus there is only a single inheritance chain for each object, and the collection hierarchy must be a tree.

In many systems, an entity must be modeled by an object in a single base *collection*. So for example, if an entity is in both the collection *person* and *stockholder*, then there also must be a collection *personStockholder* to hold it. Such a collection is called an *intersection collection*. There are three difficulties with such collections. First, they are artificial. They provide no new behavior to their instances, and exist only to satisfy the need for a base collection. Second, they are legion. Creating a new collection for every combination of roles that an entity plays results in an overwhelming number of collections. Third, they require multiple inheritance, since an intersection collection inherits from each of its supercollections. In VISION, we have seen how object specialization avoids all of these problems, by allowing collections like *stockholder* to be nonhomogeneous.

Although the more common examples of multiple inheritance can be reduced to intersection collections, there are situations that cannot; Fig. 9.6*a* contains such an example. Here, an object in collection *TA* is both a student and a teacher. If we assume that *TA*s are given special performance ratings, then these ratings must be a function defined in the collection *TA*. The VISION model of this application is shown in Fig. 9.6*b*. That figure models three entities, one of which is just a student, one is just a teacher, and one is a

FIGURE 9.6
MULTIPLE INHERITANCE

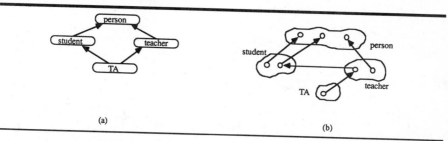

(a)

(b)

TA. Again, object specialization allows inheritance to be performed via object superchains, without the need for complex multiple inheritance machinery.

For a detailed discussion of the many advantages of object specialization, see Sciore [1987].

9.3.6 Functions as Objects

An important feature of VISION is that functions are treated as first-class objects. In VISION, there are two types of message: extensional and intensional. An *extensional message* yields the result of evaluating the function it selects. For example, the message *gm sales* yields 96371.63. An *intensional message* yields the function itself. Intensional messages are expressed by placing a colon before the function name. For example, the message *gm :sales* yields the function that connects the object *gm* to its sales value.

Since functions are objects, they also belong to collections, respond to messages, and are organized into subtypes. Refer to Fig. 9.7, which shows a portion of the VISION hierarchy for functions. Every function responds to the message value, so the method value is defined in the collection *function*. The effect of the value message is to yield the extension of the message. Thus *gm :sales value* is the same as *gm sales*.

Functions can be *computed* or *enumerated*. Enumerated functions get their values explicitly; that is, they respond to the assignment message ←. The most common enumerated function is a *property* (or *attribute*). For example, since sales is an enumerated function, we can say *gm :sales* ← 96391.2. Computed functions are either *methods*, which are user-defined, or *primitive*, which are provided by the system.

By providing functions as first-class objects, VISION avoids many of the anomalies and restrictions of other languages. The most obvious example is assignment. In VISION, assignment is not a special operation on objects. Instead, it is a normal operation on functions. For another example, the VISION approach to function types can avoid having to use methods to describe the behavior of a collection and properties to describe the internal structure of its instances. Such a distinction is made in many object-oriented languages, and seems undesirable for several reasons. First, it overlooks the fact that both are just different types of functions. Second, it does not allow

FIGURE 9.7
THE FUNCTION HIERARCHY

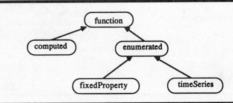

for adding other types of functions into the language. And third, it mixes in the concept of data hiding inappropriately; the issue of which functions are private and which are public should be independent of their type.

An important example of the usefulness of function types is in the modeling of historical data. In VISION, the history of an object is a function of its properties. Each property may have its own history, which may be sensitive to time in different ways [Clifford & Tansel, 1985]. In most applications, this sensitivity should be transparent to the user. In order to support this transparency, part of the global configuration of the system is its *temporal context*.

Function types are used to model the relationship between objects and the temporal context in an extensible way. For example, fixed properties are insensitive to temporal context, while timeseries properties maintain a series of events in an object's history. Thus the extensional message *gm sales* is a request for the current value of *sales* for *gm*. Intensional messages provide more control over the time property of functions, by exposing the time-specific operations associated with a given function type. For example, *gm:sales asOf:1984* dynamically rebinds the temporal context to 1984 before evaluating the function *sales*.

The issue of function-objects and their use as a history mechanism is presented in more detail in [Caruso & Sciore, 1988; Sciore].

9.3.7 Environments and Program Execution

In VISION, behavior is encapsulated by means of procedural *blocks*. A block is a parameterized sequence of statements. As an example, the expression $!p \leftarrow [|:x|x + 2]$ binds p to the block that adds 2 to its argument. Blocks and methods are similar. Essentially, if f is a method, its value is a block which is shared by all instances of the collection. Blocks respond to the value message similarly to functions: *p value:3* returns 5.

Blocks obey lexical scope rules. In the expressions

```
!sales <-- 10;
!q <-- [sales];
```

for example, the function sales referred to in the block is the one accessible at the time of definition. Thus *q value* returns 10. It is possible to invoke dynamic scoping by means of the *send* function. For example, *gm send:[sales]* rebinds the environment of the block to *gm*; thus it is equivalent to *gm sales*.

The execution of a block is implemented by a *context* (or *environment*) object. The local variables of the block become properties in the environment. In order to achieve lexical scoping, this context object must be a subobject of the object in which the block is defined. That is, in order to execute a block, the system creates a new collection containing one function for each local variable. It then extends the object that owns the block to this new collection, and executes the body of the block in the context of this new object.

The most recent context at any time is known as ∧*current*. The value of
∧*current* is constantly changing, as blocks are invoked. In particular, each user
session has a system-defined environment, which serves as the initial value of
∧*current*. We have seen that the local variables of a block become functions
in the environment. Similarly, all variables created in a user session are just
functions in the initial ∧*current*. That is, the expression *!gm* ← *company new*
creates a function called *gm* in ∧*current*. Consequently, except for certain system-defined names like ∧*current*, names in VISION do not refer to objects;
instead, all references are to functions. Thus the expression *gm sales* is techni-
cally not legal. It is treated by VISION as a shorthand for the correct expression ∧*current gm sales*.

It is interesting to see how the mechanism for block execution is related to
object specialization. For example, consider the following use of the function
extendBy:

```
!x <-- gm extendBy:[!pe <-- price/earnings]
```

Here, *x* is a specialization of *gm*, which is a member of a new collection
having the function *pe*. The effect of executing the function *extendedBy* is to
create a new environment; however, instead of returning the value of the
block, the environment itself is passed back as the value of the expression.

9.4 THE PHYSICAL ARCHITECTURE

Physically, the VISION system is divided into two components: the language interpreter, and the object manager. Although this division superfi-
cially resembles the traditional division between the programming language
and the database, there is much more cooperation in the VISION system. In
particular, both components work together toward encapsulating iteration;
both the virtual machine interpreter and object manager operate on collections as their basic unit of computation and structural organization.

9.4.1 The VISION Virtual Machine

Three performance bottlenecks have traditionally dominated the design of
object-oriented systems—message dispatch, function (or method) activation,
and garbage collection. While techniques such as method caching and stack-
based allocation can reduce the overhead associated with these operations,
these optimizations are intrinsically serial in their approach. While serial
optimizations reduce the absolute time to perform individual operations,
they still interact multiplicatively with common types of collection iteration.
Consequently, when traditional object-oriented systems try to scale up from
small collections to large ones, performance drops dramatically.

Addressing this multiplicative interaction requires an architecture capable
of factoring the computational process in nontraditional ways. In particular,

one must look for an alternative to the standard element-at-a-time iteration over collections. The VISION virtual machine solves this problem by physically partitioning a collection by the behaviors of its elements. Messages are viewed as being sent in parallel to all the elements of a collection, so message dispatch needs only to be performed once per behavior, not once per element. Moreover, the message dispatch process will identify only one function per behavior; consequently, the overhead of function activation need only be paid once per behavior. For similar reasons, garbage collecting the method activation states can also be coupled to unique behaviors, not unique individuals.

The pipelined, parallel execution of VISION programs provides a basis for another key optimization. As long as the virtual machine can determine the behavior associated with the extension of a function—a possibility for a number of function types—the result of the pipeline can be intensional. This allows the system to compose intensions, and use them in algebraic query optimization. Because the intensional structure generated can look beyond language level abstractions, it can perform optimizations not possible at the abstract type level. Although similar algorithms can be envisioned for nonparallel environments, their effectiveness in exploiting structures such as indices will be limited by their inability to explicitly recognize the iteration.

Although the specifics of its architecture are beyond the scope of this document, the VISION virtual machine is conceptually a pipe-lined parallel processor. The basic unit of computational state is a *task*. Tasks consist of a single instruction stream (typically a VISION function) that defines a pipelined computation and multiple data streams to which that pipeline applies. Beyond the parallelism associated with the pipeline execution, two additional sources of parallelism are implicit in this architecture. First, each task will be applied in parallel to all objects in a collection having the same behavior. Second, each operation on a collection will divide into several parallel tasks, one for each unique behavior represented in the collection's instances.

9.4.2 The VISION Object Manager

The goal of the VISION object manager is to provide storage that is compatible with the pipelined, parallel function application model of the VISION virtual machine. Additionally, the object manager must support databases containing millions of objects efficiently. To these ends, the object manager does not store objects in the traditional, record-oriented manner. Instead, the VISION database is transposed, or "vertically partitioned." Each enumerated function for a collection is stored together. Thus a VISION object such as *gm* is not stored as such, but is distributed in the various functions for the collection *company*. The reasons for this design decision are twofold: First, by storing entire functions, the object manager can better support the virtual machine as it composes functions and executes them in parallel. Second, experience has shown that most queries do not request entire objects, but only a small portion of them; consequently, by storing functions the object manager increases clustering and reduces the reading of unneeded information.

The VISION object manager uses an identical representation for transient and persistent data. This strategy allows the virtual machine to not care about the location of an object, and whether it is persistent or transient. The common format eliminates all conversion penalties associated with access to persistent data. As a result, persistent data can be viewed by a process as virtual memory resident. Object faulting is handled as a by-product of hardware load and store instructions and standard virtual memory paging operations. Because faulting is triggered by hardware load and store instructions, access to VISION objects does not require mediation by a separate software buffering layer.

The VISION object manager currently uses a multiversioned optimistic concurrency control method for persistent data. This strategy guarantees that a read-only transaction will always be able to see a consistent view of the database, and will never abort. Optimistic concurrency control appears to be especially appropriate for interactive modeling applications, where a large percentage of transactions are either read-only or affect only a user's private data.

9.5 THE FUTURE

VISION currently is in active commercial use, supporting the interactive use of databases containing several hundred megabytes. In practice, the pipelined parallel architecture of its interpreter has proven effective at reducing the overhead of message dispatch, context switching, and garbage collection associated with operations that iterate over collections. The treatment of functions as first-class objects along with the notion of dynamically bound temporal context has allowed time to be treated in a natural and compact manner.

Current research efforts involve extensions to the function type hierarchy to accommodate type specific concurrency control mechanisms, type-specific query optimization strategies, and object versioning. Additionally, we are investigating mechanisms for extending the global context to areas other than time in order to unify the treatment of encapsulation of objects and access control.

REFERENCES

Codd, (1979). "Extending the Database Relational Model to Capture More Meaning," *ACM TODS*, December, pp. 397–434.

Caruso and Sciore, (1988). "Contexts and Meta–Messages in Object-oriented Database Programming language Design," *Proceedings ACM SIGMOD Conference*, pp. 56–65.

Clifford and Tansel, (1985). "On an Algebra for Historical Relational Databases: Two Views," *Proceedings ACM SIGMOD Conference*, pp. 247–267.

Derret, Kent, and Lynbaek, (1985). "Some Aspects of Operations in an Object-Oriented Database," *Database Engineering*, December.

Goldberg and Robson, (1983). *Smalltalk-80: The Language and it Implementation*, Reading, Mass.: Addison-Wesley.

Lieberman, (1986). "Using Prototypical Objects to Implement Shared Behavior in Object Oriented Systems," *Proceedings ACM OOPSLA Conference*, pp. 214–223.

Maier, Stein, Otis, and Purdy, (1986). "Development of an Object-Oriented DBMS," *ACM OOPSLA Conference*, pp. 472–482.

Schmidt, (1977). "Some High-Level Language Constructs for Data of Type Relation," *ACM TODS*, September, pp. 247–261.

Sciore, (1987). "Object Specialization," TR 87-012 Boston University, submitted for publication.

Sciore, "A Language Framework for History, Versioning, and Other Meta-Information," submitted for publication.

Sciore and Warren, (1986). "Towards an Integrated Prolog/Database System," in *Expert Database Systems*, Menlo Park: Benjamin Cummings, pp. 293–305.

Unger and Smith, (1987). "SELF: The Power of Simplicity," *Proceedings ACM OOPSLA Conference*, pp. 227–242.

Wasserman, (1979). "The Data Management Facilities of PLAIN," *Proceedings ACM SIGMOD*, pp. 60–70.

CHAPTER 10

IMPLEMENTING FUNCTIONAL DATABASES

Guy Argo
John Hughes
Philip Trinder
Jon Fairbairn
John Launchbury

10.1 INTRODUCTION

In this paper we explore the feasibility of implementing a database management system in a purely functional language. Others have already argued for a purely functional database interface [Atkinson & Kulkarni, 1983; Buneman, 1985; Folinus, et al., 1974]. For simplicity we consider a database consisting of a single binary tree, and assume that transfers to and from disc are handled by a persistent memory manager at a lower level. The result has a number of desirable properties. Abortable transactions and snapshots of the database at a particular time come as a result of ordinary functional language behavior. Multiple transactions can run concurrently, even if started sequentially, with locking being performed automatically by data dependency. Interestingly, assuming that the functional language implementation performs one or two well-known optimizations, the operational behavior of our functional database is very similar to the behavior of a conventional database management system.

On closer inspection our database turns out to have some serious bottlenecks, which could drastically limit concurrency. We examine ways of alleviating these by making some results available earlier than straightforward lazy evaluation would do. We use three unusual primitives to do so: a form of parallel **if** introduced by Friedman and Wise [1978]; an "optimistic" **if** related to the conventional database technique of optimistic concurrency; and a nondeterministic "but if you have time" operator. Once again, the resulting operational behavior corresponds closely with conventional techniques. We have also discovered applications of lazy memo functions in checkpointing transactions. The techniques we have developed are interesting for two reasons. Firstly, database management systems may be required for parallel functional machines. Secondly, there may be other concurrent applications where our new primitives can be used to eliminate concurrent bottlenecks.

10.1.1 Trees as Databases

For simplicity, we shall treat a database as a collection of <name, value> pairs. While this is too naïve a model on which to base a practical database, it is sufficient to illustrate our ideas. We present two operations on our database, insert and lookup. Insert adds a new <name, value> association to the database. Lookup returns the value associated with the name supplied as an argument. Other operations may either be defined in terms of these, or may be defined directly in a similar style. To implement these abstract operations we shall use an ordered binary tree. We use the symbols <, =, > to express the ordering of the name values.

Our binary tree can be represented by the Miranda datatype (with Greek letters instead of asterisks)

bintree α :: = Node (bintree α) α (bintree α) |Nil

The intention is that the type α will be the cross product of two other types: one representing names, and the other representing values.

Polymorphic versions of insert and lookup can be written as

```
insert new Nil = Node Nil new Nil

insert (n2,v2) (Node left (n 1, v1) right)
         = Node (insert (n2, v2) left) (n1, v1)
                               right    IF n2 < n1
         = Node left (n1, v1) (insert (n2, v2)
                               right)   IF n1 < n2
         = Node left (n2,v2) right
                               OTHERWISE


lookup key Nil = error

lookup n2 (Node left (n1, v1) right)
            =lookup key left        IF n2 < n1
            =lookup key right       IF n1 < n2
            =v1                     OTHERWISE
```

Notice that insert does not modify the existing database: it returns an entirely new database in which the modification has been performed. This may appear expensive but it involves creating only d new nodes, where d is the depth of the key in the tree. The new nodes point into the original database to share any unchanged nodes (Fig. 10.1). Thus the insert operation has the same order of complexity as an imperative version, (but with a larger constant factor because copying is more expensive than updating in place).

As common nodes in the different versions of the tree are shared, we can cheaply retain a copy of an old database by keeping a pointer to it. Old nodes are reclaimed by the garbage collector when they are no longer referred to. This property has several useful applications. For instance, a large read-only transaction can be given a pointer to the database (which effectively gives it a private copy) and carry out its interrogations in parallel with other transactions. Any updates performed by these other transactions produce new versions of the database, and will not affect the original.

10.1.2 Abortable Transactions

Suppose that we have a transaction made up of two functions f and g such that, if the result of evaluating g with the database as an argument is *True*, then f is to be applied to produce an updated database. Otherwise the transaction is to be aborted, and the original database returned. In a functional language this could be written

```
if_g_then_f    db        = f db        IF g db
                         = db          OTHERWISE
```

Neither f nor g can alter the original database, so if the transaction is to abort (because g returns *False*) then the original may be returned unchanged.

FIGURE 10.1
COMMON PARTS OF THE DATABASE ARE SHARED

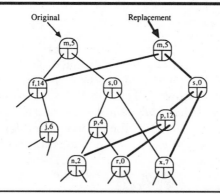

This means, for example, that an interactive shell with an undo command (to revert the database to an earlier state) would be trivial to implement by maintaining a stack of database pointers.

10.1.3 The Relationship to Conventional Databases

In our example we have modeled the database with a binary tree. But, as conventional database implementations rely heavily on secondary storage, B-trees are preferred to binary trees. The difference is not an important one. We are not bound to a binary tree implementation; it merely makes the description simpler.

In conventional databases updates are done in place. While this doesn't give the sharing advantages discussed previously, it does provide an increase in performance. If our implementation uses a reference counting garbage collector, we can ensure all nodes with a reference count of 1 (i.e., those nodes not shared) are updated in place. This will not alter the semantics of our model, and in such cases will execute almost as efficiently as the imperative version. This combines the advantages of both approaches. The result is like shadow paging [Hecht & Gabbe, 1983], a technique used in conventional databases to support abortable transactions. The transaction writes to unused pages and commits by overwriting the root. If the transaction aborts, the root remains unchanged.

10.2 MULTIPLE USERS

To cope with multiple requests a DBMS must be able to handle asynchronous inputs. The issue of combining input from many sources has already been tackled in work on functional operating systems [Henderson, 1982; Stoye, 1984]. These use variants of Henderson's nondeterministic merge. We assume a similarly appropriate solution is employed in our DBMS and therefore restrict ourselves to regarding the input to the manager as a list of requests.

10.2.1 Requests Are Functions

What appears in the input stream? In other words, what sort of operations would we want of the shared database? We must still be able to interrogate it with general queries. A query may always be expressed as a function from the database to a domain of answers. This function can be passed to the database manager, which returns the result of applying the function to the database.

We must also be able to update the database. In this case a function from database to database will suffice. The function takes the database as an argument and returns a new database as the result. The database manager retains this new database and uses it for the next request. Rather than distinguish between the two kinds of request, we shall define a request to be a function of type $db \rightarrow$ (output x db). Given such request functions, what will the database manager (i.e., the stream processing function) look like?

A very simple version is

```
manager   ::   database   --> [request] --> [answer]
manager   db   [fn : fns] = out : manager db' fns
                      WHERE    [out, db'] = fn db
```

The request is applied to the database and a pair is received as the result. The output part of the pair is returned in the output stream for communication with the outside world. The resulting database (db') is given as the first argument to the recursive call of manager. We partially apply the function **manager** to an initial database db_0 to obtain the stream processing function. Thus the expression (manager d_0) has the type [request] $\rightarrow$ [answer]. As **manager** retains the new databases produced by the request functions, it effectively has an evolving state.

10.2.2 Noninterference between Transactions

Suppose that we have two requests f and g, and that the action of f depends crucially on the action and result of g. In other words, we intend to submit g to be processed and then to submit f *without any other request in between*. This is apparently hard to ensure given that a request from another user may arrive in between them. However, if we can combine the two requests into one then atomicity is guaranteed. This combination can be achieved with functional composition. A new function is defined in which the result of the first request is passed to the second, which is in turn evaluated.

As an example, suppose we have a database of airline bookings, and that we are given two functions:

```
available   ::   flight --> integer --> db --> boolean
         [returns True if the flight has sufficient free
         seats available], and
book           ::   flight --> integer --> db --> db
         [will book the seats on the flight -- that is,
         the new database will have the bookings recorded].
```

We could define a function if_ok_book by

```
if_ok_book   flt n dbs
      = [''Ok'', book flt n dbs]    IF available flt n dbs
      = [ ''No room'', dbs]         OTHERWISE
```

This simple definition will ensure that no two attempts to book the same seats can occur because there is no chance for the database to change between the query and the action. Notice that this is another example of an abortable transaction.

In practice it may turn out that certain ways of combining requests into transactions occur particularly frequently. If so, we could take advantage of this and define combining forms using higher-order functions.

In the rest of this paper the terms request and transaction will be used interchangeably. These differ only in the way that one might think about them. In particular they are both functions of the same type, so no confusion should result.

10.2.3 Integrity of the Database

Since a transaction is just a function, there could be transactions that do not terminate, take too long (according to some criterion), or corrupt the data in some way. How can we defend the database against rogue transactions? Consider long and nonterminating transactions first. In conventional databases, transactions may be timed out and aborted if they take too long. At first sight, it seems that time-outs cannot easily be fitted into the semantics of functional programming. However, if we are willing to accept nondeterminism we can introduce a primitive that decides nondeterministically whether to apply a transaction or not. On a machine level the guiding factor would be the time taken by the function. From the standpoint of the user, the database appears just like a conventional database, in that any transaction submitted may or may not be performed. What we have altered here is not the semantics of the user's functions, but laws that the database satisfies. However, there may be some important long transactions that should not be subject to time-out.

There is an alternative approach to the problem. We may define an abstract data type (ADT) of transactions. Objects of the ADT will be represented by a function just as before. However, the ADT mechanism allows restrictions to be imposed on the sort of transaction that can be written. For example, we may restrict the transactions to be terminating without restricting the time that they take to execute. Or we could limit execution time by including in the ADT some sort of complexity bound that cannot be exceeded. Then we have a guarantee that all transactions will be completed with a certain time.

The ADT approach can also help solve the data corruption problem. The key issue here is that of privilege. While one user may be allowed read and update access to the whole of the data, another may be restricted to read access only. It is possible to have a number of ADTs all representing transactions of differing privilege, and impermissible operations could either be caught by the type checker, or at run-time by the database system.

10.3 CONCURRENCY

It has been known for some time that functional programs have scope for automatic concurrency [Darlington & Reeve, 1981; Clack & Peyton-Jones, 1985]. In the absence of side effects it is possible to evaluate many expressions in parallel, since the evaluation of one expression cannot affect the evaluation of another. This means that a transaction can potentially start before the previous one has finished, with no risk of wrong behavior. This contrasts well with the imperative approach, where the problem of ensuring correct handling of dependencies between transactions is difficult.

Pure demand-driven evaluation of the database tree would not lead to any concurrency between transactions because the parts of the tree would only be evaluated when their contents were required. This would hold up the process needing the value. We therefore use an eager constructor to build the tree so that it may be evaluated in parallel with incoming transactions. As a result, many database operations proceed in parallel.

Suppose one transaction updates part of the data, and a later transaction depends on the new data. The second transaction cannot be allowed to read the database until the first transaction has finished with it—the data must be locked. The imperative solution is for a transaction to mark all the nodes that it may change, so denying access to other transactions until the updates are performed. In the functional approach, locking takes place automatically, as a result of data dependency. If part of the tree is still being evaluated by one function then no other function can read the value until the tree (or enough of it) has been computed. In a later section we discuss ways of minimizing locking. In contrast to the conventional case, "locking" applies to any datum—even individual fields of records.

10.3.1 The Drawbacks

Unfortunately, some things do not work so easily. Some of the methods we described previously can severely limit concurrency. For example, an abortable transaction effectively locks the entire database throughout its execution. This is because neither the original nor the replacement database is returned until the decision whether to abort has been made. Therefore, no other transaction may use any part of the data until after this decision. Only then will one of the roots be returned. This applies even if the first does not affect the data required for the second.

A similar problem arises if we use balanced trees. Insertion may require rotations anywhere along the path to the inserted item in order to maintain the balance. Usually such rotations are performed deep in the tree, near the point of insertion. But, occasionally, the root of the whole tree is rotated. It is only possible to recognize whether or not this will occur after all the other rotations have been performed. As a result, the insertion function will lock the root throughout its execution, preventing any concurrent operation. An alternative is to leave the tree unbalanced after an insertion, but then rebalance the whole tree periodically. This has problems too: rebalancing a large tree is a time-consuming operation, during which no other access to the database is possible.

Any of these problems is sufficient to drastically reduce concurrency. In the next few sections we explore methods for solving the problems.

10.3.2 Friedman and Wise If

As we mentioned before, abortable transactions lock the root of the database until after the decision has been made whether to abort or not. But, in most cases the two will have the bulk of the database in common. This common part will eventually be returned whatever the result of the abort decision. If there were some method of returning this part early, then the performance of our approach would be greatly enhanced. The evaluation of other functions could begin (and possibly complete) on the common part.

Our solution is to use the modified if statement introduced by Friedman and Wise [1978] (henceforth referred to as **fwif**). The action of **fwif** can be seen in the following reductions:

$$
\begin{array}{ll}
\textbf{fwif } \text{True } \textbf{then } x \textbf{ else } y & \Rightarrow x \\
\textbf{fwif } \text{False } \textbf{then } x \textbf{ else } y & \Rightarrow y \\
\textbf{fwif } p \textbf{ then } a \textbf{ else } a & \Rightarrow a \\
\textbf{fwif } p \textbf{ then } q{:}r \textbf{ else } s{:}t & \Rightarrow (\textbf{fwif } p \textbf{ then } q \textbf{ then } s) : \\
& \quad (\textbf{fwif } p \textbf{ then } r \textbf{ else } t)
\end{array}
$$

(and similarly with other data constructors).

The last reduction is not as inefficient as at first appears. The two occurrences of p share the same expression. Because of lazy evaluation, this expression will only be evaluated once and its result used in both instances.

Semantically, **fwif** is identical to the standard **if** except when the predicate fails to terminate (has the value $\bot$). Normally the value of an **if** expression is $\bot$ if the value of the predicate is $\bot$ (**if** is strict in its first argument), whereas **fwif** returns common parts of the **then** and **else** branches even in this case. Note if the **then** and **else** parts are identical no part of the result will be $\bot$. **fwif** is implemented by concurrent evaluation of the predicate and the two conditional branches. Any common parts of the two branches are returned as soon as they are found. And when any part is found not to be common to both then evaluation of that part ceases. Once the predicate is evaluated, the chosen branch is returned and the evaluation of the other is canceled.

fwif can be defined in terms of domain theory. Leaving out the **then** and **else** keywords, we have

$$\textbf{fwif } axy = \textbf{if } axy \sqcup (x \sqcap y)$$

FIGURE 10.2
Fwif RETURNS COMMON PARTS EARLY

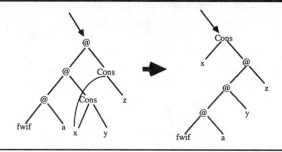

Then, to take the example shown in Fig. 10.2,

$$\textbf{fwif } a(x:y)(x:z) = \textbf{if } a(x:y)(x:z) \sqcup ((x:y) \sqcap (x:z))$$

$$= \textbf{if } a(x:y)(x:z) \sqcup x : (y \sqcap z)$$

$$= (\textbf{if } axx \sqcup x) : (\textbf{if } ayz \sqcap (y \sqcap z))$$

$$= x : \textbf{fwif } ayz$$

10.3.3 Optimistic If

Often abortable transactions have the form:

```
if predicate db
then transform db
else db
```

It may be that in most cases the predicate will return *True* allowing the transaction to proceed. In other, rarer, cases the predicate will return *False* and the transaction will be aborted. Normally the predicate is evaluated, and only when its value is known is one of the branches evaluated. This is a sequential process. In order to increase the level of concurrency, we may take advantage of the supposition that the **then** branch is the most likely to be chosen and start evaluating it immediately. To do this we propose to use an "optimistic" if (**optif**). **Optif** begins the evaluation of the **then** branch at the same time as the predicate. When, as in most cases, the predicate eventually evaluates to *True*, the evaluation of the result will be well on the way to completion. In the cases when the value of the predicate is *False*, evaluation of the **else** branch is started as usual, and evaluation of the **then** branch is arrested. Notice that the denotational semantics of **optif** are the same as for **if**—the only difference is operational. This approach bears a close resemblance to optimistic concurrency in conventional databases. The advantage gained from using **optif** is that in most cases concurrency has been increased. The disadvantage is that in some cases unnecessary calculations have been performed. This is not serious as we expect these cases to be rare. Also, an implementation could give optimistic calculations a lower priority: to be performed if there are spare processors, but not otherwise.

Why not optimistically evaluate both branches? If we did, the number of optimistic evaluations would be exponential in the depth of nesting of **optifs**. If we only evaluate one branch—the 'likely' one—then the number of evaluations will be linear in the depth of nesting. As a result, the machine is less likely to be swamped.

We may increase concurrency further by allowing subsequent transactions to start under the assumption that the present one succeeds. We may make use of the following equivalence

$$f(\text{if } axy) = \text{if } a(fx)(fy) \qquad (\text{if } f \text{ is strict, or } a \neq \perp)$$

and optimistically begin the evaluation of (fx). The required transformation of a reduction graph is shown in Fig. 10.3, and is performed whenever a function f demands the value of an optimistic if.

Notice that no results can be returned from such transactions until the predicate is evaluated. If the predicate returns *False* then evaluation of the **else** branch will automatically restart subsequent transactions.

10.3.4 Long Transactions

If one user submits a long transaction, and then submits another that relies on the result of the first, then he or she must expect a delay while the first completes. But, if two users submit interrelating transactions simultaneously, it is not reasonable to expect the shorter transaction to wait on the longer. Instead it would be desirable to impose the ordering that the short transaction is to be dealt with first, and then the longer. How do we decide which is shorter? The solution is to evaluate both transactions concurrently. As soon as one has completed we arrest the other and reevaluate it on the new database. This gives us the ordering that we require. However, the second transaction may already have been largely evaluated on the old tree, and it may be that

FIGURE 10.3
DISTRIBUTE FUNCTIONS OVER OPTIMISTIC if

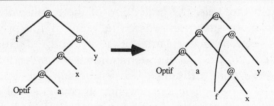

the new tree is not very different from the old, which means that computation is repeated. We claim that although some repetition of work is unavoidable, it may be reduced with the use of lazy memo functions [Hughes, 1985]. If the long transaction is memoized, then any intermediate results from unchanged parts of the database are preserved. When the transaction is reevaluated, these results may be used immediately. In the best case the second transaction may be almost instantaneous.

10.3.5 Balancing

To guarantee good access time, we must keep the database tree balanced. One method would be to schedule a transaction to rebalance the whole tree from time to time. If this is always allowed to run to completion we risk locking the database when other more useful work is available. A solution to this is to make the rebalancing transaction abort if another transaction arrives while it is running. The problem with this is that the rebalancing may never be completed in a busy system, because it would always be aborted by the arrival of a new transaction. Even memoization cannot guarantee that the rebalancing is ever completed. Worse, since the "live" version of the database is not replaced until rebalancing is complete, it may become progressively unbalanced. The traditional alternative to bulk rebalancing is to maintain the balance criterion incrementally, as part of performing transactions. As mentioned before, the problem then is that the root of the tree will be locked throughout the transaction, prohibiting concurrency.

To solve this problem we introduce a new nondeterministic operator called ButIfYouHaveTime. The expression (a **ButIfYouHaveTime** b) returns the value b if given sufficient time to compute it, but returns a if an answer is required before b has completed. Insert could then be written in the form

```
insert (n2,v2)  (Node left (n1, v1) right)

        = Node insert_left (n1,v1) right
               ButIfYouHaveTime
          balance (Node insert_left (n1,v1) right)
                 IF n2 < n1
        = ....

          WHERE
                insert_left = insert (n2,v2) left
```

If a part of the database is accessed while rebalancing is still going on, the rebalancing is cancelled and the data is made available immediately. In other parts of the database the balancing will continue. The behavior of the database using this operator mimics the conventional approach of treating local rebalancing as a "spare-time" task.

10.3.6 Conclusion

We have described the implementation of a very simple database management system in a purely functional language. Several standard operations turned out to have very natural implementations, whose operational behavior closely mimics that of a conventional DBMS. We also discovered unexpected bottlenecks that could restrict concurrency severely. We overcame these by introducing unusual concurrent and nondeterministic operators.

We conclude that functional languages are promising for database implementations; and also that new primitives may be necessary if functional languages are to make full use of concurrent machines.

References

Atkinson, M. P., and Kulkarni, K. G., (1983). "Experimenting with the Functional Data Model," *Persistent Programming Research Report 5*, Department of Computing Science, Glasgow University, September.

Buneman, P., (1985). "Datatypes for Database Programming," *Proceedings of the Persistence and Data Types Workshop*, Appin, August, pp. 295–307.

Clack, C., and Peyton-Jones, S. L., (1985). "Generating Parallelism from Strictness Analysis," *Proceedings of the Workshop on Implementation of Functional Languages*, University of Goteborg & Chalmers University of Technology Report 17, February, pp. 92–131.

Darlington, J., and Reeve, M., (1981). "Alice, A Multi-Processor Reduction Machine for the Parallel Execution of Applicative Languages," *Conference on Functional Programming and Computer Architecture*, Portsmouth, New Hampshire.

Folinus, J. J., Madnick, S. E., and Shultzmann, H. B., (1974). "Virtual Information in Database Systems," *FDT, SIGFIDET* Volume 6.

Friedman, D. P., and Wise, D. S., (1978). "A Note on Conditional Expressions," *CACM*, Vol. 21, No. 11, November, pp. 931–933.

Hecht, M. S., and Gabbe, J. D., (1983). "Shadowed Management of Free Disk Pages with a Linked List," *ACM ToDS*, December, pp. 503–514.

Henderson, P., (1982). "Purely Functional Operating Systems," *Functional Programming and its Applications*, Darlington, Henderson, and Turner (eds.), pp. 177–189, Cambridge University Press.

Hughes, R. J. M., (1985). "Lazy Memo Functions," *Proceedings of the Workshop on Implementation of Functional Languages*, University of Goteborg & Chalmers University of Technology Report 17, February, pp. 400–421.

Nikhil, R., (1985). "Functional Databases, Functional Languages," *Proceedings of the Persistence and Data Types Workshop*, Appin, August, pp. 209–330.

Stoye, W., (1984). "A New Scheme for Writing Functional Operating Systems," Technical Report 56, University of Cambridge Computer Laboratory.

CHAPTER 11

Data Abstraction and Transaction Processing in the Database Programming Language RAPP

J. G. Hughes
Michelle Connolly

11.1 INTRODUCTION

During the past decade a number of database programming languages have emerged which are an integration of aspects of the relational data model and Pascal-like languages. The pioneering work of Schmidt [1977] on Pascal/R led the way in this area, and languages such as PLAIN [1980], RIGEL [1979], and Modula/R [1984] have followed. This paper describes some recent developments in the implementation of another language in this category, called RAPP [1987], which extends the modular, multiprocessing language Pascal Plus [1979] with the relation data type and relational algebraic operations. RAPP incorporates features that have been borrowed from some of the languages mentioned above, particularly Pascal/R and PLAIN, but offers some significant advantages that may be summarized as follows:

1. Sophisticated facilities for the construction of abstract data types and for data encapsulation.
2. High-level constructs for representing and scheduling database transactions.
3. A relatively small, two-pass compiler that generates 'portable' P-code.

The following sections summarize the nature and form of the database programming facilities provided by RAPP, and outline the current implementation status of the system.

11.2 RELATIONAL DATABASE CONSTRUCTS

In common with other Pascal-based database programming languages, the relation data type in RAPP is based on the existing record data type. For example, a relation students with attributes *st#* (the key attribute), *stname*, *status*, and *dateofbirth* might be defined by the following declarations:

```
type
        strange         = 0..9999 ;
        string          = packed array [1..30] of char ;
        statustype      = (undergrad, postgrad, research) ;
        datetype        = packed array [1.6] of char ;
        studentrec      = record
                                st#             :strange ;
                                stname          :string ;
                                status          :statustype ;
                                dateofbirth     :datetype
                          end;
        studentrel      = relation [st#] of studentrec;
var
        students   :   studentsrel;
```

RAPP differs from many of the database programming languages previously mentioned in that it permits an attribute type to be an abstract data type. This facility is similar to that provided in ADT-INGRES [1984] and RAD [1986], both of which permit abstract data types to be defined for domains and allow operations to be defined on these types. The construction of such types in RAPP is described in the next section.

The operators provided by RAPP for manipulating relations are (in common with the language PLAIN) based on the relational algebra [1970]. These operators consist of selection, projection, natural join, Cartesian product, and the set operators of union, intersection, and difference. A full description of these operators is given in Hughes and Connolly [1987]. The advantage of the relational algebra is that there are a relatively small number of operations necessary for relational completeness, and effort can be concentrated on the efficient implementation of these operations.

Relations in RAPP may be indexed on any attribute by means of an index relation. Index relations are created by the user, but subsequently they are automatically maintained by the system when the base relation is updated. This relieves the user of the often complex and mundane responsibility of index maintenance.

11.3 ABSTRACT DATA TYPES FOR DOMAINS

There are many database application areas where the data structures are of such complexity that the primitive typing facilities offered by commercial database management systems are found to be totally inadequate. In the design of large applications, data abstraction has long been recognized as a means to develop high-level representations of the concepts that relate closely to the application being programmed and to hide the inessential details of such representations at the various stages of program development. Thus many modern programming languages such as Ada and Modula-2 offer very general algorithmic facilities for type definition. Module or 'information-hiding' mechanisms are provided so that arbitrary new types can be defined by both the necessary details for representation, which are hidden from the surrounding program, and the allowable operations to be maintained for objects of that type. Furthermore, since these mechanisms may be applied repeatedly, types may be mapped, step by step, from higher, user-oriented levels to lower levels, ending with the built-in language constructs. At each level, the view of the data may be abstracted from those details which are unnecessary for data usage, that is, details with regard to representation, constraints, access rights, and so on. This leads to a decoupling of the data structures that define the database, and the application programs that operate on them.

This approach is consistent with the relational model of data in which, at the abstract level, attributes are viewed as atomic or nondecomposable objects. However, for a database management system to actually store and manipulate attribute values, the details of their machine representation must be incorporated into that part of the system which is normally hidden from a user's view.

In RAPP the programmer may introduce arbitrary new data types into a relational database and define arbitrary operations on objects of these new types. Such data abstraction and modularity are provided for in RAPP via the *envelope* and *envelope module* constructs. An envelope may be thought of as a parameterized data type, together with associated operations, of which multiple instances may be declared. The actual parameters are passed whenever an instance is declared. If only one instance of an envelope is required the definition and instantiation may be combined into a single envelope module. An envelope module in RAPP is very similar to the module or package facility found in languages such as Modula/2 and Ada. An envelope also defines a control structure that envelopes the execution of any block in which an instance of the envelope is declared. This control structure may be used to enforce correct initialization and finalization of data structures.

For example, an integer set abstraction in RAPP could be represented by an envelope of the following form:

```
Envelope Integer Set  (size : integer);

        Procedure *Insert (i: integer) ;
           {Inserts value i into the set}

        Procedure *Remove (i : integer) ;
           {Removes value i from the set}

        Function *Present (i: integer) : Boolean ;
           {Tests if i is a member of the set}

    begin
           {initialize empty set} ;
           *** ;
           {finalization code (if any)}
    end;
```

Instances of *IntegerSet* may be declared as follows:

```
    Instance S1 : IntegerSet (10) ;
            S2 : IntegerSet (25) ;
```

The effect of declaring an instance of *IntegerSet* in any block *B* is to make available to that block an integer set data structure and an associated set of operations, that is, those operations which are "starred" in the envelope declaration. In addition, the block *B* is implicitly enveloped by the code in the body of the envelope. Thus the set is first initialized and when the "inner statement" (***) is encountered block *B* is executed. On termination of block *B* any finalization code following the inner statement will be executed. The inner statement has full status and may be executed conditionally or repetitively. This enables a variety of tracing, monitoring, and recovery strategies at block level which few other languages support [Schmidt, 1977]. For example, we could make the execution of block *B* conditional on the successful initialization of the integer set by replacing the body of the envelope with the following code:

```
begin
    { initialize empty set } ;
    if {set successfully initialized}
    then begin
                *** ;
            { finalization code }
        end .
end;
```

11.3.1 An Alternative Abstraction Mechanism

Abstract data types which are to be employed as attribute types in RAPP may be constructed as "starred" type declarations within envelope modules. As a simple example, let us consider the attribute *dateofbirth* which was declared to be of type *packed array [1..6] of char* in the preceding example. This is a rather inadequate type and we may wish to define a more structured type for *dateofbirth* and provide operations on objects of that type, such as

1. Compute the number of days between two dates.
2. Given a date *d*, compute the date *n* days later.
3. Return the day of the week corresponding to a given date.

An envelope module for the abstract data type *datetype* providing the preceding operations might take the following form:

```
Envelope Module DateModule ;
type
   *DateType = {the structure of Datetype is hidden}
   *DayType = (*Sunday,*Monday,*Tuesday,*Wednesday,
               *Thursday,*Friday,*Saturday);

   Function *NoOfDays (d1,d2 : DateType) : Integer ;
      { Computes the number of days between dates d1
        and d2 }

   Procedure *NewDate (d:DateType; n:Integer; var
                       result:DateType} ;
      { Given a date d, computes the date n days later }

   Procedure *DayofWeek (d : DateType ; var day :
                         DayType) ;
      { Returns the day of the week on which date d
        falls }

begin
     ***
end{  DateModule } ;
```

A user of the module *DateModule* may declare variables and attributes of type *DateType* in his program and apply the operations *NoOfDays*, *NewDate*, and *DayOfWeek* to those variables. He does not know, and does not need to know, how *DateType* is implemented.

11.4 MODELING DATABASE TRANSACTIONS

The facilities for concurrent programming in RAPP are based on the ideas of Hoare [1974]. From the point of view of database programmer the most useful concepts are those of the process module and the monitor module. A process module is identical in structure to a standard Pascal procedure but represents a program activity that may be executed in parallel with other processes. Thus it is an ideal representation for a database transaction. (The implementation must of course take responsibility for treating processes as units for recovery and concurrency). A monitor module is a module that holds the declarations of items of data which are accessed by more than one process and guarantees exclusion on that data. That is, only one process at a time is capable of modifying data that has been declared local to a monitor. However, starred monitor variables may be *inspected* by any number of processes at the same time.

If a transaction requires a data item that is not currently available it will suspend itself until some other transaction gives up its exclusive access to that data item. This synchronization of transactions is achieved using instances of a built-in monitor called *Condition*. The interface provided by the *Condition* monitor is as follows:

```
Monitor Condition;
Type
      Range = 0..maxint ;

    Procedure *PWait (P : Range) ;

    Procedure *Wait ;

    Procedure *Signal ;

    Function *Length : Range ;

    Function *Priority : Range ;

  End{Condition} ;
```

Each instance of *Condition* defines a queue on which transactions may be temporarily suspended until the data item they require is available. The action of the procedure *PWait* is to suspend the transaction calling it on the condition queue in a position behind those transactions with the same or smaller values of *P*. The action of procedure *Wait* is to call *PWait* with a priority value of *(MaxInt div 2)*. When a transaction is suspended on a condition queue all monitor exclusions held by that transaction are released. When a transaction signals, it passes control to the transaction at the head of the queue. Since only one transaction may be active in a monitor, *Signal* delays the transaction calling it until the signalled transaction has released its exclusion on the monitor. Function *Length* returns the number of transactions in the queue, while function *Priority* returns the priority of the process at the head of the queue.

As a simple example let us consider the particular case of providing access to a relation that is treated as a single resource and for which each transaction obtains either read or write access as required, and where several transactions are allowed to read simultaneously. Ignoring priority, the form of the corresponding relation management module might be as follows (adapted from Bustard, et al. [1987]):

```
Monitor RelationAccess ;

type
    *AccessMode = (*Read, *Write, None) ;
instance
    readers, writers : Condition ;
var
    CurrentAccessMode: AccessMode ;
    NoOfReaders : 0..Maxint ;

    Procedure * Acquire (AccessRequired : AccessMode);
    begin
        case CurrentAccessMode of
            None:   begin
                        CurrentAccessMode :=
                        AccessRequired ;
                        ifAccessRequired = Read
                        then NoOfReaders: = 1
                    end;
            Read:   ifAccessRequired = Write
                    then writers.wait
                    else if writers .Length = 0
                        then NoOfReaders :=
                        NoOfReaders + 1
                        else readers.wait;
            Write:  if accessRequired = Read
                    then readers.wait
                    else writers.wait;
        end{case}  ;
    end{Acquire}  ;
```

```
Procedure *Release ;
var
        NoCurrentReaders : Boolean ;
begin
        if CurrentAccessMode = Read
        then begin
                NoOfReaders : = NoOfReaders - 1 ;
                NoCurrentReaders : =
                (NoOfReaders = 0) ;
                ifNoCurrentReaders
                then if writers .Length > 0
                        then writers .Signal

            end
          else
            if readers .Length > 0
            then begin
                while readers .Length > 0 do
                begin
                    readers.Signal;
                    NoOfReaders : = NoOfReaders + 1
                end;
                CurrentAccessMode : = Read
            end
          else if writers .Length > 0
            then begin
                writers .signal ;
                CurrentAccessMode : = Write
            end
end{Release} ;
    begin
        CurrentAccessMode : = None;
        NoOfReaders : = 0;
        ***
    end {RelationAccess} ;
```

This monitor provides read-sharable and write-exclusive locks. That is, any
number of readers may share access to a relation but a writer (an updating
transaction) is given exclusive access. A process may have read access to the
database if there are no processes using the database, or if other processes
have read access *and* there are no processes waiting to write. This latter
condition is necessary to ensure that a process waiting to write does not wait
forever.

A reader releasing access to the relation allows any waiting writer to proceed provided there are not other current readers. A writer releasing access
allows all waiting readers to proceed. If there are no waiting readers then
any waiting writer is activated. This allocation scheme should be adequate in

practice, but obviously alternative strategies are easily programmed. Note that this simple example shows the locks to be at the relation level but that higher degrees of granularity can also be achieved with the monitor construct.

11.5 IMPLEMENTATION

The major changes to the Pascal Plus system were concerned with the analysis of relational algebraic statements and the generation of code for their implementation. At the lowest level, this involves calls to procedure imported from the common file system for opening and closing relations and reading and writing blocks of data to and from relations. Relations are stored as direct access files with a dense primary index organized as a B^+ tree. User-defined index relations are also organized as B^+ trees and the implementation of retrieval operations on these indices (i.e., using the selection operator) takes advantage of this multilevel structure.

The join operation is implemented by means of the classic sort-merge-join algorithm. In this method, the two relations to be joined are sorted on their common attribute values using a multiway merge sort. The two resulting sorted files are then merged and tuples with matching common attribute values are output to the resultant relation. No attempt as yet has been made to optimize algebraic expressions involving non-index relations. The philosophy adopted in the development of RAPP is that, instead of providing a large and complicated optimizer, we provide appropriate programming tools with which the programmer can improve on efficiency directly. Index relations provide the programmer with a powerful means for optimizing the performance of database systems written in RAPP. For this reason, a great deal of effort, during the development of RAPP, was devoted to the efficient storage and maintenance of indices, and to providing the programmer with a simple interface to these structures. Thus, index relations can be created or re-created simply by a call to the procedure rewrite (<index-name>). The system subsequently maintains indices automatically, thereby absolving the programmer from the complicated procedure of updating indices following insertion or deletion operations on the base relation. Also, since indices are treated as relations, the programmer can combine and manipulate them using the normal algebraic and set operators.

The RAPP system has been in use over the past year as a teaching aid on final-year and post-graduate database courses, and also for general purpose database development. It has proven to be reliable and efficient. The system consists of a relatively small two-pass compiler, written in standard Pascal, which generates P-code. P-code interpreters have been written for a variety of machines including VAX and ICL ranges. Work is continuing on providing additional run-time support facilties and on improving the performance of the system.

REFERENCES

Bustard, D. W., Elder, J. W. G., and Welsh, J., (1987). *Concurrent Program Structures*, London: Prentice-Hall.

Codd, E. F., (1970). "A Relational Model of Data for Large Shared Data Banks," *Comm. ACM*, Vol. 13, pp. 377–387.

Hoare, C. A. R., (1974). "Monitors: An Operating System Structuring Concept," *Comm. ACM*, Vol. 17, pp. 549–557.

Hughes, J. G., and Connolly, M., (1987). "A Portable Implementation of a Modular Multi-Processing Database Programming Language," *Software—Pract & Exper.*, Vol. 17, pp. 533–546.

Ong, J., Fogg, D., and Stonebraker, M., (1984). "Implementation of Data Abstraction in the Relational Database System INGRES," *SIGMOD Rec.* Vol. 14, No. 1, pp. 1–14.

Osborn, S. L., and Heaven, T. E., (1986). "The Design of A Relational Database System with Abstract Data Types for Domains," *ACM TODS*, Vol. 11, No. 3, pp. 357–373.

Reimer, M., (1984). "Implementation of the Database Programming Language Modula/R on the Personal Computer Lilith," *Software—Pract. & Exper.*, Vol. 14, pp. 945–956.

Rowe, L. A., and Shoens, K. A., (1979). "Data Abstraction, Views and Updates in RIGEL," Proceedings ACM SIGMOD Conference, Boston, pp. 71–81.

Schmidt, J. W., (1977). "Some High Live Language Constructs for Data of Type Relation," *ACM TODS* Vol. 2, pp. 247–261.

Wasserman, A. I., Sheretz, D. D., Kersten, M. L., van de Riet, R. P., and Dippe, M. D., (1980). "Revised Report on the Programming Language PLAIN," University of California San Francisco, Technical Report Number 42.

Welsh, J., and Bustard, D. W., (1979). "Pascal Plus—Another Language for Modular Multiprogramming," *Software—Pract. & Exper.*, Vol. 9, pp. 947–958.

CHAPTER 12

INTEGRATION ISSUES IN IMPLEMENTING SEMANTIC DATA MODELS

Brian Nixon
John Mylopoulos

12.1 INTRODUCTION

We are interested in a performance theory for semantic data model implementations, that is, a theory for the development of systems based on an Entity-Relationship data model and that manage a large and complex information base (see Borgida, et al. [1985a], Albano [1985a], Atkinson, et al. [1987], Hull & King [1987], and Peckham & Maryanski [1988] for recent overviews of semantic data models). A natural starting point for such a theory is to apply results from existing technologies, including databases, compilers, and systems modeling. This has in fact happened with several prototype semantic data model implementations (e.g., Galileo [Albano, et al., 1985b], ADAPLEX [Chan, et al., 1982; Smith, et al., 1983], and GEM [Tsur & Zaniolo, 1984]). The application of existing technologies, however, has not been totally trouble-free as many *integration* problems arise from the *interaction* of data model features, implementation techniques, and design goals. Thus the cumulative effect of design decisions (relating to a data model and its implementation) often results in difficulties for the implementor of a semantic data model. So while we can build a reasonably robust and efficient relational database system, characterize its performance, and analytically choose among implementation alternatives, using a well-established body of techniques, we do not have such *systematic tools* for building semantic data models. This chapter examines some of the interaction difficulties in implementing a semantic data model, and considers some areas where systematic methods could apply to the development of a theory for semantic data model implementation.

Semantic data models, like all data models, offer a logical data structure along with appropriate operations for accessing and revising it. To build an information system, one needs to write, in some programming language, application programs that use the data model operations. Some proposals for semantic data models address this need by offering a full programming language with an embedded and integrated semantic data model (e.g., Taxis [Mylopoulos, et al., 1980b; Wong, 1981], ADAPLEX [Chan, et al., 1982; Smith, et al., 1983], and Galileo [Albano, et al., 1985b]). Others ignore this need altogether (e.g., SDM [Hammer & McLeod, 1981]). We propose to focus on the former type of semantic data model, which permits optimized implementations of information systems that simultaneously take into account the data structures constituting the database as well as the applications programs. The rest of the discussion treats the problem of implementing a semantic data model as a special case of the implementation problem for programming languages, particularly languages supporting persistent data types (see Atkinson & Buneman [1987] for a thorough survey).

A programming language implementation usually involves the construction of a compiler that translates programs written in the language into code that executes *faithfully* (reflecting the semantics of the programming language) and *efficiently* (at least in the sense that compiled code executes more efficiently than its interpreted counterpart). Accordingly, implementation of a semantic data model also involves the construction of a compiler that generates data structures constituting a database and translates programs accessing that database into code that executes faithfully and efficiently.

The construction of a compiler for a semantic data model is influenced by three sets of issues:

1. *Features of the semantic data model (including programming language features):* abstraction mechanisms, data manipulation operations, and programming constructs, among others.
2. *Implementation techniques:* including management of processes, static type checking, and efficient use of secondary storage.
3. *Design goals:* including reliability, safety, and uniformity.

When applying "off-the-shelf" technology from areas such as compilers and databases to the implementation of semantic data models, *integration problems often arise due to interactions among semantic data model features, implementation techniques, and design goals.* Such interactions often lead to trade-off dilemmas and suboptimal implementations. (See Fig. 12.1.)

FIGURE 12.1

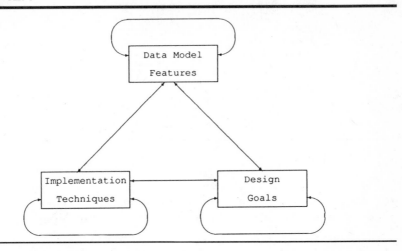

Moreover, such interactions are often discovered in the middle of an implementation, necessitating some redesign work. This motivates our desire for a more systematic methodology for the selection of implementation techniques based on the features of the semantic data model and the design goals of a particular implementation.

The purpose of this chapter is to describe some of the interactions that arise, to illustrate with examples the problems entailed by these interactions, and to suggest some solutions that have been offered in the literature. Much of our experience on the subject has been derived from an ongoing implementation project for Taxis [Nixon, 1983; Nixon, et al., 1987a,b; Chung, 1984; Chung, et al., 1988]. In the remainder of the chapter, we assume that the reader has some familiarity with semantic data models. Sections 12.2 through 12.5 of the chapter list potential interactions, discuss the problems they create for the semantic data model designer and implementor alike, and suggest possible solutions to these problems. Finally, Section 12.6 presents conclusions and directions for future research.

12.2 INTERACTING DATA MODEL FEATURES

The features of a semantic data model often interact. First consider a semantic data model, such as Taxis, which offers isA hierarchies, transactions,[1] and exceptions. (See Fig. 12.2.)

---

[1]In this chapter, "transaction" means an atomic operation on a database, with or without facilities for recovery.

FIGURE 12.2

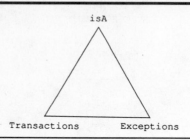

When *generalization (isA) hierarchies* are applied to several different kinds of classes, the semantics of generalization need to be refined on a case-by-case basis in order to capture intuitions. Consider, for example:

☐ *Integer classes.* A natural starting point for integer classes is the Pascal definition of integer type, which requires a contiguous range of integers. One option requires a specialized integer class to be one contiguous subrange of the range of the more general class:

```
define integerClass Grade := { | 0 :: 100 |}
define integerClass PassingGrade := { | 50 :: 100 |}
   isA Grade
```

While this disallows some potentially useful definitions, such as

```
define integerClass ThresholdGrade :=
   { | 49, 59, 69, 79 |} isA Grade
```

the contiguity restriction does allow an implementation to optimize type checking by exploiting work done on efficient testing of the legality of an assignment to a target whose values are within one single subrange [Wortman, 1979]. But as we'll see later, even with the contiguity restriction, integer specialization complicates type checking.

☐ *Enumeration classes.* While again starting with Pascal-like types, a different specialization rule can be obtained. One option is to require a specialized enumeration to consist of a (not necessarily contiguous) subset of the general class.

```
define enumerationClass Department :=
   { | Math, History, Physics, Latin |}
define enumerationClass ScienceDepartment:=
   { | Math, Physics |} isA Department
```

This reflects the notion that specialization of concepts implies smaller extensions or less-frequent cases. In some situations, ordering may be important, in which case an additional requirement is that the specialized enumeration keep the same relative ordering of elements as the general class.

☐ *Entity classes.* These classes group entities that can be created, modified, and removed in the course of their lifetimes. The specialization rules will reflect the inherent semantic integrity constraints of the data model. For example, most semantic data models use a version of the so-called *structural isA constraint* which requires subclasses to inherit the attributes of their superclasses, and to have attribute value ranges (whether integer, enumeration, entity, etc.) the same as, or specializations of, the general attribute value range. Additional attributes may also be associated with subclasses.

```
define entityClass Student ...
    name: String
    area: Department
    . . .


define entityClass ScienceStudent isA Student ...
    area: ScienceDepartment
    laboratoryDesk: {| 1 :: 1000 |}
    . . .
```

It appears from these examples that the "natural" definition of specialization is different for each kind of class. Note that even with such differences, there is a common underlying theme in all these uses of specialization which dictates that specialization leads to smaller extensions (fewer instances) and larger intensions (more attributes). The latter property of specialization is captured by the aforementioned *structural isA constraint.*

Consider next the problem of introducing into a semantic data model the notion of *isA hierarchies of transactions.* Clearly, this is a desirable feature from a uniformity point of view, and in fact has appeared in one form or another in many object-oriented languages going back to SIMULA [Dahl & Nygaard, 1966]. To this end, transactions need to be treated as classes, while the (procedural) body of a transaction, its parameters, prerequisites, and local variables are defined through attributes (much in the spirit of attaching "methods" and instance variables to object classes in an object-oriented programming language such as SMALLTALK [Goldberg & Robson, 1983]). The specialization rules discussed earlier, involving inheritance of attributes, then apply for parameter and local variable attributes. But what does it mean to specialize an action? There are several possible rules [Mylopoulos & Wong, 1980a; Borgida, 1981]. One can consider whether the "net side effects" of a specialized action constitute a superset of those of a more general action. For example,

```
actionA: j <- 7
```

could be specialized to

```
actionA: begin
            j <- 7
            k <- 24
         end
```

in that the specialization "does more" than the more general action. Unfortunately, this specialization rule is undecidable. It can be tested, however, for individual cases to ensure that it will never be violated during the execution of a program. Note how this "semantic" form of action specialization contrasts with SIMULA's textual inheritance of code from a superclass to a subclass [Dahl & Nygaard, 1966] and with SMALLTALK's default inheritance, where methods of subclasses can override those of superclasses without any consideration of the semantics of the methods involved [Goldberg & Robson, 1983].

A related issue that arises in treating transactions as classes concerns the (relative) order of execution of action attributes. If an ordering is given for the more general class, it would make sense to require that the ordering given for its specializations should be compatible. This, however, can lead to trouble when *multiple inheritance* is allowed, where a class has more than one immediate superclass. In that case, it is possible to inherit incompatible orderings on action attributes from superclasses. For example, in the following transaction T3, should actionA precede or follow actionB?

```
define transactionClass T1 ...
   actionA: ...
   actionB: ...

define transactionClass T2 ...
   actionB: ...
   actionA: ...

define transactionClass T3 ... isA T1 ..., T2 ...
```

Yet another interaction that needs to be dealt with by the designer of a semantic data model concerns the interaction between *exceptions* and *transactions*. Some data models have procedural exception handling, which closely interrelates the two data model features. Exception classes can be arranged in isA hierarchies:

```
define ExceptionClass CourseFull isA
   RegistrationProblem ...
```

Exceptions are "raised" by a transaction on failure of a condition:

```
define TransactionClass enrol (s:Student, c:Course) ...
    prerequisite
        notFull: (c.enrolment < c.maxSize)
            elseRaiseException CourseFull(...)
```

Each transaction call (such as the call to enrol(...), following) can associate an exception handler (which is a transaction, such as Petition(...)) with each exception (such as CourseFull) that can be raised by the transaction.

```
[JohnSmith, Math1000].enrol exceptionHandler for
CourseFull is Petition
```

If a transaction raises an exception, the associated exception handler will be invoked. But what should happen once the exception handler completes its execution? One possibility is for control to be returned to the transaction that raised the exception in the first place. This makes sense when the exception handler is viewed as having "repaired" the problem. Another possibility, widely adopted by programming languages supporting exception handling, is to return control to the caller of the interrupted transaction [Goodenough, 1975]. This control structure is appropriate when the exception handler accomplishes what the interrupted transaction set out to do. It seems then that the control structure for exception handlers is dependent on what the exception handler is set out to do. It is fair to add that in some ways, recovery mechanisms based on exception handling constitute a more flexible recovery mechanism than the standard "undo all" mechanism usually offered by database transactions [Borgida, 1985b].

IsA hierarchies of exceptions introduce additional flexibility in the selection of exception handlers. When an exception is raised for which no handler has been specified, one can look for a handler higher up in the isA hierarchy of actions and exceptions, instead of using the static or dynamic scope rules used by conventional programming languages. For instance, if no handler is specified for the CourseFull exception, one could see if a handler has been specified for the more general exception RegistrationProblem.

This interaction between transactions and exceptions should not be unexpected, since exception handling can be reexpressed in terms of control-flow constructs such as if—then—else. For example:

```
if (c.enrolment < c.maxSize)
    then ... /* continue with enrol(...) transaction */
    else ... /* invoke transaction corresponding to
                CourseFull exception */
```

12.2.1 Interacting Programming Constructs

Yet another kind of complication can arise when two *programming constructs* result in unusual semantic constraints. Consider the interaction between *iteration* and the *entity deletion* operation. A reasonable semantic requirement is that iteration through the instances of a class should not depend on the system-determined order of fetching the entities. However, if an entity is deleted within a loop, the exact number of iterations may vary, causing a conflict with our initial requirement. For example, suppose one wants to remove each instance of Person where the spouse's name begins with the letter J, and at the same time compute the average age of persons. One could write:

```
n <- 0
ageSum <- 0
for each instance p in Person do
    begin
        n <- n + 1
        ageSum <- ageSum + p.age
        if p.spouse.name.firstLetter = 'J'
                then deleteEntity p.spouse
    end
averageAge <- ageSum / n
```

Suppose the married couples are

```
Bill & Jane,    Bob & Jill,    Beth & Joe
```

If the system orders the iteration as

```
Jane, Jill, Joe, Bill, Bob, Beth
```

then six iterations will be performed, but if the order of iteration is

```
Bill, Bob, Beth, Jane, Jill, Joe
```

then there will be only three iterations, and there will be a different value for the average age.[2] The problem arises because one is deleting instances of the class (Person) through which the iteration is being performed. It would seem advisable for a compiler to statically detect this case and inform the programmer of the possible problem. However, this is in general undecidable if nested transactions are allowed. So there is a choice here between clear semantics and the uninhibited combination of programming constructs.

---

[2]Of course, this reflects an ambiguity in the problem specification; that is, whether none, some, or all of the persons to be deleted should be included in the calculation of average age.

There are two general observations to be made, on the basis of the issues raised. Firstly, the incorporation of two features that are not completely orthogonal can cause problems. Secondly, *formal* semantic data models (e.g., Abiteboul & Hull [1984] and Houtsma & Balsters [1988]) may be more amenable to logic-based techniques for detecting underlying interaction of features during data model design. Related work from the program verification field includes Elliott [1982], which derives conditions for the absence of errors, by way of rewrite rules applied to (possibly interacting) programming language constructs. In general, however, the problem of detecting interaction is very difficult.

12.3 INTERACTING FEATURES AND IMPLEMENTATION TECHNIQUES

Experience shows that when trying to apply existing techniques to implement data model features, the "obvious" techniques are sometimes inadequate or inefficient. Let us give a few examples.

12.3.1 Attribute Storage

When storing large amounts of persistent data, a natural first choice is relational database technology. If we can represent attribute values within a relational schema, we can exploit the efficient storage and access techniques already developed for relational databases. However, inheritance hierarchies result in collections of attribute values whose appearance is more like a "staircase" than a table:

	name	age	laboratoryDesk	advisor
GraduateScienceStudent				
ScienceStudent				
Student				

As a result, a simple relational representation may waste space. For example, one alternative for representing all attributes is to use a universal relation that has one tuple per entity, one column per attribute, and null values for attributes not applicable to an entity. Obviously, such a representation would be highly inefficient with respect to space usage. Let us compare with some alternative proposals.

A second, more interesting alternative involves using one relation per class [Smith & Smith, 1977], while another uses one relation for each generalization sublattice that is part of the conceptual schema [Zaniolo, 1983]. When using one relation per class, one may store all attributes (newly defined or

TABLE 12.1
HORIZONTAL SPLITTING

	entity	age	laboratoryDesk	advisor
OnlyGraduateScienceStudents	Grad0036	24	38	ProfSmith
	Grad0035	28	37	ProfJones

OnlyScienceStudents	Scie0034	19	43
	Scie0033	23	97

OnlyStudents	Stud0032	20
	Stud0031	22

TABLE 12.2
VERTICAL SPLITTING

AllStudents		AllScienceStudents		AllGraduateStudents	
entity	age	entity	laboratoryDesk	entity	advisor
Grad0036	24	Grad0036	38	Grad0036	ProfSmith
Grad0035	28	Grad0035	37	Grad0035	ProfJones
Scie0034	19	Scie0034	43		
Scie0033	23	Scie0033	97		
Stud0032	20				
Stud0031	22				

inherited) of a particular class in the corresponding relation (*horizontal splitting*), or only the newly defined attributes, as done in Smith & Smith [1983] (*vertical splitting*). For example,[3] see Tables 12.1 and 12.2. Some implementations give the system designer more flexibility in selecting storage mechanisms to meet more selectively the needs of a particular application. ADAPLEX [Chan, et al., 1982] supports a form of both vertical and horizontal partitioning of entities and their attribute values. In fact, arbitrary predicates, specifying which entities to include in which partition, are available to the system designer.

Another alternative (which was considered for Taxis [Nixon, et al., 1987b]) stores a tuple of "triples": for every attribute value of every entity, one stores the entity identifier, the attribute name, and the attribute value. The example would be represented by Table 12.3. The "triples" method does

---

[3] In the examples, we assume that entities are implemented by assigning a unique internal identifier to each entity. Also note that only some attributes are shown in the diagrams.

TABLE 12.3
ATTRIBUTE TRIPLES

entity	attribute	attributeValue
Grad0036	age	24
Grad0036	laboratoryDesk	38
Grad0036	advisor	ProfSmith
Grad0035	age	28
Grad0035	laboratoryDesk	37
Grad0035	advisor	ProfJones
Scie0034	age	19
Scie0034	laboratoryDesk	43
Scie0033	age	23
Scie0033	laboratoryDesk	97
Stud0032	age	20
Stud0031	age	22

not offer the best performance, but does permit translation to a schema with a small, fixed number of relations, which requires no refinement or reformatting, even when additional classes and attributes are defined.

An analysis of the different alternatives for attribute storage is presented in Nixon, et al. [1987b]. While there are trade-offs, it is clear that one needs to go beyond a simple relational representation in order to obtain efficiency.

12.3.2 Integrity Constraint Enforcement

When implementing semantic integrity constraints, one must consider how the system searches among all the constraints that may be violated. Since the system will be continually looking for unsatisfied constraints, an important performance issue is whether the search is exhaustive or selective.

Consider a constraint that every employee must have a salary that does not exceed the budget of his or her department. Exhaustive search involves the repeated checking of every constraint after any change to the system; in the example, every employee's salary could be examined, and this entire process might be done frequently. It would be better to analyze the condition at compilation, and produce code with *selective* checking; in the example, a compiler would emit code that does not check this condition for any salary *decrease*. See Chung [1984] and Nixon, et al. [1987a] for details. It turns out that there are trade-offs among the different techniques for selective checking

[Chung, et al., 1988]; this points out the need for a methodology to choose among alternative implementations.

In some cases, existing techniques need to be *extended*. For example, techniques for semantic integrity constraint enforcement developed for Entity-Relationship data models [Sarin, 1977] have been extended [Chung, 1984] to handle arbitrary nesting of attribute selections. For instance, a constraint could refer to the size of the desk of the manager of a department. A related implementation issue concerns *temporal* integrity constraints, which requires some form of a triggering mechanism. The implementation offered in Chung, et al. [1988] suggests yet another feature-implementation trade-off: a restriction on the form of assertions permits efficient checking. In fact, Chung, et al. [1988] states that, with some restrictions, enforcement of the class of constraints considered by Chung depends *linearly* on the extension of the class being constrained; more precisely, it is proportional to

(cardinality of source class) × *(length of expression)*

On the other hand, the particular implementation technique offered by Chung does not address the problem of inconsistent constraints (which can lead to classes with no instances). Contrasting this with a data model allows the full power of first-order logic for its constraint language.

12.3.3 Long-Term Processes

Another related issue concerns the efficient implementation of concurrency provided by a data model. Consider, for example, the process of a student going to university, that is, the states and state changes a student goes through, such as being admitted, taking courses, and graduating, which can be modeled by a Taxis *script* (see Fig. 12.3).

FIGURE 12.3
A SAMPLE SCRIPT

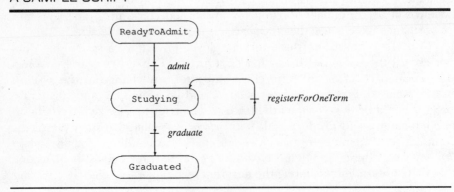

Scripts offer a Petri net-like graphical formalism, inspired by Zisman [1978], but incorporate significant extensions, among them (*i*) the molding of scripts into the framework of classes, instances, and attributes, and (*ii*) the addition of interprocess communication primitives based on Communicating Sequential Processes [Hoare, 1978]. As with Petri nets, scripts have two node types, one representing *states* (in Fig. 12.3 indicated by ovals: ReadyToAdmit, Studying, and Graduated) which will be instances of their respective *state classes* each time the script is instantiated, and the other representing *transitions* (indicated by directed arcs: *admit, registerForOneTerm*, and *graduate*). The description of a state[4] includes *assertions* which must be true in that state, while the description of a transition includes a list of activation *conditions* that must be true for the transition to fire and a list of *actions* that are to be executed in this case. For example, the transition *RegisterForOneTerm* has a condition that the student has paid the fees for the term, and an action that calls the enrol transaction, which was described previously. Scripts can invoke other scripts, communicate with them, and can also reference any entity.

There are several problems in the management of the type of concurrency introduced by a modeling construct such as that of scripts. In general, there will be a large number of active script instances, states, and transitions at any one time, and it is important to use a strategy for process scheduling that is both fair and efficient. The key to any such strategy is the determination and management of transitions that are eligible for activation or are currently active. One needs to consider techniques for both scheduling (such as those available from systems programming) *and* optimized detection of condition satisfaction. If an implementation uses an "off-the-shelf" technique which *only* provides scheduling (such as monitors provided by an operating system), but does not incorporate optimizing techniques (such as selective checking), then performance will be poor. For example, if the condition that fees have been paid by a particular student is translated to a monitor-like "wait" construct, the result could be very inefficient, as the condition would be evaluated repeatedly. Now if there are 20,000 instances of the script (one for each student at the university), the tremendous amount of checking may stop the system altogether. Again *selective* checking will improve the situation. For example, the condition on *registerForOneTerm* could be checked for a particular student when that student is paying fees.

To evaluate the efficiency of a proposed implementation for a construct as complex as that of scripts, one may have to develop an analytic model of the performance of a proposed implementation. For the problem of modeling long-term processes, a reasonable starting point is operating systems modeling. However, the length of, and variance in, the lifetimes of persistent entities is much greater in an information system than in an operating system [Rios-Zertuche, forthcoming], making it more difficult to apply existing results. Moreover, in an information system, one cannot use the operating

---

[4]Not all details are shown in the diagram.

system assumption that older (persistent) entities are more likely to be deleted than younger ones [Butler, 1987]. Once again, the moral is that existing tools and techniques are not quite applicable.

12.4 INTERACTING FEATURES AND DESIGN GOALS

An implementor will wish to satisfy a set of software design goals (such as reliability, safety, portability, and readability). These goals are bound to influence the implementations considered for particular data model features.

Consider the design goal of providing a portable implementation. To avoid having an implementation deal with machine dependencies (such as bookkeeping for procedure calls), while permitting software to be used on several kinds of hardware, a high-level target language can be used. However, one must still deal with data model features that are not present in the target language. For example, a Pascal-like target language was used for the Taxis compiler. However, a number of Taxis features could not be translated directly to Pascal [Barron, 1981] because Taxis transactions have several features not offered by Pascal procedures:

1. Exception handling, which requires an additional mechanism to alter flow of control, in what otherwise appears to be "straight-line code."
2. A transaction hierarchy, which requires methods of inheriting code (Due to the expected large schema size, the analysis of time-space trade-offs is quite significant).
3. A transaction call rule, which requires a run-time mechanism to invoke a particular transaction specialization, depending on the actual parameter values.
4. Run-time access to meta-knowledge (e.g., the type of a variable or the names of fields of a record).

Now consider the design goal of providing safety with respect to a type system. This also interacts with the provision of data model features. For example, in order to avoid some type security problems, all local variables can be initialized. Now if the data model provides a distinguished null value which is an instance of every type, local variables can be initialized to this value. But if the null value is also used in other contexts (to indicate an absent value, an unknown value, an error value, etc.), the result can be that the null value is severely "overloaded."

12.5 MORE COMPLEX INTERACTIONS

We close this discussion with a look at interactions among data model features, implementation techniques, design goals, and the cumulative effect of previously made decisions. We give three examples.

12.5.1 Referential Integrity

First consider three data model constraints, and the resulting interaction with their implementations. Let us start with the referential integrity constraint, an important constraint for entity-based modeling frameworks, that prohibits deletion of an entity that is participating in relationships with other entities. For example, if Fred is Mary's advisor, and Fred leaves the university, the entity Fred cannot be deleted until the value of advisor of Mary is changed. To enforce the constraint, a "reference count" can be maintained (See (1) in Fig. 12.4), indicating the number of times an entity (e.g., Fred) is used as an attribute value; deletion is allowed only when the count is zero. Now suppose that the actual "inverse references" (back pointers, such as a link from Fred to advisor of Mary) are also maintained by the *implementation* (2). This allows access to inverse references to be made available as a *data model feature* (3); for example, a programmer can examine all relationships Fred participates in—advisor of Mary, manager of Joe, and so on. It also attains a *design goal* (4) of letting the *programmer handle* a violation of the referential integrity constraint (by modifying relevant relationships and then deleting an entity), rather than only having the *system detect* the violation.

A seemingly independent feature of some semantic data models is that every entity must have a unique "minimum class"—the unique lowest class in the isA hierarchy which contains the entity.[5] Assume that an implementation gives each entity a unique internal identifier. Observe that encoding the minimum class of an entity in its internal identifier can reduce access to secondary storage, thus helping achieve the goal of increasing efficiency of run-time operations (5 and 5'). The run-time savings can be compounded by storing the schema (isA hierarchy, definitions of classes, their attributes, and constraints) in main memory. Consider a transaction with parameter s of type Student, which prints the names and most specialized type definitions of the attributes of the entity. Now s might in fact refer to a ScienceStudent, which has additional attributes. The correct result will be obtained by first determining the minimum class of the value of s, and then accessing the definition of that class, all of which can be done without reference to secondary storage.

Now consider a third data model constraint that the minimum class of an entity be fixed over time. It would be very desirable from a modeling point of view to relax this constraint, so that a Person entity could start as a Child, and then become an Adult, ceasing to be a Child, but remaining a Person. Assuming that the minimum class would still be unique at any one time, how hard would it be to permit an entity to dynamically change its minimum class? First we have the problem that an entity's internal identifier occurs in many places throughout a database; *each* occurrence contains the minimum class

---

[5] For example, if the entity John is an instance of both the Student and Employee classes, it must also be an instance of a class (say Tutor) that is a specialization of both Student and Employee.

FIGURE 12.4
CUMULATIVE INTERACTION: AN EXAMPLE

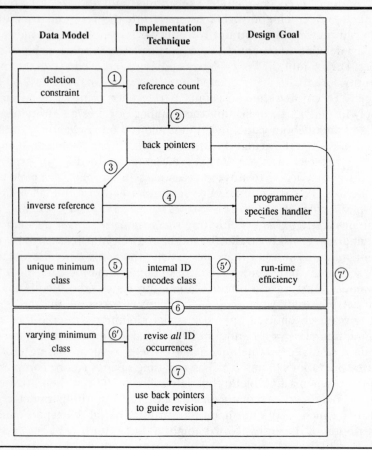

and would have to be changed (6 and 6′). However, this otherwise expensive operation becomes quite feasible if *inverse references* have been implemented— the system simply finds and modifies the appropriate internal identifiers (7 and 7′). So we have quite an intricate interaction among three data model constraints, their associated implementations, and design goals and decisions.

12.5.2 Static Typing

Can type checking for a semantic data model be performed statically? And what are the corresponding implications for implementation? Answers to these questions can be explained as the cumulative result of a sequence of decisions concerning the data model and design goals.

There is a conflict between increasing the expressiveness of the data model and meeting the design goal of having static typing. To illustrate, we compare the trade-offs made for two languages: a data-oriented language described by Cardelli [1988], and Taxis [Nixon, et al., 1987a]. Different design choices were made for each language. As we will see, each approach is consistent with its own goals, yet the consequences for static type checking and the features of the data models are quite different. We will compare the resulting data models with respect to

- ☐ specialization for transactions.
- ☐ specialization for attributes in the presence of side effects.
- ☐ the kinds of constraints allowed.
- ☐ whether levels of types can be collapsed.

Cardelli's design goals were to first and foremost provide reliability via static type checking; and then also allow as much data model expressiveness and implementation efficiency as possible, noting that these goals are conflicting. Cardelli's language is a multilevel type system, with a fixed number of levels (entities, types, and metatypes).

The goal of static checking leads to an "inverted" function specialization rule: to specialize a function, the return type is specialized but the parameter type is generalized:

```
define transactionClass f(p:A) returns B'
   isA   f(p:A') returns B
      (where A' isA A,   B' isA B)
```

The consequence is that a function that applies to an argument type without failing can also be applied to a more general argument type.

Cardelli motivates static type checking as being very desirable for designing systems that change over time: when a (revised) program is accepted by the type checker, the absence of type errors at run-time is (again) guaranteed.

On the other hand, there can be other (nontype) constraints, which may have to be checked at run-time. For example, suppose a data model provides integer subranges. If a type checker has found that the right-hand side of an assignment is of type integer, it may still not be possible to statically show that the expression is within a particular subrange to make the assignment to the target valid. In this case an assertion may have to be checked at run-time (This assumes that the data model treats subranges as all having the same type—integer—and not as separate subtypes). Of course, in many cases the amount of run-time checking can be minimized by utilizing information known during compilation.

In information systems, one frequently needs atomic transactions that update the (global) information base and then return a value, such as a routine to make a deposit and return the new bank account balance. While mathematical functions have no side effects, some programming languages and semantic data models allow functions with global side effects (as well as the local side effects of variable assignment). Whether written as functions, or as procedures with output parameters, these routines are still needed. Now consider a language that combines an assignment statement with Cardelli's function specialization rule. To maintain static typing, one seems to require that local variables not be specialized, *and* that parameters not be generalized.

```
define integerClass A   := { | 1..15 |}

define integerClass A' := { | 1..10 |} isA A

define transactionClass f(p:A') returns B with
  locals
    w:  { | 2..20 |}
  actions
    a1: w <- 2*p
  return ...
```

In the preceding general transaction, the assignment statement can be statically checked, since the range of the right-hand-side expression is within the range of the target variable. But in the specialized transaction below, the expression can be out of range, causing the assignment statement to fail at run-time. To cause this error, it suffices to generalize the parameter *or* specialize the local variable. Hence there are limitations on what can be expressed while maintaining static checking.

```
define transactionClass f(p:A) returns B' with
  locals
    w:  { | 6..20 |}
  actions
    a1: w <- 2*p
  return ...
```

When a data model provides more general integrity constraints (such as a constraint on the relationship between two attribute values of an entity), more run-time constraint checking may be needed. Again, some optimization is possible, as shown in Chung, et al. [1988].

Cardelli's language keeps type levels distinct. If, however, type levels are "collapsed" so that a variable can range over entities, types, and metatypes, then static typing is lost. In the design of the Taxis data model, it was felt desirable to provide certain special classes containing instances from two or more levels, such as AllClasses, which has all generic entities in a Taxis database as instances, including itself. Of course, there is an implementation cost associated with this feature.

The design goals for Taxis were to first provide expressiveness of modeling and then reliability and efficiency. Concerning reliability, it was decided

that *all* violations of type rules and other constraints must be detected, preferably at compilation, but otherwise at run-time.

In order to understand the Taxis rule for transaction specialization, and
the implications for type checking, consider some data model constraints
and design goals which were considered as essential parts of the language.
Recall the *structural isA constraint*, which requires subclasses to inherit the
attributes of their superclasses, and to have attribute values that are the same
or specializations of the general attribute value. In addition, the Taxis data
model requires the most specialized constraint to be applied to an entity. For
example, it is not possible to override constraints by saying something like:
"Update the age of John as if he were just a Person, even though he is also a
Student." A design goal was to apply constraints uniformly to all attributes,
regardless of the attribute value.

```
define entityClass Person with ...
    age: {| 0::120 |}
    friend: Person

define entityClass Student isA Person with ...
    age: {| 5::120 |}
    friend: Student
```

Here Person has an integer-valued attribute and an entity-valued one, each
of which is specialized in the definition of Student. Note that both the integer subrange and the specialized entity class are treated as true subclasses.
Now what are the implications for implementation of (static) type checking?
Again, assignment statements interact with specialization. Consider a transaction fragment:

```
locals
    x:   Person
    y:   Person
actions
    ...
    a2:  x.age <- y.age
```

If Person had no specializations, one could statically determine that the
attribute assignment operation will always work. But the local variable x could
also be a Student, in which case a run-time check would be needed to ensure
that the right-hand side evaluates to a smaller integer subrange suitable for
the restricted values for x.age. So the result of the data model constraints
and design goal is that implementation of type checking will require additional static analysis[6] and some run-time checks. Taxis does some type check-

---

[6]Thorough type checking for a single-parameter transaction could require repeated analysis
for each specialization of the parameter. For multiple-parameter transactions, however, the work
can grow as the cross product of the specializations of each parameter, causing an unexpected
computational cost.

ing statically (for example, ensuring that a general transaction is correct with respect to the general parameters, and that specialized actions are correct with respect to specialized parameters), while leaving some checking for run-time (such as checking general actions with respect to specialized parameters; see Nixon [1987a,b] for details). Attribute values which are entities (instead of integers) cause exactly the same problem, so that the same kind of run-time check will be needed for

```
x.friend <- y.friend
```

Another design goal was to apply the data model constraints uniform-ly, whether the attribute was stored or computed. The preceding age and friend are stored; suppose we want yearOfBirth to be a computed attribute of Person, with values in the range 1868 to 1988, and to be spe-cialized for Student:

```
define transactionClass yearOfBirth(p:Person)
   returns { | 1868::1988 |} ...
      return (1988 - p.age)

define transactionClass yearOfBirth(p:Student)
   returns { | 1868::1983 |} ...
```

Now what is the implication for the data model's specialization rule for transactions? For consistency with the stored definitions, the Student trans-action should be a specialization of the Person one. So specialized transac-tions in Taxis have specialized values for both the parameter (subject) value and the return (attribute) value:

```
define transactionClass f(p:A') returns B'
   isA  f(p:A) returns B
      (where A' isA A,  B' isA B)
```

We also claim that this corresponds naturally to taxonomic modeling where constraints are added or strengthened as more refined levels are defined in the isA hierarchy [Borgida, et al., 1984]. For example, consider a general transaction which, given a student, determines the student's major field of study:

```
define transactionClass MajorField(q:Student)
   returns Department
```

Now this could have a more specialized version for science students:

```
define transactionClass MajorField(q:ScienceStudent)
   returns ScienceDepartment
```

Note that static type checking for usage of parameters in expressions (such as the preceding p) will not be possible, for the same reasons discussed before for local variables.

An overall observation concerning trade-offs in the kinds of specialization provided by a semantic data model is that if attribute values (whether entity attributes, transaction parameters, or local variables) can be specialized, or parameter values generalized, *and* assignment statements (causing side effects) are provided, then it seems difficult to provide static type checking.

The cumulative interaction is not quite over, though. What happens when a run-time check fails? Suppose the design goal of avoiding fatal run-time errors (which would cause "down time" in the information systems designed) is coupled with the provision in the data model of exception handling facilities to deal with over-abstraction (e.g., Borgida, et al. [1984]). Standard operations (such as attribute value modification) can be modeled as transactions, and the associated error conditions (such as a value out of range) as exceptions. If the data model provides exception handling facilities, they can be used to deal with run-time failures. This has the nice feature that standard operations and user-defined transactions are treated uniformly, but can have the disadvantage of creating a plethora of built-in exceptions.[7]

12.5.3 Type Checking

The implementation of type checking interacts with decisions made about design goals and data model features. We give three examples.

Informative Messages

Type checking can interact with the design goal of providing informative messages regarding possible run-time errors. Suppose a data model permits a general class (say Person) which does not have a particular attribute (say advisor) defined, to have two or more specializations (say Student and Politician) which do. When checking usage of an attribute selection (say x.advisor where x is a Person), the compile-time message

    Persons do not have advisors

is quite misleading, and certainly less helpful than

    Many Persons do not have an advisor, but Students and
    Politicians do.

---

[7]There is also the difficult problem of finding the possible source(s) of run-time failure, and then retroactively correcting them. In the earlier example, for instance, the assignment of a value *to* y.age could be the real source of the problem.

To produce the more informative message, an implementation cannot simply analyze an expression with respect to the declared classes of variables; instead, it must also consider their subclasses. We feel the extra checking and reporting is needed even if code is not generated for the "possible error" case.[8] If, however, code is generated, some run-time type checking will be needed. We also note that the (compile-time) type checking mechanism would be further complicated by the possibility of having to propagate more than one value for an expression; in the example, the expression could have three distinct *values*: `illegal` (indicating no value at all), a `StudentAdvisor` or a `PoliticalAdvisor`. As Bancilhon [1988] points out, finding good support for multiple usage of attribute names is a main issue for object-oriented systems: "This is where the fusion between databases and programming languages is interesting and hard to do."

Iteration

Consider a data model that facilitates access to several levels of classes or types.[9] For example, the familiar iteration construct can be extended to retrieve all instances of a metaclass (e.g., `PersonClass`), which will access classes (such as `Person`, `Student`, etc.) and then to retrieve all the entities that are instances of each such class:

```
for each instance c of PersonClass do
    for each instance x of c do
        ... x   ... /* reference to entity */
        ... x.f ... /* call to function f with entity
                       x as argument */
```

Now when providing such a powerful feature, an important design goal will be to provide type safety; this may require restricting the data model. Observe that if all the instances of `PersonClass` are arranged in a lattice with a unique highest element—a "most general instance" (say `Person`)—then the outer iteration is comparable to

```
for each subclass c of Person do
    ...
```

We compare two approaches that are variations on this theme.

☐ The provision of statically typed polymorphism is very promising. Cardelli [1988] achieves this by constraining the language, using suitable definitions of specialization, and exploiting certain typesafe forms of polymorphism. One particular form of metatype offered by the language is the set of subtypes of a specified general type (here, `Person`),

---

[8] An implementation that requires static checking will not generate code when a run-time error is possible.

[9] Entities are arranged into classes, and classes are arranged into metaclasses.

which can be used as the parameter type of a function (here, f). Assume that the call to the function is safe when applied to instances of the general type. When combined with Cardelli's specialization rule for functions, we conclude that any instance of a specialization of the general type may safely be applied to the function. This is an example of subtype polymorphism.

☐ The data model can be constrained to require that every metaclass have a unique most general instance, as was done for Taxis [Nixon, et al., 1987a]. In this case, iteration through instances of a metaclass will always be comparable to iteration through subclasses of its most general instance. This approach can be applied to languages that are statically typed, as well as those that are not. When the language's function specialization rule (discussed previously) does not statically guarantee the safety of all function invocations (thus requiring run-time checks), reasonable compile-time checking can still be achieved by using the most general instance as a first approximation to the type structure of all the relevant classes.

Multiple Inheritance

For a data model supporting multiple inheritance, an important design goal is to ensure that attribute names not be ambiguous. Suppose Student and Employee both have an office attribute, but Person does not. Let the specialized class Tutor inherit the attribute from two classes, Student and Employee. Now asking for the office of a particular tutor will be ambiguous— do we want the office where a tutor studies or the one where that tutor works? An additional constraint on multiple inheritance, based on Schneider [1978], can be imposed: every attribute that is multiply inherited must have a unique, most generalized class where it is declared. Thus, for the office attribute to be associated with both Student and Employee, it must be declared in Person (or at least in one class somewhere higher than both Student and Employee). This constraint makes sure that there will be no ambiguity in interpreting an attribute or an attribute value, since the multiply inherited values have a common source. Of course there are implementation implications:

☐ If the Schneider constraint is not enforced, then the storage of attribute values may be harder to manage. If the previously mentioned "vertical splitting" method is used, an attribute value may be stored in more than place. For example, updating the office of a particular tutor may require changing the office value in the Employee tuple as well as the Student tuple.

☐ When the Schneider constraint is combined with the goal of providing informative messages concerning possible run-time errors (discussed previously), some subtle cases must be detected by a type checker (see Nixon, et al. [1987a] for details).

12.6 RESEARCH DIRECTIONS AND CONCLUSIONS

This chapter has reviewed some integration problems arising in the design and implementation of semantic data models. The obvious conclusion of this discussion is that we need to make a systematic study of the interactions between features, implementation techniques, and design goals, to simplify the job of the semantic data model designer and implementor. It is noteworthy that many of these concerns have also been raised for object-oriented databases [Bancilhon, 1988].

Some progress has already been made toward this goal. A partial list of topics that have been or currently are being addressed in the literature is given as follows.

Physical Storage Design

An important first step toward a performance theory for semantic data models has been made in Weddell [1987] where database performance analysis techniques are used. Weddell considers a semantic data model that permits multiple inheritance, and studies the problem of generating optimal physical designs. For example, he shows that the problem of obtaining an optimal alignment of records to permit static determination of the location of an attribute value, in a schema with horizontal splitting, is NP-hard, but that reasonable suboptimal solutions can be found relatively easily. His work focuses on main memory databases; of course many more problems arise in the context of a two-level storage implementation for a semantic data model.

Query Processing

For query optimization, there is a wealth of database results to draw on [Jarke & Koch, 1984]. However, generalization hierarchies can complicate the analysis, as they permit an entity to be an instance of more than one class. In addition, powerful facilities for traversing a database and its metaknowledge make it harder to narrow down the range of values to which an expression can refer, thus decreasing opportunities for optimization.

It would be desirable for semantic data model implementations to support recursive queries, with predictable performance. Since semantic networks are directed graphs, one approach would be to adapt recent work on a query language [Cruz, et al., 1988] that has been designed to handle a certain class of recursive queries over directed graphs. This work is notable for providing (*i*) a simple-to-use graph-based notation for expressing recursive queries, and (*ii*) results on query evaluation costs.

Long-Term Schema Changes

The ability to modify a schema over a period of time is useful in both a design environment [O'Brien, 1982, 1983; Mylopoulos, et al., 1986; Kambanis, 1988] and in a "production" system. Again, generalization hierarchies cause complications. Addition or removal of a class is relatively straightforward in the case of a "leaf" class (at the bottom of an isA hierarchy). However, in the case of a nonleaf class, one must consider the impact on its specialization classes [Banerjee, 1987]. When entity and transaction definitions are both changing, the impact on instances as well as on transactions should be minimized [Zdonik, 1987].

Modules

The provision of modules in a semantic data model presents a trade-off between the features of hiding information and of allowing uniform, global access to a database and its metaknowledge. In the context of object-oriented databases, Bancilhon [1988] has observed the trade-off between hiding information in modules and providing visibility of internal structures in a query language. Concerning separate compilation, the PS-algol project [Atkinson, et al., 1983, 1985] proposes using modules to improve the efficiency of separate compilation of persistent databases; recompilation can often be limited to a particular module.

Type Theory

As we have seen, the selection of data model features and design goals will directly influence the type system. This in turn has immediate implementation implications for type checking. We see this as an example of a trade-off between the expressiveness of a semantic data model and performance of its associated implementations. We see the need for continued development of formal type theories for semantic data models (e.g., Ait-Kaci [1984]). Not only will they clarify semantics, but they could also be used to aid proofs of correctness of the type checking component of a compiler, and using specification and verification techniques such as those in Gries [1981].

Concurrency Control

If a semantic data model supports concurrent execution of multiple, communicating, long-term processes which interact with an information base, as in the case of Taxis, the need for concurrency control arises. Consider the problem of avoiding concurrent access to an attribute value of an entity, while maximizing parallelism among transactions. Concurrency control for a large information base is a major problem. Relational databases can offer a variable granularity of locking, whose units are all "simple" parts (field, tuple, relation) of the one data structure offered, the relation. However, semantic data models have the problem that it is hard to ensure locality of reference of an expression. First, the *aggregation* abstraction mechanism interrelates several entities; as a result, not only an entity, but also all the other entities participating in any relationship with it, may also need to be locked. Second, the *specialization* abstraction mechanism (isA hierarchies), with the consequent overlap of class extensions, makes it harder to detect cases that increase possible concurrency, such as disjoint extensions. For both these reasons, it is harder in a semantic data model to lock a single, simple, small region of a data structure. So it is difficult to obtain a generic concurrency control algorithm that has reasonable performance on a large knowledge base, unless one can constrain the range of values to which an expression can refer.

Given a semantic data model that provides multiple inheritance, Rios-Zertuche [forthcoming] describes a concurrency control method that provides correct shared access to information. If the implementation strategy for physical storage management is to map a semantic data model to a relational database which provides physical locking at the tuple (or higher) level, Rios-Zertuche shows how to correctly map a concurrency control mechanism at the semantic data model level (based on two-phase locking) to the relational database level.

Performance Analysis

A major purpose of performance analysis is to answer questions concerning the size and complexity of intended application systems and the capacity and behavior of the implemented system. In order to obtain some acquaintance with what resources are needed to handle an application, a workload model should provide the expected number of input-output operations, and also some idea about the computational demands.

The problem of determining workload is expected to be much harder for semantic data models than for traditional data models, since the workload model must be more detailed in order to account for data model features that enhance expressive power but have not been directly addressed by previous performance analyses. Some of the features that we expect to cause difficulties include:

- ☐ An *isA* hierarchy, which skews the distribution of entities among classes, especially in the presence of multiple inheritance, making it harder to estimate class cardinalities.
- ☐ The referential integrity constraint, which induces additional hidden cost factors, such as the maintenance of back pointers, which must be considered in the workload model.
- ☐ Explicit integrity constraints, whose analysis is complicated by the presence of multiple inheritance. When considering a constraint that relates two classes, the model of system load must be kept to a manageable size, while accounting for the entities that are shared by two classes (and need only be fetched once from the database during constraint enforcement) [Chung, 1988; Rios-Zertuche, forthcoming].
- ☐ Allowing several *prerequisite conditions* per transaction, which implies that they can all be checked in parallel. But spawning a large number of independent subtransactions makes it hard to estimate the number of active processes at any one time, thus making system workload more difficult to estimate.

One of the benefits of performance analysis is the ability to compare difference implementation strategies. For example, a semantic data model can be mapped to a standard relational database system or to specifically designed physical storage structures. Rios-Zertuche [forthcoming] is able to compare the execution costs expected to be obtained for both strategies.

Two basic approaches to development of semantic data models have been identified [Brodie & Mylopoulos, 1985]. One is the evolutionary approach, in which advanced features are added *incrementally* to a programming language (e.g., Galileo [Albano, et al., 1985b]) or to a relational database management system (e.g., POSTGRES [Stonebraker & Rowe, 1986]). The other is the revolutionary approach, which attempts to tightly integrate powerful modeling techniques from artificial intelligence with database management technologies, without making an a priori commitment to existing data models or database implementation techniques (see the discussion in Brodie & Mylopoulos [1986]). In either case, interaction issues need to be addressed.

Acknowledgements

We would like to thank Lawrence Chung, David Lauzon, Alex Borgida, Daniel Rios-Zertuche, John Kambanis and other present and former members of the Taxis project for continued advice and assistance in the preparation of this chapter. We also thank Raj Verma, Isabel Cruz, and Matthias Jarke for helpful comments and discussions. The Taxis project has been supported by an ongoing Operating Grant to John Mylopoulos as well as a three-year Strategic Grant from the Natural Sciences and Engineering Research Council of Canada.

References

Abiteboul, Serge, and Hull, Richard, (1984). "IFO: A Formal Semantic Database Model," *Proceedings of the Third ACM SIGACT-SIGMOD Symposium on Principles of Database Systems*, Waterloo, Ontario, April 2–4, pp. 119–132.

Ait-Kaci, Hassan, (1984). "Type Subsumption as a Model of Computation," In Kerschberg, Larry (ed.), *Proceedings of the First International Workshop on Expert Database Systems*, Kiawah Island, SC, October 24–27, pp. 124–150.

Albano, Antonio, (1985a). "Conceptual Languages: A Comparison of ADAPLEX, Galileo and Taxis," *Proceedings of the Workshop on Knowledge Base Management Systems*, Crete, June, pp. 343–356.

Albano, Antonio, Cardelli, Luca, and Orsini, Renzo, (1985b). "Galileo: A Strongly Typed, Interactive Conceptual Language," *ACM TODS*, Vol. 10, No. 2, August.

Atkinson, M. P., Bailey, P. J., Chisholm, K. J., Cockshott W. P., and Morrisson, R., (1983). "An approach to persistent programming," *Computer Journal*, Vol. 26, No. 4, November.

Atkinson, Malcolm P., and Morrison, Ronald, (1985). *Integrated Persistent Programming Systems*. Persistent Programming Research Project Report 19, University of Glasgow, Dept. of Computing Science.

Atkinson, Malcolm P., and Buneman, O. Peter, (1987). "Types and Persistence in Database Programming Languages," *Computing Surveys*, Vol. 19, No. 2, June, pp. 105–190.

Bancilhon, Francois, (1988). "Object-Oriented Database Systems," *Proceedings, Seventh ACM Symposium on Principles of Database Systems*, Austin, Tex., March, pp. 152–162.

Banerjee, Jay, Kim, Won, Kim, Hyoung-Joo, and Korth, Henry F., (1987). "Semantics and Implementation of Schema Evolution in Object-Oriented Databases," In Dayal, Umeshwar, and Traiger, Irv (ed.), *ACM SIGMOD '87, Proceedings of Association for Computing Machinery Special Interest Group on Management of Data, 1987 Annual Conference*, San Francisco, CA, May 27–29, 1987, *SIGMOD Record*, Vol. 16, No. 3, December, pp. 311–322.

Barron, David William (ed.), (1981). *Pascal—The Language and its Implementation*. Chichester: John Wiley & Sons.

Borgida, Alexander, (1981). "On the Definition of Specialization Hierarchies for Procedures," *Proceedings of the Seventh International Joint Conference on Artificial Intelligence*, Vancouver, B.C., August 24–28, pp. 254–256.

Borgida, Alexander, Mylopoulos, John, and Wong, Harry K. T., (1984). "Generalization/Specialization as a Basis for Software Specification," In Brodie, Michael L., Mylopoulos, John, and Schmidt, Joachim W. (eds.), *On Conceptual Modelling: Perspectives from Artificial Intelligence, Databases, and Programming Languages*, New York: Springer-Verlag, pp. 87–117.

Borgida, Alexander, (1985a). "Features of Languages for the Development of Information Systems at the Conceptual Level," *IEEE Software*, Vol. 2, No. 1, January, pp. 63–73.

Borgida, Alexander, (1985b). "Language Features for Flexible Handling of Exceptions in Information Systems," *ACM TODS*, Vol. 10, No. 4, December, pp. 565–603.

Brodie, Michael L., and Mylopoulos, John, (1985). "Knowledge Bases and Databases: Semantic vs. Computational Theories of Information," In Ariav, Gad, and Clifford, Jim (eds.), *New Directions for Database Systems*, Ablex Publishing.

Brodie, Michael L., and Mylopoulos, John (eds.), (1986). *On Knowledge Base Management Systems*, New York: Springer-Verlag.

Butler, Margaret H., (1987). "Storage Reclamation in Object Oriented Database Systems," In Dayal, Umeshwar, and Traiger, Irv (eds.), *ACM SIGMOD '87, Proceedings of Association for Computing Machinery Special Interest Group on Management of Data, 1987 Annual Conference*, San Francisco, CA, May 27–29, 1987, *SIGMOD Record*, Vol. 16, No. 3, December, pp. 410–425.

Cardelli, Luca, (1988). "Types for Data-Oriented Languages," In Schmidt, J. W., Ceri, S., and Missikof, M., (eds.), *Advances in Database Technology—EDBT '88*, International Conference on Extending Database Technology, Venice, Italy, March 1988, *Proceedings, Lecture Notes in Computer Science*, No. 303, Berlin: Springer-Verlag, pp. 1–15.

Chan, Arvola, Danberg, Sy, Fox, Stephen, Lin, Wen-Te K., Nori, Anil, and Ries, Daniel, (1982). "Storage and Access Structures to Support a Semantic Data Model," *Proceedings, Eighth International Conference on Very Large Data Bases*, Mexico City, September 8–10, pp. 122–130.

Chung, Kyungwha Lawrence, (1984). "An Extended Taxis Compiler," M.Sc. Thesis, Dept. of Computer Science, University of Toronto, January. Also CSRG Technical Note 37, 1984.

Chung, K. Lawrence, Rios-Zertuche, Daniel, Nixon, Brian A., and Mylopoulos, John, (1988). "Process Management and Assertion Enforcement for a Semantic Data Model," In Schmidt, J. W., Ceri S., and Missikof, M. (eds.), *Advances in Database Technology — EDBT '88*, International Conference on Extending Database Technology, Venice, Italy, March 1988, *Proceedings. Lecture Notes in Computer Science*, No. 303. Berlin: Springer-Verlag, pp. 469–487.

Cruz, Isabel F., Mendelzon, Alberto O., and Wood, Peter T., (1988). "G$^+$: Recursive Queries Without Recursion," In Kerschberg, Larry (ed.), *Expert Database Systems*, Proceedings of the Second International Conference on Expert Database Systems, Tysons Corners, Va., April 25–27, pp. 355–368.

Dahl, Ole-Johan, and Nygaard, Kristen, (1966). "SIMULA — an ALGOL-Based Simulation Language," *CACM*, Vol. 9, No. 9, September, pp. 671–678.

Elliott, W. David, (1982). "On Proving the Absence of Execution Errors," Technical Report CSRG–141, Computer Systems Research Group, University of Toronto, March. Also Ph.D. Thesis, Dept. of Computer Science, 1980.

Goldberg, Adele, and Robson, David, (1983). *SMALLTALK–80: The Language and its Implementation*, Reading, Mass.: Addison-Wesley.

Goodenough, John B., (1975). "Exception Handling: Issues and a Proposed Notation," *CACM*, Vol. 18, No. 12, December, pp. 683–696.

Gries, David, (1981). *The Science of Programming*, New York: Springer-Verlag.

Hammer, Michael, and McLeod, Dennis, (1981). "Database Description with SDM: A Semantic Database Model," *ACM TODS*, Vol. 6, No. 3, September, pp. 351–386.

Hoare, C. A. R., (1978). "Communicating Sequential Processes," *CACM*, Vol. 21, No. 8, August, pp. 666–677.

Houtsma, Maurice A. W., and Balsters, Herman, (1988). *Formalizing the Data and Knowledge Model*, Memorandum INF–88–23, University of Twente, Dept. of Computer Science, July.

Hull, Richard, and King, Roger, (1987). "Semantic Database Modeling: Survey, Applications, and Research Issues," *Computing Surveys*, Vol. 19, No. 3, September, pp. 201–260.

Jarke, Matthias, and Koch, Jürgen, (1984). "Query Optimization in Database Systems," *Computing Surveys*, Vol. 16, No. 2, June, pp. 111–152.

Kambanis, John, (1988). "An Information Systems Design Environment Based on a Semantic Data Model," Technical Report CSRI–210, Computer Systems Research Institute, University of Toronto, June.

Mylopoulos, John and Wong, Harry K. T. (1980a). "Some Features of the Taxis Data Model," *Sixth International Conference on Very Large Data Bases, Proceedings*, Montreal, October, pp. 399–410.

Mylopoulos, John, Bernstein, Philip A., and Wong, Harry K. T., (1980b). "A Language Facility for Designing Database-Intensive Applications," *ACM TODS*, Vol. 5, No. 2, June, pp. 185–207.

Mylopoulos, John, Borgida, Alex, Greenspan, Sol, Meghini Carlo, and Nixon, Brian, (1986). "Knowledge Representation in the Software Development Process: A Case Study," In Winter, H. (ed.), *Artificial Intelligence and Man-Machine Systems*, Lecture

Notes in Control and Information Sciences, No. 80. Berlin: Springer-Verlag, pp. 23–44.

Nixon, Brian Andrew, (1983). "A Taxis Compiler," M.Sc. Thesis, Dept. of Computer Science, University of Toronto, April. Also CSRG Technical Note 33, May 1983.

Nixon, Brian A., Chung, K. Lawrence, Lauzon, David, Borgida, Alex, Mylopoulos, John, and Stanley, Martin, (1987a). *Design of a Compiler for a Semantic Data Model*, Technical Note CSRI—44, Computer Systems Research Institute, University of Toronto, May. Also in Schmidt, J. W., and Thanos, C. (eds.), *Foundations of Knowledge Base Management*, Berlin: Springer-Verlag, 1989, pp. 293–343.

Nixon, Brian A., Chung, K. Lawrence, Lauzon, David, Borgida, Alex, Mylopoulos, John, and Stanley, Martin, (1987b). "Implementation of a Compiler for a Semantic Data Model: Experiences with Taxis," In Dayal, Umeshwar, and Traiger, Irv (eds.), *ACM SIGMOD '87, Proceedings of Association for Computing Machinery Special Interest Group on Management of Data, 1987 Annual Conference*, San Francisco, May 27–29, 1987, *SIGMOD Record*, Vol. 16, No. 3, December, pp. 118–131.

O'Brien, Patrick, (1982). "Taxied: An Integrated Interactive Design Environment for Taxis," M.Sc. Thesis, Department of Computer Science, University of Toronto, October. Also CSRG Technical Note 29.

O'Brien, Patrick D., (1983). "An Integrated Interactive Design Environment for Taxis," *Proceedings, SOFTFAIR: A Conference on Software Development Tools, Techniques, and Alternatives*, Arlington, Va. July 25–28. Silver Spring, MD: IEEE Computer Society Press, pp. 298–306.

Peckham, Joan, and Maryanski, Fred, (1988). "Semantic Data Models," *Computing Surveys*, Vol. 20, No. 3, September, pp. 153–189.

Rios-Zertuche, Daniel, M.Sc. Thesis, Dept. of Computer Science, University of Toronto, forthcoming.

Sarin, S. K., (1977). "Automatic Synthesis of Efficient Procedures for Database Integrity Checking," M.Sc. Thesis, Dept. of Electrical Engineering and Computer Science, Massachusetts Institute of Technology, September.

Schneider, Peter F., (1978). "Organization of Knowledge in a Procedural Semantic Network Formalism," Technical Report 115, Dept. of Computer Science, University of Toronto, February.

Smith, John Miles, and Smith, Diane C. P., (1977). "Database Abstractions: Aggregation and Generalization," *ACM TODS*, Vol. 2, No. 2, June, pp. 105–133.

Smith, John M., Fox, Stephen A., and Landers, Terry A., (1983). "ADAPLEX: Rationale and Reference Manual," Technical Report CCA–83–08, Computer Corporation of America, Cambridge, Mass, May.

Stonebreaker, Michael, and Rowe, Lawrence A., (1986). "The Design of POSTGRES," In Zaniolo, Carlo (ed.), *Proceedings of ACM SIGMOD '86 International Conference on Management of Data*, Washington, D.C., May 28–30, 1986, *SIGMOD Record*, Vol. 15, No. 2, June, pp. 340–355.

Tsur, Shalom, and Zaniolo, Carlo, (1984). "An Implementation of GEM—Supporting a Semantic Data Model on a Relational Back-end," In Yormark, Beatrice (ed.), *SIGMOD '84 Proceedings*, Boston, June 18–21, 1984, *SIGMOD Record*, Vol. 14, No. 2, pp. 286–295.

Weddell, Grant E., (1987). "Physical Design and Query Optimization for a Semantic Data Model (assuming memory residence)," Ph.D. Thesis, Dept. of Computer Science,

University of Toronto, April. Also Technical Report CSRI-198, Computer Systems Research Institute, University of Toronto.

Wong, Harry K. T., (1981). "Design and Verification of Interactive Information Systems Using TAXIS," Technical Report CSRG–129, Computer Systems Research Group, University of Toronto, April. Also Ph.D. Thesis, Department of Computer Science, 1983.

Wortman, David B., (1979). "On Legality Assertions in Euclid," *IEEE Transactions on Software Engineering*, Vol. SE–5, No. 4, July, pp. 359–367.

Zaniolo, C., (1983). "The Database Language GEM," *Proceedings, 1983 ACM SIGMOD Conference on Management of Data*, May, pp. 207–218.

Zdonik, Stanley B., (1987). "Can Objects Change Type? Can Type Objects Change?" *Proceedings of the Workshop on Database Programming Languages*, Roscoff, France, September.

Zisman, Michael D., (1978). "Use of Production Systems for Modeling Concurrent Processes," In Waterman, D. A., and Hayes-Roth, Frederick (eds.), *Pattern-Directed Inference Systems*, New York: Academic Press, pp. 53–68.

PART III

OBJECT-ORIENTED SYSTEMS AND PERSISTENCE

CHAPTER 13

SHARING, PERSISTENCE, AND OBJECT-ORIENTATION: A DATABASE PERSPECTIVE

Setrag Khoshafian
Patrick Valduriez

13.1 INTRODUCTION

In this paper we clarify different aspects of persistence and sharing in an object-oriented framework from a database perspective. These terms (including object orientation) mean different things to different people. The AI, database, object-oriented, and programming languages communities have been using these concepts in a conflicting and sometimes contradictory manner.

Sharing

In a database framework "sharing" relates to synchronizing concurrent accesses to objects to ensure the consistency of information stored in the database. The database is accessed and updated through transactions, where a transaction is a program that is either executed entirely or not executed at all (i.e., transactions are *atomic*). Serializability of transactions is required [Eswaran, et al., 1976; Papadimitriou, 1979], and is typically achieved through locking. Shared locks on an object allow multiple "readers" to access it, whereas an exclusive lock grants access to only one user ("writer"). Objects that are accessed concurrently by multiple users (transactions) will henceforth be called *concurrently shared objects*.

In an object-oriented framework "sharing" relates to the support and maintenance of the *references* of the shared object [Rentsch, 1982]. A reference to an object implies (shared) ownership by all referencing objects. An object that becomes nonaccessible from any other object is "garbaged" and should be removed from the object space [Lieberman & Hewitt, 1983; Ungar, 1984]. So unlike the database perspective, where the "users" of an object could be thought of as concurrently executing transactions, the "users" in the object-oriented world are themselves objects *owning* or *referencing* the same shared entity. Objects that are accessible (and hence "shared") by other objects will be called *referentially shared objects*.

Persistence

A similar confusion exists with the term *persistent*. The term is rarely used in traditional database literature. The intended meaning is that an object will *persist* after the termination of the program that manipulates it. The classic example of persistent programming languages is PS-Algol [Atkinson et al., 1983]. The most important contribution of PS-Algol is the demonstration that persistence is orthogonal to the type of an object. In other words, *any* type of object should be allowed to persist. This is in contrast to, say, the Pascal language, where only certain data types (such as files of restricted record types) can be persistent. Other examples of persistent languages are Amber [Cardelli, 1984] and Galileo [Albano, et al., 1985]. Similar to PS-Algol, these languages, though allowing any type to persist, do not handle in their current implementation transaction concurrency and recovery [Albano, et al., 1986]. The "persistence" provided by these languages would seem rather naïve and weak from a database perspective!

From a database perspective, the problem of "persistence" primarily deals with the resilience of the database to failures. Thus, a whole range of *recovery* strategies have been developed for three types of failures [Gray, 1978]:

1. *Transaction Failures*: usually caused by concurrent transactions conflict-ing in their accesses to the "shared" database. When such conflicts are detected, the DBMS aborts one or more of the conflicting transactions. (Note that the assumption here is that the persistent objects are also concurrently shared.) Transaction failures could also arise due to error conditions in the transaction execution.
2. *System Failures*: usually caused by software errors in the operating system or the DBMS or by hardware failure other than the disk media.
3. *Media Failures*: usually caused by hard disk crashes.

There exists a fundamental relationship between sharing and persistence in databases. Transaction updates of the database must persist. But since the persistent database is concurrently accessed (i.e., it is shared), we must serialize the execution of the transactions. Recovery techniques typically require the use of logs [Gray, 1978]. These logs record before and after images of updated objects. If a transaction must be aborted due to conflicts, its effects are *undone* using the log. The log is also used for system and media recovery. Another technique to achieve high resilience is through data replication as in the Tandem transaction processing systems [Borr, 1981]. Some attempts have been made to extend programming languages such as PS-Algol, to provide support of concurrent transactions and deal with transaction failures [Krablin, 1985].

Most commercially available DBMS's attempt to deal with all three types of failures. In fact, the recovery manager and the exception handler represent a substantial part of the DBMS code. For this reason the programming language perspective on *persistence* in terms of the data being maintained on secondary storage after a program terminates, appears as rather naïve from a database perspective.

Object Orientation

Even the notion of object orientation has different connotations and meaning for the different communities.

From a database perspective, object orientation is a rather novel concept being incorporated in recent database data models. Dittrich [1986] has identified three levels of object orientation for DBMS's:

1. *Structurally object-oriented*: implies the capability of representing arbitrarily structured complex objects.
2. *Operationally object-oriented*: implies the ability to operate on complex objects in their entirety, through generic complex object operators.
3. *Behaviorally object-oriented*: implies typing in the object-oriented programming sense (classes), with the specification of the types and operations (messages) which can manipulate objects of the given types, without the caller of the operator knowing the internal structure of the object being manipulated (data abstraction).

Thus a whole range of data models, such as non–first normal form relational models [Abiteboul and Bidoit, 1984], semantic data models [King & McLeod, 1985], entity relationship data models [Chen, 1976], functional data models [Shipman, 1981; Kuklarni & Atkinson, 1986], logical data models [Kuper and Vardi, 1984], and data models manipulating complex objects [Bancilhon and Khoshafian, 1986], fall into the first and sometimes the second categories. To call some of the structurally object-oriented models "object-oriented" might sound *naïve* or even *heretical* by some standards such as the one given in [Cardelli and Wegner, 1985] which defines object orientation through the formula:

object oriented = data abstractions + object types + type inheritance

This is closer to behavioral object orientation, although other perspectives would emphasize the notion of "messages" as being fundamental to the object-oriented paradigm [Stefik & Bobrow, 1986]. In fact, object-oriented languages such as Smalltalk-80 [Goldberg & Robson, 1983], and C++ [Stroustrup, 1986] possess all three features, with strong emphasis on behavioral object orientation.

Integration and Differentiation

Although there are many attempts to incorporate database features (such as persistence) in programming languages and object-oriented systems, and object-oriented as well as general purpose programming power in database data models, there are still fundamental differences in perspectives and priorities. The fundamental drive directing database research is high *performance concurrent transaction processing* for large *disk-based databases*. The fundamental drive directing the nondatabase communities is *the computational power of the underlying model* as well as *high performance for RAM-based, mostly CPU bound execution environments*. This is not to say that database research is not concerned with computational power nor that AI, object-oriented, and programming languages research is not concerned with performance of disk accesses. The point here is that the *overall* emphasis of databases has been performance in disk-based systems for concurrent transactions. On the other hand, the primary concern and justification of the design of novel languages and compilers is computational power and performance in a RAM-based, CPU-bound environment.

An interesting arena where these differences show up quite clearly is the special-purpose machine architectures, microcode implementations, as well as software algorithms and technologies developed for the different paradigms. For AI, the special purpose architectures as well as the software algorithms and technologies tend to be *language-oriented*. Thus, LISP machines attempt to support symbolic list processing through tagged architectures [Moon, 1985]. Other features provided by these LISP machines include run-time type checking, large virtual address spaces, and efficient garbage collection [Creeger, 1983; Hayashi, et al., 1983]. For object-oriented languages, the microcoded implementation of Smalltalk-80 on the Dorado provides interpretation of the language with good performance [Deutsch, 1983]. Special-purpose architectures for Smalltalk-80 such as Swamp [Lewis, et al., 1986], which, among other features, supports Smalltalk contexts directly in hardware, have demonstrated even better performance. These architectures and technologies demonstrate that the main problems being dealt with are primarily processing (CPU) but sometimes primary storage (RAM) bottlenecks.

In contrast, the main bottleneck of DBMS's is the I/O [Boral & DeWitt, 1983] (i.e., the secondary storage accesses). It should be noted that DBMS applications usually deal with much larger disk-resident persistent databases. An extreme case in point is the United Airlines Apollo reservation system based on IBM's Transaction Processing Facility, which uses 135 IBM 3380 disk drives and services 55,000 terminals [Krause, 1985]! Hence, many of the proposed Database Machine architectures attempt to alleviate the I/O bottleneck through increasing the I/O bandwidth. Similar to the commercially available Teradata machine architecture [Neches, 1985], the de facto architecture of these machines is a collection of processing units that "share nothing" [Stonebraker, 1986] and each of which has its own disk (or I/O subsystem). The persistent data itself is horizontally partitioned (*declustered*) [Livny, et al., 1987] across the disks of the processing units. A fast interconnection network provides the inter-processing unit communication. Examples of shared nothing database machine architectures currently investigated by researchers are GAMMA [DeWitt, et al., 1986], GRACE [Fushimi, et al., 1986] and MBDS [Demurjian, et al., 1986]. It is important to emphasize that unlike many AI and object-oriented architectures, the processing elements of these database machines are not special purpose. Off-the-shelf, state-of-the-art microprocessors are used (as is the case with the Intel 80286 based Teradata).

Organization of the Paper

In this paper we present our database-oriented perspective, through lessons learned from our experiences in the design and ongoing implementation of a prototype of a structurally and operationally object-oriented database system. For each of the concepts presented in the subsequent sections, we shall explain different aspects of sharing, persistence, and object-orientation. It will be shown that referential and concurrent sharing can occur both in the system and user spaces. Different types of persistent objects characterized by the duration of the persistence will also be described.

The rest of the paper is organized as follows: in Section 13.2 we present aspects of sharing and persistence in the conceptual and internal model of our DBMS; in Section 13.3 we describe sharing and persistence in the transaction, session, and execution environments of the DBMS. In Section 13.4, we demonstrate the storage and representation of the referentially and concurrently shared objects. In Section 13.5 we give the summary.

13.2 SHARING AND PERSISTENCE IN THE OBJECT MODELS

At a gross level, the architecture of our DBMS consists of a *conceptual layer* and an *internal layer*. The conceptual model is the interface to the conceptual layer and consists of a language and a data (knowledge) representation which together constitute the user interface and programming environment. In other words, user transactions will be written in the conceptual language, manipulating objects in the persistent database, which is structured according to the conceptual schema. The conceptual layer is responsible for the in-RAM representation and manipulation of the conceptual objects.

The internal model, on the other hand, is the interface of the internal layer. This layer is responsible for the physical secondary storage representation of the conceptual objects and provides, among other things, accelerators (such as B-trees) for fast associative accesses to the stored objects.

In this section we discuss persistence, sharing, and object representation in the conceptual model, as well as some aspects of the conceptual to internal mapping.

The conceptual object model described here is that of FAD [Bancilhon, et al., 1987]. FAD has a rich set of operations and structures, and supports the notion of object identity [Khoshafian & Copeland, 1986]. FAD is structurally and operationally object-oriented. In FAD, objects are defined as follows:

Assume we are given a set of attribute names A, a set of identifiers I, and a collection of base atomic types.

An *object* o is a triple (*identifier, type, value*) where the identifier is in I, the type is in (*atom, set, tuple*), and the value is one of the following:

- ☐ If the object is of type *atom*, then the value is an element of a user-defined domain of atoms.
- ☐ If the object is of type *set*, then the value is a set of distinct identifiers from I.
- ☐ If the object is of type *tuple*, then the value is of the form $[a1 : i1, a2 : i2, \ldots, an : in]$ where the ais are distinct attribute names, and the ijs are identifiers. ij is the value taken by the object on attribute aj. It is denoted $o.aj$.

An *Object System* is a set of objects. An object system is *consistent* "iff" (i) no two distinct objects have the same identifiers (unique identifier assumption) and (ii) for each identifier present in the system there is an object with this identifier (no dangling identifier assumption).

The notion of *persistence* is also built in FAD through a **database** root (where **database** is a reserved key word of FAD). Every object "reachable" from **database** is persistent. More specifically, objects reachable from **database** are defined recursively as follows:

1. **database** is reachable from itself.
2. If O is a set object reachable from **database**, then so is every o in O.
3. If O is a tuple object reachable from **database**, then so is $O.a$ for all a.

Objects not reachable from **database** are called *transient*. In order to avoid confusion with other sorts of persistent objects, the conceptual FAD objects reachable from the **database** root will be called *recoverable* objects.

Note that since FAD supports object identity, referential sharing of objects is possible. In fact, objects can be shared in either the persistent conceptual object space or the transient object space.

13.2.1 Graphical Representation

An object system can be represented by a *graph*. The graph of an object system is defined as follows.

1. Each object is represented by a node, labeled by its type. Atomic types are labeled by their value. A node representing a set type is denoted by *. A node representing a tuple type is denoted by •.
2. There is an arc labeled a from node n to node n' if node n represents object o and node n' represents object o' and object o is of type *tuple* and $o.a$ is the identifier of o'.
3. There is an unlabeled arc from node n to node n' if node n represents object o, and node n' represents object o' and object o is of type *set* and the identifier of object o' is in the value of object o.

Consistent object systems are represented by graphs such that from each tuple node there is at most one arc with a given label and terminal nodes (i.e., nodes that do not have any out arcs) are either empty set nodes, empty tuple nodes, or atom nodes.

The following example gives the graphical representation of an object where $s1$ and $s2$ are set identifiers, and $t1$, $t2$, $t3$, and $t4$ are tuple identifiers. To simplify the presentation, we shall not indicate the identifiers of the atomic object in the graphical representations.

This graphical representation clearly illustrates referential sharing of objects. Note that both persistent and transient objects can have referential object sharing. Needless to say, object identity is the feature that enables this type of object sharing.

13.2.2 Mapping to the Internal Model

In our implementation, transactions expressed in FAD are compiled into the language of the internal layer. Programs in this language manipulate *stored physical* objects which correspond to and are determined by the conceptual

FIGURE 13.1
CONCEPTUAL OBJECT REPRESENTATION

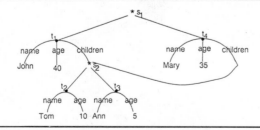

objects of FAD. The recoverable objects of the conceptual layer are actually stored as recoverable files, tuples, sets, and so on in the internal layer. An important feature of the internal model is the fact that it is "value based." This means objects are identified through "key" attributes, such as the *EmployeeNumber* in an *Employees* relation, or *DepartmentName* in a *Departments* relation. Furthermore, the internal layer supports the direct representation and storage of complex objects (similar to some implementations of non–first normal form relational models [Deppisch, et al., 1986]). Similar to the conceptual model, the objects in the internal model are constructed through sets, tuples, and atomic objects. *Surrogates*, which are system-generated unique identifiers independent of physical addressability or content [Khoshafian & Copeland, 1986] are introduced to support the conceptual model's identity. Thus, one possible representation of the conceptual object in Fig. 13.1 is given in Fig. 13.2, where *S1*, *S2*, *T1*, *T2*, *T3*, and *T4* are surrogates.

In fact, there are three important aspects of the compilation process from the conceptual to the internal layer:

1. Implementation of identity through the introduction of surrogate attributes for sets and tuples as shown in Fig. 13.2.

2. Incorporation of the algorithms for mapping graph-structured objects in the conceptual model to trees or flat files in the physical layer. Therefore a *referentially shared object* in the conceptual layer will be either decomposed and both "owners" of the object will be given links (logical or physical) to the shared object, *or* the object will be stored with one of the parents and the other parent(s) will be given link(s) to the shared object as in Fig. 13.2. The conceptual to internal mapping strategy specifies the actual algorithms and strategies for supporting the conceptual object sharing in the internal layer.

3. The internal layer supports accelerators for enhanced associative accesses to the physical objects. These accelerators consist of B^+ trees, hash tables, and so on. Furthermore, *multiple copies* of the same set

FIGURE 13.2
INTERNAL OBJECT REPRESENTATION

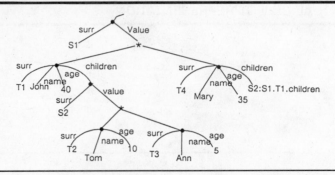

object might exist, where each copy is *clustered* (i.e., sorted or hashed) on a different attribute. Given these representation and clustering schemes, the compiler attempts to generate optimal [Selinger, et al., 1979] internal code for a given conceptual transaction.

In Section 13.4, we shall demonstrate the different structures supporting transient and persistent objects in the internal as well as conceptual object spaces, and show how referentially and concurrently shared objects are manipulated in these spaces.

13.3 TRANSACTIONS, SESSIONS, AND THE EXECUTION ENVIRONMENT

In this section we describe different aspects of persistence and sharing in the transaction workspace, sessions, and the execution environment.

13.3.1 Transactions

A *transaction* is a program that (1) maintains a database in a consistent state and (2) is either executed entirely or not executed at all (i.e., transactions are *atomic*). Underlying this definition are (*i*) a database that is persistent (in fact *recoverable*) and (*ii*) a set of integrity constraints which should not be violated by the transaction updates. In this paper we have not concerned ourselves with integrity constraints.

With each transaction we associate a transaction *workspace*. These workspaces contain images of database objects as well as data structures which are generated by the DBMS and which persist for the duration of the transaction. The concurrency control/recovery system uses a *shadowing* [Lorie, 1977] mechanism for the persistent database. This means database objects updated by the transaction will be shadowed and maintained (persist) in the workspace of the transaction since the transaction needs to see the effects of its updates in subsequent accesses. The scheme is similar to the one used in Gemstone [Maier, et al., 1986]. There are also system structures (i.e., structures generated by the DBMS on behalf of the transaction) which only persist for the duration of the transaction. One example is the data structure, which maintains the correspondence between the shadow and persistent pages. Another example is the list of transaction identifiers which could potentially conflict with the currently executing transaction.

As far as persistence is concerned, the database is resilient to transaction, system, and media failures. Transaction failures arise due to conflicting accesses to concurrently shared objects by different transactions. A certification-based [Kung & Robinson, 1981] concurrency control synchronizer aborts one of the conflicting transactions. The user interacting with the system is informed of the abort and might choose to retry (reexecute) the transaction.

13.3.2 Sessions

A user interacts with transaction management systems in *sessions*. Simply stated, a session refers to the duration that a user is logged into the database management system. During the session a certain environment (expressed in *session variables*) is established and the user submits one or more transactions to the DBMS in this environment.

Some examples of session variables are the terminal/window parameters of the user interface, statistics on number of transactions executed and duration of each, as well as trace options set and reset at different points of time during the sessions. These session variables are shared by all the transactions that get executed during the session, and persist for the duration of the session.

As for running transactions within a session, three types of interaction schemes are feasible. We present these schemes as follows in increasing order of "optimism" in concurrent accesses.

1. *Checkout-Checkin*: in this scheme, after starting a session, the user submits simple transactions that retrieve "large" objects from the database, *explicitly checking out objects from the database*. Two modes are supported: Shared and Exclusive. In shared mode the user gets a version of the objects that could change without notification. In exclusive mode the user prevents access (and hence changes) to the checked out objects. If some of the desired objects are checked out by someone else, the transaction is aborted. The user will manipulate the object and, after performing all the necessary updates to them, the objects will be checked in through a transaction. This scheme is commonly used in CAD/CAM databases.

2. Transaction Programs: with this scheme, whenever transactions (which are typically more complicated than accesses to single objects) need be executed to get results or update persistent (recoverable) objects, they are submitted in **Begin TX ... End TX** delimited programs. If the transaction succeeds, its results are returned to the user. If the transaction fails, an "aborted" message is returned.

3. Interactive Commits: the most "optimistic" approach is to have conceptual object space "buffers" in the workspace of the user. The workspace will contain both user- (or session-) generated temporary *and* persistent objects. Every now and then a user will submit a "commit" request. The system will either reject the request (due to conflicts) or accept it, in which case the transaction will be committed.

The main difference between (1) and (2) is that with the first scheme the checked-out objects are manipulated locally at the user's site (e.g., a personal workstation). With the second scheme the transaction manipulating the objects is executed at the site(s) of the DBMS (e.g., a Database Machine).

Note that (3) (which is the scheme used in Gemstone [Maier, et al., 1986]) is the most optimistic since the user might end up doing a lot of interactive work, attempt a commit, and then be told that the commit can not go through due to conflicts with other transactions.

13.3.3 The Execution Environment

Sessions are created in the execution environment of the DBMS whose interface, among other things, provides the user with a **start session** menu option. There are numerous data structures maintained by the DBMS which persist as long as the system is up and operational (i.e., as long as there are no system or media failures). The DBMS software is organized into several layers and each of these layers maintains data structures that are part of a transaction workspace (and hence persist for the duration of the transaction), belong to the set of session variables, or pertain to the execution environment (and hence persist as long as the system is up). We already described examples of the former two. For execution environment data structures, perhaps the most important is the *Buffer* table, which contains the page identifiers of all the physical persistent and concurrently shared data base pages buffered by the buffer manager. The disk image describing the free and used pages of the disk and access tables used for determining conflicting accesses are other examples of execution environment persistent data structures. These execution environment structures are shared by all the sessions created during an *activation* of the execution environment. These activations correspond to system re-starts.

13.4 REPRESENTATION AND STORAGE OF PERSISTENT/SHARED OBJECTS

We mentioned in the previous section the transaction workspace and the session variables in the run-time execution environment. Parts of these workspaces will be allocated to storing FAD objects in the conceptual model's format. These conceptual FAD objects will be either transient or persistent (i.e., accessible from the **database** root). Another portion of the workspaces will be storing paginated objects in the internal model's format. These internal storage objects in the workspace of a transaction will consist of those objects that reside in pages updated by the transaction.

The DBMS also buffers concurrently shared data pages of the indexed files which store the internal database objects. However, these pages are shared across all currently executing transactions and do not belong in the private workspace of any particular transaction (the private transaction workspace disappears once the transaction terminates).

Figure 13.3 illustrates these different object storage areas. Thus, among other things, the transaction workspace contains conceptual objects stored

FIGURE 13.3
TRANSACTIONS WORKSPACE AND SHARED BUFFER POOL

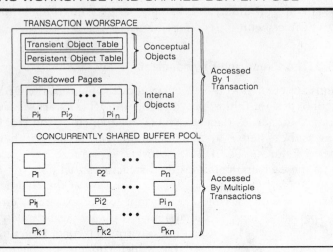

in *Transient Object* and *Persistent Object Tables*. The *Persistent Object Table* is retrieved either from the shadow pages in the workspace of the transaction or the shared *Buffer Pool*.

Each of the shadow pages $Pi'_1, \ldots, Pi'_n$ corresponds to a concurrently shared storage page either in the shared *Buffer Pool* ($Pi_1, \ldots, Pi_n$ in Fig. 13.3) or on disk. If the transaction commits, the shadowed pages ($Pi^{1i}, \ldots, P^i$) replace the concurrently shared pages ($Pi'_1, \ldots, Pi_n$) on disk and in the *Buffer Pool*.

13.4.1 The Object Tables

The entries in the *Transient* and *Persistent Object Tables* consist of triplets:

   [ObjectType, ReferenceCount, ObjectValue]

where *ObjectType* is one of: *SET, TUPLE*, or *ATOMIC*. *Reference Count* is due to the referential sharing of objects and is used to reclaim the space allocated to unreferenced objects. The representation of *ObjectValue* is, in general, a pointer. This is discussed further as follows. Fixed-length atomic values are stored directly in an object table.

Objects are referenced through an *identifier* that specifies the table (*Persistent* or *Transient*) and a table entry corresponding to an object:

   [TableSelector, **Index**]

Hence, *TableSelector* is either *TRANS* or *PERS*. **Index** is an index to the corresponding object table.

Associated with each of the object tables we have an *Object Value Table*. This table stores the actual values of objects. The values of string atomic objects are stored as self-describing:

[STRING, ValueByteString]

The value of a set or tuple is a list of the form

([AttrName, Identifier])

If the object is a set, the *AttrName* field is *NIL*.

Small fixed-size atomic objects (like integers) will be stored directly in the *Object Tables* (versus object *Value Tables*).

Figure 13.4 gives a more detailed description of the conceptual transaction object space. We should also emphasize that it is permissible to have persistent objects referenced from the *Transient Object Table* or the *Transient Object Value Table*. However, *all* references from the *Persistent Object Table* or the *Persistent Object Value Table* must be to entries in these *Persistent Tables* only.

13.4.2 Example

Next we illustrate some of these concepts through an example. Assume we have a couple, John and Mary Smith, who referentially share their children, in the persistent database. Also assume we have derived some statistics concerning a person and his/her number of children, as well as all the children of the database in the transient object space. We assume the database contains only John, Mary, and their children. For simplicity, persistent identifiers will be represented as *Ij*'s and transient identifiers will be represented as *ij*'s.

FIGURE 13.4
CONCEPTUAL OBJECT TABLES

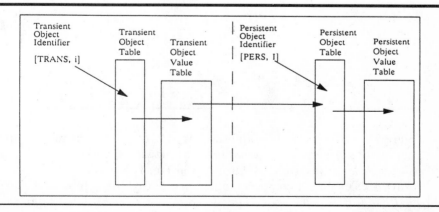

FIGURE 13.5
GRAPHIC REPRESENTATION OF THE OBJECTS

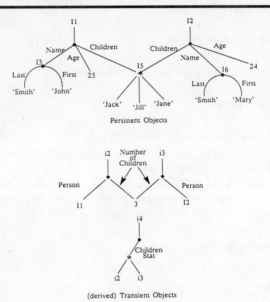

Persistent Objects

(derived) Transient Objects

FIGURE 13.6
OBJECT REPRESENTATION IN THE PERSISTENT OBJECT TABLES

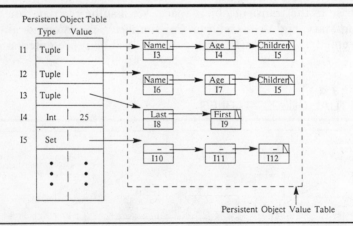

Figure 13.5 gives a simple graphical representation of the persistent and the transient objects. The persistent objects are actually stored in the *Persistent Object/Value Tables* respectively, as illustrated in Fig. 13.6 and 13.7.

Figure 13.8a shows a compact storage of the tuples for John and Mary in page *P1* of a *Persons* database. The interpretation of the byte string representing these tuples will use the schema of *Persons* given in Fig. 13.8c. The

FIGURE 13.7
OBJECT REPRESENTATION IN THE TRANSIENT OBJECT TABLES

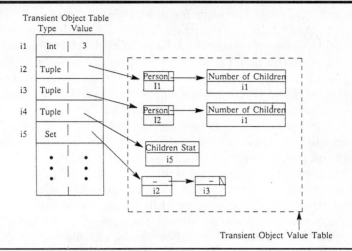

FIGURE 13.8
OBJECT REPRESENTATION IN THE INTERNAL LAYER

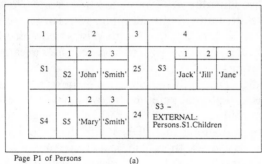

Page P1 of Persons   (a)

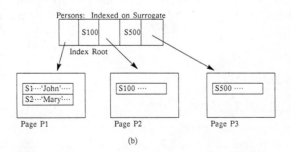

(b)

Schema of Persons

Surrogate	Name:Tuple		Age:	Children:Set	
	Surrogate	Last:String	First:String	Integer	Surrogate	String

(c)

numbers 1, 2, ... in Fig. 13.8a are for illustrative purposes and indicate the 1st, 2nd, ..., attribute of a tuple or the 1st, 2nd, ..., element of a set. For example, for *Name* (tuple valued) attribute of tuple $s1$ in *Persons*, the first attribute is a surrogate ($S2$), the second is a string (*John*) and the third is also a string (*Smith*). These numbers will **not** be stored in $P1$. Instead *separators, pointer arrays,* or *linksets* [Batory, 1985] will be used to cluster all the subobjects of the same object in the same page. If an object is "large" (i.e., cannot fit in a page), its subobjects need to be partitioned and segmented across multiple page nodes (disk storage of complex objects requires innovative engineering techniques and is being investigated extensively (Batory [1985], Maier & Stein [1986], Valduriez, et al. [1986], and Deppisch, et al. [1986]).

Note that the children field of *Mary* stores an *external* reference to children attribute of tuple with surrogate value $S1$ in *Persons*. In the internal model we need such external references since with our strategy a referentially shared object in the conceptual model would be stored with only *one* of the objects referring to it. The other object will store the *path* of the external reference. These paths consist of sequences where attribute names and keys for set valued attributes alternate. In the *Persons* database, $S1$ identifies a unique tuple and children an attribute of that tuple.

In Fig. 13.8b we illustrate a B^+ tree structure which clusters the *Persons* tuples on surrogate attributes. Thus, all tuples with surrogate values between 0 and 100 are stored in page $P1$, those with values between 100 and 500 are stored in $P2$, and tuples of *Persons* with surrogate values greater than or equal to 500 are stored in page $P3$.

Strictly speaking, Fig. 13.8 is telling half the story: we also need to store all the paths of external references to an object in order to be able to efficiently support updates (e.g., deletes) of either the shared object or the object currently containing the referentially shared object. Furthermore, associated with the *Persons* set, there will be a cluster index (on the surrogate field) and a number of *inverted* indices for fast associative access through, say, the *Name* or *Age* attributes of the *Persons* complex tuples. Finally, other copies of *Persons* with an alternative organization and clustering are also not shown in Fig. 13.8.

13.5 ,SUMMARY

In this paper we have attempted to present aspects of sharing and persistence, in an object-oriented framework. The perspective given to these concepts was database oriented and influenced from the design and implementation of one particular DBMS.

We saw an increasing degree of persistence going from a transaction workspace, to session variables, to the execution environment, and finally to the recoverable persistent database.

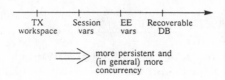

As far as concurrently shared objects are concerned, we can similarly characterize objects and data structures shared within a transaction (such as shadowed pages), within the session of a user (such as the session variables), within an execution environment, and finally the most important space, namely the recoverable database. Therefore, similar to persistence, there is an increase in the degree of concurrency in going from transaction workspace to the recoverable database.

We should note that, although in general the recoverable database and the database shared concurrently across multiple transactions are one and the same, there are numerous DBMS's that restrict user accesses to certain subsets of the recoverable database, depending upon access grants [Fernandez, et al., 1981]. In other words, it is conceivable to have portions of the recoverable database accessed by, say, only one "special" type of transaction. The bottom line is that recoverable does not necessarily mean concurrently shared. Of course, session and execution environment variables show that concurrent sharing does not automatically imply recoverability either. However, the concurrently shared variables of these environments *do* persist as long as the environment is operational.

We demonstrated different aspects of the mapping between the conceptual recoverable object space and the internal recoverable object space. We have discovered that the most interesting (and difficult) issue here is the mapping of a graph structured object space to an object space that allows no referential object sharing.

We explained some of the data structures in the transaction workspace, which are used to store transient and persistent conceptual object images. Similarly, we showed the shadowed representation of internal storage blocks in the same transaction workspace. The internal objects that are concurrently shared and recoverable were "paginated" and stored in storage blocks on disk. Some of these blocks were cached in the concurrently shared buffer pool.

Therefore, "persistence" and "sharing" in an object-oriented framework have different facades spanning the object models and the different software modules of a DBMS. Furthermore, the *degree* of persistence and sharing varies.

From our perspective, *the* implementation issue is to build high performance DBMS's whose conceptual model supports structural (hence referential object sharing) and operational object orientation, with concurrent accesses to the recoverable **database**.

Acknowledgment

We would like to thank Haran Boral for numerous helpful comments on an earlier draft of the paper. Also thanks to Mike Franklin, Ted Briggs, and Dick Tsur for their helpful suggestions and to Ted Briggs and Brian Hart for their efforts in the implementation of the system.

References

Abiteboul, S., and Bidoit, N., (1984). "Algebra for Non-Normalized Relations," *Int. Symposium on PODS.*

Albano, A., Cardelli, L., and Orsini, R., (1985). "Galileo: A Strongly-Typed Interactive Conceptual Language," *ACM Transactions on Database Systems,* Vol. 10, No. 2, June.

Albano, A., Gheli, G., Occhiuto, M. E., and Orsini, R., (1986). "A Strongly Typed, Interactive Object-Oriented Database Programming Language," *Proceedings of the International Workshop on Object-Oriented Database Systems,* Pacific Grove, Calif., September.

Atkinson, M., Bailey, P., Cockshott, W., Chisholm, K., and Morrison, R., (1983). "An Approach to Persistent Programming," *Computer Journal,* Vol. 26, No. 4.

Bancilhon, F., Briggs, T., Khoshafian, S., and Valduriez, P., (1987). "FAD, A Powerful and Simple Database Language," MCC report submitted for publication.

Bancilhon, F., and Khoshafian, S., (1986). "A Calculus for Complex Objects," *Int. Symposium on PODS,* March.

Batory, D. S., (1985). "Modeling the Storage Architectures of Commercial Database Systems," *ACM Transactions of Database Systems,* Vol. 10, No. 4.

Boral, H., and DeWitt, D. J., (1983). "Database Machines: An Idea Whose Time has Passed? A Critique of the Future of Database Machines," *Int. Workshop on DBM,* Munich, September.

Borr, A. J., (1981). "Transaction Monitoring in ENCOMPASS: Reliable Distributed Transaction Processing," *Int. Conf. on VLDB,* Cannes, September.

Cardelli, L., (1984). "Amber," AT&T Bell Labs, Technical Memorandum 11271-840924-10TM.

Cardelli, L., and Wagner, P., (1985). "On Understanding Types, Data Abstraction, and Polymorphism," *ACM Computing Surveys,* Vol. 17, No. 4, December.

Chen, P. P., (1976). "The Entity-Relationship Model—Toward a Unified View of Data," *ACM Transactions on Database Systems,* Vol. 1, No. 1.

Creeger, M., (1983). "Lisp Machines Come Out of the Lab," *Computer Design,* November.

Demurjian, S., Hsiao, D., and Menon, J., (1986). "A Multi-Backend Database System for Performance Gains, Capacity Growth and Hardware Upgrade," *Int. Conf. on Data Engineering,* Los Angeles, February.

Deppsich, U., Paul, H-B., and Schek, H-J., (1986). "A Storage System for Complex Objects," in *Proceedings of 1986 Intl. Workshop on Object-Oriented Database Systems,* Pacific Grove, Calif., September.

Deutsch, L. P., (1983). "The Dorado Smalltalk-80 Implementation: Hardware Architecture's Impact on Software Architecture," in *Smalltalk-80: Bits of History, Words of Advice,* Krasner, Glenn (ed.), Reading, Mass.: Addison-Wesley.

DeWitt, D. J., et al., (1986). "GAMMA—A High Performance Dataflow Database Machine," *Int. Conf. on VLDB,* Kyoto, August.

Dittrich, K. R., (1986). "Object-Oriented Database Systems: The Notion and the Issues," *Proceedings of the International Workshop on Object-Oriented Database Systems,* Pacific Grove, Calif., September.

Eswaran, K. P., Gray, J. N., Lorie, R. A., and Traiger, I. L., (1976). "The Notions of Consistence and Predicate Locks in a Database System," *Comm. ACM,* Vol. 19, No. 11.

Fernandez, E. B., Summers, R. C., and Wood C., (1981). "Database Security and Integrity," Reading, Mass.: Addison-Wesley.

Fushimi, S., Kitsuregawa, M., and Tanaka, H., (1986). "An Overview of the System Software of a Parallel Relational Database Machine GRACE," *Int. Conf. on VLDB,* Kyoto, August.

Goldberg, A., and Robson, D., (1983). "Smalltalk-80: The Language and Its Implementation," Reading, Mass.: Addison-Wesley.

Gray, J., (1978). "Notes on Database Operating Systems," IBM research report RJ2188, IBM Research Center, San José, Calif.

Hayashi, H., Hattori, A., and Akimoto, H., (1983). "ALPHA: A High Performance LISP Machine Equipped with a New Stack Structure and Garbage Collection System," *Proceedings of the 10th Annual Int. Symposium on Computer Architecture.*

Khoshafian, S., and Copeland, G., (1986). "Object Identity," *Proceedings of OOPSLA,* Portland, Ore.

King, R., and McLeod, D., (1985). "Semantic Database Models," in Yao, S. B. (ed.), *Database Design,* New York: Springer-Verlag.

Krablin, G. L., (1985). "Building Flexible Multilevel Transactions in a Distributed Persistent Environment," *Persistence and Data Types,* Papers for the Appin Workshop, U. of Glasgow, August.

Krause, J., (1985). Presentation, Int. Workshop on High-Performance Transaction Systems, Pacific Grove, Calif., September.

Kulkarni, K. G., and Atkinson, M. P., (1986). "EFDM: Extended Functional Data Model," *The Computer Journal,* Vol. 29, No. 1.

Kung, H. T., Robinson, J., (1981). "On Optimistic Methods for Concurrency Control," *ACM TODS,* Vol. 6, No. 2, June.

Kuper, G., and Vardi, M., (1984). "A New Approach to Database Logic," *Int. Symposium on PODS,* April.

Lewis, D. M., Galloway, D. R., Francis R. J., and Thomson B. W., (1986). "Swamp: A Fast Processor for Smalltalk-80," *OOPSLA-86 Proceedings,* Portland, Ore.

Lieberman, H., and Hewitt, C., (1983). "A Real-Time Garbage Collector Based on the Lifetimes of Objects," *Comm. ACM,* Vol. 26, No. 6, June.

Livny, M., Khoshafian, S., and Boral, H., (1987). "Multi-Disk Management," to appear in *Proc. of ACM-SIGMETRICS Int. Conf.*

Lorie, R. A., (1977). "Physical Integrity in a Large Segmented Database," *ACM TODS,* Vol. 2, No. 1, March.

Maier, D., and Stein, J., (1986). "Indexing in an Object-Oriented DMBS," *Proceedings of 1986 International Workshop on Object-Oriented Database Systems*, Pacific Grove, Calif.

Maier, D., Stein, J., Ottis, A., and Purdy, A., (1986). "Development of an Object-Oriented DBMS," *OOPSLA-86*, Portland, Ore., September.

Mattson, R., et al., (1970). "Evaluation Techniques for Storage Hierarchies," *IBM Systems Journal*, Vol. 3, No. 2, June.

McLeod, D., Narayanaswamy, K., and Rao Bapa, K., (1983). "An Approach to Information Management for CAD/VLSI Applications," *ACM-SIGMOD Int. Conf.*, San José, May.

Moon, D. A., (1985). "Architecture of the Symbolics 3600," *Proceedings of the 12th Annual Int. Symposium on Computer Architecture*.

Neches, P., (1985). "The Anatomy of a Database Computer System," *COMPCON 85*, San Francisco, Calif., February.

Papadimitriou, C. H., (1979). "Serializability of Concurrent Database Updates," *Journal of the ACM*, Vol. 26, No. 4.

Rentsch, T. (1982)., "Object-Oriented Programming," *SIGPLAN Notices*, September.

Selinger, et al., (1979). "Access Path Selection in a Relational Database Management System," *ACM-SIGMOD*, Boston.

Shipman, D., (1981). "The Functional Data Model and Data Language DAPLEX," *ACM Transactions on Database Systems*, Vol. 6, No. 1.

Stefik, M., and Bobrow, D. G., (1986). "Object-Oriented Programming: Themes and Variations," *The AI Magazine*, Vol. 6, No. 4.

Stonebraker, M., (1986). "The Case for Shared Nothing," *Database Engineering*, Vol. 9, No. 1, March.

Stroustrup, B., (1986). "The C++ Programming Language," Reading, Mass.: Addison-Wesley.

Ungar, D., (1984). "Generation Salvaging: A Non-Disruptive High Performance Storage Reclamation Algorithm," *ACM Software Eng. Notes/SIGPLAN Notices Software Engineering Symposium on Practical Software Development Environments*, Pittsburgh, Pa., April.

Valduriez, P., Khoshafian, S., and Copeland, G., (1986). "Implementation Techniques of Complex Objects," *Proceedings of Very Large Databases: 12th International Conference*, Kyoto, Japan.

CHAPTER 14

POLYMORPHIC NAMES AND ITERATIONS

Malcolm Atkinson
Ronald Morrison

14.1 INTRODUCTION

Names are used for many categories of objects within programming languages—for example, to name constants, variables, points in the program, exceptions, and so forth. When they name fields of records, then it is often the case that some input and output operations could use those names; for example, in a form-filling system, or in a browser [Dearle & Brown, 1987]. Diagnostic tools and program construction aids need to manipulate, input, and output these names.

In operating system command languages, editors, and other user interfaces, names are used to identify objects from different sets of categories, especially file directories and files. At present these names may obey different rules from those in the programming language. As we attempt to develop a single coherent system in which long- and short-term data (code, objects, etc.) are treated consistently [Atkinson, et al., 1981, 1983; Atkinson & Morrison, 1985a], it has been necessary to consider carefully the treatment of names.

Unfortunately, during the development described in those cited papers there were two flaws in our treatment of names:

1. The interpretation of field names in the type checking rules implied a single universe of names for fields—which is known to be unmanageable in large evolving systems.

2. Program identifiers were used to name some things (e.g., procedures and structure classes) while strings were used to name other things (notably databases and entries in databases).

The former problem appears in many systems as we note in various surveys [Atkinson & Buneman, 1988; Buneman & Atkinson, 1986; Atkinson, et al., 1987]. The latter problem manifests itself in most languages as the use of strings for file names. It has the inconvenience of introducing a quite different, dynamic, binding rule for the interpretation of these names. Normally, the operating system is responsible for providing this rule. The inconsistency introduced makes programming more difficult and requires program alteration when programs are moved between operating systems.

In PS-algol and its descendents we have wished to encompass more of the semantics that affect the execution of programs to give the programmer a consistent world for the total computation. We have therefore sought to remove these anomalous string-names and their inconsistent interpretation. A similar motivation has influenced other work [Buhr & Zarnke, 1987; Richardson, et al., 1987]. We envisage that by continuing this development most of the functions of an operating system can be given a consistent semantics, which is also consistent with the command languages and the programming languages provided. The task of learning to use the composition of these languages, and of implementing them, is then much simplified. For example, in many programming environments there are naming systems for files, databases, schema components within the database, command language variables, commands, parameters, programs, processes, procedure libraries, modules within these libraries, and so on. Often different rules apply to the name management for each of them, which have to be both implemented and understood.

Within this motivation we proposed namespaces [Atkinson & Morrison, 1985a] and have subsequently refined them and renamed them environments in our implementation of Napier [Atkinson, et al., 1986, 1987; Atkinson & Morrison, 1987]. These ameliorate the two problems previously identified but do not permit all aspects of an operating system to be modeled. At the first Appin workshop [Atkinson & Morrison, 1985a] we noted our inability to iterate over structures containing names. Interaction, that is, data transfer across the inevitable boundary between the computation described by the language and the environment of that computation, was also incomplete. For example, names could not be communicated to and from the user without treating them as strings. The lack of iteration meant operating system functions like browsing a directory of files could not be implemented. The lack of interaction meant that generic I/O (e.g., forms packages) could not be implemented easily, though Dearle and Cooper have developed a use of the callable compiler which overcomes this deficiency [Dearl & Brown, 1987; Cooper, et al., 1986, 1987; Cooper & Atkinson, 1987].

This paper shows how the new language construct *polymorphic name types* allows us to define iterators and transport operations and hence code these hitherto problematic functions. First the polymorphic name type, the universal extensible union type, the polymorphic I/O construct, and the iterator construct proposed for Napier are defined. Then example program fragments illustrate how they are used.

14.2 THE POLYMORPHIC TYPE NAME

Like procedures and abstract types in Napier [Atkinson & Morrison, 1987], names may be parameterized by any type, thus specifying the type of objects they may name. Syntactically there is a name type constructor **name** that when parameterized with a type yields a type. For example,

name[string]

is a set of all names which may name a string. More precisely, we consider all environments (those produced explicitly and manipulable with the **env** construct, those corresponding to records, and those associated with the lexical block structure) to be sets of quadruples. Each quadruple is a name, type, constancy, and value. The type with which a name value is parametrized must match under the type rules the second element of this tuple when the name value is matched with the first element.

The operations on names are type test, input and output, type consistent assignment, and lexical ordering.

Names may be used to index a **struct** or **env** object, and to construct new quadruples to insert into an **env** object.

These operations are further defined as follows. There are also two transfer functions on names:

let *nameToString* = **proc**[*t* : **type**] (*n* : **name**[*t*] → *string*)

and

let *stringToName* = **proc**[*t* : **type**] (*s* : *string* → **name**[*t*])

The type test has the form

<exp> is <ptype>

and type rule

∀*t* : *t* is ptype ⇒ bool

where ptype is

    a. Any one of the predefined types (e.g., *int, real, bool*).

    b. Any user-defined type name (i.e., an in-scope occurrence of <type_name> from **type** <type_name> **is** . . .).

    c. Any type expression (i.e., such as may appear after **is** in **type** . . . **is** . . .).

    d. Any type *constructor* (e.g., **abstype**, which might have been used in **type** *stack* **is abstype** . . .).

Figure 14.1 illustrates the use of the type test.

The equality test on name is **true** if they both are represented by the same sequence of characters and if they are both restricted to exactly the same type. Thus the program

    let $p1$ = **name** [*real*] *floccinaucinihilipilification*
    let $p2$ = *stringToName* [*real*] ("floccinaucinihilipilification")
    print $p1 = p2$

would print **true**.

FIGURE 14.1
A PROCEDURE TO GIVE A STRING CORRESPONDING TO THE TYPE OF ITS PARAMETER

```
let typeName = proc[t : type](x : t → string)
        begin
      case true of
                        x is int                : "int"            !base types
                        x is real               : "real"
                        x is bool               : "bool"
                        x is string             : "string"
                        x is picture            : "picture"
                        x is pixel              : "pixel"
                        x is image              : "image"          !constructors
                        x is vector             : "vector"
                        x is structure           "structure"
                        x is union              : "union"
                        x is proc               : "proc"
                        x is env                : "env"
                        x is abstype            : "abstype"
                        x is name               : "name"
                        x is any                : "any"
                        default "impossible"
                        end
```

Input and output are discussed in a subsequent section, and assignment is identical with all other assignments in the language.

Lexical ordering is defined for the corresponding strings and is irrespective of type.

$$<exp_1 >\,<\,<exp_2 >$$

for

$$\forall t,\, t'\ \textbf{name}\ [t]\ <\ \textbf{name}[t']$$

is exactly equivalent to

$$nameToString\ (<exp_1 >)\ <nameToString\ (<exp_2 >)$$

We use this ordering when defining iterators.

14.3 THE UNIVERSAL EXTENSIBLE UNION TYPE

In PS-algol we had an extensible union type, **pntr**, and we grew to appreciate its utility; indeed much of the database programming, including the interface to persistent data and data model implementation, depended on it [Atkinson, et al., 1987; Cooper, et al., 1987].

We refer to it as a *union* type because it may refer to an instance of *any* structure class. We refer to it as *extensible*, as new classes declared after the use of **pntr** are eligible as referends, thus the set of possible referends is increased when each structure class is declared. It was not *universal* as there were types, for example, **int**, which were excluded from its set.

It was valuable because it allowed a type check to be delayed, because it allowed us to limit the traversal of the type match algorithm, and because it allowed generic code to be written applicable to future types, possibly with the execution taking into account the actual type. It was, however, overused, as no more specific alternative was available when referend types were predetermined. It was also unfortunate as its pronunciation 'pointer' evoked connotations of other languages where such things provide a loophole in the type system and even pointer arithmetic. Of course, these horrors do not exist in PS-algol.

In Napier we therefore allow proper constraint of referend type where appropriate in data structures, and we use polymorphism to implement most generic code. We have retained the valuable properties of **pntr** in a type **any**, but removed an irksome restriction by making it universal.

There are few operations on values of type **any** (only equality, inequality, and assignment), thus it is safe. To gain access to other operations on the values it is necessary to project out of the union, just as one projects out of a statically defined union. A delayed type check is needed in both cases. We now make this projection explicit. (The implicit projection from **pntr** was one of the causes of a single namespace of field names.) Thus our **any** is similar to Cardelli's **dynamic** [Cardelli & MacQueen, 1985; Cardelli, 1985].

Note **name** [**any**] is the type that includes all possible names.

14.4 POLYMORPHIC INPUT AND OUTPUT

The output statement **print** in PS-algol [PPRR-12] is already polymorphic, handles multiple fonts and multiple destinations, and its default actions may be replaced by other code. In Napier we retain the essence of this **print** clause but we are revising details [Philbrow, et al., 1987].

Thus

> **print** 4 + 3
> **print** "freedom is never achieved by violence"
> **print** 14.2 + 3.7

would print the values in the accepted format. Logically the print statement would be written as

> **print**[*int*] 4 + 3

et cetera, to be consistent with our other polymorphic constructs, however in this case we have decided that the explicit type parameter is so tedious we prefer to omit it and tolerate the inconsistency. (There is some hope that we may be able to return to consistency by omitting the type parameters elsewhere c.f. Poly [Matthews, 1985]).

In PS-algol input was performed by special functions indicating the type expected, for example, *readstring*. This cannot be data type complete since the type space is infinite, and so is inconsistent with our design principles. It also masks the projection and dynamic type check from the sequence of user actions (e. g., key strikes, mouse clicks, etc.) to the internal type. A dynamic type check, prevalent in languages, we believe should be properly visible and parametric. **read** therefore takes a type parameter, as is shown following:

> **let** i :=   **read**[int]   ! create an integer variable i and
> ! initialize it to the next input integer
> **let** r =   **read** [real]   ! declare real constant r
> **let** vs =   **read** [*string]   ! vs string becomes a constant referring to a
> ! vector of strings which are read in.

A consequence of this treatment is the **read** operation, which corresponds to a call of the compiler on the relevant input source seeking the specified type.

FIGURE 14.2
A PROGRAM FRAGMENT COLLECTS DATA DESCRIBING
WHAT TO PLOT

. . .		
print	"n supply initial X"	
let Xi	= **read** [real]	
print	"n supply final X"	
let Xf	= **read** [real]	
print	"n supply f(X)"	
let f	= *real* [proc (*real* → *real*)]	

Parts of a program to plot an arbitrary function is shown as Fig. 14.2. But it may also receive an already typed object via *cut & paste* actions, since, if we capture the system within one semantics, the structure and type information is invariant over these operations.

14.5 POLYMORPHIC ITERATIONS

When a polymorphic procedure is defined this indicates that different applications of the procedure may have parameters of a different type, but that for each application the procedure body will be executed with a consistent and constant substitution of the type variables. The polymorphic iterator is defined correspondingly. Each traversal of the iteration may be with a different type substitution, but within each execution of the controlled statement the type substitution is constant and consistent.

There are iterators to perform defined sequences of operations in the language, for example,

for i = 1 **to** 10 **do** . . .

with the usual semantics and options. Note that i is a constant declared here with the scope of this **for** statement.

There is a similar iteration construct, introduced by **for each**, which iterates over compound objects. Each of the compound objects may be considered a map, for example, a vector of type *t is a stored map from *int* to t. Identifiers may be provided in the iteration statement to range over the sequence of values in the map, and for every type of map the iteration sequence is defined. For example,

for each k → u **in** vs **do** . . .

where vs is a vector of strings, would apply the controlled clause first with k set to the lower bound of vs and u set to the first string, and repeat for increasing index up to the upper bound. Either control variable may be omitted, for example,

for each k **in** vs **do** . . .

and

for each $\rightarrow u$ **in** vs **do** . . .

Similar arrangements are available for iterating over indexes, with multiple keys having corresponding multiple control variables.

The other major classes of compound object (**struct & env**) all encapsulate environments (maps from names to values with different types for different names). Consequently the first control variable is a polymorphic name, and the second of the corresponding type, which constitutes polymorphic iteration, for example,

for each $[t : \textbf{type}]$ $aName : \textbf{name}[t] \rightarrow aValue : t$ **in** . . .

where $aValue$ is of type t. Note t is available as a type variable in the controlled clause. The iteration substitutes from the quadruple with the least name first.

14.6 ILLUSTRATING THE USE OF CONSTRUCTS TO MANIPULATE ENVIRONMENTS

Our environments have been described elsewhere [Atkinson, et al., 1987; Atkinson & Morrison, 1987]. They may be used to provide extensible objects, and one such application of those would be as file directories—where files are now properly typed.

FIGURE 14.3
INSERTING A NEW QUADRUPLE IN AN ENVIRONMENT

```
      . . .
            print        "n What is the name?"
            let          newName = read[name [*int]]
            print        "n What is the initial value for", newName, "?"
            let          initalValue = read [*int]
            print        "n is the filed updateable?"
            let          constantField = replyAffirmative ()
            if           constantField then
                         insert newName : = initialValue in anEnv
      else
                         insert newName = initialValue in anEnv
```

Figure 14.3 shows the insertion of a new quadruple in an environment, equivalent to adding a file (with or without write protection) to a directory, *anEnv*.

To illustrate the iterator construct more fully suppose that environments have been chosen to represent some entity, and that now a new property is to be recorded for every instance. The programmer/data designer has decided that such transitions are likely, and considered it worth incurring the additional costs of using **envs** rather than static records. The iteration in Fig. 14.4 would then achieve this.

That example has assumed the existence of a procedure, *envShow*, capable of printing any environment. A simple implementation, utilizing polymorphic iteration, is shown in Fig. 14.5.

Figure 14.6 shows a procedure to copy one element of an environment, then Fig. 14.7 shows how that and polymorphic iteration can be used to construct a backup copy of any environment.

Figure 14.8 shows how two environments may be combined using the same facilities, and Fig. 14.9 shows how a user-controlled directory (environment) editor might be built.

Finally a program to emulate the *ls* shell command (a simple version) as in UNIX^{TM} is shown as Fig. 14.10. Note that *NameToString* is used explicitly because otherwise the name would be printed like a name literal expression, for example,

name [*int*]*fred*

since a language must be able to read its own handwriting.

FIGURE 14.4
AN EXAMPLE PROGRAM FRAGMENT TO ADD TO A NEW INTEGER FIELD TO ALL THE ENVIRONMENTS IN AN INDEX

```
. . .
      print "n is the field updateable?"
      let constantField = replyAffirmative()
      print "n What is the name of the new integer field?"
      let newName = read [name[int]]
      for each →      anEnv in theIndexToEnvs do        !don't care about the key
                      begin                             !once for each env
                            !show the user the environment
                      envShow (anEnv)
                  print "nWhat is the initial value for", newName, "?"
                      let initialValue = read[int]
                      if constantField then
                              insert newName = initalValue in anEnv
                      else
                              insert newName = initialValue in anEnv
                      end                             ! of iteration through index
```

FIGURE 14.5
PROCEDURE TO PRINT ANY ENVIRONMENT

```
let  envShow = proc (theEnv: env)
  begin
  for each [t:type] aName:name[t]  ---> aValue in theEnv do
    begin
    print '''n'', nameToString (aName) using xor
                !invert name
    print ''='' using copy
    if  aValue is int or aValue is real or aValue is bool
        or aValue is string then
        print aValue
    else
        begin       !here print type name rather than value
        let typeString = typeName [t] (aValue)
                !see Fig 1.1
        if typeString = ''pixel'' or typeString =
           ''picture'' then
           print typeString
      else
        printEnboldened(typeString)
    end
  end
end
```

FIGURE 14.6
A PROCEDURE TO MAKE AN EXACT COPY INCLUDING CONSTANTS
OF ONE BINDING FROM ONE ENVIRONMENT TO ANOTHER

```
let copyOneEn-
try = proc [t:type] (el,e2: env, n: name [t])
     if constant el (n) then
         insert n = el (n) in e2
     else
         insert n:= el (nn) in e2
```

14.7 TYPING RELATIONAL JOIN

At the workshop in Appin in 1985 Peter Buneman [Buneman, 1985] posed the problem of declaring a procedure that implements join. There were three subproblems.

1. To provide a type that will pass the parameters, that is, the two relations and the names of the columns on which the join is to be performed.

2. To check the mutual consistency of these parameters, for example, that the columns named appear in both relations and have the correct type.

3. To generate the type of the result relation.

These language features provide a *partial* solution to the posed problem. Figure 14.11 shows a polymorphic procedure to perform an *equijoin* on two relations over a list of columns of type *t*. Each relation is presumed to be a vector of environments, and the columns are identified by a vector of names. The procedures used by *equijoin* are shown in Figs. 14.11 to 14.14.

Subproblem (1) is solved using this type system. We consider as follows whether the solution is adequate. The check (subproblem (2)) has been programmed—Fig. 14.12—verifying that all the columns appear in each relation. The dynamic specification of this condition is acceptable since the check is inherently dynamic; the relevant properties of the parameters may not be determined until the code that calls *equijoin* is executed. The result type (3) is statically specified and consequently the third subproblem is avoided.

FIGURE 14.7
A PROCEDURE TO PRODUCE A COPY OF AN ENVIRONMENT WITH ALL THE FIELDS CONSTANT

```
let snapshortEnvs=proc (e: env --> env)
    begin     ! make a constant snap-shot of its argument
    let res = emptyEnv ()
    for each [t:type] n:name [t] --> v in e do
        insert n = v is res
    res
    end
```

FIGURE 14.8
A PROCEDURE TO ADD THE CONTENTS OF ONE ENVIRONMENT TO ANOTHER

```
let mergeEnvs = proc (envl, env2: env)
    begin     !adds to envl all the bindings in env2
    let duplicates = emptyEnv ()
    for each [t:type] n:name [t] in env2 do
        if n in envl then
            copyOneEntry [t] (env2, duplicates, n)
        else
            copyOneEntry [t] (env2, envl, n)
    if size duplicates = o do raise name-
Clashes (duplicates)
    end
```

FIGURE 14.9
PROCEDURE THAT ALLOWS THE USER TO CONTROL THE PARTS
OF AN ENVIRONMENT COPIED

```
let userControlledCopy = proc (e: env --> env)
    begin
    let res = emptyEnv ()
    for each [t:type] n: name [t] in e do
        begin
        print '''n include'', n, ''?''
        if replyAffirmative () do
            copyOneEntry [t] (e,res,n)
        end
    res
end
```

FIGURE 14.10
PROCEDURE TO LIST THE CONTENTS OF A NAMESPACE
c.f. ls IN UNIX™

```
let  listEnv = proc (e: env)
        for each [t:type] n:name [t] in e do
            print nameToString (n)
```

When the quality of this solution is considered, the problems re-arise.
The type of a relation ***env** is unsatisfactory for a number of reasons:

a. Its cardinality is inflexible, leading to the final copy phase of the algorithm.
b. It is not space or update efficient, as the use of **env** rather than **struct**
requires a flexible map to be stored and maintained.
c. It does not indicate that every tuple in a relation is over the same
columns, thus factoring out the check that columns are valid depends
on programmers complying with this *unwritten* convention (it also
repeats the type and name information redundantly with every tuple).

These new subproblems are not entirely a result of pedagogical simplifi-
cation, nor is the naïve algorithm. Subproblem (a) could be overcome by a
better data structure, for example, a list of vectors. Suppose we used ***struct**
(. . .) to overcome subproblem (b). Then we lose the polymorphism and name
abstraction of *equijoin*. This could be solved if we say that **env** ⊃ **struct** so that
*env would type match ***struct** for the relation parameters. But this does not
deal with the result type, as somewhere we need to compute the appropriate
struct (. . .) of the result type, which is dependent on the two input relation

FIGURE 14.11
DECLARING A POLYMORPHIC EQUIJOIN PROCEDURE IN NAPIER

```
let equijoin = proc [type t]
  (rel1, rel2:*env; cols:*name[t] --> *env)
  begin
      ! check column names are present in each relation
  allIn[t] (rel1(1), cols)
      !each env in a rel has some set of names
  allIn[t] (rel2(1), cols)
      !set up temporary result structure

  let resSize: = 0
  type tupleList is struct (tuple: env; next: tupleList)
  let tl: = tupleList (emptytuple (), nil)
                                  !n*m naive algorithm
  for each --> e1 in rel1 do  !each tuple in rel1
  for each --> e2 in rel2 do  !each tuple in rel2
  if match [t] (e1, e2, cols) do
      begin
      resSize: = resSize + 1
      tl: = tupleList (merge (e1, e2), tl)
      end
                                  !final result
  let res = vector 1:: resSize of tl (tuple)
  for i = 2 to resSize do
      begin tl: = tl (next); res (i):= tl (tuple) end
  res
  end
```

parameters. The equivalent calculation takes place on each iteration in procedure merge (Fig. 14.14) in the presented solution. At present we have no mechanism for calculating this result type at the start of *equijoin* and using it (statically) for each iteration. If this deficiency were overcome ***struct** (...) would also deal with subproblem (c), but variants of this subproblem then tend to reappear as solutions to subproblem (a) are constructed.

FIGURE 14.12
CHECK ALL THE COLUMNS NAMES ARE IN THE
FIRST ENVIRONMENT

```
let allIn = proc [type t] (rel: *env; names: *names[t])
       for each --> n in names do
          if not (n in rel(1)) do
             raise wrongColumn
```

FIGURE 14.13
TEST TWO TUPLES FOR EQUALITY

```
let match = proc [type t]
(t1, t2: env; cols:*name [t] --> bool)
  begin
  let equal := true
  for each --> in cols do
        equal: = equal and t1(n) = t2(n)
  equal
  end
```

The $n * m$ algorithm should be replaced by sort merge, or use of indexes, but the polymorphic requirement militates against this. The type parameter t could be **image** or **proc (int, string** $\rightarrow$ **real)** or **any** and so on. To use indexes we need to either calculate a hash code or perform a 'less than' comparison operation. This leads us to identify another unsolved subproblem:

d. Either a generic operation *hashcode* [**type** t] $(x : t \rightarrow int)$ or a generic comparison *lessthan* [**type** t] $(x, y : t \rightarrow$ **bool**) is required to achieve efficiency, but we do not know how to define and implement it.

Because of these outstanding problems we built a polymorphic index type constructor into Napier that is, **index** $t_1, t_2, \ldots t_n \rightarrow t$. Using this we can overcome subproblems (a) to (d) but we have achieved this by passing them to their implementor. Even then we cannot properly type *equijoin*, since, if the parameters and the results were to include indexes, these types are static and the result type cannot be computed.

FIGURE 14.14
GENERATE THE NEW TUPLE FROM THE TWO THAT MATCHED

```
Let merge = proc(t1, t2: env --> env)
  begin
  let newTuple = emptyEnv ()
  mergeEnvs (newTuple, t1)
          !all columns from rel1 — see Fig 1.8
  for each [t:type] n: name [t] in t2 do
     if not (n in t1) do
          copyOneEntry [t] (t2, newTuple, n)
                              !see Fig 1.6
  newTuple
  end
```

For the moment we remain unable to define an adequate type system for generic applications, and we overcome the problem by synthesizing a specific procedure for each type parameterization of join when it is needed, and then using the callable compiler to build the operation before applying it. Persistence and the universal extensible union type allow us to memorize this operator construction [Cooper, et al., 1987]. It is not clear whether a type system that does better than this is achievable.

14.8 CONCLUSIONS

The sequence of examples shows that scanning directories is now possible, and that other data-dependent generic algorithms can be written. The constructs introduced to achieve this—polymorphic name types, type-constrained name values, environments, and polymorphic iterators—are individually simple to understand and use, they combine well, and they do not result in a loss of type control or incomprehensible computations.

Use of these constructs to build replacement operating system structures will eliminate strings as names. We need to start the bootstrap as a program binds to its environment, and do this by introducing one standard variable *PS* (Persistent Space).

These structures need to be updated to reflect changes in the environment, for example, addition of new network addresses, new discs, and so on. It does not appear possible to include these within the language. However we extend the scope of the language there will always be external agents affecting the computation, and consequently a closed universe is impossible, that is, *deus ex machina* will occur. If we wish to use the same naming system for everything, then we need to expand the type system to contain everything we wish to name. Examples might be machines, devices, et cetera, if they may be explicitly manipulated or selected by the user/programmer. But this makes it difficult to adhere to the principle of data type completeness.

The section on the implementation of a join procedure is included to show that type systems are *still* not adequate for all we wish to do. We pose the question: "Can we do better than synthesis of code followed by calling the compiler?" for these remaining generic tasks. The advantage of that approach is that more than type checking may be 'statically' determined, that is, factored out of the operator's iterations.

REFERENCES

Atkinson, M. P., and Buneman, O. P., (1988). "Types and Persistence in Database Programming Language Design," to be published in *ACM Computing Surveys*.

Atkinson, M. P., and Morrison, R., (1985a). "Procedures as Persistent Data Objects," *ACM TOPLAS*, Vol. 7, No. 4, October, pp. 539–559.

Atkinson, M. P., and Morrison, R., (1985b). "Types, Bindings and Parameters in a Persistent Environment," in *Proceedings of the 1st International Workshop on Persistent Object Systems: Data Types and Persistence*, Appin, Scotland, August, PPRR-16-85*, pp. 1–24.

Atkinson, M. P., and Morrison, R., (1987). "Polymorphism, Type Checking and Labels in a Persistent Object Store," in *Proceedings of the 2nd International Workshop on Persistent Object Systems: Their Design, Implementation and Use*, Appin, Scotland, August, PPRR-44-87*.

Atkinson, M. P., Buneman, O. P., and Morrison, R., (1987). "Delayed Binding and Type Checking in a Database Programming Language," to be published in *The Computer Journal*, April 1988.

Atkinson, M. P., Chisholm, K. J. and Cockshott, W. P., (1981). "PS-algol: An Algol with a Persistent Heap," *ACM SIGPLAN Notices*, Vol. 17, No. 7, July, pp. 24–31.

Atkinson, M. P., Morrison, R., and Pratten, G. D., (1986). "Designing a Persistent Information Space Architecture," in *Proceedings of Information Processing '86*, Dublin, Ireland, September, pp. 115–119.

Atkinson, M. P., Bailey, P. J., Chisholm, K. J., Cockshott, W. P., and Morrison, R., (1983). "An Approach to Persistent Programming," *The Computer Journal*, Vol. 26, No. 4, pp. 360–365.

Buhr, P. A., and Zarnke, C. R., (1987). "Persistence in an Environment for a Statically Typed Programming Language," in *Proceedings of the 2nd International Workshop on Persistent Object Systems: Their Design, Implementation and Use*, Appin, Scotland, August, PPRR-44-87*.

Buneman, O. P., (1985). "Data types for Database Programming," in *Proceedings of the 1st International Workshop on Persistent Object Systems: Data Types and Persistence*, Appin, Scotland, August, PPRR-16-85*, pp. 285–298.

Buneman, O. P., and Atkinson, M. P., (1986). "Inheritance and Persistence in Database Programming Languages," in *Proceedings of ACM SIGMOD Conference, '86*, Washington, D.C., May.

Cardelli, L., (1984). "Amber," Technical Report, AT&T Bell Laboratories, Murray Hill, N.J.

Cooper, R. L., and Atkinson, M. P., (1987). "Requirements Modeling in a Persistent Object Store," in *Proceedings of the 2nd International Workshop on Persistent Object Systems: Their Design, Implementation and Use*, Appin, Scotland, August, PPRR-44-87*.

Cooper, R. L., Atkinson, M. P., Dearle, A., and Abderrahmane, D., (1987). "Constructing Database Systems in a Persistent Environment," in *Proceedings of the 13th International Conference on Very Large Data Bases*, Brighton, England, September, pp. 117–125.

Dearle, A., and Brown, A. L., (1987). "Safe Browsing in a Strongly Typed Persistent Environment," in *Proceedings of the 2nd International Workshop on Database Programming Languages*, Salishan, Oregon, May 1989, PPRR-33-87*.

Philbrow, P., Armour, I., Atkinson, M. P., and Livingstone, J., (1987). "A Device-Independent Output Statement," to be submitted to *ACM SIGPLAN Notices*.

PPRR-12. "The PS-algol Reference Manual: Fourth Edition," PPRR-12-87*.

Richardson, J. E., Carey, M. J., Dewitt, D. J., and Schuh, D. T., (1987). "Persistence in Exodus," in *Proceedings of the 2nd International Workshop on Persistent Object Systems: Their Design, Implementation and Use*, Appin, Scotland, August, PPRR-44-87*.

CHAPTER 15

O₂, AN OBJECT-ORIENTED DATA MODEL

Christophe Lecluse
Philippe Richard
Fernando Velez

15.1 INTRODUCTION

One of the objectives of the *Altair* Group is to develop a new generation database system. The target applications are traditional business applications, transactional applications (excluding very high performance applications), office automation, and multimedia applications.

The system we are designing is object-oriented. We briefly recall the main features of the object-oriented paradigm:

1. Object identity. Objects have an existence that is independent of their value. Thus, two objects can be either identical, that is, they are the same object, or they can be equal, that is, they have the same value.
2. The notion of *type*.[1] A type describes a set of objects with the same characteristics. It describes the structure of data carried by objects

---

[1] The term *class* is frequently used; however, in addition to the intensional notion of type, it contains an extensional aspect, as it denotes the set of all objects of the system which conforms to the type at a given time.

as well as the operations (*methods* in the object-oriented terminology) applied to these objects. Users of a type only see the interface of the type, that is, a list of methods together with their signatures (the type of the input parameters and the type of the result): this is called *encapsulation*.

3. The notion of *inheritance*. It allows objects of different structures to share methods related to their common part. Types are organized in an inheritance (or *subtype*) hierarchy that factorizes common structure and methods at the level at which the largest number of objects can share them[2].

4. *Overriding* and *late binding*. The body of a method in a given type may be redefined at any moment in any of its subtypes, yet keeping the same name. This frees the programmer from remembering the name of an overridden method in a given type, and therefore the code is simpler and reusable because it is independent of the types that existed at the time the program was written. To offer this functionality, the system has to bind method names to binary code at run-time.

There is clear interest in the database community for the object-oriented technology. First of all, types and inheritance are a powerful tool to model the real world. They also make systems extensible: by adding new types in a system, one can extend its capabilities. Object identity allows modeling object sharing and provides a natural semantics for object updates [Copeland & Khoshafian, 1986]. Second, this technology provides a framework to represent and manage both data and programs. It is a promising paradigm to solve the so-called *impedance mismatch*—the awkward communication between a query language and a programming language that results when developing applications with a database system. Third, it provides good software engineering tools that make the programming task much easier.

Object-oriented database systems are currently being built. Most of them are prototypes [Banerjee, et al., 1987; Zdonik, 1984; Nixon, et al., 1987; Bancilhon, et al., 1987] and few of them are commercial products [Copeland & Maier, 1984; Andrews & Harris, 1987]. The overall objective of these systems is to integrate database technology (such as data sharing, data security, persistency, disk management, and database query languages) with the object-oriented approach in a single system.

However, there is a lack of a strong theoretical framework for object-oriented systems. This paper is a step in this direction. It proposes the data model foundations for an object-oriented database system. The originality of this model, called O_2, is its type system defined in the framework of a set and tuple data model. We think that what makes our approach different from other object-oriented approaches is that we use set and tuple constructors

---

[2]Another mechanism allowing objects to share operations is called *delegation*. It is the basis of the so-called "Actor languages." We will not consider it in this paper.

to deal with arbitrary complex objects, and the type system enforces strong typing, yet overriding is allowed.

There already exist models dealing with inheritance such as Bruce and Wegner [1986] and Cardelli [1984]. In Bruce and Wegner, types are modeled as many-sorted algebras. A type is a subtype of another if there exist suitable (not necessarily injective) "coercion" operators that behave as homomorphisms between the algebras. In Cardelli [1984], a safe, strongly typed system is proposed in which the semantics of subtyping for tuple-structured types corresponds to set inclusion between the corresponding type interpretations (this semantics is different from the previous one). Functions are typed and rules for subtyping among functional types are also given.

We have borrowed Cardelli's interpretation for tuple types, as it leads to an intuitive notion of subtyping of tuple structures. Our model is different from these proposals in that (*i*) we propose a different rule for inheritance of methods (for functional subtyping, in Cardelli's terms), (*ii*) set-structured objects are introduced, and objects may form a directed graph in which cycles are allowed, and (*iii*) methods can be directly attached to objects.

Our "tuple-and-set" construction of objects is similar to that of Bancilhon and Khoshafian [1986] and especially to that of Kuper and Vardi [1984] where identifiers (called addresses) are also introduced.

This paper is organized as follows. Section 15.2 gives an informal overview of our approach and exposes it through examples. Section 15.3 gives a definition of objects. Section 15.4 gives the semantics of types and inheritance relationship. Finally, the notion of database is introduced in Section 15.5. Section 15.6 contains some concluding remarks and open problems.

15.2 INFORMAL OVERVIEW

Let us introduce some of the notions of this model using examples. Objects represent our (computer) world. They are made up of an object identifier (a name for the object) and a value. Values can be atomic (string, integers, reals, . . .), tuple-structured, or set-structured.

$(ob_1, <$name : "Smith", age 32$>)$
$(ob_2, <$name : "Doe", age : 29, salary : 9700$>)$
$(ob_3, \{ob_1, ob_2\})$

The first two objects are examples of tuple objects and the last one is a set object. Atomic objects here are ages and names (they actually also have identifiers, as shown later). Objects can, of course, reference other objects and this allows the definition of complex objects. We can have mutually referencing objects, as shown in the following example:

$(ob_4, <$name : "john", spouse : $ob_5>)$
$(ob_5, <$name : "mary", spouse : $ob_4>)$

This possibility makes our objects more general than the simple nested tuple-and-set-objects.

A type has a name and it contains a structure and a set of methods applying to these objects. A structure will be either a basic structure (string, integer, real, for example), tuple structures, or set structures. The following example of type structures will be used throughout the paper:

```
Person = <name: String, age: Integer, sex: String>
Employee = <name: String, age: Integer, sex: String,
    salary: Integer>
Male = <name: String, age: Integer, sex: ''male''>
Persons = {Person}
Employees = {Employee}
Married-Person = <name: String, spouse: Married-Person,
    children: Persons>
```

The type structure of Person represents the sort of all tuple objects having a name field that is a string, and an age field that is an integer. The type structure of Male is as Person except that the sex field is restricted to contain the string male. The type structure of Persons represents all objects that are sets of persons. Given a set of objects Θ, we shall call the interpretation of a type structure (say Person) the set of all objects of this set having the corresponding structure. If Θ is the set of all objects ob_1 to ob_5, then the interpretation of Persons will be the object ob_3, whereas the interpretation of Person will be the two objects ob_1 and ob_2. Indeed, these two objects have name and age fields with the corresponding structures (string and integers). Notice that we allow the objects to have additional fields (the object ob_2 also has a salary field). In the same manner, the interpretation of the Employee structure is the set containing only the ob_2 object. So the interpretation of Employee is included in the interpretation of type structure Person. This is an intuitive result, because we want to say that every employee is a person. This is-a relationship between type structures is what is called inheritance in the object-oriented terminology.

The notion of inheritance also deals with methods. As employees are persons, a method defined for every person can be applied to an employee. Moreover, if a method (say name) is defined for both persons and employees, then we shall put some constraint on these methods, in order to make them "compatible." Such a compatibility is necessary to be able to perform type checking.

15.3 OBJECTS

In this section, we define the notion of objects. We suppose given:

- ☐ A finite set of *domains* $D_1, \ldots, D_n$, $n \geq 1$ (for example, the set **Z** of all integers is one such domain). We note **D** the union of all domains $D_1, \ldots, D_n$. We suppose that the domains are pairwise disjoint.

☐ A countably infinite set **A** of symbols called *attributes*. Intuitively, the elements of **A** are names for structure fields as we shall see later.

☐ A countably infinite set **ID** of symbols called *identifiers*. The elements of **ID** will be used as identifiers for objects.

Let us now define the notion of *value*.

DEFINITION 15.1.   [Values]

1. The special symbol *nil* is a value, called a *basic value*.
2. Every element v of **D** is a value, called a *basic value*.
3. Every finite subset of **ID** is a value, called a *set value*. Set values are denoted in the usual way using brackets.
4. Every finite partial function from **A** into **ID** is a value, called a *tuple value*. We denote by $<a_1 : i_1, \ldots, a_p : i_p>$ the partial function t defined on $a_1, \ldots, a_p$ such that $t(a_k) = i_k$ for all k.

We denote by V the set of all values.

We can now define the notion of object.

DEFINITION 15.2.   [Objects]

1. An *object* is a pair $o = (i, v)$, where i is an element of **ID** (an identifier) and v is a value.
2. We define, in an obvious way, the notion of *basic* objects, *set-structured* objects, and *tuple-structured* objects.
3. O is the set of all objects, that is $O = \textbf{ID} \times V$.

This "tuple-and-set" construction of objects is similar to that of Bancilhon and Khoshafian [1986] and especially to that of Kuper and Vardi [1984] where identifiers (called addresses) were also introduced.

In the following, we need some technical notations: If $o = (i, v)$ is an object then *ident(o)* denotes the identifier i and *value(o)* denotes the value v. We will denote by *ref* the function from O in 2^{ID} which associates to an object the set of all the identifiers appearing in its value, that is, those referenced by the object. We can use a graphical representation for objects as follows.

DEFINITION 15.3.   [Object graph] If Θ is a set of objects, then the graph *graph(Θ)* is defined as follows:

1. If o is a basic object of Θ then the graph contains a vertex with no outgoing edge. The vertex is labeled with the value of o.
2. If o is a tuple-structured object .bf $(i, <a_1 : i_1, \ldots, a_p : i_p>)$, the graph of o contains a vertex, say v, represented by a dot (.) and labeled

FIGURE 15.1

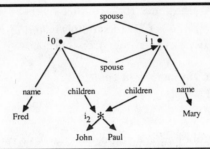

with i, and p outgoing edges from v labeled with $a_1, \ldots, a_p$ leading respectively to the vertex corresponding to objects $o_1, \ldots, o_p$, where o_k is an object identified by i_k (if such objects exist).

3. If o is a set-structured object .br $(i, \{i_1, \ldots, i_p\})$, the graph of o contains a vertex, say v, represented by a star (*) and labeled by i, and p unlabeled outgoing arcs from v leading respectively to the vertex corresponding to objects $o_1, \ldots, o_p$, where o_k is an object identified by i_k (if such objects exist).

We illustrate this definition with an example. Let Θ be the set consisting of the following objects:

$$o_0 = (i_0, <\text{spouse} : i_1, \text{name} : i_3, \text{children} : i_2>)$$
$$o_1 = (i_1, <\text{spouse} : i_0, \text{name} : i_4, \text{children} : i_2>)$$
$$o_2 = (i_2, \{i_5, i_6\}), \ o_3 = (i_3, \text{“Fred”}), \ o_4 = (i_4, \text{“Mary”})$$
$$o_5 = (i_5, \text{“John”}), \ o_6 = (i_6, \text{“Paul”})$$

Θ is represented by Fig. 15.1.

It is important to note that, referring to Definition 15.3, we cannot build the graph representation of any set of objects. For example, if an identifier i appears in a value, there must be an object identified by it. Intuitively speaking, identifiers are pointers on objects and there must be no dangling pointers in our set of objects. This leads us to introduce the notion of consistency for a set of objects.

DEFINITION 15.4.   [Consistent set of objects] A set Θ of objects is consistent "iff":

1. Θ is finite.
2. The *ident* function is injective on Θ (i.e., there is no pair of objects with the same identifier).
3. For all $o \in \Theta, ref(o) \subseteq ident(\Theta)$ (i.e., every referenced identifier corresponds to an object of Θ).

In the following, we denote by $\Theta(i)$ the value v such that the object (i,v) is in Θ.

In value-based systems (i.e., in systems where no object identity exists, such as relational systems) there is no need to distinguish between identical objects and equal objects since the two notions are the same. On the contrary, object-oriented systems need to distinguish them as there is a sharp distinction between values and objects.

DEFINITION 15.5. [Equalities]

1. *0-equality*: two objects o and o' are 0-equal (or *identical*) "iff" $o = o'$ (in the sense of mathematical pair equality).

2. *1-equality*: two objects o and o' are 1-equal (or simply *equal*) "iff" value(o) = value(o').

3. *σ-equality:* two objects o and o' are σ-equal (or *value-equal*) "iff" span-tree(0) = span-tree(o') where span-tree(o) is the tree obtained from o by recursively replacing an identifier i (in a value) by the value of the object identified by i.

Equality implies value-equality, but the converse is not true since many distinct objects may have the same span tree. These definitions of equality correspond to identity, shallow-equality, and deep-equality of Smalltalk 80 [Goldberg & Robson, 1983]. We must notice that the span-tree build from an object may be infinite (in the case of cyclic objects). So, this construction cannot be used (directly) as a decision procedure for testing value-equality.

15.4 TYPES

A type is an abstraction that allows the user to encapsulate in the same structure data and operations. In our model, the static component of a type is called a type structure. As we shall see later, our notion of type bears some similarity to abstract data types. Users of a type only see its abstract part, that is, the interface of its methods, whereas the programmer of the type is concerned with the implementation. However, a type has only one implementation.

In what follows, we shall decompose the process of defining the syntax, semantics, and subtype relationship among types in two steps. First, in Section 15.4.1, we shall define the syntax of type structures as well as the notion of schema. Then, we shall give the semantics of a schema with respect to a consistent set of objects. A partial order among type structures will be defined using this semantics. Second, in Section 15.4.2, the same treatment will be given to methods. We shall bring up pieces together in Section 15.4.3 with the notion of "type systems." We begin by defining the set of type names.

DEFINITION 15.6.   [Type names] *Bnames* is the set of names for basic types containing:

1. The special symbols *Any* and *Nil*.
2. A symbol d_i for each domain D_i. We shall note $D_i = \mathrm{dom}(d_i)$.
3. A symbol $'x$ for every value x of D.

Cnames is a set of names for constructed types which is countably infinite and disjoint with *Bnames*. *Tnames* is the union of *Bnames* and *Cnames* and it is the set of all names for types.

In order to define types, we assume that there is a finite set MT whose elements are called methods and which shall play the role of operations on our data structures. For the moment, we can think of the elements of MT as uninterpreted symbols. We shall define them in Section 15.4.2.

DEFINITION 15.7.   [Types] *Basic types* (Btypes): a basic type is a pair (n,m) where n is an element of *Bnames* and m a subset of MT^3.
Constructed types (Ctypes): A constructed type is one of the following:

1. A triple (s,t,m) where s is an element of Cnames, t is an element of Tnames, m a subset of MT. We shall denote such a type by $(s = t, m)$.
2. A triple (s,t,m) where s is an element of Cnames and t is a finite partial function from A to Tnames and m a subset of MT. We shall denote such a type by $(s = <a_1 : s_1, \ldots, a_n : s_n>, m)$ where $t(a_k) = s_k$ and call it a *tuple-structured type*.
3. A triple (s, s', m) where s is an element of Cnames and s' an element of Tnames and m a finite subset of MT. We shall denote such a type by $(s = s', m)$ and call it a *set-structured type*.

A *type* is either a basic or a constructed type. The set of all types is denoted by T.

15.4.1 Type Structures

In this subsection we are interested in the static part of a type, that is, in its structure.

DEFINITION 15.8.   [Type structures] *Basic type structure:* let $T = (n, m)$ be a basic type. We call n the *basic type structure* associated to t.

---

[3]The link between basic types and domains D_i will be given in the following section, in the definition of interpretations.

Constructed type structure: let $t = (s = x, m)$ be a constructed type. We call $s = x$ the *constructed type structure* associated to t.

Given a type t, its structure part will be denoted by *struc*(t) and its methods part by *Methods*(t). Intuitively, a type structure is a type in which the methods part is hidden, that is, it is the data part of the type. Note that recursion (or transitive recursion) is allowed in type definitions, that is, one of the s_i may be s. The type structure Married-Person is an example of recursively defined type.

Type structures are analogous to GALILEO's concrete types [Albano, et al., 1985] except that type structures only exist within types.

For the same reasons as in Section 15.2, we need a notion of consistency for a set of expressions defining type structures. In order to define it formally, we need some technical notations:

1. If t is a type, then *name*(t) is the name of the type, that is, the first component in its definition.
2. If st is a type structure associated to the type t, we call "name of the type structure" st, the name of t, and we note *name*(st) = *name*(t).
3. If st is a type structure (associated to a type t), we call "set of types references for st" and denote by *refer*(st) the set of all types names appearing in the structure st.

DEFINITION 15.9. [Schemas] A set Δ of constructed type structures is a *schema* "iff"

1. Δ is a finite set.
2. *name* is injective on Δ (only one type structure for a given name).
3. For all $st \in \Delta$, *refer*(st) $\cap$ Cnames $\subseteq$ *name*(Δ) (i.e., there are no dangling identifiers).

Note Bene: In a schema, we can identify a *type name* of name(Δ) with the corresponding type structure in Δ, and we shall use this convention in the sequel of the paper.

We illustrate the notion of a schema with two examples: Let Δ be the set consisting of the following type structures:

```
age   =   integer,
person =   <name : string, age : age>
```

Δ is a schema. If we take off the type structure *age* from Δ, it is no longer a schema. On the other hand, the following set of type structures is also a schema:

person = human
human = person

This set of type structures may be not useful but it is well defined and has an interpretation as we shall see in what follows.

Interpretation. This section deals with the definition of the semantics of the type structure system just presented. It will be given by a particular function which associates subsets of a consistent set of objects to type structure names.

DEFINITION 15.10. [Interpretations] Let Δ be a schema and Θ be a consistent subset of the universe of objects O. An *interpretation* I of Δ in Θ is a function from Tnames in $2^{ident(\Theta)}$, satisfying the following properties:

Basic Type Names

1. $I(Nil) \subseteq \{i \in ident(\Theta)^4/(i, Nil) \in \Theta\}$.
2. $I(d_i) \subseteq \{id \in ident(\Theta)/\Theta(id) \in D_i\} \cup I(Nil)$.
3. $I('x) \subseteq \{id \in ident(\Theta)/\Theta(id) = x\} \cup I(Nil)$.

Constructed Type Names

4. If $s = <a_1 : s_1, \ldots, a_n : s_n>$ is in Δ then $I(s) \subseteq \{id \in ident \, (\Theta)/\Theta(id)$ is a tuple-structured value defined (*at least*) on $a_1, \ldots, a_n$ and $\Theta(id)(a_k) \in I(S_k)$ for all $k\} \cup I(Nil)$.
5. If $s = \{s'\}$ is in Δ then $I(s) \subseteq \{id \in ident \, (\Theta)/\Theta(id) \subseteq I(s')\} \cup I(Nil)$.
6. If $s = t$ is in Δ then $I(s) \subseteq I(t)$.

Undefined Type Names

7. If s is neither a name of basic type nor a name of the schema Δ, then $I(s) \subseteq I(Nil)$.

DEFINITION 15.11. [Model of a schema]

1. *Partial order on interpretations:* An interpretation I is *smaller* than an interpretation I' "iff" for all $s \in Tnames, I(s) \subseteq I'(s)$.
2. *Model:* Let Δ be a schema and Θ be a consistent set of objects. The model M of Δ is Θ, which is the greatest interpretation of Δ in Θ.

As we shall show later, this definition is well founded. Some important remarks are in order at this point. Intuitively, the model $M(s)$ of a constructed type structure of name s is the set consisting of all objects (identifiers of objects) having this structure. For example, if

$$\Theta = \{(i_o, Nil), (i_1, \{i_2, i_3\}), (i_2, 1), (i_3, 4), (i_4, <a : i_2>), (i_5, <a : i_2, b : i_3>)\}$$

and

$$\Delta = \{s_1 = \ <a : Integer>, s_2 = \ <a : Integer, b : Integer>, s_3 = \{Integer\}\}$$

then

$M(s_1) = \{i_0, i_4, i_5\}$
$M(s_2) = \{i_0, i_5\}$
$M(Integer) = \{i_0, i_2, i_3\}$
$M(s_3) = \{i_0, i_1\}$

We can notice that the value of an interpretation of a *Basic type name* does not depend on Δ, which is an intuitive result. Moreover, if (the identifier of) an object belongs to the model $M(s)$ of a tuple structure, then it also belongs to the models of tuple type structures which are substructures of s. In the following example, i_5 is in $M(s_2)$ but also in $M(s_1)$. This property will allow us to give a simple set-inclusion semantics for the subtyping relation among type structures defined in the following subsection. This interpretation is derived from an interpretation originally proposed in Cardelli [1984]. Note that any attribute could be added to a tuple-structured object and the latter would still have a well-defined type. Such "added" attributes will be referred to as "exceptional," and their manipulation is considered in Section 15.4.4.

We now have to prove that our definition of the model of a schema is well founded. Given a schema Δ and a consistent set of objects Θ, there is a finite number of interpretations of Δ defined on Θ. Therefore, in order to prove that the greatest interpretation exists, we just have to prove that the union of two interpretations is an interpretation.

Let I_1 and I_2 be two interpretations, and I be the function defined by $I(s) = I_1(s) \cup I_2(s)$, for every type name s. This function I clearly verifies properties 1, 2, and 3 of the definition of interpretations. If $s = \ <a_1 : s_1, \ldots, a_n : a_n>$ and id is an element of $I(s)$ (for example, an element of $I_1(s)$), then $\Theta(\text{id})(a_k)$ is in $I_1(s_k)$ for all k, because I_1 is an interpretation. So $\Theta(\text{id})(a_k)$ is in $I(s_k)$ for all k, and I verifies the property 4 of Definition 15.10. We can show in the same manner that I also verifies properties 5 and 6.

In conclusion, there is a greatest interpretation M, and we have

$$M(s) = \bigcup_{I \in INT(\Delta)} I(s)$$

for every type name s, where $INT(\Delta)$ denotes the set of all interpretations of Δ (in Θ).

Partial Order Among Type Structures

DEFINITION 15.12. [Partial order $\leq$ st] Let s and s' be two type structures of a schema Δ. We say that s is a substructure of s' (denoted by $s \leq$ st s') "iff" $M(s) \subseteq M(s')$ for all consistent sets Θ.

For example, if Δ consists of the following type structures

$s_1 = <a : Integer>$
$s_2 = <a : Integer, b : Integer>$
$s_3 = <c : s_1>, s_4 = <c : s_2>$
$s_5 = \{s_1\}, s_6 = \{s_2\}, s_7 = <a : '1>$

then the following relationships hold among these structures:

$s_2 \leq$ st s_1 $s_4 \leq$ st s_3
$s_7 \leq$ st s_1 $s_6 \leq$ st s_5

The first relationship ($s_2 \leq$ st s_1) comes from the interpretation of tuple type structures. Let us establish the second one ($s_4 \leq$ st s_3). Let id be the (identifier of an) object belonging to $I(s_4)$. We know from the definition that $\Theta(\text{id})(c)$ belongs to $I(s_2)$ and so to $I(s_1)$ because we have $s_2 \leq$ st s_1. We conclude that id belongs to $I(s_3)$ and so $I(s_4) \subseteq I(s_3)$. The inequality $s_6 \leq$ st s_5 can be established in the same manner and the relation $s_7 \leq$ st s_1 is obviously true.

Definition 15.12 gives a semantic definition for the subtyping relationship $\leq$ st. The following theorem gives a syntactic characterization of it.

THEOREM 15.1. Let s and s' be two type structures of a schema Δ. s is a substructure of s' ($s \leq$ st s') "iff"

1. Either s and s' are tuple structures $s = t$ and $s' = t'$, such that t is more defined than t' and for every attribute a such that t' is defined, we have $t(a) \leq$ st $t'(a)$.
2. Or s and s' are set structures $s = \{s_1\}$ and $s' = \{s'_1\}$ and we have $s_1 \leq$ st s'_1.
3. Or $s = 'x$, s' is a basic type structure, and x is in dom(s').

Proof. The validity of this characterization can be easily established by induction. The completeness can be established with a case study, inspecting successively tuple-structured types, set-structured types, and basic types.

This theorem gives a syntactical means for checking type structure subtyping.

15.4.2 Methods

In Section 15.4.1, we have presented the syntax and semantics of type structures. In this subsection, we define, in the same way, the syntax and semantics of operations, which we call methods in this context. These operations will consist of (first-order) functions.

Definition. We assume that we have a countable set Mnames of symbols that will be used as names for methods.

DEFINITION 15.13. [Signatures] Let Δ be a schema. A *signature* over Δ is an expression of the form

$$s_1 \times s_2 \times \cdots \times s_n \to s$$

where $s_1, s_2, \ldots, s_n$, and s are type names corresponding to type structures in Δ or basic type names.

A *method* m is a pair $m = (n, \sigma)$ where n is a method name (an element of Mnames) and σ is a signature. We shall denote by *name(m)* the name of the method m and by *sign(m)* the signature of the method m.

In the object-oriented formalism, methods are related to types (or type structures) using the first argument of their signature, so we have:

DEFINITION 15.14. [Methods] Let $m = (n, s_1 \times \cdots \times s_n \to s)$ be a method. We say that *m is defined on* s_1.

Interpretation. In this subsection, we define the model of a signature σ.

DEFINITION 15.15. [Model of a signature] Let Δ be a schema and σ a signature over $\Delta (\sigma = s_1 \times \cdots \times s_n \to s)$. If Θ is a consistent set of objects, then the *model of σ in* Θ is the set of all **partial** functions from $M(s_1) \times \cdots \times M(s_n)$ into $M(s)$ where $M(s_k)$ is the model in Θ of the structure of Δ identified by s_k.

Let us illustrate these definitions by an example. Let Δ be the schema introduced in Section 15.2 restricted to the type structures Person, Persons, Employee, Employees, and Male. We consider now the following signatures:

$\sigma_1 = $ Persons $\times$ Person $\to$ Boolean
$\sigma_2 = $ Employees $\times$ Employee $\to$ Boolean
$\sigma_3 = $ Person $\to$ Person
$\sigma_4 = $ Male $\to$ Employee
$\sigma_5 = $ Employee $\to$ Integer

We shall take the following set of objects Θ as interpretation domain:

(i_0, nil), $(i_1, <\text{name} : i_{16}, \text{age} : i_7, \text{sex} : i_8>)$,
$(i_2, <\text{name} : i_{17}, \text{age} : i_9, \text{sex} : i_{10}>)$
$(i_3, <\text{name} : i_{18}, \text{age} : i_9, \text{sex} : i_8, \text{salary} : i_{11}>)$,
$(i_4, <\text{name} : i_{19}, \text{age} : i_{13}, \text{sex} : i_{12}, \text{salary} : i_{11}>)$
$(i_5, \{i_1, i_2\})$, $(i_6, \{i_3, i_4\})$, $(i_7, 20)$, $(i_9, 25)$, $(i_{11}, 130000)$,
$(i_{13}, 35)$, $(i_8, \text{"male"})$, $(i_{10}, \text{"varying"})$, $(i_{12}, \text{"female"})$,
(i_{14}, false), (i_{15}, true), $(i_{16}, \text{"Smith"})$
$(i_{17}, \text{"Blake"})$, $(i_{18}, \text{"Jones"})$, $(i_{19}, \text{"Nash"})$

Using Definition 15 in the previous subsection, we can build the models of the type structures defined in Δ:

$M(\text{Person}) = \{i_0, i_1, i_2, i_3, i_4\}$
$M(\text{Persons}) = \{i_0, i_5, i_6\}$
$M(\text{Employee}) = \{i_0, i_3, i_4\}$
$M(\text{Employees}) = \{i_0, i_6\}$
$M(\text{Male}) = \{i_0, i_1, i_3\}$
$M('\text{"male"}) = \{i_0, i_8\}$
$M(\text{String}) = \{i_0, i_8, i_{10}, i_{12}, i_{16}, i_{17}, i_{18}, i_{19}\}$
$M(\text{Integer}) = \{i_0, i_7, i_9, i_{11}, i_{13}\}$
$M(\text{Boolean}) = \{i_0, i_{14}, i_{15}\}$

The model of the signature σ_1 is the st of all **partial** functions from $\{i_0, i_5, i_6\} \times \{i_0, i_1, i_2, i_3, i_4\}$ into $\{i_0, i_{14}, i_{15}\}$. Intuitively, the model of the signature σ_1 is the set of functions assigning a Boolean object to some pairs (i, j) where i is (the identifier of) a set of person objects and j is (the identifier of) a person object.

We shall use this interpretation of signatures in the following subsection, which introduces an ordering among signatures.

Partial Order Among Signatures

DEFINITION 15.16. [Partial order $\leq$ m] Let Δ be a schema and f and g two signatures over Δ. We say that f is smaller than g (or that f *refines* g) "iff" $M(f) \subseteq M(g)$ for all consistent sets Δ. This ordering will be denoted by $\leq$ m.

Looking at the schema of the previous example, we can see that the following inequalities hold:

$$\sigma_2 \leq m\sigma_1 \text{ and } \sigma_4 \leq m\sigma_3$$

In fact, let Θ be any consistent set of objects and f be a partial function in $M(\sigma_2)$. f is a (partial) function from $M(\textit{employees}) \times M(\textit{employee})$ in $M(\text{Boolean})$. We have seen in Section 15.4.2 that employees $\leq$ st person, and hence, $M(\text{employees}) \subseteq M(\text{persons})$ and $M(\text{employee}) \subseteq M(\text{person})$. f is also a partial function from $M(\text{persons}) \times M(\text{person})$ in $M(\text{boolean})$, so f is in $M(\sigma_1)$. A similar proof can be constructed for the inequality $\sigma_4 \leq m\sigma_3$.

Intuitively, $\sigma \leq m\sigma'$ means that we can use a method of signature σ' "in place of" a method of signature σ_1 to a set of employees and an employee because employees are persons. This partial order models inheritance of data structures. In the following section, we put data structures and methods together to define type systems and we use the ordering $\leq$ st which models inheritance of data structures. In the following section, we put data structures and methods together to define type systems and we use the ordering $\leq$ st and $\leq$ m to define inheritance of types. The following theorem gives an easy syntactical equivalence to the definition of the partial order $\leq$ m among signatures.

THEOREM 15.2. Let f and g be two signatures over a schema Δ. Then, $f \le mg$ "iff"

$$f = s_1 \times \ldots \times s_n \to s$$
$$g = s'_1 \times \cdots \times s'_n \to s'$$
$$s_k \le st\, s'_k \text{ for } k = 1, 2, \ldots, n$$
$$s \le st\, s'.$$

Proof. In order to clarify the proof, we assume, without loss of generality, that the methods signatures are of the form: $\sigma = s_1 \to s$, and $\sigma'_1 \to s'$. Suppose that $\sigma \le m\sigma'$. Every partial function from $M(s_1)$ to $M(s)$ is then a partial function from $M(s'_1)$ to $M(s')$. So, we necessarily have $M(s_1) \subseteq M(s'_1)$ and $M(s) \subseteq M(s')$.

Conversely, if these two inclusions hold, then every partial function from $M(s_1)$ to $M(s)$ is clearly also a partial function from $M(s'_1)$ to $M(s')$.

In the part concerning methods, our definition differs from the "classical" definitions of data type theory [Bruce & Wegner, 1986; Cardelli, 1984; Albano, et al., 1985]. In these settings, functional types may be constructed: the type $r \to s$ has as instances functions having r as domain and s as co-domain. The general rule of subtyping among functional types can be expressed as follows:

If $r' \le r$ and $s \le s'$ then $r \to s \le r' \to s'$.

This means that a function with domain r and co-domain s can always be considered as a function from some smaller domain r' to some larger co-domain s'. This is a necessary condition for the type system to be *safe*, that is, to guarantee that a run-time error will never be caused by a syntactically well-typed expression. If we had adopted this rule in our framework, the subtype relation would be inverted between the right-hand sides of the signatures in Theorem 2, that is, $s' \le s$ instead of $s \ge s'$.

Our choice leads to a less restrictive type system, but we give up safety. There are three main reasons for such a choice. First, we want to be able to inherit an "add" method defined on sets. Suppose there are two types S and T such that $S \le st\, T$. Then we have $\{S\} \le st\{T\}$. Let $add_S \le m\, add_T$, which is a necessary condition to have $\{S\} \le \{T\}$ (see Definition 15.18). Second, this model is intended to be a foundation for an object-oriented layer on top of C which itself is not type safe. Third, we shall implement run-time checking for the cases where static type checking is not sufficient.

15.4.3 Type Systems

DEFINITIONS 15.17. [Type systems] A set of types Π is a *type system* "iff"

1. The set of structures associated to Π is a schema.
2. For all type $t \in \Pi$, and for all methods $m \in$ Methods$(t)^4$, m is defined on *struct(t)*.

Now, given a type system Π, we must be able to compare two types t and t', with respect to their structures and to the methods they contain.

DEFINITION 15.18.   [Subtyping] Let Π be a type system and t and t' two types of Π. We say that *t is a subtype of t'* and we note $t \leq t'$ "iff"

1. struct(t) $\leq$ st struct(t').
2. For all $m \in$ Methods(t), there exist $m' \in$ Methods(t') such that name(m) = name (m') and sign(m) $\leq$ m sign(m').

We illustrate this by the following example: Let Π be the type system of the example of Section 15.4.2 where

Methods(Person) = {(husband, σ_3)}
Methods(Persons) = {(parent, σ_1)}
Methods(Employee) = {(husband, σ_3), (salary, σ_5)}
Methods(Employees) = {(parent, σ_1), (manager, σ_2)}
Methods(Male) = {(hire, σ_4), (husband, σ_3)}

In this type system, the following subtype relationships hold: employee $\leq$ person, male $\leq$ person, and employees $\leq$ persons.

15.4.4 Objects Revisited

We shall now extend the definition of an object in order to encapsulate in the same structure data and operations.

DEFINITION 15.19.   [Objects revisited] An *object o* is a triple (i, v, m) where i and v are as in Definition 2 and m is a set of methods. The first component of the signature of every method of m is a type structure whose interpretation contains o.

The set of methods of an object can be empty, and in this case, it will be manipulated through the methods of the type it possesses. This notion is useful in the following cases:

1. When handling exceptions. For example, let us assume that we define in type Employee a method increase salary to compute the salary of an

---

[4] We recall that *Methods(t)* denotes the set of methods of type t.

employee. Suppose that one of these employees is the CEO and that his or her salary has to be computed in a different way than for regular employees. One could create a specific subtype of employee in order to override the increase salary method of type employee. This would be heavy and it is more natural to define a specific method for the CEO object.

2. "Exceptional" attribute handling (see Section 15.4.2). As full encapsulation is preserved, the only way to access and/or modify an exceptional attribute of an object is via a method attached to the object.

3. Still another application is when representing the data model in terms of itself. This kind of self-representation is very frequent in object-oriented frameworks (the predefined classes "class" and "metaclass" of Smalltalk 80 are a good example). Types could be represented as objects belonging to a predefined type "type" and "type methods" could be easily defined attaching them to these objects. An example of a type method for a type T is a customized method for instanciating instances of T.

15.5 DATABASES

In this section, we introduce the notion of database. Informally, a database is a type system together with a consistent set of objects representing the instances of the types at a given moment.

DEFINITION 15.20. [Databases] A database is a tuple $(\Pi, \Theta, < db, \mathbf{ext}, \mathbf{impl})$ where

1. Π is a type system, and Δ is the associated schema.
2. Θ is a consistent set of objects.
3. $< db$ is a strict partial order among Π.
4. $\mathbf{ext}$ is an interpretation of Δ in Θ.
5. $\mathbf{impl}$ is a function assigning a function to every method m of a type t.

Moreover, we impose that the following properties hold:

1. $t < db\ t'$ implies $t \le t'$.
2. If $t < db\ t'$ and $t < db\ t''$ then t' and t'' are comparable.
3. $\Theta = \cup_{t \in \Pi} ext(t)$.
4. $\mathbf{ext}(t) \cap \mathbf{ext}(t') = \varnothing$ if t and t' are not comparable.
5. If t is a type of Π and m a method of t having signature $t \times \cdots \times s_n \to s$, then $\mathbf{impl}(m)$ is a function defined at least from $\mathbf{ext}(t) \times \cdots \times \mathbf{ext}(s_n)$ in $\mathbf{ext}(s)$.

This definition deserves some comments. The extension of a type is an interpretation but may not be a model. Indeed, a model contains all the possible objects that satisfy a given structure. For example, there may be two types of structure "integer" (say age and weight) in a database. These types have the same model but a given extension as defined by a user will not contain the same objects. The $\leq$ ordering of Definition 15.18 models the notion of subtyping. That is, two types t and t' are comparable using $\leq$ if one *can be* a subtype of the other. The ordering $\leq$ db is the actual inheritance types hierarchy, as *defined* by the user. This ordering must satisfy property 1, that is, the user can declare that t is a subtype of $t'(t <$ db $t')$ only if it is allowed by the model ($t \leq t'$). For example, the type system may contain the types:

Age = (Integer, $\{+, -\}$)
Weight = (Integer, $\{+, -\}$)

with corresponding signatures for the methods $+$ and $-$. We have the inequalities (Age $\leq$ Weight) and (Weight $\leq$ Age) but the user does not intend to consider an age as a weight nor a weight as an age, and Age and Weight will be incomparable for $<$ db. Property 2 says that we do not allow multiple inheritance. This is a constraint we introduced for the O_2 system because it is still an open problem to decide whether **multiple** inheritance is a useful modelization tool. In any case, our semantics would still be valid in the context of multiple inheritance. Property 3 says that Θ is the union of all type extensions. There are no database objects not belonging to any type extension. Property 4 says that an object o cannot belong to the extension of two types t and t' if they are incomparable for $<$ db. Consider the preceding types Age and Weight. The object $(i_1, 1)$ belongs to the model of Age and to the model of Weight, but if we allow this object to belong to both ext(Age) and ext(Weight), we violate the user intention, which was to isolate these two types.

15.6 CONCLUDING REMARKS

The main contribution of this paper is to propose a data model for an object-oriented database system. The model includes the following features:

1. Objects may have a tuple or set structure (or be atomic). They form a directed graph in which cycles may appear. Consistent sets of objects are used as interpretation domains for type structures and method signatures.
2. Types consist of a type structure and a set of methods. Their structure may be recursively defined. The interpretation of tuple-structured types is unusual in the database world and follows the original pro-

posal of Cardelli [1984]. It allows to give a simple set inclusion semantics to the partial order among type structures ($\leq$ st). Methods are
defined as a name together with a signature and are interpreted as
a function. The interpretation of method signatures allows again a
simple set inclusion semantics for the partial order among signatures
($\leq$ m). The subtyping relationship is defined using the ordering $\leq$ st
and $\leq$ m. Notice that although our database definition restricts inheritance to simple inheritance, our model deals with multiple inheritance.

3. The $\leq$ m relation differs form other proposals [Cardelli, 1984; Bruce
& Wegner, 1986] in that it is less restrictive, but the type system is no
longer safe (that is, run-time errors may be caused by a syntactically
well-typed expression). This decision was mainly motivated because of
its increased flexibility and by the fact that we are not building a new
language, but rather an object layer according to this model on top of
existing programming languages with unsafe type systems, such as C
and Lisp.

4. The notion of "database" is introduced. A database is a type system,
together with a consistent set of objects (database instances) and a
subtyping relationship satisfying some constraints.

We are currently working on some extensions of the model. The first one
concerns object naming. Up to here, the only handle that a programmer has
on a object is through the name of one of its types. So, to retrieve an object
from the database, the programmer has to send a message to the extension
of the type with some key as argument. Such a problem is introduced by
persistency: in standard programming languages, we name objects using
temporary variable names. Object names seem to be needed, and they have
to be introduced in the model.

A second extension concerns the introduction of variables in the construction of types in order to model genericity (also called "parametric polymorphism") of types and methods. Genericity can be simulated with inheritance
[Meyer, 1986], but in a heavy and nonintuitive way.

A third extension is to increase the modeling power of the model: a
list constructor should be included in order to model ordered collections of
data (it could be implemented as a recursive tuple type, but we would lose
expressiveness). Finally, in this model, we made the simplifying assumption
that the methods are not objects of the model. So methods have to be modeled
as first-order functions. It should be interesting to extend the model to treat
methods as objects and to allow higher-order methods.

REFERENCES

Albano et al 85, "GALILEO: A Strongly Typed, Interactive Conceptual Language,"
A. Albano, L. Cardelli, and R. Orsini, *ACM TODS*, Vol. 10, No. 2, March 85.

Andrews & Harris 87, "Combining Language and Database Advances in an Object-oriented Development Environment," T. Andrews and C. Harris, *Proc. OOPSLA*, 1987.

Bancilhon and Khoshafian 86, "A Calculus for Complex Objects," F. Bancilhon and S. Khoshafian, *ACM PODS Conference*, 1986.

Bancilhon et al 87, "The O$_2$ Object Manager Architecture," F. Bancilhon, V. Benzaken, C. Delobel, and F. Velez, *Altaïr Technical Report*," 14/87, November, 87.

Banerjee et al 87, "Data Model Issues for Object-Oriented Applications," J. Banerjee et al., *ACM TOOLS*, Vol. 5, No. 1, January 1987.

Bruce & Wegner 86, "An Algebraic Model of Subtypes in Object-Oriented Languages," K. B. Bruce and P. Wegner, *SIGPLAN notices*, Vol. 21, No. 40, October 86.

Cardelli 84, "A Semantics of Multiple Inheritance," L. Cardelli, in *Semantics of Data Types, Lecture notes in Computer Science*, Vol. 173, pp. 51–67, Springer Verlag, 1984

Copeland & Maier 84, "Making Smalltalk a Database System," G. Copeland and D. Maier, *ACM-SIGMOD*, 1984.

Copeland & Khoshafian 86, "G. Copeland and S. Khoshafian, "Object Identity," *OOPSLA 86*, Portland, Oregon, September 1986.

Goldberg and Robson 83, "*Smalltalk 80: The Language and Its Implementation*," A. Goldberg and D. Robson, Addison-Wesley, Reading, Mass, 1983.

Kuper and Vardi 84, "A New Approach to Database Logic," G. M. Kuper, M. Y. Vardi, *ACM PODS Conference*, Waterloo, Canada, 1984.

Meyer 86, "Genericity versus Inheritance," B. Meyer, *OOPSLA 86*, Portland, September 1986.

Nixon et al 87, "Implementation of a Compiler for a Semantic Data Model: Experience with Taxis," B. Nixon et al., *ACM SIGMOD*, 1987.

Zdonik 84, "Object Management System Concepts," S. Zdonik, *Proc. ACM SIGOA on Office Systems*, Toronto, 1984.

CHAPTER 16

OBJECT-ORIENTED TYPE EVOLUTION

Stanley B. Zdonik

16.1 INTRODUCTION

One of the major challenges in the engineering of large-scale software systems is to provide mechanisms that allow for evolution and change. This change can take many forms. Some aspects of this problem have been addressed by modern programing languages and environments. For example, data abstraction makes it easier to change the implementation of a module without having to make changes to the modules that use it.

Database systems represent an environment in which these problems are particularly severe. After all, databases are concerned with data that will survive for a very long time. This data may have been created with one set of assumption, and as the system develops, those assumptions will shift. How can the database systems provide support for this inevitable process?

Some proposals [Liebenman, 1986] have advocated the use of prototypes. In these schemes, there is no notion of type. Therefore it appears that these systems are more able to change. We feel that the flexibility offered by the prototype approach has one very serious drawback for use in database systems, that is, that database systems rely on the uniformity that is imposed by a typed universe in order to achieve high performance. For example, the fact that all employees have an employee number (defined by the type *Employee*) allows us to compute an index on this attribute.

We are, therefore, interested in trying to balance these two views. We wish to retain a notion of typing while at the same time allowing for more flexibility in system evolution. This paper will explore some of the problems and possible solutions to this view of types. We will first examine the problem of allowing the type of an individual object to change, and then we will present a mechanism that allows type definitions themselves to change.

16.2 OBJECTS THAT CHANGE TYPE

For long-lived systems such as databases, a given object will evolve and change state over time. In an object-oriented database, objects are capable of reacting to messages that are defined by their type, some of which mutate their state. This state is usually thought of as capturable by the object's instance variables and as observable by a subset of the basic methods. The methods that are available are always uniquely determinable from the object's type.

Polymorphism allows an object to be created as an instance of a set of types. For example, if we create an instance of the type *Toyota*, that instance is also an instance of the types *Car, Vehicle*, and *Movable Object*. Another way in which an object can change state is by a mutation of the set of types that it possess. Consider an object that is currently a *Person*. As time passes, it might naturally become an instance of the type *Person*. At time passes, it might naturally become an instance of the type *Student* and then later an instance of the type *Professor*. This kind of modification is usually not directly supported by type systems. It may be possible to create another object of the new type and somehow copy information from the old object to it, but one loses the identity of the old object.

We would like to be able to design a type system for a database that allows this kind of evolution. However, we would also like to be able to control the way in which it happens and to be able to control thee type checking problems that it presents. The rest of this section will examine these issues.

16.2.1 Rules for Type Changes

Our comments will assume that we have a type lattice that allows for multiple supertypes. As stated previously, an object x can have a set of types S. We will call a member of S that has no subtype in S a *most immediate subtype* of x. We will call the supertype and the subtype that is one step away from a type T the *direct supertype* and the *direct subtype* of T, respectively.

We view thee change from one type to another as a process of selectively applying the following two operations:

add-type $(x : T, t : \text{subtype } (T))$ **returns** $y : \text{subtype } (T)$
delete-type $(x : T, t : \text{supertype } (T))$ **returns** $y : \text{subtype } (t)$

Add-type takes an object x of type T and ads to it a specified type t. This subtype must be a direct subtype of the most immediate subtype of T. This corresponds to moving down the type hierarchy. *Add-type* will likely take more than two arguments to initialize the storage that must be added. *Delete-type* removes one of the direct supertypes from x. This corresponds to moving up the type hierarchy. The second argument names the direct supertype of the result. We adopt this convention to accomodate a type with multiple parents. Changing an object from type $T1$ to type $T2$ involves finding a path in the type lattice and using the preceding operations to move along this path, one type at a time. Notice that we have not taken a position on whether or not $x = y$ in these two operation specifications.

Essential Types.   If we think about how objects change type in the real world, we notice that some transitions cannot occur. For example, it is not possible to change a person into a frog (except in fairy tales). In order to capture this kind of knowledge, we need a simple mechanism for expressing these constraints at the type level.

A simple observation can help to explain this phenomenon. Some types cannot be lost. If an object is created as an instance of type *Student*, that instance might change to type *Professor*, but both *Student* and *Professor* share a common supertype, type *Person*. Any instance that has type *Person* as a supertype can never lose that type. We say that type *Person* is an *essential type*, that is, it defines the essence of its subtypes and must always be present in the list of types of an individual that was created as an instance of it.

Designating a type as an essential type is an activity that would be done by the type designer. It adds some extra semantics about the potential behavior of instances of that type. It builds a simple constraint into the information provided by the type definitions. It is similar to constraints related to object uniqueness (i.e., keys) and referential integrity.

It is possible to have more than one essential type. If our type system allows for multiple inheritance, we might have several essential types contributed by different paths in the lattice. For example, type *Car* might be subtype of both *Movable_Object* and *Sellable_Object*. Moreover, both of these types might be essential. That is, it might be possible to make a car into a truck by modifying the body, but it must always remain movable and sellable.

Exclusionary Types.   In a similar way, we might also designate a type T as *exclusionary* if an object can only acquire T at the time of its creation. T is called exclusionary because in moving an object x from some type R to some other type S, it is illegal to move through a type that would have T as a supertype. We are therefore excluded from it as a new type.

Notice that essential types are not exclusionary. It is possible to add a type that is essential to an object. Of course, once it has been added, it cannot be lost. Moreover, an exclusionary type is not essential because it can be removed. Of course, the definition of an exclusionary type requires that once it has been removed, it can never be regained.

Often an object must change types in come predefined sequence. For example, a person starts out as a child, becomes a student, graduates and becomes a professor, and then retires. It is possible to use exclusionary types to stimulate this requirement. Suppose that the hierarchy in Fig. 16.1 is used to model this situation.

It is possible to create an object *x* as an instance of type *Child*, which is exclusionary. We can remove the type *Child* and then add the type *Student*. Although we can remove the type *Student*, we cannot add the type *Child* at this point because it is exclusionary. We can, however, remove the type *T2* and add the type *Professor*. In a similar way, we cannot return to type *Student*. This arrangement allows us to enforce a direction to type changes, however, it is possible to skip any of the intermediate types. We can move from being a child to a retiree directly.

16.2.2 Problems with Type Checking

Allowing objects to change their type presents a potential problem for type checking. The problem has to do with changing the type of an object that is assigned to a variable such that the new type violates the typing requirements of the variable. This could occur in a programming language in which objects are assigned to typed variables or in a database in which the files of an object can have type constraints associated with them.

Because of the problem of aliasing, changing the type of an object in a way that is consistent with one variable might introduce a problem with some other variable. As an example, assume that type *Person* has a property called *friend* that takes another person as a value. Further assume that type *Enrollment* has a property called *student-of* that takes a student as a value.

FIGURE 16.1
EXCLUSIONARY AND ESSENTIAL TYPES

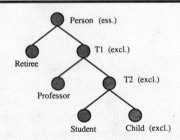

Further assume that type *Person* has two subtypes, *Student* and *Drop_out*. Fred has a friend, John, who is a student. John is also the value of the *Student_of* enrollment *E1*. The function *types: Object → {Type}* takes an object as an argument and returns a set of types corresponding of all types of which that objects is an instance. We can then execute the following program:

```
p:Person
P:=Fred.friend
If[Student in types (p)] then {delete_type (p, Person)
                               add_type (p, Drop_out)}
```

Nothing illegal has happened with respect to *Fred, John,* or the variable *p*, but the value of the *student_of* property of *E1* now has an instance of the type *Drop_out* assigned to it. This is a type violation.

The problem in this example actually occurred when we removed the *Student* type from *John*. At that point *John* was only a *Person*, while *E1* required him to be a *Student*. Adding types does not cause this problem since the result will never be inconsistent with any previously assigned type specification; it is only deleting types that causes this kind of type check failure.

16.2.3 THE DELETION PROBLEM

This is similar to a common problem that comes up in database programming languages. The problem concerns the ability to explicitly delete objects. In database systems, it is common to have an explicit command that deletes an object (e.g., removes a tuple from a relation). We will call this view the explicit deletion view. In many modern programming languages, there is no facility for explicitly deleting objects. Instead, one can only destroy references, and the system then reclaims the storage for an object (i.e., garbage collection) when there is no longer any reference to it. We will call this the garbage collection view.

These two views are hard to reconcile in a database programming language. In databases, and in some languages (e.g., Galileo [Albano, et al., 1985] through its class mechanism) there is always some way to refer to an object. The object can be named through its container (e.g., its class object). In the case of relations, one can always get a tuple through the relation that contains it. In models like this, since the relation provides a reference that cannot be broken by other means (i.e., reassignment) there is a need for an explicit delate.

In languages for which there is a uniform referencing mechanism, all references can be broken. When there are no more references left, the object is effectively deleted. The garbage collector performs a space optimization by actually reclaiming the inaccessible storage. It has been argued that this kind of approach simplifies programming because programmers do not have to keep track of when an object is referenced by other objects. It is impossible with this approach to get dangling references.

In the explicit delete case, one can place a "tombstone object" in place of the deleted object. This eliminates the problem of dangling pointers because a pointer can never be dereferenced to another real object. It will always produce the original object or that object's tombstone. The remaining problem with the tombstone solution is that all programs that do pointer dereferencing would have to able to handle the case in which the expected object has been deleted out from under a given reference. This complicates application code since expressions as simple as $x.p$ (which should return the object referred to by the p field or x has to be prepared to handle an exception generated by the object's not being there (i.e., a tombstone is there instead).

As we saw in a previous section, a similar problem can occur when we delete a type T from an object x. There might still be other objects that are referring to x with the expectation of its having type T.

16.2.4 Changing an Object's Type

In an object-oriented language, objects can have many types. For a given object, there is a piece of state that corresponds to each of its type. We will call each of these fragments of state a *type piece*. For example, if we have types *Toyota*, *Car*, and *Vehicle* in the obvious relationship to each other, then an instance of type *Toyota* will have a type piece for its Toyota part as well as a type piece for each of its car and vehicle parts. We will now look at the problem of modifying an object's type from two different perspectives.

Global Type Modifications.   One view of how to allow objects to change type allows operations that add and delete type pieces directly on the instance. That is, a type change involves modifying the state of the object. Removing a type would correspond to deleting a type piece. If we perform the following operation on c, a variable of type *Car* that holds an instance of the type *Toyota*

```
delete-type (c, Car)
```

this removes the *Toyota* type piece of c. There might be other objects or variables that still refer to its *Toyota* type piece. If *delete-type* actually removes the storage, then we would have to have some way to alert other programs that use that object. This might be implemented by placing a tombstone in the c object to indicate that it once was a *Toyota*, but that that type piece has been removed.

This is completely analogous to the case of deletion semantics described previously. When a program attempts to access the *Toyota* part of an object, it must be prepared to receive a signal that indicates that that type piece is no longer available.

Deleting the type of an object is useful when the intent is to change the type state of the object for all other objects that reference it. Using that semantics for type deletion, we require that adding a type have a global effect as well. That is, if we execute the following code,

```
t:Toyota
delete-type (t, Car)
add-type (t, Toyota, importer = ''Foreign Motors'')
```

any object that refers to this *Toyota t* will see the modification. The modification involved removing the *Toyota* type piece (which lost any information contained therein) and adding a new type piece for *Toyota* to the *Car* object that resulted from the type deletion.

Local Type Modifications.   Another approach involves having the *delete-type* operation only produce a different "view" of the object. In this way, *delete-type* will produce a reference to the object that is of a higher (in the type lattice) type. For example, in the person example in the previous section, we could write

```
e:enrollment
p:person
p:=delete-type (e.student, person)
```

Here, *e.student* and *p* both refer to the same object, but each of the references provides a different type. The variable *p* provides a view as a person, and *e.student* provides a view as a student.

In this view, adding a type would return a new object reference that had the additional type and shared all of the state (including the types) of the original object. In this way, the following code would produce several views of the same object.

```
t:Toyota
p1,p2: Person
p1.owns:-t
p2.drives:=delete-type (p1.owns, Car)
```

The reference *p1.owns* will produce a *Toyota* while *p2.drives* will produce a *Car*. If we then execute the additional code,

```
p2.drives:=add-type (p2.drives, Toyota,
                     importer=''Foreign Motors'')
```

p2.drives will be referencing a *Toyota* that is different from the *Toyota* that is referenced by *p1.owns*, even though they both share the same *Car* type pieces.

When a type piece is no longer referenced, that part of the object can be garbage collected. A type p is said to be referenced by a variable r when $type\ (r) \leq type(p)$. Garbage collection of type pieces can be implemented by reference counts.

16.3 CHANGES TO TYPE DEFINITIONS

Many of the applications that object-oriented databases have been designed to address involve highly volatile information. CAD systems, programming environments, and office information systems are good examples of this type of application. In these environments many of the basic definitional concepts will evolve as well as the data. In an electrical CAD environment, one's notion of how to model a particular kind of circuit may change rapidly as one's understanding of the design space improves and as new technologies are employed.

16.3.1 The Problem

Data abstraction [Liskov, et al., 1977] provides a way to change the implementation of a type and not affect the programs that use that type. This is achieved by defining an interface that captures the abstract behavior of the type and hides the implementation details.

In long-lived application, it is often necessary to change the interface to a type as well. As the interface evolves, two problems are introduced:

1. Keeping old programs working on instances of new versions of a type.
2. Allowing new programs to work with instances of an old version of a type.

We say that a solution to these problems preserves *type change transparency*. Ahlsen, et al. [1984] and Skarra and Zdonik [1987] have looked at solutions that attempt to achieve this goal.

Others [Banerjee, et al., 1986; Penny & Stein, 1987] have looked at this problem from the point of view of how to make sure that the type definitions remain consistent in the face of different classes of change to the type interfaces and to the type lattice structure itself.

16.3.2 Why Not Convert?

Converting all instances of an old type version to be consistent with a new version of that type has three problems:

1. It might not be possible. There might not be enough information in the old version or information might be lost in the conversion.

2. It might not be feasible. It might take too long.

3. It would require converting all existing application programs to be consistent with the new interface.

16.3.3 The Exception Handler Approach

A solution has been proposed [Skarra & Zdonik, 1987] that uses exception handling to achieve type change transparency. In this scheme, as a type evolves, new versions of that type are created. The old versions of the type are not removed. Each object is connected to the type object under which it was created. When a new version of a type is added, the type designer must also add code fragments to other type versions to handle the cases for which there is a conflict between the old versions and the new version.

16.3.4 The Multiple Views Approach

Another approach has an object as a more complex entity. Each time a type changes, the object acquires another layer that reflects those things that are peculiar to the new type. We can think of each layer as a view on the previous layers. A layer can introduce new representation, it can define new definitions for operations, it can suppress (i.e., delete) the availability of an operation, or it can make use of operations in a previous layer. In this way, types are treated as objects that can have versions [Zdonik, 1986]. An object's state reflects all of the versions that its type currently possesses. Figure 16.2 of an object x illustrates this concept. $T1$ and $T2$ are versions of type T. The $f1$, ... ,$f6$ are operations that are defined on their respective type versions.

Notice that the object x is the entire skinny rectangle that spans three type versions. $T1$ is the part of the object defined by the first version of type T. It has a representation used to store its state. It also has four operations used to access this state. $T2$ is the part of the object that is defined by the second version of T. It adds some additional state to support its new operations. One of the new operations $f5$ uses a piece of state from $T1$. Operation $f5$ might do nothing more than invoke operation $f4$. In this way, we have $f4 = f5$ and their names might be the same thereby indicating that there is no change in

FIGURE 16.2

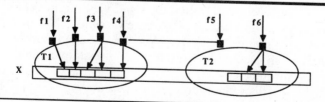

this operation. Operations $f1$ through $f3$ are not available in the $T2$ version of T.

It is important to note that this approach is purely additive in the sense that no information is ever thrown away. Each time an object is expanded to reflect new versions of its underlying type, that expansion is very similar to a conversion. Unlike a conversion, however, the old state is retained as a part of the object.

Whenever a type change occurs, all old instances are, at least conceptually, converted to the new form. Note that the actual conversion of storage may be deferred until the object is referenced. Allocation of type versions consists of two steps. The first expands the storage for the object to make room for additional instance variables that its operations will require, and the second initializes these variables based on values that are possibly derived from previously allocated type chunks.

As an example of new type chunk allocation, assume that the type version $Car1$ supports an mpg (miles per gallon) property whose value is stored in an instance variable called *mpg*. Further, assume that type version $Car2$ supports a kpl (kilometers per liter) property that is stored in an instance variable called *kpl*. If we have an object that was created as an instance of $Car1$, we should have to allocate more storage when that object is passed to a context that attempts to use it as if it were an object of type $Car2$. The code for allocating this space might look as follows:

```
Car2$alloc(c:Car)=
          <allocate space>
          c.Car2$kpl:=c.Car1$mpg
```

The notation *x.T$mpg* represents the *mpg* instance variable defined by type version T for object x. This allocation procedure creates the appropriate space and copies the value of the *mpg* instance variable for $Car1$ into the *kpl* instance variable for $Car2$.

Notice that it is possible to have an operation from one type version use a previous type version. It should be pointed out that it is dangerous to have the newer type view access the instance variables from the previous type view directly. This can be illustrated with a simple example. Suppose that the first type version $Car1$ defines an instance variable called *mpg* to support an abstract property of the same name that is restricted to be in the range 0 . . . . The second type version $Car2$ might also have an abstract property called mpg that is defined to be in the range 0 . . 40. If $Car2$ shared the storage for the mpg property with $Car1$, then the $Car1$, view might get a value that is out of its range if a program set that instance variable to 35 through the $Car2$ view. We therefore require that a type version use the resources of another type version through its abstract interface. In our example, $Car2$ could set the value of the *mpg* instance variable in $Car1$ by calling the *set-mpg* operation that is defined in $Car1$. This will disallow values that are out of range for $Car1$.

The model, then, consists of multiple versions of a type T ordered chronologically as $T1, \ldots, Tn$. An object x is created as a version of one of the n type versions Ti. This causes allocation of the state (i.e., the representation) for all type versions $T1, \ldots, Ti$. Whenever x is accessed in a context that expects a type version Tj such that $j > i$, then the state for all type versions $Ti + 1, \ldots, Tj$ is allocated. In other words, the system ensures that all type views from $T1$ to Tj exist, where Tj is the type version expected by the current executing context.

The requirement to allocate all type version $T1, \ldots, Tj$ less than or equal to the type version Tj expected by the current executing program reflects the fact that type version Tj might use the resources defined on any type version $Ti(1 \le i \le j)$. In practice, we could follow a slightly more conservative method. We could simply allocate storage on demand. If Tj is required by object x, the system would allocate the storage for Tj on object x.

When a program uses an object of a particular type it is able to use the appropriate interface in a consistent way. If a program is expecting an object of type $T2$, it will use the $T2$ interface, even if the object was created as an instance of $T1$. With this approach, an object is not an instance of a single type version as in Skarra and Zdonik [1987].

This usage can be illustrated by the following example. Suppose that we have the following two programs:

```
prog p (x)                      prog p' (x)
    x: Ti                           x: tj

    . . .                           . . .
    f(x) // use f in Ti             g (x) // use g in Tj
```

In fact, the Ti and the Tj would not be distinguished in the program text. The programming environment would be responsible for keeping track of which type version the individual programs were compiled with. The system mechanism for invoking functions would use the interface expected by the using program. It would further be responsible for doing the appropriate allocation.

16.4 SUMMARY

We have suggested a couple of ways in which our notion of type might be relaxed to increase the flexibility of our type systems. We have also looked at a couple of problems that these more flexible models introduce and have sketched some preliminary solutions to these problems. It is clear that there is a need for this kind of capability in many application areas. The challenge is to stretch our notions of type as far as we can in these directions without decreasing our understanding or eliminating the advantages of current type systems.

We need to gain more experience with these models and investigate the feasibility of implementing them in the context of a real object-oriented database programming language. The theoretical ramifications of these proposals deserve further study.

REFERENCES

Ahlsen, M., Bjonerstedt, A., Britts, S., Hulten, C., and Soderlund, L., (1984). "Making Type Changes Transparent." University of Stockholm, SYSLAB Report No. 22, February.

Albano, A., Cardelli, L., and Orsini, R., (1985). "Galileo: A Strongly-Typed, Interactive Conceptual Language." *ACMM Transactions on Database Systems*, Vol. 10, No. 2, June, pp. 230–260.

Banerjee, J., Kim, H. J., Kim, W., Kim and Korth, H. F., (1986). "Schema Evolution in Object-Oriented Persistent Databases." Proceedings of the Sixth Advanced Database Symposium, August.

Katz, R., and Lehman, T., (1982). "Storage Structures for Versions and Alternatives." Computer Science Department, University of Wisconsin—Madison, Technical Report No. 479, July.

Liebermann, H., (1986). "Using Prototypical Objects to Implement Shared Behavior in Object-Oriented Systems," *Proceedings of the Conference on Object-Oriented Programming Systems, Languages, and Applications*, Portland, Ore., September.

Liskov, B., Snyder, A., Atkinson, R., and Shaffert, C., (1977). "Abstraction Mechanisms in CLU." *Communications of the ACM*, Vol. 20, No. 8, August, pp. 564–576.

Penny, D. J., and Stein, J., (1987). "Class Modification in the GemStone Object-Oriented DBMS," *Proceedings of the Conference on Object-Oriented Programming Systems, Languages, and Applications*, Orlando, Fla. October.

Stein, L. A., (1987). "Delegation is Inheritance." *Proceedings of the Conference on Object-Oriented Programming Systems, Languages, and Applications*, Orlando, Fla., October.

Skarra, A. H., and Zdonik, S. B., (1987). "Type Evolution in an Object-Oriented Database," in *Research in Object-Oriented Databases*, Shriver, B., and Wegner, P., (eds.), Reading, Mass.: Addison-Wesley.

Zdonik, S. B., (1986). "Version Management in an Object-Oriented Database." *Proceedings of the IFIP 2.4 Workshop on Advanced Programming Environments*, Trondheim, Norway, June.

CHAPTER 17

Semantics for Transactions in Shared Object Worlds

J. Eliot B. Moss

17.1 INTRODUCTION

One of the motivations for object-oriented databases is nontraditional database applications such as computer-aided design (of many varieties) and office automation. An interesting aspect of design applications is that they are cooperative, and frequently distributed (at least locally). Current database models for managing the consistency, integrity, and permanence of design data are poor. Either these functions are not dealt with at all (relying on an underlying file system and backup procedure, perhaps), handled in an ad hoc fashion, or traditional database techniques are applied. Even the check-in and check-out model is rather weak, though quite helpful in practice.

Past and current work has focused more on specific mechanisms that permit users to accomplish a reasonable subset of their goals. These mechanisms have met with varying success. I believe that what is required is an appropriate model that can capture the desired application semantics—a counterpart in the design domain to serializability in traditional database applications. In short, we need models suitable for applications in which the users are cooperating, and hence may share data in nonserializable ways. While such a model might be implemented using some of the mechanisms others have already designed, the model would provide guidance as to the most appropriate manner in which to use the mechanisms.

Devising such a model for cooperative, data-oriented applications is a major goal of my ongoing research. At present I am working on a model that I call the *shared object world*. The model is incomplete, and I am interested in obtaining criticism and suggestions on the work in progress.

17.2 OBJECTS, VERSIONS, AND WORLDS

An *object* is best defined through its properties. Each object has a *state*, which may (or may not, for some kinds of objects) change over time. Every object has an *identifier (id)*, which is unique over all time (at least as far as we can tell). Once an object is created, it persists until it can no longer be accessed from any world.

The details of the possible kinds of states of objects are probably not that important, but I suggest one possibility for concreteness. An object can consist of either an array of bytes, or an array of *slots*. Every slot contains the ID of an object. Thus, the object corresponds roughly to objects in a language such as Smalltalk, except that the author is ignoring classes and subclass relationships. Even this simple object world presents enough interesting features, however.

Though an object is thought of as changing state over time, I consider an object to be a set of *versions*, where each version represents the state of the object at some point in time (in some world). In the normal course of affairs we get a linear sequence of versions, with the most recent one being of primary interest.

A *world* is, on the one hand, a set of objects, and, on the other hand, a mapping from IDs to versions. If we are operating "within" a given world, and we modify some object x, then we are really just changing the binding between x's ID and its version *for this world only*. Thus, typical computation causes a world to evolve, presumably toward some state that is more useful than its current state.

If every object had a unique world, then worlds would simply partition the objects. However, I believe that it is quite useful to allow objects to reside in multiple worlds, simultaneously. In this state of affairs, when we change an object we need to know which worlds should be affected, of the many worlds that might contain the object. Suppose that at any point in time there is established a list of worlds, and when a given object is modified, we modify it in the first world on the list in which the object appears. This is similar to a search path in a file system. An interesting question is how should this list be maintained during computation, and whether there are reasonable schemes other than a simple list for organizing the worlds.

New worlds are created by copying old ones. When such a copy is made, the copy and the original can and will evolve separately. This might be implemented by copying the object table of the original world, and copying the objects only when they are actually modified (a kind of per-object, copy-on-write facility).

17.3 SUBWORLDS AND VERSIONS OF WORLDS

The model as described so far supports diverging worlds only. This could be very useful for "what if" computations, but is of limited utility unless we can install results from a separate computation back into the mainstream. To allow merging, I introduce the notion of *subworlds*. A subworld is contained within another world, and maintains (versions for) a set of objects. Objects can be created in the subworld and are freely accessible from the containing world. However, I add an additional twist: subworlds have versions, and we can dynamically choose which version of a subworld is the one meant when references are made from the containing world.

To clarify, suppose we start with a world w and create a subworld s within w. Suppose we make a new version of s somehow (discussed later); call it s'. We can install s' for s within w, and then the versions of s world objects represented by s' will be used when those object are accessed within w.

There is a potential consistency problem with this notion of subworlds. Suppose we start with a subworld s, and then evolve a copy of it, s'. In particular, we create some new objects in s'. We then install s', and references to these new objects begin to "escape" into the containing world w. Finally, for some reason we decide to revert to s. At this point the escaped references are meaningless.

There are two ways out of this problem. First, we can try to prevent the escaping of references. This seems impractical and overly restrictive, though perhaps consistent with the notion that a subworld should strongly protect its objects and allow access only through a distinguished root object (or set of roots). This may be an interesting direction to pursue, but may add undesirable complexity. The alternative is to prevent reversion to earlier worlds, and to support only the installation of "future" worlds: ones evolved from the current world. This is consistent with the philosophy of pushing ahead rather than rolling back, but it is not clear if it is entirely practical.

Another thing we need to be able to do is to install an evolved subworld as a "new" subworld, maintaining both the original and new subworlds as alternatives, rather than forcing a choice between them. Exactly how this would work and what it would mean are questions I have yet to answer, but it appears necessary to be able to do something of this nature.

17.4 SIMPLE TRANSACTIONS

This mechanism can be used to support simple transactions in the following way. To begin a transaction, make a copy of the subworld to be modified. Suppose the original is s, and the copy is s'. In performing the transaction, make changes in s' freely. When satisfied that s' is what is needed, make the substitution of s' for s within the containing world. This is the transaction commit.

With no controls on subworld version installation, chaos can obviously ensue. We clearly need some sort of concurrency control. Further, a transaction might modify a number of worlds, and desire to commit only if all of the versions can be installed. Thus we need an atomicity mechanism in support of transaction commit. At this point it would appear that we have something similar to optimistic concurrency control.

17.5 COOPERATION AND SHARING

Even though subworld versioning allows tentative computations to be kept separate and then merged in later, we still have not dealt effectively with cooperation. Frankly, what I have to offer is still along the lines of mechanism rather than a real model, but perhaps it will be of some help. I propose two extensions to the mechanism as it stands.

First, when a subworld is installed, we have the option of not installing some of *its* subworlds. In particular, if someone else has modified a piece of the subworld, we may accept his or her changes. This would seem reasonable (in many cases) provided none of the changes overlap ours. However, it would definitely help to add some notion of semantics and integrity contraints. This leads to the second extension. We can support recording the operations performed on or within a (sub)world. This information could be used to determine if subworld installation is all right.

It seems that a subworld (or perhaps a world in general) might best be used to contain the pieces of an abstract object, and that the subworld gives a good way to localize and control the state of that object, even when it is spread over a number of the simple storage objects first discussed. Note that subworld installation now makes a little more sense—it represents the atomic application of some operations to a single abstract object. However, since we added the logs, we can do more then before: we can actually attempt to merge the operations, either by merging changed data (when that is possible), or by executing appropriate operations to form the logical merge state.

At the workshop it was suggested that it is not so much the notion of serializability that is wrong, but our concept of exactly what forms a transaction. I am inclined to agree, but it is difficult to make this notion precise; the difficulty is determining what collections of actions are (should be) meaningful transactions and defining consistency in a suitable way. One suggestion was that if there are multiple participants in a transaction they must (a) each have read all the others' writes, and (b) all request commit of the transaction. This captures agreement or acceptance of all changes by all parties operationally. Perhaps we can find a way to capture it more axiomatically, which would make us rather more comfortable (how does a party to a transaction decide if another party's update is all right?). Even the operational statement may not be quite right. Perhaps part (a) should read "each have read all the others' *conflicting* writes." Clearly this matter deserves further consideration in our research.

17.6 SUMMARY

Why is this (as yet incomplete) approach any better than current database techniques? One difference is that the fundamental world is a structured address space of objects rather than some other data model. I am interested in such models for two reasons. First, they are closer to programming language run-time systems than traditional data models. Second, they seem more suited to nontraditional applications. More to the point, though, the diverging worlds approach supports concurrent evolution in different directions and it allows "what if" computations. Further, it is more oriented to permitting inconsistent versions to be stored and then merged to form more consistent ones—a kind of forward error recovery, rather than the traditional backout on conflict. Thus, the proposed model seems to have some positive tendencies, even though it is disappointingly far from the mark in being a true model of cooperation.

CHAPTER 18

A PRACTICAL LANGUAGE TO PROVIDE PERSISTENCE AND A RICH TYPING SYSTEM

Deborah A. Baker
David A. Fisher
Jonathan C. Shultis

> I knew an old woman
> who swallowed a fly.
> I don't know why
> She swallowed the fly.
> Perhaps she'll die!
> —Traditional

18.1 MANIFESTO

The woeful inadequacy of current software engineering practice is widely recognized, and there is no need to belabor the problems here. However, what is not so widely recognized is that we cannot make significant progress without radically altering the way we design and build software systems.

Programming languages, operating systems, and databases, as long as they remain separate entities, create insurmountable obstacles to effective software design and maintenance. In particular, their separateness prohibits the specification and exploitation of global information about entire applications. Consequently, it is impossible to ensure the global integrity of applications, to maintain integrity over time, or to obtain efficient implementations.

A typical application currently consists of a number of programs, often written in different languages. Each program has its own view of one aspect of the application. The internal consistency of these views is ensured by the programming languages and their compilers, but there is no information about the application as a whole, which could be used to maintain global consistency among the programs and the persistent data which make up the global state of the application.

Database were invented to provide a globally consistent, representation independent state which could be shared among all of the programs in an application. Unfortunately, because the database abstractions and representations are not shared directly with the languages and their compilers, each interface between program and database is an opportunity for programmer error. Since there is usually no formal relationship between the database and the programs that use it[1], change to either the programs or the database is difficult and error phone. The database also introduces a sharp distinction between the internal program state and the external application state, thereby creating the new problem of maintaining the mutual consistency of these states[2].

In exchange for this flaccid rendition of global consistency, applications pay a high performance penalty. One source of inefficiency is that databases invariably overcommit the structure of the global state, so that only limited specialization to applications is possible. Normalization of relational databases typifies such specialization; it reduces storage requirements, but only within the confines of the relational abstract machine.

A more serious source of inefficiency in databases is their reliance on host operating systems and file systems, which introduce yet another layer of software between the application and the target hardware. Like general-purpose databases, operating systems require every application to pay for unneeded generality.

The only way to achieve reliability and economy in software systems is to integrate the functions of programming languages, databases, and operating systems, so that each application can be managed as a single, coherent body of information. In particular, the abstract properties of the global, persistent state of an application have to be made explicit and formal. Only by doing

---

[1]Cobol/Codasyl is a notable exception, though the fact that they have been integrated is due more to the weakness of Cobol than to the strength of Codasyl.

[2]Incidentally, we do not mean at all to imply that nothing of value has come out of the study of databases. In particular, we owe to database research and experience a vast wealth of data structures and algorithms for indexing, searching, concurrency control, transactions, recovery, and so forth. However, we view these things as technologies that should be called into play to solve specific problems in applications. In this way, it becomes possible to optimize the general mechanisms for the specific situations in which they are applied. Similar remarks apply to operating systems.

so can the global integrity of the application be maintained automatically. Only by doing so can requirements, specifications, designs, code, tests, versions, and so forth be composed, checked, derived, and otherwise manipulated automatically. Only by doing so can this information be used to generate efficient code specifically for each application, instead of interpreting general-purpose command languages. (Note that command language expression (query) optimization is only a halfway measure; the optimized expression is still interpreted.)

We are designing and implementing an experimental language, called **prism**, which seeks to encompass the full spectrum of concerns in a software development environment. The success of such an enterprise requires keeping tight control over the number and complexity of the language features, for fear of engendering an unwieldy monster. Our basic thesis is that there are relatively few fundamental concepts underlying all aspects of software development, and that most of the complexity and lack of integration of software development environments today results from the proliferation of incompatible special cases of these general concepts. Efficient implementation of the particular combinations of these concepts appearing in an application depends on the availablility of information about the properties of those combinations, that is, type information.

Our goal here is to sketch in general terms the features of prism, with particular attention to the issues for "database programming languages." Specifically, we address the issues of persistent data, evolving applications, types, and error handling. We close with a few remarks about the ingredients in our design, but without discussing details of syntax and semantics, which would be premature.

18.2 PERSISTENCE

If we look for an explanation of why the semantics of applications has become spread out over so many different system components, it seems that the sharp separation of the internal state of a program from its external environment is at fault.

During the execution of a program, it is the responsibility of the compiler to ensure that the programmer's intentions are carried out correctly and consistently. The programming language is the means by which the programmer expresses those intentions. By relegating the results of programs to files outside the scope of the language, the designers of our early languages implied that once a program is done processing some data, the programmer has no intentions to express, that is, is no longer interested in those data.

Operating system command languages were therefore invented, so that the programmer *could* express an interest in and concern for data in the environment. These languages have gradually evolved from the Neanderthal grunts of OS/360 JCL to the Cro-Magnon C shell of Unix, but have contin-

ually remained far behind programming languages in their ability to express
the abstract properties of data and to perform manipulations on complex data
types. Dressing up the syntax with windows, templates, and pointing may be
an improvement over awkward mnemonics and cryptic options, but it does
not alleviate the underlying semantic poverty.

Databases were invented in an attempt to make up for the inadequacies
of operating systems, in particular file systems. As time goes on, we swallow
larger and larger animals in pursuit of the original fly, separating the environment from the programming language, until now we are on the brink
of swallowing "database programming languages" and "relational operating
systems." What next, object-oriented logic programming database operating
systems?

Why did we swallow the fly? Perhaps we did not understand at the time
that a uniform abstraction does not require a uniform implementation. In
many programming languages, a program is a procedure, which is effectively
called by the environment. It contains local variables, which are "global" to
the program. What that means, of course, is that those variables exist until
the program completes. For efficiency, it makes good sense to fix the location
of those variables, relative to some fixed start address. Once that decision is
made, of course, we can dispense with the names of the variables altogether,
and use just their addresses.

Abstractly, persistent data are much like global variables, except that
they may exist until the *application* completes (which may never happen). Of
course, that time is usually much longer than the life of any variable in a
program, long enough for the device on which it resides to get broken, or
hopelessly fragmented, or upgraded, or moved from one machine to another.
When any of those things happens, the location of the data shifts; we conclude
that the correspondence between abstract names and addresses can not be
maintained for persistent data.

Faced with this situation, one might think that the only way to treat
persistent data uniformly with program data would be to devise a location-
independent naming scheme for *all* data, and use some kind of directory
system for locating things. The performance of such a scheme for program
data is clearly unacceptable; witness early Lisp and Smalltalk implementations, which do just that! Hence, one would conclude, persistent data and
nonpersistent data are different things, and should be treated differently.

The mistake in this thinking is that it confuses the abstraction with its
implementation. There is nothing at all wrong with choosing one implementation (e.g., fixed offsets) for program data, and another (e.g., directories
with modifiable location bindings) for persistent data. The compiler should
be free to choose any representation that correctly represents the intentions
of the programmer. In practice, we would expect to use many different representations for any given abstraction.

The only thing required to bring persistent data into the realm of programming is the notion of *universal extent*. Conceptually, there is a single rou-

tine, the universe, in which all things exist and take place. The entities in the universe can be counted (over time), and hence can be uniquely identified, by binding each one to a universal name. The universal name of an entity contains no information about that entity; that is, universal names are an unbounded, unordered, discrete type. Note that in order to support things like removable media and network growth, the name space has to be shared among all systems, everywhere, over all time.

The abstraction of universal names is a trivial generalization of the notion of access types (pointers). The representation of a universal name may vary considerably, depending on such things as storage device characteristics and extent. Moreover, the language implementation is free to convert between representations as it sees fit. How and when such conversions are carried out will depend on details of the application, and the intelligence of the "compiler."

Of course, it must be possible to attach a name to a value of any type in the language. That is, data of any type can be persistent. And, the scope rules of the language will dictate some obvious constraints on the relationships between persistent objects; for instance, no object can outlive its type, so types must also be capable of being persistent data, and so forth. Some examples, illustrating how universal names are used to solve persistent data problems, can be found in Baker, et al. [1987].

18.3 EVOLUTION

The distinguishing feature of large, long-lived applications is that they evolve over time. Evolution occurs through the continuing interaction of independently activated, concurrent, and distributed processes. Some applications eventually become extinct (i.e., terminate), while others are expected to continue until the universe (the *real* main program) ends.

From these remarks we see that, like routines, applications can be initiated and terminated, and have local data. Unlike ordinary routines, their data are persistent; that is, they have universal extent. Also unlike ordinary routines, the completion of their main thread of control does not correspond to termination of the application but serves only to initiate the application. In this regard, an application is more like an Ada[3] package than a routine.

Some of the data in an application may be completely passive, like integers or trees of records, which are acted on by programs. Other application data are passive programs; that is, operations that can be invoked explicitly. Other data are active programs, that is, message-driven entities; these are variously called daemons, responders, objects, actors, servers, task activations, and so forth.

---

[3]Ada is a registered trademark, U.S. Department of Defense, Ada Joint Program Office.

In ordinary operation, applications evolve through internal change. That is, the operations of the application are stimulated to create, delete, or modify its component data. Correct operation of the application as a whole amounts to a set of global properties that constrain the operation of the components. These properties constitute the "type" of the application, in a sense to be made precise in the next section.

Applications can also evolve through external change. To see how this comes about, we need to understand that applications are dynamically specified and instantiated objects of the environment, that is, the application that is the universe. For such creation to be possible, the universe has to be able to specify and manipulate all of the syntactic and semantic concepts composed to form applications (including, of course, itself). That is, one can compute with applications, including their specifications, to derive new applications that depend on (in the simplest case, inherit) properties of the original.

18.4 TYPES

The guiding principle for the design of **prism's** type system is that types convey information abut applications and their components. The kind of information should not be restricted, as it usually is, to functionality. For instance, performance specifications, characteristics for the operating environment, and statistical expectations about input data are all legitimate properties of programs, and as such should constitute type information.

The amount of information should also not be constrained unnecessarily. A programmer should not have to supply any more information than is required by the compiler to derive an implementation[4]. Nor should a programmer be prevented from specifying information that is deemed useful, whether intended for the compiler, an analysis tool, a management tool, a human reader, or for any other purpose. Information useful to the compiler, for instance, might include bounds on the length of a sequence, which could help the compiler to choose among alternative representations of sequences or to transform the program into a more efficient form.

---

[4] Just what that information is may vary from one compiler to the next. The smarter the compiler, the more it should be able to infer. Moreover, the kind of information from which it infers the implementation is allowed to vary, so that any program specification paradigm can be accommodated. For this reason, there is no required syntatic form for anything in the language, though there is a set of predefined forms which the programmer is always free to use. The basic concepts of the language can be extended by defining new semantic abstractions, including the relations between abstractions needed by the compiler. Examples of such relations are the consistency relation between Ada package specifications and bodies, the realizability relation that enables sets of ground terms satisfying a proposition to be inferred from a set of nonlogical axioms within an appropriate framework such as Horn logic. From these remarks it should be clear that the intelligence of the compiler is not fixed, but can continually accumulate programming knowledge to the benefit of all users.

Type theory has focused recently on the Curry-Howard isomorphism between types and propositions, viewing type systems as logicodeductive mechanisms. The idea is that the type of a program (expression) asserts something about the outcome (conclusion, result) of the program. The problem is that this does not apply neatly to applications which, as we pointed out in the preceding section, do not generally conclude. Moreover, when they do conclude, we have no interest in the outcome. On the contrary, we are only interested in the intermediate stages of applications.

Another aspect of applications which does not fit neatly into most of the recent work on types is that they involve concurrency. To our knowledge, the only serious attempt to treat concurrency in a logical framework is linear logic [Girard, 1986]. Even there, however, there is a serious problem associated with attaching a meaning to nonterminating deductions.

The time dependence of applications immediately suggests some kind of modal logic, if we want to adopt the idea of applications as proofs. It seems more natural to us, however, to consider applications not as proofs but as theories. The computation of an intermediate result is therefore treated as a deduction within that theory. Sound applications evolve internally by adding and deleting nonlogical axioms that are independent of both the theory and one another.

The principle formal concept underlying **prism** is therefore not *proposition*, but *theory*. Theories, in turn, are simply bodies of information which are required to be internally consistent. The criteria for consistency of theory T come partly from the theories on which T is based (including the universe), and may additionally depend on criteria defined within T itself.

The most important base theory, which is shared by all applications, is the universe, that is, the theory of **prism** core consists of a set of types that are mutually self-defining. An independent model for these types exists, and is given canonically by a realizability interpretation.

The most important types in **prism**, from a formal point of view, are those of *declaration* and *composition*. The declaration mechanisms determine the visibility and binding of names in the environment; the composition rules determine the basic inferential structure of the language. In this respect, at least, **prism** is reminiscent of the Theory Of Constructions [Coquand, 1985]. In fact, **prism** currently differs from TOC in only one formally significant way: its basic inferential structure is modeled after linear, rather than sequential, logic, to allow for concurrency.

However, a goal of **prism** is to be practical, and so there are a number of pragmatic respects in which it differs quite sharply from TOC and most other experimental type languages. For instance, arbitrary **prism** expressions can be submitted to the compiler and analyzed, instead of being laboriously synthesized (derived) by interactive application of the basic composition rules of the language. In plainer words, we do not force the programmer to derive programs at a fine grain of detail. This allows a style that is intermediate between pure program derivation and pure program verification, which is easily and widely accepted in practical settings (where it is called "separate compilation").

Another important practical respect in which **prism** differs from its formal relatives is that it includes "high-level" concepts like structured control, packages, and arrays. These types of the language are important because they convey properties that are needed by our current compiles to generate good code for real machines, and which are difficult to recognize if they are translated into a "lower level" notations like λ-calculus [Lee, 1987]. In the long term, changes in basic machine architecture or improvements in compiler technology might enable us to shrink the **prism** core, but such speculation does not help us to design a practical language today. There is also nothing sacred about the core types since any defined types have equal status. In fact we would expect the set of types that are perceived as constituting the core to evolve over time and differ among applications.

An example of a high-level declaration mechanism is provide by Ada's package construct. Formally, an Ada package specification declares a weak propositional theory; that is, it declares a set of entities and asserts that they have certain properties. These properties are expressed in a fairly weak language of propositions, where as usual we interpret such things as "integer" to be propositional constants, "record," "function," etcetera propositional connectives, and various kinds of constraints as special predicates. The theorems of this theory consist of the closure of the declarations under the composition rules of Ada, where the type checking rules serve as inference rules[5].

A package body, on the other had, declares a different kind of information; formally, it defines a representation morphism yielding a model of the theory given by the specification. As suck, it is an example of a specific deductive mechanism which is consistent with the specified theory.

Packages illustrate the two basic kinds of information in **prism** alluded to earlier. The package specification is an example of declarative (syntactic, specification) information, and the body is an example of deductive (semantic, composition) information. The example at hand illustrates mechanisms for declaring and deducing (computing) with a certain class of theories. As indicated earlier, however, **prism** allows arbitrary new types of information of both classes to be defined.

To achieve the required level of generality, the fundamental notions of declaration and composition in **prism** have a categorial flavor. Specifications are analogous to objects and deductions are categorial constructions. To some extent, therefore, we share inspiration with CAML [Curien, 1983]. However, CAML restricts itself to a very special category of sets and functions in order to fix an interpretation of composition. By making composition and its specifi-

---

[5] Note that package specifications can use a number of mechanisms for synthesizing theories, including extension and inheritance (with clauses). The particular set of theory synthesis mechanisms in Ada is, however, rather ad hoc. A clearer and more complete set of mechanisms is apparent in the Larch shared language [Guttag, et al., 1985].

cation abstract, however, **prism** programmers are free to attach any interpretation to composition that yields a model. This is perhaps the most important purpose for which multiple representations can be attached to an abstraction! That is, the crucial feature of **prism** which makes it different from all other data abstraction languages is its lack of rules about how the programmer is to give meaning to specifications, and the nature of that meaning. It follows directly from this that things can share a set of formal properties but differ considerably in the details of their meaning[6].

To drive the point home, the general concepts of declaration and deduction subsume all of the specific examples exhibited by programming systems, including

- ☐ programs as proofs of propositions; generalized realizability
- ☐ programs as constructions of resource-consumption functions
- ☐ specifications as "realizations" of requirements, designs
- ☐ parsing as syntactic derivation ("proof") discovery

In fact, they capture the essence of computation in the abstract, and any given species of information manipulation is a specialization of these general concepts.

However, category theory does not quite meet our needs, because its basic logic is not "concurrent." This is the source of our interest in linear logic, and why we are working to develop a kind of "linear category theory" as the formal foundation of **prism**. We must admit, however, that at this time our understanding of what this means in practical terms, and how to implement it, is better than our formal understanding.

18.5 ERRORS

A system is reliable to the extent that it is correct, makes proper use of computing resources, behaves predictably and appropriately when hardware of software components fail, and can be operated reliably by its users. As in any other engineering discipline, reliability is achieved by applying scientific design principles, by including safeguards and contingency mechanisms in the design, and by testing. Each of these three reliability activities contributes to our confidence in a system in different ways, and makes up for some weaknesses of the others.

---

[6] In retrospect, it is somewhat surprising, in light of the demonstrated capacity of category theory to unify so much of mathematics through abstraction, that this kind of separation of syntax and semantics has not been incorporated in programming languages before. Put another way, category theory has infinitely more polymorphism than any programming language because of its decoupling of models and theories, and we propose to follow its example.

Each activity has its own style of detecting, analyzing, and recovering from errors. Type checking and related static analysis mechanisms are the tools of scientific design. Exceptions and exception handling mechanisms are used to safeguard against possible flaws in the design or problems in the operating environment. Various forms of instrumentations (debuggers, performance monitors, psychological experiments) are used for testing operational systems and their components.

In each of the three reliability activities, the same five language issues arise: control, visibility, binding, resource allocation, and abstraction. Moreover, all five language issues relate to all three aspects of error handling: detection, analysis, and recovery.

In instrumentation, for example, control issues arise in each aspect of error handling: the triggering of probes (detection), the ability of probes to alter the control flow of the system being measured (during analysis), and the transfer of control from probes back to the system, when this is meaningful (recovery).

Here are some illustrations of how the language issues of visibility, binding, and resource allocation arise in the context of instrumentation. The environment in which a probe executes determines what user-defined types and data it can access (if any), or whether certain run-time system information is visible. Binding time determines such things as whether breakpoints can be installed interactively, or have to be "compiled in. " In performance instrumentation, resources must be apportioned among the observed system, data collection, data reduction, and analysis, and presentation and user interaction (if any) so as to minimize intrusiveness.

Currently, the **prism** core includes mechanics for raising and handling exceptions similar to those in Ada. On a more fundamental level, these mechanisms depend on synchronous and asynchronous control transfer. However, we are acutely aware that this is only a start.

The most difficult problem here is in the area of abstraction. Ideally, one would like to say "measure the X of system Y," and have any necessary probes, data reduction facilities, et cetera, generated, installed, and run automatically. Or, better yet, "determine how well system Y's behavior matches hypothesis Q," thereby tying testing back to design specifications. The realization of these ideals requires mechanisms for defining and manipulating abstract properties of systems. Unfortunately, we do not yet understand the logical/type theoretic aspects of error detection and handling well enough to know how to support the necessary abstractions.

18.6 DESIGN

Naturally, good language design practice is required in the design of any language [Weinberg, 1971; Hoare, 1973; "Ironman," 1976]. What constitutes good design depends in part on how, by whom, and for what purposes the language will be used. Some guidelines that we have adopted in the design of **prism** are the following.

Because the applications are varied and many, it is necessary to provide a small number of highly composable mechanisms, instead of a large number of mechanisms specialized to an arbitrarily chosen set of anticipated applications. To retain simplicity in the language each primitive mechanism must isolate some unique functionality in a form that is easily composed with the other primitives. Every effort should be applied to avoid language features that will lead to psychological ambiguities in programs. The design should emphasize ease of reading over ease of writing programs, emphasize the semantic integrity and completeness of the language, provide redundancy without duplication, avoid default mechanisms that obscure the meaning of programs, and use syntactic and semantic features, wherever possible, which are compatible with the traditional notations and intuitions of mathematics, engineering, and computer science. The syntax should be conservatively extensible, to allow syntactic extensions that cannot, for example, cause confusion by redefining the parsing rules for familiar phrases. And, finally, the design must strive in every way possible to provide features that will in their use (during program execution) be only as expensive as is inherent in the generality of their use.

Our design draws on four sources for inspiration and guidance: Ada, functional languages, object-oriented languages, and foundational theory. We look to each of these sources for specific contributions, as follows.

Ada is influencing many of the practical aspects of syntax and program structure. This influence is both positive and negative; we seek to take the best from Ada and avoid its mistakes. Ada is currently the most complete compendium of features needed for practical application development. As such, we use it as a baseline of capabilities for our full spectrum language; anything that exists in Ada should either be in **prism** or preferably be easily defined and integrated. If this goal is achieved, it should be easy for programmers familiar with Ada to switch to **prism** with a minimum of retraining.

Ada also contains the echoes of some very good ideas, both in its syntax and semantics. For instance, its near unification of the syntax of record literals and actual parameter lists reveals an underlying commonality that should be recognized and exploited to make the language smaller and cleaner. The question is: how?

For an answer to this particular question, we turn to functional languages such as ML [Gordon, et al., 1979], Amber [Cardelli, 1986a], Ponder [Fairbairn, 1983], and Miranda [Turner, 1985], which have explored a number of alternatives for unifying data and parameter structures. Other desirable aspects of functional languages are the use of highly composable, small-grained components; ease of formal analysis and transformation; the functional character of abstract data types and modules; and an extensive body of interactive/incremental implementation technology. The most important contribution of functional languages, however, is higher-order programming.

The application designer often faces the dilemma of not knowing a good general solution to a problem, though a good solution can be generated for any particular case, given some additional information. Higher-order programming in a language like Common Lisp enables the designer to implement an algorithm for deriving a good solution, but at the cost of getting an unacceptably inefficient implementation of that solution. A static language like Ada, on the other hand, provides efficient mechanisms which can be combined to obtain an efficient implementation, but at the loss of the general solution.

The problem is that the Common Lisp programmer cannot convey enough information about the application to the compiler for it to obtain an efficient implementation, while an Ada programmer cannot avoid conveying so much information about the details of his particular solution that the compiler is unable to abstract the general solution. In a full-spectrum language, the programmer should be able to communicate to the compiler, as part of the program, any information it needs to derive an efficient implementation of a specialized solution.

Typed functional languages enable more efficient implementations by including type information in programs. Types constrain the application, promote checking and representation decisions to an earlier point in the computation, and enable a wide class of optimization transformations.

The more intricate a type system is, the more information can be expressed in it. For instance, dependent types can be used to inform the compiler to represent a list as an array if the length of the list is known to depend on a numeric parameter. In the extreme, virtually any logical property that has constructive significance can be embodied in type information (at which point we say we are doing "logic programming").

The information a compiler needs is not restricted to functionality, however. To cite a few examples, the criteria to be used in optimization, expected statistical characteristics of input data, and complexity measures of components can all be used to guide the compiler's selection of algorithms and data structures.

As language implementors, we know how to make compiler components that are driven by user-supplied information and are hence open-ended. What is less clear is what high-level syntactic mechanisms should be supplied to enable the application designer to express information and convey it to the portions of the compiler that need it. This is the most difficult syntax design challenge we face. Although we have worked out some prototype models of the language, we are not yet sufficiently satisfied with any of them to expose their details.

Object-oriented languages, operating systems, and databases are currently experiencing the greatest experimental activity in the areas of inheritance mechanisms and persistent data issues, and so we look to them to supply perspectives and mechanisms in these areas. In particular, these languages contribute a third baseline of features, in addition to those found in Ada and functional languages.

The fourth source of inspiration for our design comes from the formal foundations of semantics, type theory, logic, and category theory as they relate to program development. These formal foundations we see as giving the formal outlines to such things as the type system, notions of component composability, computing with semantic components, and the functors relating the various concepts in the language. They give us insight into what is theoretically possible, as well as warnings about potential difficulties. Most importantly, the formal foundations tell us what properties the language as a whole must have in order to assimilate the mechanisms required by tools for formal program manipulation. It is through the application of such tools that we expect the real gains in software productivity and reliability to be realized.

Our thesis is that the features we include in the language core should be adequate for any application. As a partial validation of this thesis, the language is completely self-defining. In particular, use of the language to implement its own run-time system should test its ability to support systems programming, and use of the language to support its own development should test its ability to support software engineering. It should be noted that we already have experience with this approach, since we use it in our existing Ada development environment.

References

Atkinson, M. P., Bailey, P. J., Chisholm, K. J., Cockshott, P. W., and Morrison, R., (1983). "An Approach to Persistent Programming," *The Computer Journal*, Vol. 26, No. 4, pp. 360–365.

Baker, D. A., Fisher, D. A., and Shultis, J. C., (1987). "Persistence and Type Integrity in a Software Development Environment," Workshop on Persistent Object Systems: Their Design, Implementation and Use, Appin, Scotland, August.

Bernstein, Philip A., (1987). "Database System Support for Software Engineering," *Proceedings of the Ninth International Conference on Software Engineering*, IEEE Computer Society Press, Monterey, Calif., March, pp. 166–178.

Brookes, S. D., (1985). "On the Axiomatic Treatment of Concurrency," CMU-CS-85-106, Department of Computer Science, Carnegie-Mellon University, Pittsburgh, Penn.

Cardelli, L., (1986). "Amber," Combinators and Functional Programming Languages, *Lecture Notes in Computer Science #242*, New York: Springer-Verlag.

Cockshott, W. P., (1983). "Orthogonal Persistence," Thesis CST-21-83, Department of Computer Science, University of Edinburgh, February.

Constable, R. L., et al., (1986). "Implementing Mathematics in the NuPrl System," Englewood Cliffs, NJ: Prentice-Hall.

Coquand, T., (1985). "Une Théorie des contructions," Thése de Troisiéme Cycle, L'Université de Paris VII, January.

Curien, P. L., (1983). "Combinateurs Catégoriques, Algorithmes Séquentiels et Programmation Applicative," Thése de Doctorat d'Etat, L'Université de Paris VII, December.

Fairbairn, J., (1983). "Ponder and Its Type System," Polymorphism, Vol. 1, No. 2, The ML/LCF/Hope Newsletter, April.

Fisher, D. A., and Standish, T. A., (1979). "Initial Thoughts on the Pebbleman Process," Institute for Defense Analyses (IDA) Paper P-1392, June.

Ganziner, H., and Jones, N. D. (eds.), (1986). "Programs as Data Objects," (Workshop Proceedings), **LNCS 217**, New York: Springer-Verlag, April.

Girard, J. Y., (1986). "Linear Logic," L'Université de Paris, October.

Goldberg, A. T., (1986). "Knowledge-Based Programming: A Survey of Program Design and Construction Techniques," *IEEE Transactions on Software Engineering*, Vol. 12, No. 7, July, pp. 752–768.

Goldberg, A., and Robson, D., (1986). *Smalltalk-80: The Language and its Implementation*, Reading, Mass.: Addison-Wesley, 1983.

Goldsack, S. J. (ed.), (1985). *Ada for Specification: Possibilities and Limitations*, Cambridge, England: Cambridge University Press.

Gordon, M. J., Milner, A. J., and Wadsworth, C. P., (1979). "Edinburgh LCF," *Lecture Notes in Computer Science*, No. 78, Berlin: Springer-Verlag.

Guttag, J. V., Horning, J. J., and Wing, J. M., (1985). "Larch in Five Easy Pieces," Report #5, Digital System Research Center Reports, July.

Hailpern, B., (1986). "Multiparadigm Languages and Environments," *IEEE Software*, Vol. 3, No. 1, January.

Hoare, C. A. R., (1973). "Hints on Programming Language Design," *SIGACT/ SIGPLAN Symposium on Principles of Programming Languages*, October.

Howard, W. A., (1980). "The Formulæ-As-Types Notion of Construction," Unpublished manuscript 1969. Reprinted in Curry, H. B., *Essays on Combinatory Logic, Lambda Calculus and Formalism*, Seldin, J. P., and Hindlay, J. R. (eds.), New York: Academic Press, 1980.

Huet, G., (1987). "A Uniform Approach to Type Theory," INRIA.

"Ironman," (1976). Department of Defense Requirements for High Order Computer Programming Languages, HOLWG Report, June.

Khoshafian, S. N., and Copeland, G. P., (1986). "Object Identity," *Object-Oriented Programming Systems, Languages and Applications Conference Proceedings*, October, (also *SIGPLAN Notices*, November 1986), pp. 406–416.

King, R. M., (1985). "Knowledge-Based Transformational Synthesis of Efficient Structures for Concurrent Computations," Ph.D. Thesis, Rutgers University, Kestrel Institute Report, KES.U.85.5, April.

Lampson, B. W., and Schmidt, E. E., (1983). "Organizing Software in a Distributed Environment," *Proceedings of the ACM Symposium on Programming Languages Issues in Software Systems*, San Francisco, June, pp. 1–13.

Lee, P., (1987). "The Automatic Generation of Realistic Compilers from High-level Semantic Descriptions," Ph.D. Thesis, University of Michigan.

Leivant, D., (1983). "Reasoning About Functional Programs and Complexity Classes Associated with Type Disciplines," Twenty-fourth Annual Symposium on Foundations of Computer Science, Tuscon, Ariz., pp. 460–496.

MacQueen, D. B., and Burstall, R. M., (1987). "Structure and Parameterization in a Typed Functional Language," MSS, August.

Manes, E., (1987). "Program Expressions in a Category," *Third Workshop on the Mathematical Foundations of Programming Language Semantics*, New Orleans, April.

Martin-Löf, (1984). "Intuitionistic Type Theory," Studies in Proof Theory, Bibliopolis.

Meyrowitz, Norman (ed.), (1986). *Object-Oriented Programming Systems, Languages, and Applications Conference Proceedings, ACM SIGPLAN*, ACM, Portland, Ore. September. *SIGPLAN Notices*, Vol. 21, No. 11, November 1986.

Mitchell, J. C., (1986). "Representation Independence and Data Abstraction," *Thirteenth Annual ACM Symposium on Principles of Programming Languages*, St. Petersburg Beach, Fl., January, pp. 263–276.

Phillips, J., (1983). "Self-Described Programming Environments," Ph.D. Thesis, Stanford University Computer Science Department, Kestrel Institute Report, KES.U.83.1, March.

Powell, M. L., and Linton, M. A., (1983). "Database Support for Programming Environments," *Proceedings of ACM SIGMOD International Conference on Databases for Engineering Design*, San José, May, pp. 63–70.

Scherlis, W. L., and Scott, D. S., (1983). "First Steps Towards Inferential Programming," Carnegie-Mellon University Technical Report CMU-CS-83-142, July.

Scott, D., (1987). "Domains in the Realizability Universe," Third Workshop on the Mathematical Foundations for Programming Language Semantics, New Orleans, La., April.

Shultis, J. C., (1983). "A Functional Shell," *Proceedings SIGPLAN '83 Symposium on Programming Language Issue in Software Systems,* June, pp. 202–211.

Shultis, J. C., (1985). On the Complexity of Higher-Order Programs," Technical Report CU-CS-288-85, University of Colorado, February.

Shultis, J. C., (1986). "The Design and Implementation of Intuit," IEEE Conference on Logic in Computer Science, June.

Sintzoff, M., (1980). "Suggestions for Composing and Specifying Program Design Decisions," International Symposium on Programming, *Lecture Notes in Computer Science*, New York: Springer-Verlag.

Taylor, R. N., Baker, D. A., Belz, F. C., Boehm, B. W., Clarke, L. A., Fisher, D. A., Osterweil, J., Selby, R. W., Wileden, J. C., Wolf, A. L., and Young, M., (1987). "Next Generation Software Environments: Principles, Problems, and Research Directions," submitted for publication.

Turner, D. A., (1985). "Miranda: A Non-Strict Functional Language with Polymorphic Types," *Functional Programming Languages and Computer Architecture*, Jouannaud, J. P. (ed.), New York: Springer-Verlag, LNCS 201, pp. 1–16.

Warren, D., (1977). "Applied Logic—Its Use and Implementations as a Programming Tool," Ph.D. Thesis, University of Edinburgh.

Weinberg, G. M., (1971). "The Psychology of Computer Programming," New York: Van Nostrand Reinhold.

Zdonik, S. B., (1986). "Maintaining Consistency in a Database with Changing Types," Object-Oriented Programming Workshop, June, (also *SIGPLAN Notices*, October 1986), pp. 120–127.

PART IV

LOGIC

CHAPTER 19

SEMANTICS OF UPDATES IN LOGIC PROGRAMMING

Shamim Naqvi
Ravi Krishnamurthy

Par ma foi! il y a plus de quarante ans que je dis de la prose sans que j'en susse rien.

— MOLIÈRE, Le Bourgeois Gentilhomme (1670), II.iv

19.1 PREAMBLE

Oscar Wilde, writing about a country gentleman chasing a fox, once described it as "the unspeakable in full pursuit of the uneatable." Logic programming and database updates have a similar relationship. Recognizing that nobody would speak for a database language without update constructs, logic programming has actively sought a declarative update facility but has found it to be uneatable for the declarative programming palate. The solution proposed in this paper relies on imparting a new semantics, based on Dynamic Logic [Harel, 1979], to logic programs with updates. Dynamic logic semantics, in the absence of updates, reduce to the classical semantics of logic programs.

We claim that our dynamic semantics coincide with the operational and intended semantics of logic programmers. Is it the case then, we may ask ourselves as logic programers, that, like M. Jourdain, we have been using the formalism of Dynamic Logic without knowing it?

Note that the notion of a state is inherent in any notion of updates. Why not then assign state transition semantics to logic programs? One could then view updates as transitions of a state through a state space. Immediately, it becomes obvious that in the absence of updates, a classical logic program, that is, one without updates, has only one state and that queries map this state to itself. Thusly to the hope that the new semantics would reduce to the classical semantics. The question remains: What is the notion of a state of a logic program? We observe that the closure operator T_p [Apt & van Emkden, 1982] associated with a logic program P computes a state of P in the sense that it assigns valuations to the variables of P. This notion of a state of a logic program suggests the modeling of updates as actions causing state transitions in a state space.

As for simplifying assumptions, we start by restricting ourselves to updates to base relations through a notion of a logic query. Thus a logic program with updates is a triple of a set of ground facts (alternatively viewed as instances of a finite set of *base relations*), a set of rules, and a query. Updates in our simplified context apply only to the set of base relations in the program and are specified only in the query. These assumptions are not fundamental to our thesis; indeed the avid are referred to [Naqvi & Krishnamurthy, 1988] wherein the presentation is devoid of any such simplifications. If a new (ground) fact is added to a state then we could view this operation as a transition from a state to a new state, one which contains all the previous facts as well as the newly added fact. For example, consider a program whose canonical meaning is characterized by a state s of the program. The update $I1$: *insert eds(john,db,10K)* takes state s into a new state, say t, such that t contains all the ground facts in s and the newly inserted fact. That is, t is the minimal change from s in that every fact of s is a fact of t and additionally t contains the fact *eds(john,db,20K)*. Similarly, a deletion operation takes a state to a new state that does not contain the deleted fact, leaving all remaining facts unchanged.

The central notion in Propositional Dynamic Logic (PDL) [Harel, 1979] is that of a set W, whose elements are called *states* in which certain facts are true and others are false. Our semantics will indicate, for a formula Q and state $s \in W$, whether Q is true in s (s *satisfies* Q) or not. It is then plausible to define the meaning of such a formula Q to be the subset of W consisting precisely of those states that satisfy it. When viewing updates as actions that can change a state, it is also plausible to define, by paraphrasing [Harel, 1979], "the meaning of an update as a binary relation on states, including the pair (s,t) in that relation "iff" the update in question started in state s can terminate in state t." For example, the formula $+P$ where P is some ground fact asserts that $+P$ is true in some state if it is possible to reach a state in which P is true. Similarly, $-P$ asserts that the formula is true if it is possible to reach a state in which $\neg P$ is true. The nature of our updates is such that for a given state s there is a unique state t such that (s, t) is in the meaning relation of that action. Thus, update actions are deterministic.

The basic insert and delete update commands are used to define a rich set of commands for multiple, iterative, and conditional updates. Initially, we define updates containing ground predicates only and then extend these to the case of predicates with variables. We discuss syntactic conditions for safety of updates with variables and outline an execution strategy. We show examples of update programs highlighting their usage and the manner in which the declarative and imperative aspects are mixed. We introduce the notion of a model of programs and define truth values of formulas with respect to models. We show that in the absence of updates these semantics reduce to the classical model semantics of logic programs. The paper ends with a pointer to future research plans and references.

19.2 SYNTAX

> since feeling is first
> who pays any attention
> to the syntax of things
>
> —e. e. cummings, XLI Poems, FOUR, VII

A *program* P is a triple (R, F, Q) where R is a finite set of rules, F is a finite set of ground facts, and Q is a query. The *universe* U of a program is the set of all possible terms constructed from all possible constant symbols in the program closed under function application. The *Herbrand Base* B of a program P is the set of all possible ground atoms constructed from the terms in U and the predicate symbols in P. These concepts are defined rigorously in the literature, for example [Lloyd, 1987]. A *rule* is a formula of the form

$$A \leftarrow B_1, \ldots, B_n$$

where A is a positive atomic formula, and $B_1, \ldots, B_n$ are positive or negative atomic formulas. A *fact* is a ground atom. If $p(t_1, \ldots, t_n)$ is a fact in F then p is called an n-ary base predicate symbol. A *query* is a comma-separated list of formulas, say $Q_1, \ldots, Q_n$, where $\forall i (1 \leq i \leq n) Q_i$ is either an atomic formula or an *update predicate*.

Update predicates, for a program $P = (R, F, Q)$, are defined as follows (let $\mathcal{P}$ be the set of base predicate symbols in F).

BASE PREDICATES Φ_{-3}. $\Phi_{-3} = \{p(t_1, \ldots, t_n) \mid p \in \mathcal{P}, p$ is of arity n, and $\forall i (1 \leq i \leq n) t_i \in U\}$.

QUERY PREDICATES Φ_{-2}. $\Phi_{-2} = \{p(t_1, \ldots, t_n) \mid p$ is a positive or negative n-ary predicate symbol from the universe U of the program, and $\forall i (1 \leq i \leq n), t_i \in U\}$. If $A \in \Phi_{-2}$ and $B \in \Phi_{-2}$ then $A, B \in \Phi_{-2}$. Note that $\Phi_{-3} \subseteq \Phi_{-2}$.

BASIC UPDATE PREDICATES Φ_{-1}. $\Phi_{-2} \subseteq \Phi_{-1}$. If γ either $+$, $-$ and $A \in \Phi_{-3}$ then $\gamma A \in \Phi_{-1}$. Note that since $A \in \Phi_{-3}$, only base predicates can be updated.

COMPOUND UPDATE PREDICATES Φ_0. $\Phi_{-1} \in \Phi_0$. For $\alpha \in \Phi_0, \beta \in \Phi_0$, and $Q \in \Phi_{-2}$,

$\alpha, \beta \in \Phi_0$
$(\alpha) \in \Phi_0$
$*(\alpha) \in \Phi_0$
$(Q?\alpha) \in \Phi_0$
$(\alpha; \beta) \in \Phi_0$

The update predicates have the following intuitive meanings:

☐ $+\rho(\bar{t})$ asks for the insertion of the tuple $(\bar{t})$ into the base relation p. Similarly, $-p(\bar{t})$ asks for deleting the indicated tuple from base relation p.

☐ α, β means *do α and β nondeterministically*, that is, in any order, but the final state must be the same. Note that this construct requires that the semantics of α and β be independent of the order of execution.

☐ $*(\alpha)$ means *repeat α an unbounded number of times*.

☐ $(Q?\alpha)$ means *do α if Q is true, otherwise do nothing*.

☐ $(\alpha; \beta)$ means *do α followed by β*.

For convenience of writing short programs, we allow two additional compound update predicates: For $Q \in \Phi_{-2}$, and $\alpha, \beta \in \Phi_0$,

☐ $[Q?\alpha] \equiv (*(Q?\alpha), \neg Q?)$ (this stands for "while Q do α").

☐ $\{Q, \alpha, \beta\} \equiv ((Q?\alpha), (\neg Q?\beta))$ (this stands for "if Q then do α else do β").

Examples of syntactically valid queries are shown as follows:

$\leftarrow +eds(john,db,20K)$.
$\leftarrow (+eds(john,db,20K), -eds(peter,db,30K))$.
$\leftarrow eds(john,db,20K)$.
$\leftarrow (eds(john,db,20K)? + eds(peter,db,30K))$.
$\leftarrow (-eds(john,db,20K); + eds(john,db,30K))$.

The careful reader must have noticed that update predicates are defined to be ground, restricting the class of update programs to an uninteresting set. We can relax this restriction by admitting variables in an update predicate provided these variables obtain bindings from some query predicates. This requires that an ordering on the predicates in a query be found such that any variables in an update predicate receive bindings from preceding query predicates. But what does the phrase "preceding query predicates" mean in the context of pure logic programs? This will require us to make precise the notion of *covering*.

We define a conjunct C_1 to be equivalent to another conjunct C_2 if C_1 is of the form

$$\ldots, \alpha, \beta, \ldots$$

and C_2 is of the form

$$\ldots, \beta, \alpha, \ldots$$

that is, C_1 and C_2 differ in only one comma-separated adjacent position, or there exists a conjunct C_3 such that both C_1 and C_2 are equivalent to C_3. What this means intuitively is that conjuncts C_1 and C_2 reach the same final state if started out from the same initial state. Note that this notion of equivalence is a syntactic notion. We shall provide its semantic counterpart later.

A *well-ordering* of a conjunct is any *left-to-right* predicate occurrences of an equivalent conjunct. A variable in an update predicate is said to be *covered* if it occurs in some query predicate occurrence preceding it in a well-ordering. A rule is *well formed* if all variables in an update or compound predicate are covered. For example, the rule

$$r(X) \leftarrow +p(X), q(X).$$

is well formed since $q(X)$, $+p(X)$ is a conjunct equivalent to the body of the rule, and the variable X is covered.

19.3 EXAMPLES OF UPDATE PROGRAMS

Take for example this:
—e. e. cummings, &, A (Post Impressions), IV

Somewhat more interesting programs can be written using the notion of covered variables. Insert a tuple $(john, db, 20K)$ in the relation *eds*.

$$\leftarrow +eds(john, db, 20K).$$

Delete a tuple $(peter, db, 30K)$ from the relation *eds*.

$$\leftarrow -eds(peter, db, 30K).$$

Give every database employee a 10% salary increase.

$$\leftarrow eds(X,db,S),S1 = S*1:1,$$
$$(-eds(X,db,S); + eds(X,db,S1)).$$

Continue increasing salaries by 10 percent until François' salary exceeds 300K.

$$\leftarrow [\,(eds(francois,db,S),S \leq 300K)?$$
$$eds(X,db,Y),S1 = Y*1.1,$$
$$(-eds(X,db,Y); + eds(X,db,S1))]$$

Fire all employees who make more than their managers.

$$mgr(X,Y)\leftarrow emp(X,M,S), \; mgr(M,Y).$$
$$mgr(X,Y)\leftarrow emp(X,Y,S).$$
$$\leftarrow emp(N,X,S1), \; mgr(N,M),$$
$$emp(M,Y,S2), \; S1 > S2, -emp(N,X,S1).$$

Add to the base relation $p(X,Y)$ all tuples $p(U,V)$ for which $q(U,V)$ is true.

$$\leftarrow q(U,V), + \rho(U,V).$$

For the conjunction of base relations $r(X,Y)$, $t(X,Z)$ interchange for each result tuple (X,Y,Z) the values of Y and Z.

$$\leftarrow r(X,Y),t(X,Z),(-r(X,Y); -t(X,Z); +r(X,Z); +t(X,Y)).$$

Simultaneously, replace the second argument of $r(a,\_)$ with c and the first argument of $r(\_,b)$ with d. This is an interesting update. Note that for a tuple (a,b) in r the result must be a composition of the two updates. The procedural way of specifying this update is as follows:

```
if (a,b) is in r then
  replace (a,b) with (d,c)
  else if (a,X) is in r
    then change X to c
      else if (X,b) is in r
        then change X to d fi
  fi
fi
```

This can be stated as follows:

$$\leftarrow \{r(a,b),(-r(a,b); +r(d,c)),$$
$$\{r(a,X),(-r(a,X); +r(a,c)),$$
$$\{r(X,b),(-r(X,b): + r(d,b))\}\}\}$$

Alternatively, we may state the preceding program as follows:

$$p(a,b,c,d).$$
$$p(a,X,C,D) \leftarrow X \neq b, C = a, D = X.$$
$$p(X,b,C,D) \leftarrow X \neq a, C = X, D = b.$$
$$\leftarrow r(X,Y), p(X,Y,C,D), -r(X,Y), +r(C,D).$$

19.4 ORDER ON PREDICATES

Stand not upon the order of your going
But go at once.

—-SHAKESPEARE, Macbeth, I.iv.24

In general update actions depend on the order of execution in that different orders of execution may yield differing final states. The meaning we have chosen for the $(\alpha; \beta)$ construct in this report places the responsibility of the order of execution on the user. The semantics of the language make no use and no claim that α executed before and after β gives the same result. However, for the conjunction of two compound update predicates $\dots, \alpha, \beta, \dots$ the semantics require that all different orders of execution yield the same final state, that is, the Church-Rosser property for updates is satisfied.

We define two update predicates α and β to be *equivalent* if their meaning relations are the same. Using this equivalence relation, we define the *Church-Rosser Property* (CRP) of a predicate as follows:

- ☐ if $P \in \Phi_{-1}$ then P satisfies CRP.
- ☐ If $P \in \Phi_0$ then the following cases apply:

    If $P = \alpha, \beta$ then P satisfies CRP "iff" $p(\alpha, \beta) = p(\beta, \alpha)$, that is, both α and β satisfy CRP.

    If $P = (\alpha; \beta)$ then P satisfies CRP "iff" both α and β satisfy CRP.

    If $P = (Q?\alpha)$, $Q \in \Phi_{-2}$, then P satisfies CRP "iff" α satisfies CRP.

    If $P = (*(\alpha))$ then P satisfies CRP "iff" α satisfies CRP.

This property is the semantic counterpart of the syntactic equivalence of conjuncts defined earlier. Intuitively, CRP guarantees that the meaning of a given predicate is independent of the order in which the predicate is executed. Since this property is required by the semantics, we need to show a syntactic test for ensuring this property.

First, we recall a well-known definition from logic programming literature. The *definition* of a predicate symbol p is defined to be the set of all rules with head predicate symbol p.

Next we define *def(p)* to be the set of all base predicate symbols that can recursively occur in the definition of p.

$def(p) = \{q \mid$ Either q is base predicate symbol in the definition of p or for r, a (derived) predicate symbol in the definition of p, q is a base predicate symbol in the definition of $r\}$.

We define the *reference set*, $\delta(\alpha)$, of an update predicate α as the set of all facts that α can possibly reference. The set $\delta(\alpha)$ is defined in terms of an intermediate set $\delta'(\alpha)$ as follows.

For $\alpha \in \Phi_0, \beta \in \Phi_0, \gamma \in \{+, -\}$, and P and $Q \in \Phi_{-2}$,

$$\delta'(\alpha, \beta) = \delta'((\alpha; \beta)) = \delta'((\alpha, \beta)) = \delta'(\alpha) \cup \delta'(\beta)$$
$$\delta'(*(\alpha)) = \delta'(\alpha)$$
$$\delta'(P?\alpha) = \delta'(P) \cup \delta'(\alpha)$$
$$\delta'(\gamma P) = \delta'(P)$$
$$\delta'(P) = def(P)$$
$$\delta'(P, Q) = def(P) \cup def(Q)$$
$$\delta'(P) = r \text{ where } r \text{ is the predicate symbol of } P$$
$$\delta(\alpha) = \{p(t_1, \ldots, t_n) \mid p \text{ is predicate symbol of arity } n, p \in \delta'(\alpha) \text{ and } (\forall 1 \le i \le n)t_i \in U\}$$

We use this notion of reference sets to state the syntactic condition, assuring the satisfaction of CRP by the predicates α, β as follows: α, β satisfies CRP if $\delta(\alpha) \cap \delta(\beta) = \phi$. We now proceed to prove this condition by way of first showing some preliminary lemmata.

LEMMA 19.1.   For some state s, ground fact f and predicate α, let $\delta(\alpha) \cap s = s$ and $f \notin \delta(\alpha)$. Then, if $(s \cup \{f\}, t) \in p(\alpha)$ then $(s, t - \{f\}) \in p(\alpha)$.

Proof.   First note that if $f \notin \delta(\alpha)$ then $f \notin s$. Further note that, as $f \notin \delta(\alpha)$, the fact f must also be a member of t since t is the minimally changed state from s. In other words, any transition from state s must reach a state in which the fact f is a member. Similarly, we can argue that any transition from a state not containing f will reach a state that also does not contain f, because α can not insert f since $f \notin \delta(\alpha)$. Therefore, $(s, t - \{f\}) \in p(\alpha)$.

COROLLARY 19.1.   For states s, s' and predicate α, let $\delta(\alpha) \cap s = s$ and $\delta(\alpha) \cap s' = \phi$. If $(s \cup s', t) \in \rho(\alpha)$ then $(s, t - s') \in \rho(\alpha)$.

COROLLARY 19.2.   For states s, s' and predicate α, let $\delta(\alpha) \cap s' = \phi$ and $s \cap s' = \phi$. If $(s \cup s', t) \in \rho(\alpha)$ then $(s, t - s') \in \rho(\alpha)$.

LEMMA 19.2.   For some state s, fact f, and predicate α, let $f \notin s$ and $f \notin \delta(\alpha)$. Then, if $(s, t) \in p(\alpha)$ then $(s \cup \{f\}, t \cup \{f\}) \in p(\alpha)$ and $f \notin t$.

Proof. Any state reachable from $s \cup \{f\}$ must contain the element f; let that state be $t' \cup \{f\}$ where $t' \neq t$. Assume, for the sake of deriving a contradiction, that $(s \cup \{f\}, t' \cup \{f\} \in p(\alpha))$ where $t \neq t'$. Then, from Corollary 19.2, we can conclude that $(s, t') \in p(\alpha)$. As $t \neq t'$, both (s, t) and (s, t') cannot be in $p(\alpha)$ since this contradicts Proposition 1 and 2, that is, the determinism of the update predicates, whose proofs are shown in the next section. Also, since $f \notin \delta(\alpha)$, any transition from state s must reach a state that does not contain f.

COROLLARY 19.3. For states s and s' and predicate α, let $\delta(\alpha) \cap s' = \phi$. Then, if $(s, t) \in p(\alpha)$ then $(s \cup s', t \cup s') \in p(\alpha)$, and for any $f \in s'$, $f \notin t$.

THEOREM 19.1. α, β satisfies CRP if $\delta(\alpha) \cap \delta(\beta) = \phi$.

Proof. An update α is said to be *executable* in a state s if there exists a state t such that $(s, t) \in p(\alpha)$. If there is no state in which α and β are executable then CRP is satisfied. Hence, assume that there exists a state s in which α and β are executable. Let $s = s\alpha \cup s\beta \cup s'$, where $s\alpha = s \cap \delta(\alpha), s\beta = s \cap \delta(\beta)$, and $s' = s - s\alpha - s\beta$. Thus, s is a disjoint union of $s\alpha, s\beta$ and s'.

First, we show the following two propositions.

1. $(s\alpha, s\alpha') \in p(\alpha)$ such that $s\alpha' \cap s\beta = \phi$, and $s\alpha \cap s' = \phi$.
2. $(s\beta, s\beta') \in p(\beta)$ such that $s\beta' \cap s\alpha = \phi$, and $s\beta' \cap s' = \phi$.

As α is executable in s, there exists some $s\alpha'$ such that $(s\alpha, s\alpha') \in p(\alpha)$. As $s\alpha \subseteq \delta(\alpha)$, it must also be that $s\alpha' \subseteq \delta(\alpha)$. This is because for any $f \in s\alpha'$ such that $f \notin \delta(\alpha)$ f must also be in s, that is, $f \in s$, which contradicts $s \subseteq \delta(\alpha)$. Consequently, $s\alpha' \in s' = \phi$. Further, for any fact $f \in s\beta$, $f \notin s\alpha$ because $\delta(\alpha) \cap \delta(\beta) = \phi$; therefore, $s\alpha' \cap s\beta = \phi$. Thus we can conclude (1) from before. In a similar fashion we can show (2).

Using (1) and (2), we show the following two propositions:

3. $(s\alpha \cup s\beta \cup s', s\alpha' \cup s\beta \cup s') \in p(\alpha)$.
4. $(s\beta \cup s\alpha \cup s', s\beta' \cup s\alpha \cup s') \in p(\beta)$.

Propositions (3) and (4) are direct consequences of Corollary 19.3 to Lemma 19.2 and (1) and (2) respectively. From (3) and (4) we can directly show that

5. $(s\alpha' \cup s\beta \cup s', s\alpha' \cup s\beta' \cup s') \in p(\alpha)$.
6. $(s\beta' \cup s\alpha \cup s', s\beta' \cup s\alpha' \cup s') \in p(\beta)$.

Thus confirming the commutativity property shown in Fig. 19.1. This concludes the proof of $p(\alpha, \beta) \equiv p(\beta, \alpha)$.

FIGURE 19.1
COMMUTATIVITY DIAGRAM FOR THE PREDICATES α AND β

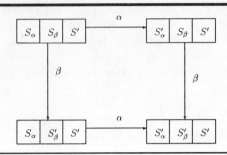

19.5 MEANING, TRUTH, AND MODELS

> But, as for certain truth, no man has known it,
> Nor shall he know it, . . .
> For all is but a woven web of guesses.
>
> —-XENOPHANES (428–354 B.C.)

The semantics of programs are given by a structure $M = (W, p)$ where W is a set of *states*, and p is a mapping

$$p : \Phi \to 2^{W \times W}$$

called the *meaning relation*, which assigns to each update, say α, some binary relation on states with the intended meaning $(s, t) \in p(\alpha)$ "iff" execution of α in state s can lead to the state t.

We shall now provide the details of the mapping p. Let α be a ground predicate. A *state s* of a program P is a subset of the Herbrand Base of P such that if $p(t_1, \ldots, t_n) \in s$ then p is a base predicate symbol.

$$p(\alpha) = \{(s, s) \mid \alpha \in s\}$$
$$p(\neg \alpha) = \{(s, s) \mid \alpha \notin s\}$$
$$p(+\alpha) = \{(s, t) \mid t = s \cup \{\alpha\}\}$$
$$p(-\alpha) = \{(s, t) \mid t = s \setminus \{\alpha\}\}$$

Thus + and − respectively add and delete a ground fact from the given database leaving all other facts unchanged. The states s and t above are minimally different from each other. The following proposition shows that the + and − are deterministic, that is, there is a unique final state for each basic update predicate.

PROPOSITION 19.1. For $\alpha \in \Phi_{-1}$, that is, α is a basic update predicate, if $(s, t) \in p(\alpha)$ and $(s, t') \in p(\alpha)$ then $t = t'$.

Proof. Let A be a base fact. Assume, for the sake of deriving a contradiction, that $t \neq t'$. If $\alpha = +A$ then $t = s \cup \{A\}$ and $t' = s \cup \{A\}$. This implies that $s \cup \{A\} \neq s \cup \{A\}$ which is an impossibility. A similar argument holds for the case of α being a delete action.

We now turn our attention to compound update predicates and define the semantics of compound update predicates in terms of the basic update predicates from before.

Let α and $\beta \in \Phi_0$ be arbitrary update predicates and $P \in \Phi_{-2}$ be a query predicate, or a conjunction of query predicates.

$$p((\alpha)) = p(\alpha)$$
$$p(*\alpha) = \{(s, t) \mid \exists k \exists s_0, \ldots, s_k \ (s_0 = s \text{ and } s_k = t) \text{ and } (\forall \ 1 \leq i \leq k)(s_{i-1}, s_i) \in$$
$$p(\alpha)) \text{ and } \forall s' \neq t(s_k, s') \notin p(\alpha)\}$$
$$p((P?\alpha)) = \{(s, t) \mid (s, s) \in p(P), (s, t) \in p(\alpha)\} \cup \{(s, s) \mid (s, s) \notin p(P)\}$$
$$p((\alpha; \beta)) = \{(s, t) \mid \exists u(s, u) \in p(\alpha), (u, t) \in p(\beta)\}$$
$$p(\alpha, \beta) = p(\alpha; \beta) = p(\beta; \alpha)$$

PROPOSITION 19.2. Let α be a compound update predicate. Then if $(s, t) \in p(\alpha)$ and $(s, t') \in p(\alpha)$ then $t = t'$.

Proof. Since compound update predicates are defined as compositions of basic update predicates, the proof follows directly from Proposition 19.1.

We now define truth values of formulas. Given a state s let $R(s)$ denote the least fixpoint [Apt & van Emkden, 1982; Berri et al., 1987] of the program (R, s, Q).

Define a mapping

$$\tau: \Phi_0 \rightarrow 2^W$$

which returns the set of states in which a predicate is true as follows. If A is a query predicate, that is, $A \in \Phi_{-2}$, then A is true in a state t with respect to a program P if $A \in R(s)$. Thus

$$\tau(A) = \{t \mid A \in R(t)\}$$

If A is an update predicate, $A \in \Phi_0 - \Phi_{-2}$, then A is true in state t if t is reachable from some state s by taking the action indicated by the update, that is, if the pair of states (s, t) is in the meaning relation of A, Thus,

$$\tau(A) = \{t \mid (s, t) \in p(A)\}$$

We use the truth of predicates to define truth values of rules in the usual manner. Thus a conjunct is true in a state if each of the individual predicates in the conjunct are true in that state. A rule is true in a state if whenever the *body* of the rule is true in that state the *head* is also true in that state; otherwise it is false in that state.

We now define models for the language of programs and queries. A model will be a directed graph structure in which two nodes will play an important part. A *start* node is one without any incoming edges; a node is a *final* node if it does not have any outgoing edges. The notion of models for programs associates program states with nodes and updates with the edges of a directed graph.

We consider programs on a case-by-case basis. Case 19.1 applies to programs in which the query satisfies CRP and is free of the semicolon action. The second case applies to CRP programs in which the query may contain semicolons. The final case applies to programs that do not satisfy CRP.

Case 19.1. CRP programs with query free of ";".

Consider a program $P = (R, F, Q)$ such that Q satisfies CRP and does not contain the ";" action. Then a graph $M = (W, p)$, where W is a set of nodes and p is a set of edges connecting these nodes, is a model of P

1. If $s \in W$ is a distinguished start state and every fact in F is true in s.
2. There exists a final state $t \in W$ transitively connected to s such that every $r \in R$ is satisfied by t.
3. For every update predicate $\alpha \in Q$ there exists a pair of states $(s_1, s_2) \in p(\alpha)$.

As an example consider a program $P = (R, F, Q)$ in which Q has no update predicates. Then the definition entails a graph without any edges; it expects a node representing a distinguished start satisfying the facts in F. The final state $t = s$.

For a program $P = (R, F, Q)$ where Q contains a single update predicate, say α, the definition entails a graph with a start state satisfying the facts in F, some state k such that $(k, t) \in p(\alpha)$, where t is the final state. Note that s and t have to be distinct in this case but k can be equal to s.

For a program with many update predicates in the query Q the definition requires that there be a start state containing the facts in F, a final state t satisfying all the rules of R, and many intermediate states connecting s to t representing the updates that take s to t.

Case 19.2. CRP programs with query containing ";".

We shall define the notion of models recursively with the basis of recursion at programs whose queries are free of semicolons. Let $P = (R, F, Q)$ be a program and Q a query such that Q can be split into conjuncts $Q_1, Q_2, \ldots, Q_n$ such that $Q \equiv Q_1; Q_2; \ldots; Q_n$ where each Q_j is free of ";". A graph $M = (W, p)$ with W and p as before, is a model for P if

☐ $M_1 = (W_1, p_1)$ is a model of the program (R, F, Q_1) with start state s and final state t_1.

☐ $M_2 = (W_2, p_2)$ is a model of the program (R, t_1, Q_2) with start state t_1 and final state t.

$\vdots$

☐ $(M_n = W_n, p_n)$ is a model of the program (R, t_{n-1}, Q_n) with start state t_{n-1} and final state t.

☐ $M = (W_1 \cup W_2 \cup \ldots \cup W_n, p_1 \cup p_2 \cup \ldots p_n)$

In other words, we split the query into conjuncts $Q_1, Q_2, \ldots, Q_n$, each individual Q_j being free of the semicolon action. Then we find models $M_1, M_2, \ldots, M_n$, using the definition of Case 19.1 above, such that M_1 is a model for the program with query Q_1, M_2 is a model of the program with query Q_2 and whose start state is the final state of M_1, and so on. Finally, the start state of M_n is the final state of M_{n-1}. The final state of the model M is the final state of the submodel M_n.

Case 19.3. Programs that do not satisfy CRP.

Consider a program $P = (R, F, Q)$ such that Q is not a Church-Rosser conjunct. Let $Q = Q_1, Q_2, \ldots, Q_n$. We impose an ordering on the predicates of Q, say a left-to-right ordering. Thus, Q becomes the conjunct $Q_1; Q_2; \ldots; Q_n$ which satisfies CRP and the model for such a program is defined as in the preceding Case 2.

We now define the notion of minimal models of an extended program. Let t_M denote the final state of model M. $M = (W, p)$ is a minimal model of $P = (R, F, Q)$ "iff" it is a model of P, and there is no $M' = (W', p')$ different from M such that

a. M' is model of P.

b. $t_{M'} \subset t_M$.

c. $p' \subset p$.

In other words, M is a minimal model of P "iff" it is a model, and the final state in the model is as "small" as possible, and the number of edges (representing the updates) is as "small" as possible.

19.6 FUTURE RESEARCH DIRECTIONS

Always the beautiful answer who asks a more beautiful question
—e. e. cummings, Introduction, New Poems

In this paper we have presented a subset of our work on providing updates and procedural constructs in LDL. We have limited our discussion to update and procedural notion in queries only. LDL allows update predicates in the bodies of rules. This necessitates a stratification of the rule base and complicates the notion of models. Details are provided in [Naqvi & Krishnamurthy, 1988; Naqvi & Tsur, 1988].

We believe that a formal basis has been established to look at some traditionally hard problems. The first that comes to mind is to extend this approach to handle updates to derived relations. This would immediately bring to the fore issues concerning stratified logic programs and will require a different notion of the models of a program with updates.

The subject of integrity constraints has received scant attention in the logic programming literature. But of course updates go hand in hand with integrity constraints and this is certainly one subject we plan to investigate in the near future.

Quelqu'un pourrait dire de moi que j'ai seulement fait ici un amas de fleurs étrangères, n'y ayant fourni du mien que le filet à les lier.
—Montaigne, Essais (1533–1592), III.xii

ACKNOWLEDGMENTS

We thank Shalom Tsur, Oded Shmueli, and Carlo Zaniolo for helpful suggestions, and Haran Boral and Patrick Valduriez for a careful review of the manuscript. Some update examples were taken from a private manuscript by S. Tsur and D. Maier.

REFERENCES

Apt, K., Blair, H., and Walker, A., (1988). "Towards a theory of declarative programming," in Minker, J. (ed.), *Foundations of Deductive Databases and Logic Programming*, Morgan-Kaufman.

Apt, K., and van Emkden, M., (1982). "Contributions to the theory of logic programming," *Journal of the Association of Computing Machinery*, Vol. 29, No. 3., pp. 841–862.

Bancilhon, F., Maier, D., Sagiv, Y., and Ullman, J., (1986). "Magic sets and other strange ways to implement logic programs," in *Proceedings of the 5th Annual Association of Computing Machinery Symposium on Principles of Database Systems*.

Beeri, C., Naqvi, S., Ramakrishan, R., Shmueli, O., and Tsur, S., (1987). "Sets and negation in a logic database language (ldl1)," in *Proceedings of the 6th Annual Association of Computing Machinery Symposium on Principles of Database Systems*.

Harel, D., (1979). *First-Order Dynamic Logic*, New York: Springer-Verlag, LNCS 68.

Lloyd, J., (1987). *Foundations of Logic Programming*, 2nd ex. ed., New York: Springer-Verlag.

Naqvi, S., (1986). "A logic for negation in database system," in *Proceedings Workshop on Logic Databases*.

Naqvi, S., and Tsur, S., (1988). "A logic language for data and knowledge bases," submitted for publication.

Naqvi, S., and Krishnamurthy, R., (1988). "Database updates in logic programming," in *Proceedings 7th ACM Conference on Principles of Database Systems*, Austin.

Tsur, S., and Zaniolo, C., (1986). "LDL: a logic-based data-language," in *Proceedings 12th Conference on Very Large Data Bases*.

Ullman, J., (1985). "Implementation of logical query languages for databases," *Association of Computing Machinery Transactions on Database Systems*, Vol. 10, No. 3, pp. 127–139.

Van Gelder, A., (1986). "Negation as failure using tight derivations for general logic programs," in *Proceedings 3rd IEEE Symposium on Logic Programming*, pp. 127–139.

CHAPTER 20

CONTROL AND OPTIMIZATION STRATEGIES IN THE IMPLEMENTATION OF LDL

R. Krishnamurthy
Carlo Zaniolo

20.1 INTRODUCTION

The Logic Data Language, LDL, combines the expressive power of a high-level, logic-based language (such as Prolog) with the nonnavigational style of relational query languages, where the user need only supply a correct query, and the system (i.e., the compiler/optimizer) is expected to devise an efficient execution strategy for it. Consequently, the optimizer is given the responsibility of choosing an optimal execution—a function similar to that of the query optimizer in a relational database system. A relational system uses knowledge of storage structures, information about database statistics, and various estimates to predict the cost of execution schemes chosen from a predefined search space and to select a minimum cost execution in such a space.

An LDL system offers to a user all the benefits of a database language—including the elimination of the impedance mismatch between the language and the query language. In addition, its rule-based deductive capability and its unification-based pattern matching capability make it very suitable for knowledge-based and symbolic applications. The power of LDL is not without a cost, since its implementation poses nontrivial compilation and optimization problems. The various compilation techniques used for LDL are described in Bancilhon, et al. [1986], Saccá and Zaniolo [1986], Zaniolo [1985], and Zaniolo and Saccá [1987]. This paper will concentrate on the control and optimization problem, which is the problem of deriving a safe (terminating) and efficient execution plan for a given program.

The optimization of LDL programs poses a new set of challenging problems beyond those faced by relational systems. First of all, Horn clauses support, in addition to flat relational data, complex objects (e.g., hierarchies), lists, and heterogeneous structures. Secondly, new operators are needed to handle complex data, and constructs such as recursion, negation, sets, et cetera. Thirdly, the complexities of data and operations emphasize the need for new database statistics and new estimations of cost. Finally, the presence of evaluable functions and of recursive predicates with function symbols give the user the ability to state queries that are *unsafe* (i.e., do not terminate). As unsafe executions are a limiting case of poor executions, the optimizer must guarantee that the resulting execution is safe.

This paper describes a fully integrated compile-time approach that ensures both safety and optimization to guarantee the amalgamation of the database functionality with the programming language functionality of LDL. Therefore, the LDL optimizer subsumes the basic control strategies used in relational systems as well as those used in Morris, et al. [1986]. In particular, for LDL programs that are equivalent to the usual join-project-select queries of relational systems, the LDL optimizer behaves as the optimizer of a relational system [Sellinger, et al., 1979].

We limit the discussion, in this paper, to the problem of optimizing the pure fixpoint semantics of Horn clause queries [Lloyd, 1984]. After setting up the definitions in Section 20.2, the optimization is characterized as a minimization problem based on a cost function over an execution space in Section 20.3. The execution model is discussed in Section 20.4, and used to define the execution space in Section 20.5. We outline our cost function assumptions in Section 20.6. The search space is detailed in Section 20.7 by extending the traditional approach to the nonrecursive case first, and then to recursion. The problem of safety is addressed in Section 20.8, where we extend the optimization algorithm to ensure safety.

20.2 DEFINITIONS

The knowledge base consists of a *rule base* and a *database* (also known as fact base). An example of rule base is given in Fig. 20.1.

Throughout this paper, we follow the notational convention that Pi's, Bi's, and f's are *predicates, base predicates* (i.e., predicate on a base relation), and *function symbols*, respectively. The Bi's are relations from the database

FIGURE 20.1
RULE BASE

Query is P1(x,y)?

R1:(x,y)	←	P2(x,x1), P3(x1,y).
R21:P2(x,y)	←	B21(x,x1), P2(x1,y1), B22(y1,y).
R22:P2(x,y)	←	P4(x,y).
R3:P3(x,y)	←	B31(x,x1)B32(x1,y).
R4:P4(x,y)	←	B41(x,x1),P2(x1,y).

and the Pi's are the derived predicates whose tuples (i.e., in the relation corresponding to that predicate) can be computed using the rules. Note that each rule contains the *head* of the rule and the *body* that defines the tuples that are contributed by this rule to the set of tuples associated with the head predicate. A rule may be *recursive*, in the sense that the definition in the body may depend on the head predicate, either directly by reference or transitively through a predicate referenced in the body. An example of a recursive rule is $R21$.

In a given rule base, we say that a predicate P implies a predicate Q, written $P \rightarrow Q$, if there is a rule with Q as the head and P in the body, or there exists a P' where $P \rightarrow P'$ and $P' \rightarrow Q$ (transitivity). Then a predicate P, such that $P \rightarrow P$, will be called *recursive*. Two predicates P and Q are called *mutually recursive* if $P \rightarrow Q$ and $Q \rightarrow P$. Since this implication relationship is an equivalence relation, it can be used to partition the recursive predicates into disjoint subsets, which we will call *recursive cliques*. A clique $C1$ is said to *follow* another clique $C2$ if there exists a recursive predicate in $C2$ that is used to define the clique $C1$. Obviously the 'follow' relation is a partial order.

In a departure from previous approaches to compilation of logic, we make our optimization query specific. A query with indicated bound/unbound arguments (called binding) will be called a *query form*. Thus, $P1(c, y)$? is a query form in which c and y denote a bound and unbound argument, respectively. Throughout this paper we use x, y to denote variables and c to denote a constant. We say that the optimization is query specific because the algorithm is repeated for each such query form. For instance, the query $P1(x, y)$?, will be compiled and optimized separately from $P1(c, y)$?. Indeed the execution strategy chosen for a query $P1(x, y)$? may be inefficient for a query $P1(c, y)$?, or an execution designed for $P1(c, y)$? may be unsafe for $P1(x, y)$?.

In general, we can define the notion of a binding for a predicate in a rule body based on a given permutation of the literals in the body. This process of using information from the prior literals was called *sideways information passing (SIP)* in Ullman [1985]. We note here that a given permutation is associated with a unique SIP.

20.3 THE OPTIMIZATION PROBLEM

We define as follows the optimization problem, as the minimization of the cost over a given execution space (i.e., the set of all allowed executions for a given query).

Logic Query Optimization Problem. Given a query Q, an execution space E, and a cost function defined over E, find an execution pg in E that is of minimum cost; that is,

$$\underset{pg \in E}{\text{MIN}}\,[\text{cost of } pg(Q)]$$

Any solution to this optimization problem can then be described along four main coordinates, as follows:

1. The model of an execution, pg.
2. The definition of the execution space, E, consisting of all allowable executions.
3. The cost functions that associate a cost estimate with each execution in E.
4. The search strategy to determine the minimum cost execution in the given space.

The model of an execution represents the relevant aspects of the processing so that the execution space can be defined based on the properties of the execution. The designer must select the set of allowable executions over which the least cost execution is chosen. Obviously, the main trade-off here is that a very small execution space will eliminate many efficient executions, whereas a very large execution space will render the problem of optimization intractable, for a given search algorithm. In the next sections we describe the design of the execution model, the definition of the execution space, and the search algorithm. The cost formulas are in most cases system dependent. Thus we will consider the cost formulas as a black box, where the actual formulas are not discussed except for those assumptions that impact the global architecture of the system.

20.4 EXECUTION MODEL

LDL's target language is a relational algebra extended with additional constructs to handle complex terms and fixpoint computations. An execution over this target language can be modeled as a rooted directed graph, called

FIGURE 20.2
PROCESSING GRAPH

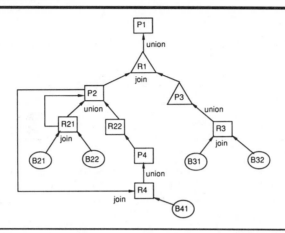

processing graph, as shown in Fig. 20.2 for the example of Fig. 20.1. Intuitively, leaf nodes (i.e., the nodes with nonzero indegree) of this graph correspond to operators and the results of their predecessors are the input operands. The representation in this form is similar to the predicate connection graph [Kellog & Travis, 1981], or rule graph [Ullman, 1985], except that we give specific semantics to the internal nodes, and use a notion of contraction for recursion as described in what follows.

In keeping with our relational algebra–based execution model, we map each AND node into a *join* and each OR node into a *union*. Recursion is implied by an edge to an ancestor or a node in the sibling subtree. We restrict our attention to *fixpoint* methods for recursion, that is, methods that implement recursive predicates by means of a *least fixpoint operator*. We assume that the fixed point operation of the recursive predicates in a clique is not computed in a piecemeal fashion (i.e., the fixpoint operation is atomic with respect to other operations in the processing tree). In order to model this property, we define the notion of a contraction. A *contraction* of a clique is the extrapolation of the traditional notion of an edge contraction in a graph. An edge is said to be *contracted* if it is deleted and its ends (i.e., nodes) are identified (i.e., merged). A clique is said to be contracted if all the edges of the clique are contracted. Intuitively, the contraction of a clique consists of replacing the set of nodes in the clique by a single node and associating all the edges in/out of any node in the clique with this new node, (as in Fig. 20.3), generically called *Contracted Clique node* (or *CC node*). As the structure of the rules in the clique will be needed for optimization, we associate the set of rules in the clique to this CC node. Intuitively, a CC node corresponds to the fixpoint operation for the clique, whose operands are the results of the predecessors.

FIGURE 20.3
CONTRACTED PROCESSING GRAPH

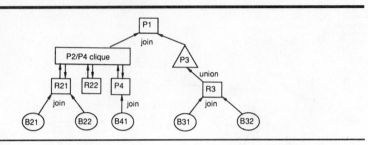

It is easy to see that a contracted processing graph is acyclic (a DAG). Moreover, for ease of exposition we also assume that this graph is converted into a tree by replicating the children with multiple successors. In the rest of the paper we assume that the processing graph has been contracted and due to the preceding stipulation, we interchangeably use the terms processing graph and processing tree.

Associated with each node is a relation that is computed from the relations of its predecessors, by doing the operation (e.g., join, union) specified in the label. We use a square node to denote materialization of relations and a triangle node to denote the pipelining of the tuples. A pipelined execution, as the name implies, computes only those tuples for the subtree that are relevant to the operation for which this node is an operand. In the case of join, this computation is evaluated in a lazy fashion as follows: using the binding from the result of the subquery to the *left* of a subtree, a tuple for that subtree is generated. This binding is referred to as *binding implied by the pipeline*. Note that we impose a *left to right* order of execution. Subtrees that are rooted under a materialized node are computed bottom-up, without any sideways information passing; that is, the result of the subtree is computed completely before the ancestor operation is started.

Each interior node in the graph is also labeled by the method used (e.g., join method, recursion method, etc.). The set of labels for these nodes are restricted *only* by the availability of the techniques in the system. Further, we also allow the result of computing a subtree to be filtered/projected through a selection/restriction/projection predicate. We extend the labeling scheme to encode all such variations due to filtering and projecting. The label for a CC node is to specify the choices for the fixpoint operation, which are the choices for SIPs and recursive method to be used.

The execution corresponding to a processing tree proceeds bottom-up left to right as follows: The leftmost subtree whose children are all leaves is computed and the resulting relation replaces the subtree in the processing tree. The computation of this subtree is dependent on the type of the root node of the subtree—pipelined or materialized—as described before. If the subtree is rooted at a contracted clique node, then the fixed point result of the recursive clique is computed, either in a pipelined fashion or in a materialized fashion; the former (i.e., pipelining) requires the use of techniques such as Magic Sets or Counting [Bancilhon, et al., 1985; Saccá & Zaniolo, 1986].

20.5 EXECUTION SPACE

Note that many processing trees can be generated for any given query and a given set of rules. These processing trees are logically equivalent to each other, since they return the same result; however very different costs may be associated with each tree, since each embodies critical decisions regarding the methods to be used for the operations, their ordering, and the intermediate relations to be materialized. The set of logically equivalent processing trees thus defines the *execution space* over which the optimization is performed using a cost model, which associates a cost to each execution. We define this space by the following equivalence preserving transformations:

1. **MP:** *Materialize/Pipeline*: A pipelined node can be changed to a materialized node and vice versa.
2. **FU:** *Flatten/Unflatten*: Flattening distributes a join over an union. The inverse transformation will be called unflatten. An example of this is shown in Fig. 20.4.
3. **PS:** *PushSelect/PullSelect*: A select can be piggy backed to a materialized or pipelined node and applied to the tuples as they are generated. Selects can be pushed into a nonrecursive operator (i.e., join or union that is not a part of a recursive cycle) in the obvious way.
4. **PP:** *PushProject/PullProject*: This transformation can be defined similar to the case of select.
5. **PR:** *Permute*: This transforms a given subtree by permuting the order of the subtrees. Note that the inverse of a permutation is defined by another permutation.
6. **PA:** *Permute & Adorn*: The recursive methods such as Magic Sets and Counting require a SIP for each rule in the clique to be specified and

FIGURE 20.4
EXAMPLE OF FLATTEN/UNFLATTEN

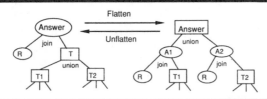

an adornment (i.e., the binding implied by the SIP) to be chosen for each recursive predicate.

7. **EL:** *Exchange Label*: Change the label of a join/union operation to another available method.

Each of the preceding transformational rules maps a processing tree into another equivalent processing tree and is also capable of mapping vice versa. We define an equivalence relation under a set of transformational rules T as follows: a processing tree $p1$ is equivalent to $p2$ under T, if $p2$ can be obtained by zero or more application of rules in T. The equivalence class (induced by said equivalence relation) defines our execution space. As an equivalence class (and therefore an execution space) is uniquely determined by a set of transformational rules, an execution space is referred to by a set notation: $\{Ti \mid Ti$ is a tranformational rule defined above$\}$. For example, $\{MP, PR\}$, $\{MP, PR, PS, PP\}$ are execution spaces.

As mentioned before, the choice of proper execution space is a critical design decision. By limiting ourselves to the preceding transformations, we have excluded many other types of optimizations like peephole optimizations (as used in traditional optimization phase of a programming language compiler), semantic optimizations, et cetera. This is a reflection of the restrictions posed in the context of relational systems from which we have generalized and is not meant to imply that they are considered less important. As in the case of relational systems, these supplementable optimizations can also be used. Even in the realm of preceding transformations, we were unable to find an efficient strategy for the entire space. Consequently, we limit our discussion in this paper to the space defined by $\{MP, PS, PP, PR, PA, EL\}$ (i.e., flattening and unflattening are not allowed). As discussed in Section 20.8, programs can be constructed for which no safe (and therefore, no efficient) executions exist without flattening. Our experience with rule-based systems, however, has been that these are artificial situations the user can be expected to avoid without any additional inconvenience.

20.6 COST MODEL

The cost model assigns a cost of each processing tree, thereby ordering the executions. Typically, the cost spectrum of the executions in an execution space spans many orders of magnitude, even in the relational domain. We expect this to be magnified in the Horn clause domain. Thus "it is more important to avoid the worst executions than to obtain the best execution" is a maxim widely assumed by the query optimizer designers. The experience with relational systems has shown that the main purpose of a cost model is to differentiate between good and bad executions. In fact, it is known from the relational experience that even an inexact cost model can achieve this goal reasonably well.

The cost includes CPU, disk I/O, communication, and so on, which are combined into a single cost that is dependent on the particular system. We assume that a list of methods is available for each operation (join, union, and recursion), and for each method, we also assume the ability to compute the associated cost and the resulting cardinality. For the sake of this discussion, the cost can be viewed as some monotonically increasing function on the size of the operands. As the cost of an unsafe execution is to be modeled by an infinite cost, the cost function should guarantee an infinite cost if the size approaches infinity. This is used to encode the unsafe property of the execution.

Intuitively, the cost of an execution is the sum of the cost of individual operations. This amounts to summing up the cost for each node in the processing tree.

20.7 SEARCH SPACE

In this section, we discuss the problem of choosing the proper search space. The main trade-off here is that a very small search space will eliminate many efficient executions, whereas a large search space will render the problem of optimization intractable. We present the discussion by considering the search spaces for queries of increasing complexity: conjunctive queries, nonrecursive queries, and then recursive queries.

20.7.1 Conjunctive Queries

An important lesson learned from the implementation of relational database systems is that the execution space of a conjunctive query can be viewed as the orderings of joins (and therefore relations) [Sellinger, et al., 1979]. The gist of the relational optimization algorithm is as follows: For each permutation of the set of relations, choose a join method for each join and compute the cost. The result is the minimum cost permutation. Note that for a given permutation, the choice of join methods becomes a local decision; that is, the EL label is unique. Further, a selection or a projection can be pushed to the first operation on the relation without any loss of optimality, for a given ordering of joins. Thus the choices of preselect, project, et cetera are incorporated in the choice of the join method. Consequently, the actual search space used by the optimizer reduces to {MP, PR}, yet the chosen minimum cost processing tree is optimal in the execution space defined by {MP, PR, PS, PP, EL}. (Note that PA is inapplicable as there are no recursions). Further, the binding implied by the pipelining is also treated as selections and handled in a similar manner.

This exhaustive enumeration approach, taken in the relational context, essentially enumerates a search space that is combinatoric on n, the number of relations in the conjunct. The dynamic programming method presented in Sellinger, et al. [1979] only improves this to $\mathbb{O}(n^*2^n)$ time by using $\mathbb{O}(2^n)$ space. Naturally, this method becomes prohibitive when the join involves many relations. Consequently, database systems (e.g., SQL/DS, commercial INGRES) must limit the queries to no more than 10 or 15 joins.

In Krishnamurthy, et al. [1986], we presented a quadratic time algorithm that computes the optimal ordering of conjunctive queries. Another approach to searching the large search space is to use a stochastic algorithm, using a technique called Simulated Annealing [Ioannidis & Wong, 1987]. The application of these techniques is discussed in Krishnamurthy and Zaniolo [1988].

20.7.2 Nonrecursive Queries

We extend the exhaustive approach that was used in the case of conjunctive queries to the nonrecursive case. Recall that the processing graph for any execution of a nonrecursive query is a tree; that is, an AND/OR tree. The optimization algorithm presented here finds an execution in the execution space corresponding to {MP, PS, PP, PR}. Here, we disallow any flattening of the tree, thus limiting the search space to the canonical structure specified in the rule base. As in the case of conjunctive query optimization, we push select/project down to the first operation on the relation and thus limit the search space to {MP, PR}. We shall propose an algorithm to enumerate this search space.

Let us first consider the case when we materialize all the temporary results for each predicate in the rule base. As we do not allow flatten/unflatten transformation, we can proceed as follows: optimize a lowest subtree in the AND/OR tree. This subtree is a conjunctive query, as all children in this subtree are leaves (i.e., base relations) and we may use the exhaustive case algorithm of the previous section. After optimizing the subtree we replace the subtree by a "base relation" and repeat this process until the tree is reduced to a single node. It is easy to show that this algorithm exhausts the search space {PR}. Further, such an algorithm is reasonably efficient if the number of predicates in the body does not exceed 10–15.

In order to allow the execution to use the sideways information by choosing pipelined executions, we make the following observation. In the algorithm of the previous paragraph, all the subtrees were materialized; as a result, the binding pattern of the head of any rule was uniquely determined. Consequently, we could outline the preceding bottom-up algorithm using this unique binding for each subtree. If we do allow pipelined execution, then the subtree may be bound in different ways (depending on the ordering of the siblings of the root of the subtree), and the subtree may be optimized differently for different binding. Observe that the number of binding patterns for a predicate is purely dependent on the number of arguments of that predicate. So, the extension to the preceding bottom-up algorithm is to optimize each subtree for all possible binding and to use the cost of the appropriate binding when computing the cost of joining this subtree with its siblings. Obviously, the maximum number of bindings is equal to the cardinality of the power set of the arguments. In order to avoid optimizing a subtree with a binding pattern that may never be used, a top-down algorithm has been devised and is reported in Krishnamurthy and Zaniolo [1988]. In any case, the algorithm is expected to be reasonably efficient for a small number of argument positions, k, and a few number of predicates in the body, n. The use of strategies other than exhaustive search is also discussed in Krishnamurthy and Zaniolo [1988].

20.7.3 Recursive Queries

In the last two sections we have seen that pushing selection and projections is a linchpin of nonrecursive optimization methods. This was used to reduce the search space from {MP, PR, PS, PP} to {MP, PR}. Unfortunately, this simple technique is frequently inapplicable to recursive predicates [Aho & Ullman, 1979]. Therefore a number of specialized implementation methods have been proposed to allow recursive predicates to take advantage of constants or bindings present in the goal. (The interested reader is referred to Bancilhon and Ramakrishnan [1985] for an overview.) Further, the same techniques are used to incorporate the notion of pipelining (i.e., sideways information passing). In keeping with our algebra-based approach however, we will restrict our attention to *fixpoint* methods, i.e., methods that implement recursive predicates by means of a *least fixpoint operator*. In particular, we use the *magic set method* [Bancilhon, et al., 1985] and *generalized counting method* [Saccá & Zaniolo, 1986] that have been shown to produce some of the most efficient and general algorithms to support recursion [Bancilhon & Ramakrishnan, 1986]. Moreover, they are compatible with the optimization framework used in this paper, since we can now map a recursive Horn clause query into an equivalent expression of extended relational algebra operators and least fixpoint operators.

We extend the algorithm presented in the previous section to include the capability to optimize a recursive query, using a divide and conquer approach. Note that all the predicates in the same recursive clique must be solved together—they cannot be solved one at a time. In the processing graph, we propose to replace a CC node by a single node (materialized or pipelined). We thus obtain a nonrecursive processing graph that can be optimized with the techniques described in the previous section.

The bottom-up optimization algorithm is extended as follows: choose a clique that does not follow any other clique. For this clique, use the nonrecursive optimization algorithm to optimize and estimate the cost and size of the result. Replace the clique by a single node with the estimated cost and size and repeat the algorithm. In Fig. 20.5 we have elucidated this algorithm for a single clique example. Note that the result of the cost and size estimates of the nonrecursive subquery are needed for the computation of the cost and size estimate for a given CC node; similarly, the nonrecursive query above the CC node uses the cost and size estimates of the recursive clique by view-

FIGURE 20.5
R-OPT EXAMPLE

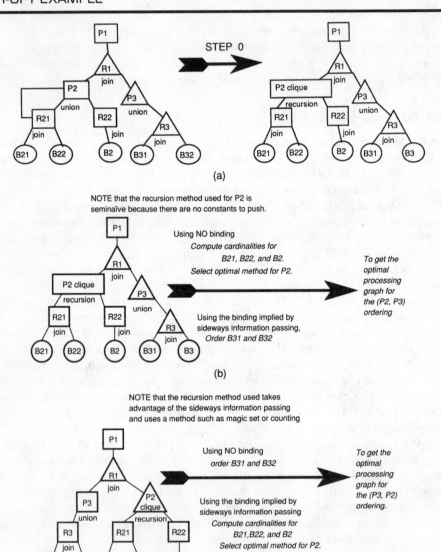

(a)

NOTE that the recursion method used for P2 is seminaïve because there are no constants to push.

Using NO binding
Compute cardinalities for
B21, B22, and B2.
Select optimal method for P2.

To get the optimal processing graph for the (P2, P3) ordering

Using the binding implied by sideways information passing,
Order B31 and B32

(b)

NOTE that the recursion method used takes advantage of the sideways information passing and uses a method such as magic set or counting

Using NO binding
order B31 and B32

To get the optimal processing graph for the (P3, P2) ordering.

Using the binding implied by sideways information passing
Compute cardinalities for
B21,B22, and B2
Select optimal method for P2.

(c)

ing the entire clique as a single node. In this manner, the executions in the search space can be enumerated. The details of the algorithm and the characterization of the search space are discussed in Krishnamurthy and Zaniolo [1988].

20.8 SAFETY PROBLEM

An important concern in implementing Horn clause queries is the issue of safety. Comparison predicates represent a first example of predicates that are potentially unsafe; recursive predicates with function symbols represent the second one. Comparison predicates include predicates such as $x > y$ and equality predicates such as $x = y + y^*z$. While comparison predicates will be executed by calls to built-in routines, they can be formally viewed as infinite relations defining, for example, all the pairs of integers satisfying the relationship $x > y$, or all the triplets satisfying the relationship $x = y + y^*z$ [Tsur & Zaniolo, 1986]. Thus, they can be used only when a sufficient number of variables is known. For instance, for $x > y$, both x and y need to be known, while bound y and z values will suffice for $x = y + y^*z$.

A similar situation occurs with recursive predicates with function symbols. Here, the Herbrand universe is infinite, and new complex terms can be generated at each step in the fixpoint computation, such that the resulting execution may not terminate. This is, for instance, the case of a list-reverse predicate, that cannot be computed unless at least one of the two arguments is instantiated. Both for comparison predicates and recursive predicates with function symbols, therefore, certain *safe binding patterns* will be given that make the predicate safe. In order to deal with safety we propose to restrict the search space of the optimization algorithm to those processing graphs where at least one safe binding pattern is satisfied for each potentially unsafe goal.

20.8.1 Derivation of Safe Binding Patterns

Patterns of argument bindings that ensure safety are simple to derive for comparison predicates. For instance, we can assume that for comparison predicates other than equality, all variables must be bound before the predicate is safe. When equality is involved in a form $x = expression$, then we are ensured of safety as soon as all the variables in *expression* are instantiated. Clearly, these are only sufficient conditions and more general ones, for example, based on combinations of comparison predicates, could be given—see for instance Maier [1984]; but for each extension, a rapidly increasing price would have to be paid in the algorithms used to detect safety and in the system routines used to support these predicates at run-time. Indeed, the problem of deciding safety for Horn clauses with comparison predicates is undecidable [Zaniolo,

1985]; even when no recursion is involved. On the other hand, safety based on safe binding patterns is easy to detect and adequate in most real-life situations.

A main advantage of using safe binding patterns for comparison predicates is that the approach also works for recursive predicates with function symbols. Here again, while the general problem of deciding safety is undecidable, sufficient safety criteria that can be checked efficiently have been given to guarantee safety of the various fixpoint methods [Bancilhon, et al., 1985; Saccá & Zaniolo, 1986]. A somewhat more complex approach is available when nested recursive predicates are involved [Ullman & Van Gelder, 1985]. In either case, however, the final outcome consists of a set of binding patterns that ensure safety, independent of the specific values of these bindings.

20.8.2 Searching for Safe Executions

As mentioned before, the optimizer enumerates all the possible permutations of the goals in the rules. For each permutation, the cost is evaluated and the minimum cost solution is maintained. All that is needed to ensure safety is that for each conditionally safe goal *its bound arguments (i.e., the arguments that contain variables appearing in goals before this) satisfy a safe binding pattern*. If this test succeeds, then the cost of each conditionally safe predicate is evaluated and the optimization algorithm proceeds as usual. If the test fails, the permutation is discarded; in practice this can be done by simply assigning an extremely high cost of unsafe goals and then letting the standard optimization algorithm do the pruning—if the cost of the end solution produced by the optimizer is not less than this extreme value, a proper message must inform the user that the query is unsafe. It is easy to show that this algorithm is correct.

20.8.3 Comparison with Previous Work

The approaches to safety proposed in Naish [1985] and Ait-kaci and Nasr [1986] are also based on reordering the goals in a given rule; but that is done at run-time by delaying goals when the number of instantiated arguments is insufficient to guarantee safety. This approach suffers from run-time overhead and cannot guarantee termination at compile time, or otherwise pinpoint the source of safety problems to the user—a very desirable feature since unsafe programs are typically incorrect ones. Our compile-time approach overcomes these problems and is more amenable to optimization.

The reader should however be aware of some of the limitations implicit in all approaches based on reordering of goals in rules. For instance, a query

```
p(x,y,z), y = 2* x?
p(x,y,z) <---- x = 3, z = x*y
```

is obviously safe ($x = 3$, $y = 6$, $z = 18$), but cannot be computed under any permutation of goals in the rule. Thus both the approaches given in Naish [1985] and Ait-kaci and Nasr [1986] and our and/or optimization cum safety algorithm will fail to produce a safe execution for this query. Two other approaches, however, will succeed. One, described in Zaniolo [1986], determines whether there is a finite domain underlying the variables in the rules using an algorithm based on a functional dependency model. Safe queries are then processed in a bottom-up fashion with the help of "magic sets" which make the process safe. The second solution consists in flattening, whereby the three equalities are combined in a conjunct and properly processed in the obvious order. In practice, however, queries such as the preceding are seldom encountered and Prolog's experience suggests that they can be omitted from the language without compromising its expressive power.

20.9 CONCLUSION

This paper has explored the new and challenging problem of optimizing a Logic-based language for data intensive applications. Thus the first contribution of the paper consists in providing a formal statement of the problem and in clarifying the main design issues involved. The second contribution is the solution approach proposed, which (*i*) cleanly integrates the search for a minimum cost execution with the safety analysis and (*ii*) is solidly rooted in the experience and know-how acquired in optimizing relational systems. Therefore the LDL optimizer includes both the conjunctive query optimization technique of relational systems [Sellinger, 1979] and the safety-oriented techniques described in Morris, et al. [1986].

Common subexpression elimination [Grant & Minkel, 1982], which appears particularly useful when flattening occurs, is one of the optimization aspects not covered in this paper. A simple technique using a hill-climbing method is easy to superimpose on the proposed strategy, but more ambitious techniques provide a topic for future research. Further, an extrapolation of common subexpression in logic queries can be seen in the following example: let both goals $P(a, b, X)$ and $P(a, Y, c)$ occur in a query. Then it is conceivable that computing $P(a, Y, X)$ once and restricting the result for each of the cases may be more efficient.

REFERENCES

Aho, A., and Ullman, J., (1979). "University of Data Retrieval Languages," *Proceedings POPL Conference,* San Antonio, Tex.

Ait-Kaci, H., and Nasr, R., (1986). "Residuation: a Paradigm for Integrating Logic and Functional Programming," submitted for publication.

Bancilhon, F., and Ramakrishnan, R., (1986). "An Amateur's Introduction to Recursive Query Processing Strategies," *Proceedings 1986 ACM-SIGMOD International Conference on Management of Data*, pp. 16–52.

Bancilhon, F., Maier, D., Sagiv, Y., and Ullman, J. D., (1986). "Magic Sets and other Strange Ways to Implement Logic Programs," *Proceedings 5th ACM SIGMOD-SIGACT Symposium on Principles of Database Systems*, pp. 1–16.

Grant, J., and Minker, J., (1982). "On Optimizing the Evaluation of a Set of Expressions," *International Journal of Computer and Information Science*, Vol. 11, No. 3, pp. 179–189.

Ioannidis, Y.E., Wong, E., (1987). "Query Optimization by Simulated Annealing," *Proceedings 1987 ACM-SIGMOD International Conference on Management of Data*, San Francisco.

Kellog, C., and Travis, L., (1981). "Reasoning with data in a deductively augmented database system," in *Advances in Database Theory: Vol 1*, Gallaire, H., Minker, J., and Nicholas, J. (eds.), New York: Plenum Press, pp. 261–298.

Krishnamurthy, R., Ramakrishnan, R., Shmueli, O., (1988). "A Framework for Testing Safety and Effective Computability," *Proceedings of 1988 ACM SIGMOD*, Chicago, pp. 154–163.

Krishnamurthy, R., Zaniolo, C., (1988). "Optimization in a Logic based Language for Knowledge and Data Intensive Applications," *in Advances in Database Technology*, EDBT '88' *Lecture Notes in Computer Science*, Vol. 303, New York: Springer-Verlag, pp. 16–33.

Krishnamurthy, R., Boral, H., and Zaniolo, C., (1986). "Optimization of Nonrecursive Queries," *Proceedings of 12th VLDB*, Kyoto, Japan.

Lloyd, J. W., (1984). *Foundation of Logic Programming*, New York: Springer-Verlag.

Maier, D., (1984). "The Theory of Relational Databases," Comp. Science Press, pp. 553–542.

Morris, K., Ullman, J. D., and Van Gelder, A., (1986). "Design Overview of the Nail! System," *Proceedings Third International Symposium on Logic Programming*, pp. 127–139.

Naish, L., (1985). "Negation and Control in Prolog," Ph.D. Thesis, Dept. of Computer Science, Univ. of Melbourne, Australia.

Naqvi, S., and Krishnamurthy, R., (1987). "Database Updates in Logic Programming," *Proceedings of 7th ACM Conference on Principles of Database Systems*, Austin, Tex.

Ramakrishnan, R., Beeri, C., Krishnamurthy, R., (1987). "Optimizing Existential Queries," MCC Technical Report (also submitted for external publication).

Saccá, D., and Zaniolo, C., (1986). "The Generalized Counting Method for Recursive Logic Queries," *Proceedings ICDT 1986 International Conference on Database Theory*, Rome, Italy.

Sellinger, P. G., et al., (1979). "Access Path Selection in a Relational Database Management System," *Proceedings 1979 ACM-SIGMOD International Conference on Management of Data*, pp. 23–34.

Tsur, S., and Zaniolo, C., (1986). "LDL: A Logic-Based Data Language," *Proceedings of 12th VLDB*, Kyoto, Japan.

Ullman, J. D., (1985). "Implementation of logical query languages for databases," *TODS*, Vol. 10, No. 3, 289-321.

Ullman, J. D., and Van Gelder, A. (1985). "Testing Applicability of Top-Down Capture Rules," Stanford Univ. Report STAN-CS-85-146.

Villarreal, E., (1987). "Evaluation of an $O(N**2)$ Method for Query Optimization," MS Thesis, Dept. of Computer Science, Univ. of Texas at Austin.

Zaniolo, C., (1985). "The representation and deductive retrieval of complex objects," *Proceedings of 11th VLDB*, pp. 458–469.

Zaniolo, C., (1986). "Safety and Compilation of Non-Recursive Horn Clauses," *Proceedings of First International Conference on Expert Database Systems*, Charleston, S.C.

Zaniolo, C., and Saccá, D. (1987). "Rule Rewriting Methods for Efficient Implementations of Horn Logic," in *Foundations of Logic and Functional Programming, Lecture Notes in Computer Science*, Vol. 306, New York: Springer-Verlag, pp. 114–139.

CHAPTER 21

COL: A LOGIC-BASED LANGUAGE FOR COMPLEX OBJECTS

Serge Abiteboul
Stéphane Grumbach

21.1 INTRODUCTION

Two approaches have been followed for defining manipulation languages for complex objects: (1) an algebraic approach [Abiteboul & Beeri, 1987; Abiteboul & Bidoit, 1986; Fischer & Thomas, 1983; Schek & Scholl, 1986, and many others], and (2) a calculus approach [Jacobs, 1982; Abiteboul & Beeri, 1987]. Recently, there has been some interest in pursuing a so-called logic programming approach to define languages for complex objects [Bancilhon & Khoshatian, 1985; Abiteboul & Grumbach, 1987; Beeri, et al., 1987; Kobayashi, 1980]. This is the approach followed here.

The language COL (*Complex Object Language*) based on recursive rules is presented. This language is an extension of Datalog which permits the manipulation of complex objects obtained using tuple and (heterogeneous) set constructors. The originality of the approach is that besides the base and derived relations, base and derived "data functions" are considered. As we shall see, data functions are multivalued functions defined either extensionally (base data functions) or intensionally (derived data functions). The introduction of these functions permits the manipulation of complex objects. Other advantages of data functions are also discussed.

The semantics for COL programs is based on minimal models. Unfortunately, because of sets and data functions, some programs may have more than one minimal model. A stratification in the spirit of the stratification introduced by Apt, et al. [1986], Van Gelder [1986], Nagvi [1986], and others is used. It is shown that for stratified programs, a canonical *causal* [Bidoit & Hull, 1986] and *minimal* model of a given program can be computed using a sequence of fixpoints of operators.

In this paper, we allow negations in the body of rules. The stratification is necessary to handle such negations [Apt, et al., 1986; Van Gelder, 1986; Nagvi, 1986; . . .]. As mentioned previously, stratification is also necessary for data functions even in absence of negation. As we shall see, negation can be simulated using data functions. Indeed, the classical notion of stratification for datalog programs with negation in the body of rules can be derived from the stratification imposed on data functions introduced here.

Data functions are natural tools to manipulate complex objects. Data functions present other advantages as well:

1. Since queries can be viewed as data functions, the inelegant dichotomy between data and queries of the relational model disappear. In particular, queries can be stored in the database as data functions. The model therefore permits the manipulation of procedural data [Stonebraker, 1986].

2. In COL, data can be viewed both in a functional and in a relational manner. As a consequence, the language can be used in a heterogeneous databases context (e.g., relational view on a functional database; integration of a relational database with a functional one).

3. COL can also be used as a kernel language for semantic database models like SDM [Hammer & McLeod, 1978], IFO [Abiteboul & Hull, 1984], or Daplex [Shipman, 1981].

4. Some evaluation techniques for datalog queries like Magic Sets or others [Beeri, et al., 1987; Gardarin & de Maindreville, 1986] make extensive use of particular functions. These functions can be formalized using our model.

As mentioned previously, two other approaches have been independently followed to obtain a rule-based language for complex objects [Beeri, et al., 1987; Kobayashi, 1980]. In Beeri, et al. [1987], they do not insist on a strict typing of objects. In Kobayashi [1980] only one level of nesting is tolerated. However, both approaches could easily be adapted to the data structures considered in this paper. Furthermore, in Abiteboul and Beeri [1987], it is argued that all these approaches yield essentially the same power (i.e., the power of the safe calculus of Abiteboul and Beeri [1987]). The preceding points (1–4) clearly indicate advantages of our approach.

The paper is organized as follows. In Section 21.2, types and typed objects are described, and examples of COL rules given. Section 21.3 is devoted to the formal definition of the language. The stratification is introduced in Section 21.4. In Section 21.5, it is shown that each stratified program has a canonical, causal, and minimal model which can be computed using a sequence of fixpoints. Advantages of the language are briefly considered in a last section. The proof of key results of Section 21.5 can be found in an appendix.

21.2 PRELIMINARIES

In this section, types and typed objects are described, and examples of COL rules given.

The existence of some *atomic types* is assumed. A set of *values* is associated with each type A. This set is called the *domain* of A, and denoted $dom(A)$. To simplify the presentation, we assume that for each A and B distinct, $dom(A) \cap dom(B) = \emptyset$. More complex types are obtained in the following way.

DEFINITION 21.1. If $T_1, \ldots, T_n$ are types ($n \geq 1$) then

1. $T = [T_1, \ldots, T_n]$ is a (tuple) *type*, and $dom(T) =$
   $\{[a_1, \ldots, a_n] \mid \forall i, 1 \leq i \leq n, a_i \in dom(T_i)\}$.
2. $T = \{T_1, \ldots, T_n\}$ is a (set) *type*, and $dom(T) =$
   $\{\{a_1, \ldots, a_m\} \mid m \geq 0, \forall i, 1 \leq i \leq m, \exists j, 1 \leq j \leq n, a_i \in dom(T_j)\}$.

An *object of type* T is an element of $dom(T)$

Note that objects of a given type can be seen as particular trees of bounded depth. Most of the results of the paper would still hold if the strict typing policy is replaced by a weaker condition which guarantees the boundedness of object trees.

Note also that the language allows the manipulation of heterogeneous set. For instance, if *CAR* and *PLANE* are two types, then, for instance, $\{747, Concorde, LeCar, Mustang\}$ is an object of type $\{CAR, PLANE\}$. However, our types are more restricted than types in Abiteboul and Hull [1984], Hull and Tap [1984], and Kuper [1987], which use a "union of type" constructor. For instance, pairs with atomic first coordinate of type *CAR*, and second coordinate of type *PLANE* or *CAR*, are not considered. On the other hand, the type corresponding to sets of such pairs (i.e., $\{[CAR, PLANE], [CAR, CAR]\}$) can be used. Since we are mainly interested in sets of objects, this limitation is not too severe. Furthermore, the language COL could be extended in a simple way to handle such types.

For each type T, the existence of an infinite set $\{x_T, y_T \ldots\}$ of *variables* of that type is assumed. When the type of a variable x_T is understood, or when this type is not relevant to the discussion, the variable is simply denoted r.

Various aspects of the language are now illustrated through three examples.

EXAMPLE 21.1.

[Sets] Sets form an important component of the data structure. The predicates $\in$ and $=$ belong to the language. It is possible to define other predicates like $\subseteq$, *disjoint, disjoint-union, union, . . .* , or functions like $\cup, \cap, \ldots$ using rules.

In this example, x is a variable of type *integer*, and X and Y are variables of type *set of integers*. The following rules define the functions $\cap, \cup$, and *Difference*:

$$x \in \cap(X, Y) \leftarrow x \in X, x \in Y,$$

$$x \in \cup(X, Y) \leftarrow x \in X,$$

$$x \in \cup(X, Y) \leftarrow x \in Y,$$

$$x \in \text{Difference}(X, Y) \leftarrow x \in X, \; \neg \; (x \in Y).$$

Intuitively, the functions $\cap, \cup$, and *Difference* define sets by stating explicitly what are the elements of each set. Thus the term $\cap(X, Y)$ for instance is interpreted as the set of all the elements x such that $x \in X$, and $x \in Y$. Using these functions, the predicates $\subseteq, \subset, Disjoint, Union$, and *Disjoint-union* are now defined:

$$\subseteq (X, Y) \leftarrow \cup(X, Y) = Y,$$

$$\subset (X, Y) \leftarrow \subseteq (X, Y), \; x \in \text{Difference}(Y, X),$$

$$\text{Disjoint}(X, Y) \leftarrow \cap(X, Y) = \varnothing,$$

$$\text{Union}(X, Y, \cup(X, Y)) \leftarrow,$$

$$\text{Disjoint-union}(X, Y, \cup(X, Y)) \leftarrow \text{Disjoint}(X, Y).$$

The language allows the manipulation of complex objects, and also of "nested relations" [Abiteboul & Bidoit, 1986; Fischer & Thomas, 1983; Jaeschke & Scheck, 1982; . . .] which are special cases of complex objects.

EXAMPLE 21.2.

[Nested relations] Let N denote the set of integers. Consider the predicate $R(N, N, N)$ and the three predicates $S(N, \{[N, N]\}), S'(N, [N, N]), S''(N, \{[N, N]\})$. (The first field of S, S', and S'' contains an integer, and the second a binary relation.) Let Z be a variable of type $\{[N, N]\}$; and F and TC be functions of the appropriate types.
Unnest:

$$R(x, y, y') \leftarrow S(x, Z), [y, y'] \in Z.$$

Nest:

$$[y,y'] \in F(x) \leftarrow R(x,y,y'),$$
$$S'(x,F(x)) \leftarrow R(x,y,y').$$

Transitive closure of the second field of S':

$$[x,z] \in TC(Z) \leftarrow [x,z] \in Z,$$
$$[x,z] \in TC(Z) \leftarrow [x,y] \in Z, [y,z] \in TC(Z),$$
$$S''(x,TC(Z)) \leftarrow S'(x,Z).$$

EXAMPLE 21.3.

[Heterogeneous sets] Let $STRING$ be a type. Consider the following typed symbols:

- $\square$ $P(\{\{N, STRING\}\})$ (i.e., P is a unary predicate, and its unique field contains a set of sets of integers and strings).
- $\square$ F is a function of type $\{N, STRING\} \rightarrow \{N\}$.
- $\square$ $Q(\{\{N\}\})$.
- $\square$ H a function of type $\{\{N, STRING\}\} \rightarrow \{\{N\}\}$.
- $\square$ x_N is a variable of type N.
- $\square$ Y is of type $\{N, STRING\}$.

The following program filters the integers from P:

$$x_n \in F(Y) \leftarrow P(X), Y \in X, x_N \in Y,$$
$$F(Y) \in H(X) \leftarrow P(X), Y \in X,$$
$$Q(H(X)) \leftarrow P(X).$$

21.3 THE COL LANGUAGE

In this section, the complex object language is defined.

The *language L* of the underlying logic is first defined. This language is based on a typed alphabet containing:

a. Typed constants and variables
b. Logical connectors and quantifiers $\wedge$, $\vee$, $\neg$, $\Rightarrow$, $\exists$, $\forall$
c. Typed equality ($=_T$), and membership ($\in_{T,S}$) symbols

d. Typed predicate symbols
e. Typed function symbols of three kinds:
   ☐ data functions
   ☐ tuple functions $[\ ]_{T1,\ldots,Tn'}$
   ☐ set functions $\{\ \}_{T1,\ldots,Tn}$

Terms of the form $[\ ]_{T_1,\ldots,T_n}(a_1,\ldots,a_n)$, will be denoted by $[a_1,\ldots,a_n]$; and terms of the form $\{\ \}T_1,\ldots,T_n(a_1,\ldots,a_m)$ by $\{a_1,\ldots,a_m\}$. The set function has an arbitrary (but finite) number of arguments. Clearly, that function could be replaced by a binary function set-cons and a particular symbol, say $\emptyset$, for the empty set. For instance, $\{\ \}_{T_1,\ldots,T_n}(a_1,\ldots,a_3)$ would stand for

$$\text{set-cons}_{T_1,\ldots,T_n}(a_1,\text{set-cons}_{T_1,\ldots,T_n}(a_2,\text{set-cons}_{T_1,\ldots,T_n}(a_3,\emptyset)))$$

In the remainder of the paper, the word "function" will only refer to data functions, and not to tuple or set functions. It is assumed that all the functions that are considered in the following are set-valued, that is, an image by a data function is always a set. In the last section, this limitation is discussed, and an extension of the language to remove it considered.

Note that $\in_{T,S}$ is a symbol of the language. Clearly, $\in_{T,S}$ is interpreted by the classical membership of set theory. Indeed, when the types are understood, $\in_{T,S}$ is simply denoted by $\in$. A constant of a certain type T is interpreted as an element of $\mathrm{dom}(T)$.

The terms of the language are now defined:

DEFINITION 21.2. A constant or a variable is a *term*. If $t_1,\ldots,t_n$ are terms and F is an n-ary data, tuple, or set function symbol, $F(t_1,\ldots,t_n)$ is a *term*. (The obvious restrictions on types are of course imposed). A *closed term* is a term with neither variables, nor data functions.

EXAMPLE 21.4.

The term $[1,\{2,3\},\{7\}]$ is a closed term. On the other hand, $[1,\{2,3\},F(2)]$ is not closed. These two terms are different, but they may have the same interpretation (if $f(2) = \{7\}$).

Literals are defined by

DEFINITION 21.3. Let R be an n-ary predicate, and $t_1,\ldots,t_n$ terms, for $n \geq 0$. Then (with the obvious typing restrictions) $R(t_1,\ldots,t_n)$, $t_1 = t_n$, and $t_1 \in t_n$ are positive literals. If ψ is a positive literal, $\neg\,\psi$ is a negative literal.

Arbitrary, well-formed formulas are defined from literals in the usual way. We have defined here the language of a first-order logic. One can define a model theory and a proof theory for this language. This is not in the scope of the present paper. We next introduce a clausal logic based on this first-order logic. A key component of that clausal logic is the notion of "atom." An *atom* is a literal of the form $R(t_1, \ldots, t_n)$ or $t_1 \in F(t_2, \ldots, t_n)$. If $t_1, \ldots, t_n$ are closed terms, the atom is said to be *closed*.

Now we have:

DEFINITION 21.4. A *rule* is an expression of the form $A \leftarrow L_1, \ldots, L_n$ where

☐ the *body* $L_1, \ldots, L_n$ *is a conjunction of literals.*

☐ the *head* A is an atom (and so contains no equality predicate). A *program* is a finite set of rules.

EXAMPLE 21.5.

Consider the following program P_0:

$R(1,2,3) \leftarrow$

$R(1,3,5) \leftarrow$

$[y,y'] \in F(x) \leftarrow R(x,y,y')$

$S(x,F(x)) \leftarrow R(x,y,y').$

The predicate R is extensionally defined, whereas the function F and the predicate S are intensionally defined.

In Datalog, rules are used to specify the extension of derived predicates. Consider the preceding third rule. The predicate in the left-hand side of the rule is $\in$, which is interpreted by the set membership. In fact, the rule is used to specify the *data function F* and not the extension of a predicate.

We are interested by Herbrand-like models of our programs. The *universe* U is formed of all the closed terms which can be built from the constants of the language. Let P be a program. The *base* B_P of P is the set of all closed atoms formed from the predicate and function symbols appearing in P, and the closed terms of U. An *interpretation* of a program P is a finite subset of the base B_P.

Continuing with the preceding example we have:

EXAMPLE 21.5.

[(continued):] An interpretation of the program P_0 is:

$I = \{R(1,2,3), R(1,3,5), [2,3] \in F(1), [3,5] \in F(1), S(1, \{[2,3], [3,5]\})\}.$

It should be noted that elements in the base (and thus, in the interpretation) have very simple form. In particular, literals like $F(2) = \{3,4,5\}$ or $F(2) \in G(2)$ are not in the base. They are not closed atoms.

In order to define the notion of satisfaction of a rule, and thus of a program, the concept of valuation is introduced. Valuations play here the role of substitution in classical logic programming. Note that the valuations are written on the left of the terms or atoms, for convenience's sake.

DEFINITION 21.5.   Let θ be a *ground* substitution of the variables, and I an interpretation. The corresponding *valuation* θ_I is a function from the set of terms to the set of closed terms defined by[1]:

1. θ_I is the identity for constants, and $\theta_I x = \theta x$ for each variable.
2. $\theta_I[t_1, \ldots, t_n] = [\theta_I t_1, \ldots, \theta_I t_n]$, $\theta_I\{t_1, \ldots, t_n\} = \{\theta_I t_1, \ldots, \theta_I t_n\}$.
3. $\theta_I F(t_1, \ldots, t_n) = \{a \mid [a \in F(\theta_I t_1, \ldots, \theta_I t_n)] \in I\}$.

The function 0_I is extended to literals by:

4. $\theta_I P(t_1, \ldots, t_n) = P(\theta_I t_1, \ldots, \theta_I t_n)$.
5. $\theta_I(t_1 = t_2) = (\theta_I t_1 = \theta_I t_2)$, $\theta_I(t_1 \in t_2) = (\theta_I t_1 \in \theta_I t_2)$.
6. $\theta_I(\neg A) = \neg \theta_I A$.

A valuation in this context depends on the interpretation that is considered. This comes from the need to assign values to terms br :lt using function symbols. As we shall see, this is a major reason for the nonmonotonicity of the operators that will be associated to COL programs.

Using valuations, we now define the notion of *satisfaction* of rules and programs:

DEFINITION 21.6.   The notion of satisfaction (denoted by $\models$) and its negation (denoted by $\not\models$) are defined by:

- ☐ For each closed positive literal, $I \models P(b_1, \ldots, b_n)$ "iff" $P(b_1, \ldots, b_n) \in I$; $I \models b_1 = b_2$ "iff" $b_1 = b_2$ is a tautology; and $I \models b_1 \in b_2$ "iff" $b_1 \in b_2$ is a tautology.
- ☐ For each closed negative literal $\neg B$, $I \models \neg B$ "iff" $I \not\models B$.
- ☐ Let $r = A \leftarrow L_1, \ldots, L_m$. Then $I \models r$ "iff" for each valuation θ_I such that for each i, $I \models \theta_I L_i$, then $I \models \theta_I A$.
- ☐ For each program P, $I \models P$ "iff" for each rule r in P, $I \models r$.

A model M of P is an interpretation that satisfies P.
A model M of P is *minimal* "iff" for each model N of P, $N \subseteq M \Rightarrow N = M$.

---

[1]The reader has to be aware of a subtlety in 3. The symbol $\in$ in $[a \in F(\theta_I t_1, \ldots, \theta_I t_n)]$ is a symbol of the language COL, whereas the other occurrence of $\in$ denotes the usual membership of set theory.

EXAMPLE 21.5.

[(end):] The interpretation I_0 is a model of P_0. Furthermore, I_0 is minimal.

A given COL program may not have a minimal model. This of course arises because of the use of negation. However, even positive COL programs may not have a minimal model as illustrated by the following example:

EXAMPLE 21.6.

Consider the program:

$1 \in F, p(F), q(2),$

$q(1) \leftarrow p(1).$

Then $\{1 \in F, p(\{1\}), q(1), q(2)\}$ and $\{1 \in F, 2 \in F, p(\{1, 2\}), q(2)\}$ are two incomparable minimal models.

21.4 STRATIFIED PROGRAMS

The notion of stratification has been used by several authors [Apt, et al., 1986; Van Gelden, 1986; Naqvi, 1986; . . .] to give a semantics to programs with negation in the body of rules. We present a similar notion for programs allowing complex objects and data functions.

Some basic notion are first defined.

In a literal $P(t_1, \ldots, t_n)$, the symbol P is the *defined* symbol. Similarly, in a literal $F(t_2, \ldots, t_n) \supseteq t_1$, F is the *defined* symbol. The *defined symbol of a rule* is the defined symbol of the head of the rule. (This clearly relates to the fact that a rule $F(t_2, \ldots, t_n) \supseteq t_1 \leftarrow \ldots$ does not participate in the definition of the predicate $\supseteq$, but in that of the function F).

A symbol that occurs in a rule not as the defined symbol of the head is called the *determinant* of the rule.

Consider, for instance, the following two rules:

$F(x) \supseteq y \leftarrow R(F(x), y)$

$S(x, F(x)) \leftarrow R(X, y)$

The symbol F is the defined symbol of the first rule; and S that of the second. The symbols R and F are determinants of the two rules.

To define the notion of stratification, we use the auxiliary concepts of "total" and "partial" determinants of a rule. We say that an occurrence of a determinant predicate P is *partial* in a rule if that occurrence arises in a positive literal. Similarly, the occurrence of a determinant function F in a positive literal $F(t_2, \ldots, t_n) \supseteq t_1$ is said to be *partial*. A determinant is *partial* (in a rule) if all its occurrences are partial; a determinant is *total* otherwise.

For instance, consider the rule:

$$F(G(y)) \supseteq x \leftarrow H(x) \supseteq y, R(x,y), \; \neg S(y,z), H'(H'(x)) \supseteq y$$

In that rule, F is the defined symbol. The symbols R and H are partial determinants, and the symbols S and G total determinants. The symbol H' has one total and one partial occurrence, and thus is a total determinant. The distinction between total and partial determinant is quite natural. To derive a new atom using the previous rule it suffices to know some partial information on R and H (i.e., $R(x,y)$ and $H(x) \supseteq y$). On the other hand, S has to be completely known to be able to assert $S(y,z)$. Similarly, $H'(x)$ must be completely known.

Intuitively, if Y is defined by the rule, and X is a total determinant, then X must be "completely defined" before Y. This is denoted by $X < Y$. If X is only a partial determinant, then X must be defined no later than Y. This is denoted by $X \leq Y$. For each program P, a marked graph G_P is constructed as follows:

- ☐ The nodes of G_P are the predicate and function symbols of P.
- ☐ There is an edge from X to Y if $X \leq Y$.
- ☐ There is a marked edge from X to Y if $X < Y$.

We are now ready to define the condition for stratification:

DEFINITION 21.7.   A program P is *stratified* iff the associated graph G_P has no cycle with a marked edge.

Remark: We have defined stratification of programs using both negation and data functions. As we shall see, negation can be simulated using data functions. We could have presented stratification only for data functions, and derived that for negation.

The stratification of the program induces an order of evaluation of the predicate and function symbols as follows:

PROPOSITION 21.1.   Let P be a program, and Q the set of predicate and function symbols of P. Then P is stratified "iff" there is a partition

$$Q = Q_1 \cup \ldots \cup Q_m$$

of Q such that

$$X \leq Y, Q_i \supseteq X \Rightarrow \exists j (i \leq j, Q_j \supseteq Y)$$

and

$$X < Y, Q_i \supseteq X \Rightarrow \exists j\,(i < j, Q_j \supseteq Y)$$

The partition of symbols induces a partitioning of a program in strata. For each $Q = Q_1 \cup \ldots \cup Q_M$, let $P = P_1 \cup \ldots \cup P_m$ where for each i, $P_i = \{r \in P \,|\, \text{the defined symbol of } r \text{ is in } Q_i\}$.

It is assumed in the following that such a partitioning is assigned to each stratified program. Indeed, one can show [Apt, et al., 1986] that the choice of that partitioning is not relevant. A program with a single stratum is called *monostratum* program, and a program with several is called *multistrata* program.

To conclude this section, we illustrate the previous definitions with an example:

EXAMPLE 21.7.

Consider the following four rules:

$$r_1 = F(x) \supseteq y \leftarrow R(x,y)$$
$$r_2 = S(x, F(x)) \leftarrow R(x,y)$$
$$r_3 = F(y) \supseteq x \leftarrow S(x, Y), Y \supseteq y$$
$$r_4 = F(y) \supseteq x \leftarrow S(y, F(x))$$

The program $\{r_1, r_2\}$ is stratified. A corresponding partition is $\{R, F\} \cup \{S\}$. Similarly, $\{r_1, r_3\}$ is stratified. A corresponding partition is $\{R, F, S\}$. On the other hand, $\{r_1, r_2, r_3\}$ and $\{r_4\}$ are not stratified.

21.5 FIXPOINT SEMANTICS OF STRATIFIED PROGRAMS

In this section, the semantics of stratified programs is defined using canonical, minimal, and causal models.

The following three well-known concepts are used:

- ☐ An operator T is *monotonic* if $I \subseteq J$ implies that $T(I) \subseteq T(J)$.
- ☐ I is a *fixpoint* of T, if $T(I) = I$.
- ☐ I is a *pre-fixpoint* of T, if $T(I) \subseteq I$.

With each program P, we associate an *operator* T_P defined as follows:

DEFINITION 21.8. Let P be a program, and I an interpretation of P. Then a closed term A is the *result of applying the rule* $A' \leftarrow L_1, \ldots, L_M$ *with* a valuation θ_I such that

□ $I \models \theta_l L_i$ for each $i \in [1..m]$
□ Either $A' = P(t_1, \ldots, t_n)$ and $A = P(\theta_l t_1, \ldots, \theta_l t_n)$, or $A' = [F(t_2, \ldots, t_n) \supseteq t_1]$, and $A = [F(\theta_l t_2, \ldots, \theta_l t_n) \supseteq \theta_l t_1]$.

The operator T_P is defined by $T_P(I) = \{A \mid A$ is the result of applying a rule in P with some $\theta_l\}$.

For a program P, T_P is not monotonic in general. For instance, consider the program P consisting of the single rule $Q(F) \leftarrow$. Then

$$T_P(\{F \supseteq 1\}) = \{Q(\{1\})\} \not\subseteq \{Q(\{1, 2\})\} = T_P(\{F \supseteq 1, F \supseteq 2\})$$

The following proposition links the notion of model of P to that of pre-fixpoint of T_P.

PROPOSITION 21.2.   Let P be a program, and M an interpretation of P. Then the next two statements are equivalent:

□ M is a (minimal) model of P
□ M is a (minimal) pre-fixpoint of T_P

Proof.   It is clearly sufficient to prove that M is a model of P "iff" M is a pre-fixpoint of T_P. M is a model of P "iff" for each rule r in P, $M \models r$; "iff" for each rule r in P, if A is the result of applying r with θ_M, then A belongs to M; "iff" $T_P(M) \subseteq M$.

The next proposition relates the notion of "causal" model to that of fixpoint of T_P. We first define the concept of causality [Bidoit & Hull, 1986].

DEFINITION 21.9.   A model M of P is said to be *causal* if for each $A \in M$, there exists a rule r in P, and a valuation θ_M, such that A is the result of applying r with θ_M.

The next proposition is a straightforward consequence of Proposition 21.2.

PROPOSITION 21.3.   Let P be a program, and M an interpretation. Then the next two statements are equivalent:

□ M is a (minimal) causal model of P
□ M is a (minimal) fixpoint of T_P

Proof.   It clearly suffices to show that M is a causal model of P "iff" M is a fixpoint of T_P. M is a causal model of P, "iff" $T_P(M) \subseteq M$ (model of P), and $M \subseteq T_P(M)$ (causality); $M = T_P(M)$, that is, M is a fixpoint of T_P.

Monostratum programs are first considered. For these programs, a model can be obtained by repeated application of the corresponding operators. This motivates the use of the classical notion of powers of an operator T.

$$T \uparrow 0(I) = I$$

$$T \uparrow (n + 1)(I) = T(T \uparrow n(I)) \cup T \uparrow n(I)$$

$$T \uparrow w(I) = \cup_{n=0}^{\infty} T \uparrow n(I)$$

We will prove the following result:

THEOREM 21.1.   Let P be a monostratum program. Then for each I,

☐ $T_P \uparrow w(I)$ is a minimal pre-fixpoint of T_P containing I.
☐ $T_P \uparrow w(\varnothing)$ is a minimal fixpoint of T_P.

This result shows that $T_P \uparrow w(\varnothing)$ can be viewed as a canonical model of the monostratum program P since by Proposition 21.3, it is a minimal causal model of P.

To prove that result, we will use three properties of monostratum programs. But, first, we introduce some notation which allows us to consider particular subsets of a given interpretation.

Notation: Let I be an interpretation, and X a set of predicate and data function symbols. We denote by $I|_X$ the following subset of I:

$$I|_X = \{P(a_1, \ldots, a_n) \in I \mid P \in X\} \cup \{[F(a_2, \ldots, a_n) \supseteq a_1] \in I \mid F \in X\}$$

To prove Theorem 21.1, we shall show that monostratum programs are "growing," "X-finitary," and "stable on X" for some X.

DEFINITION 21.10.   Let P be a program and X a set of symbols. Then:

1. T_P is growing [Apt, et al., 1986] if for each interpretation $I, J,$ and M such that $I \subseteq J \subseteq M \subseteq T_P \uparrow w(I)$, then $T_P(J) \subseteq T_P(M)$.
2. T_P is *X-finitary* if for each sequence (I_n) of interpretations such that for each $n(0 \leq n), I_n \subseteq I_{n+1},$ and $I_n|_X = I_0|_X$, then $T_P(\cup_{n=0}^{\infty} I_n) \subseteq \cup_{n=0}^{\infty} T_P(I_n)$.
3. T_P is *stable on X* if for each $I, (T_P(I)|_X \subseteq I|_X)$.

The proof of Theorem 21.1 can be found in the appendix. Indeed, it is shown there that for some X, monostratum programs are X-finitary and stable on X (Lemma 21.4), that they are growing (Lemma 21.5); and for each operator T with these three properties, and for each interpretation I,

a. $T(T \uparrow w(I)) \subseteq T \uparrow w(I)$
b. $T \uparrow w(I) \subseteq T(T \uparrow w(I)) \cup I$ (Proposition 21.4)

Theorem 21.1 is then a consequence of these results (see the appendix to this chapter).

Theorem 21.1 does not hold for multistrata programs. Indeed, the operator corresponding to a multistrata program is, in general, not growing as shown by the following example.

EXAMPLE 21.8.

Consider the program:

$$F \supseteq 1 \leftarrow,$$
$$F \supseteq 2 \leftarrow,$$
$$P(F) \leftarrow .$$

Let $I = \{F \supseteq 1\}$, $J = \{F \supseteq 1, F \supseteq 2\}$. One can show that $T_P(I) = \{F \supseteq 1, F \supseteq 2, P(\{1\})\}$, and $T_P(J) = \{F \supseteq 1, F \supseteq 2, P(\{1,2\})\}$. Thus $I \subseteq J \subseteq T_P(I)$, and $T_P(I) \not\subseteq T_P(J)$. Therefore T_P is not growing.

To prove Theorem 21.1, the X-finitarity is used. In Apt, et al. [1986], besides the growing property, finitarity is used. Finitarity corresponds here to $\varnothing$-finitarity. It should be noted that monostratum programs are not, in general, finitary as shown by the example:

EXAMPLE 21.9.

Consider the one-rule program:

$$P(F) \leftarrow$$

where F is a 0-ary function which returns a set of integers. Let (I_n) be the sequence such that $I_n = \{[F \supseteq i] \mid i < n\}$. Then $\cup_{n=0}^{\infty} T(I_n) = \{P(\varnothing), P(\{0\}), \ldots, P([0..n]), \ldots\}$; and $T(\cup_{n=0}^{\infty} I_n) = \{P([0..\infty])\}$. Then $T(\cup_{n=0}^{\infty} I_n) \not\subseteq \cup_{n=0}^{\infty} T(I_n)$. In fact, the program is $\{F\}$-finitary.

Now consider multistrata programs. Intuitively, the stratification guarantees a locality property [Apt, et al., 1986] which permits us to view them as a sequence of monostratum ones. Indeed, with each stratified program, $P = P_1 \cup \ldots \cup P_m$, a sequence $T_1, \ldots, T_m$ of operators is associated. The following construction is used:

☐ $K_0 = \varnothing$
☐ $K_i = T_i \uparrow \omega(K_{i-1})$ for each $i \in [1..m]$

The sequence $T_1, \ldots, T_m$ of operators has the locality property which allows us to conclude:

THEOREM 21.2. Let P be a stratified program. Then K_m, defined as previously, is a minimal fixpoint of $\bigcup_{i=0}^{m} T_i$. Thus K_m is a minimal causal model of P.

The proof of Theorem 21.2 can also be found in the appendix.

This is the main result for COL programs. It is interesting to note that negation can be simulated using data functions. Let P be a predicate. The following program gives an equivalent form of $\neg P$.

$$F(t) \supseteq t \leftarrow P(t),$$

$$A(t, F(t)) \leftarrow,$$

$$Q(t) \leftarrow A(T, \{\}).$$

It is easy to see that $Q(t)$ is equivalent to $\neg P(t)$. Consider the stratification condition imposed by the previous program. From the first rule, $P \leq F$; from the second, $F < A$, and from the third, $A \leq Q$. As a consequence, $P < Q$ which leads to the classical notion of stratification for negation.

21.6 DISCUSSION

In this section, we briefly consider some applications and extensions of the language. More precisely, we illustrate the following points:

1. Procedural data
2. Heterogeneous databases (functional and relational)
3. Semantic database models
4. Evaluation techniques for datalog queries

During the presentation, we encounter various extensions of the language which are left for future research.

21.6.1 Procedural Data

One of the reasons for considering a functional database model versus a relational one is to remove the dichotomy between data and queries. The removal of that dichotomy is also the motivation for introducing procedural fields in Postgres [Stonebraker, 1986]. However, if the procedural fields solution is interesting as being an extension of the popular relational model, it certainly lacks the elegance of the functional solution. We believe that COL presents the advantages of both approaches by first being a relational extension, and also by making explicit use of functions to handle procedural-like data. The purpose of this section is to briefly investigate this issue.

Procedural data is introduced in Stonebraker [1986] in order to blur the dichotomy between data and queries. Queries can be stored in the database in particular fields (called procedural fields). When the corresponding data is needed, the queries are activated.

Consider the database schema

R(employee, manager,{hobby}),
S(employee, {phone}).

Suppose that the company policy is that managers can also be reached at their employees' phone numbers. The relation S can be defined intensionally using a function PHO, the facts

PHO(John) $\supseteq$ 5555, PHO(Peter) $\supseteq$ 6666, PHO(Tom) $\supseteq$ 7777 . . .

and the rules

PHO(z) $\supseteq$ w ← $R(y, z, X)$, PHO(y) $\supseteq$ w,

$S(y,$PHO$(y))$ ←.

To continue with the same example, some facts are known on relation R:

R(John, Peter, {chess, football}), R(Peter, Max, {bridge}) . . .

Suppose that it is also known that employee Tom is managed by Peter, and does not have any hobby but the ones of his boss. Then one might want to store the fact

R(Tom,Peter,HOB(Peter))

where the HOB function is defined by

HOB(y) $\supseteq$ x ← $R(y, z, X), X \supseteq x$.

The data functions therefore bring a lot of flexibility. The query R(John, Peter, X)? is answered by a simple access to the database, whereas the query R(Tom, Peter, X)? can be translated to the query HOB(Peter) $\supseteq$ x? (if a lazy evaluation strategy is chosen). Furthermore, an update of Peter's hobbies will implicitly modify Tom's hobbies.

It should be noted that the preceding program is not stratified. Indeed, HOB $<$ R because of the statement on employee "Tom", and $R \leq$ HOB because of the HOB defining rule. However, it is clearly possible to give a semantics to such programs. Intuitively, one has to consider a partial order of a set of atoms and terms. For instance, such an order would impose:

R(Peter, Max, {bridge}) $<$ HOB(Peter) $<$ R(Tom, Peter, {bridge})

This extension of the stratification is related to the local stratification in the sense of Przymusinski [Przymusinski].

To conclude with this example, assume that it is known that Tom always has for hobbies the hobbies of his current boss. Then one might store the fact:

R(Tom,Peter,HOB_BOSS(Tom))

where the HOB_BOSS function is defined by

$$\text{HOB\_BOSS}(y) \supseteq x \leftarrow R(y,z,X), \text{HOB}(z) \supseteq x$$

The preceding program is also not stratified. Indeed, it is not even locally stratified according to [Przymusinski]. The complex structure of facts should also be taken into account. For instance, two objects, say A and B, may be both intensionally defined with a subobject of each one of them depending on a subobject of the other.

21.6.2 Heterogeneous Databases

We show how to integrate a relational database and a functional one into a COL database. It is also possible to use a similar approach to define heterogeneous views when relations and functions are considered, and to restructure a relational database into a functional one, or conversely.

The main problem encountered in this context is that functional database models like FQL [Buneman & Frankel, 1979] or Daplex [Shipman, 1981] allow monovalued functions. A not too clean solution is to represent them using multivalued ones and enforce a oneness constraint. A more interesting solution is to extend the language with monovalued data functions. Rules like

$$x = F_1(y) \leftarrow R(x,y)$$
$$x = F(y) \leftarrow R(x,y), y = H(x)$$

have to be considered. The first rule yields inconsistency if, in the extension of R, the first attribute does not functionally determine the second one. This cannot be the case in the second rule. In both rules, the derived function may be only partially defined.

We now present an example with multivalued functions only. Consider the following two databases:

a. A Relational database:
   SHOW(firm,theater,time)
   PLAYS(actor,film)
   LOCATION(theater,address)

b. A Functional database:

CASTING: film →→ actor
LOCATED: Theater →→ address
EXHIB: film →→ theater,time

The two databases can be integrated, for instance, in a COL database consisting of one function and one predicate:

c. The integrating COL Database

The schema consists of the following:

GLOB_THEA(theater,address)
GLOB_INFO: theater →→ film,time
GLOB_FILM(film,{actor})

The integrating program is as follows:

GLOB_THEA(t,a) ← LOCATION(t,a)
GLOB_THEA(t,a) ← theater( ) ⊇ t, LOCATED(t) ⊇ a
ACTSIN(f) ⊇ a ← PLAYS(a,f)
ACTSIN(f) ⊇ a ← CASTING(f) ⊇ a
GLOB_FILM(f,ACTSIN(f)) ← PLAYS(a,f)
GLOB_FILM(f,ACTSIN(f)) ← film( ) ⊇ f
GLOB_INFO(t) ⊇ [f,h] ← SHOW(f,t,h)
GLOB_INFO(t) ⊇ [f,h] ← EXHIB(f) ⊇ [t,h]

21.6.3 Semantic Database Modeling

The field of semantic database models (see Hull & King [1986] for a survey) has been primarily concerned with structures and semantics, and with notable exceptions like Daplex, language aspects have not been studied in depth. The COL language presents the advantages of dealing with complex objects, and of handling both data functions and data relations. A consequence is that the language is more suited than other languages in the context of semantic database modeling.

In this section, we consider an example taken from the IFO model [Abiteboul & Hull, 1984], and investigate what is still missing in the COL language to make it a language for the IFO model. The IFO model has been chosen here because it incorporates most structural aspects of semantic database models: it is an object-based model, with aggregation (tuple constructor), classification (set constructor), functions, specialization, and generalization. Furthermore, the IFO model has been formally defined, which simplifies the investigation.

FIGURE 21.1
AN IFO SCHEMA

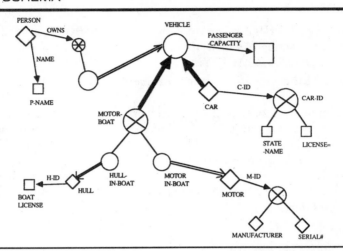

A first difficulty that is encountered comes from IFO nested functions. In IFO, the result of a function can itself be a function. Since this is a very peculiar aspect of IFO, we do not consider this feature here. We concentrate on an example given in Abiteboul and Hull [1984] without nested function. The schema is shown in Fig. 21.1. We present a corresponding COL database, and then discuss the extensions of the language that need to be considered, and the limitations of the COL representation:

a. Abstract types are represented by basic domains
   hull
   car
   person
   motor
   manufacturer

b. Constructed types are represented by base objects
   MOTORBOAT(hull,motor)
   CAR-ID(string,integer)

c. Functions
   OWNS: person → {[hull,motor],car}
   C-ID: car → [string,integer]
   M-ID: motor → [manufacturer,string]
   H-ID: hull → string PASSENGER-CAPACITY: [hull,motor] →
   binteger
   PASSENGER-CAPACITY: car → integer
   NAME: person → string

Some problems are posed by limitations of COL that were already mentioned:

☐ The type VEHICLE (i.e., either a MOTOR-BOAT or a CAR cannot be described, which yields a typing problem for the function PASSENGER-CAPACITY.

☐ Some of the functions are monovalued.

As mentioned before, these problems can be overcome by considering simple extensions of the COL language. The introduction of *name* instead of the use of the numbering of tuple fields would be a simple modification of the language that would bring it closer to the IFO model.

Perhaps a more fundamental problem is that there is no explicit way of formulating IsA relationships. An extension of the language in that direction should be considered.

21.6.4 Evaluation of Datalog Queries

It is not our purpose here to explain another technique for evaluating datalog queries. We only want to hint that the COL language provides a nice formalism for studying such questions. We briefly consider the method of Gardarin and Maindreville [1986]. Their proposal is to rewrite the relational system of equations used in a datalog query as a functional system of equations. Consider the famous Ancestor example:

$$ANC(x,y) \leftarrow PAR(x,y)$$

$$ANC(x,y) \leftarrow PAR(x,z), ANC(z,y)$$

Let us introduce the following three rules:

$$F_{PAR}(y) \supseteq x \leftarrow PAR(x,y)$$

$$F_{ANC}(y) \supseteq x \leftarrow F_{PAR}(y) \supseteq x$$

$$F_{ANC}(y) \supseteq x \leftarrow F_{PAR}(z) \supseteq x, F_{ANC}(y) \supseteq z$$

Now if the query $ANC(x,\text{Tom})$? is given, one can compute instead $F_{ANC}(\text{Tom})$ (i.e., answer the query $F_{ANC}(\text{Tom}) \supseteq x$?). In other words, a relational equation has been transformed into a functional equation:

$$F_{ANC} = F_{PAR} + F_{PAR} \circ F_{ANC}$$

where + stands for union and ∘ for the composition of multivalued functions.

In another proposal for evaluating datalog queries [Beeri, et al., 1987], namely the magic sets approach, particular terms called "grouping terms" are used. It is easy to see that these terms correspond to particular derived data functions.

21.7 CONCLUSION

The paper presents a language to manipulate complex objects based on recursive rules. The novelty is the use of data functions. The semantics of COL programs is defined as a canonical causal and minimal model using a sequence of fixpoint operators. In that sense, the semantics is constructive in nature.

We illustrated the use of the language in various database contexts: heterogeneous databases, semantic modeling, procedural data, and evaluation of datalog queries. This suggested extensions of the language: single-valued functions, explicit union of types constructor, structural stratification. Besides these issues, which were just sketched in the present paper, other important questions are raised:

- ☐ The role of inheritance in the language.
- ☐ Updates for COL databases.

Last but not least remains the issue of an efficient implementation. There has been a lot of work on nested relations and complex objects. Few of them have so far been followed by an efficient implementation (e.g., the Verso system at Inria [Verso, 1986], and the Aim project at IBM Heidelberg [Dadam, 1987]). We believe that the fixpoint semantics of COL programs makes such an implementation feasible. Indeed, the operators described in Section 21.4 can all be expressed in the algebra of complex objects of Abiteboul and Beeri [1987].

References

Abiteboul, S., and Beeri, C., (1987). "On the Manipulation of Complex Objects," abstract in *Proceedings International Workshop on Theory and Applications of Nested Relations and Complex Objects*, Darmstadt.

Abiteboul, S., and Bidoit, N., (1986). "Non-first normal form relations: an algebra allowing data restructuring," in *Journal of Computer Systems and Science*.

Abiteboul S., and Grumbach, S., (1987). "COL: a Language for Complex Objects based on Recursive Rules," abstract in *Proceedings Workshop on Database Programming Languages*, Roskoff.

Abiteboul, S., and Hull, R., (1984). "IFO: A formal semantic database model," *Proceedings ACM SIGACT/SIGMOD Symposium on Principles of Database Systems*, to appear in *ACM Transactions on Database Systems*.

Abiteboul, S., and Hull, R., (1986). "Object restructuring in semantic database models," *Proc. Intern. Conf. on Database Theory*, Roma, to appear in *Theoretical Computer Science*.

Apt, K., Blair, H., and Walker, A., (1986). "Toward a Theory of Declarative Knowledge," *Proceedings of Workshop on Foundations of Deductive Database and Logic Programming*.

Bancilhon, F., and Khoshafian, S., (1985). "A calculus for complex objects," *Proceedings ACM SIGACT/SIGMOD Symposium on Principles of Database Systems*.

Bancilhon, F., et al., (1986). "Magic Sets and Other Strange Ways to Implement Logic Programs," *Proc. ACM SIGACT/SIGMOD Symposium on Principles of Database Systems*.

Beeri, C., et al., (1987). "Sets and Negation in a Logic Database Language (LDL1)," *Proceedings ACM SIGACT/SIGMOD Symposium on Principles of Database Systems*.

Bidoit, N., and Hull, R., (1986). "Positivism vs. Minimalism in Deductive Databases," *Proceedings ACM SIGACT/SIGMOD Symposium on Principles of Database Systems*.

Buneman, P., and Frankel, R. E., (1979). "FQL—a Functional Query Language" (preliminary report), *Proceedings ACM SIGMOD Conference on Management of Data*.

Dadam, P., (1987). "History and Status of the Advanced Information Management Prototype," *Proceedings International Workshop on Theory and Applications of Nested Relations and Complex Objects*, Darmstadt.

Fischer, P., and Thomas, S., (1983). "Operators for non–first normal form relations," *Proceedings 7th COMPSAC*, Chicago.

Gardarin G., de Maindreville, C., (1986). "Evaluation of Database Recursive Logic Programs as Recurrent Function Series," *Proceedings ACM SIGMOD Conference on Management of Data*.

Hammer, M., and McLeod, D.J., (1978). The semantic data model: A modeling mechanism for database applications. In *Proc. ACM SIGMOD*, Int. Conf. Management of Data, Austin, TX, May 31–June 2, ACM, New York, 1978, pp. 26–35.

Hull, R., and King, R., (1986). "Semantic database modeling: Survey, applications, and research issues," U.S.C. Computer Science Technical Report, to appear in *ACM Computing Surveys*.

Hull, R., and Yap, C. K., (1984). "The format model: A theory of database organization," *Journal of the ACM*, Vol. 31, No. 3.

Jacobs, B., (1982). "On Database Logic," *Journal of the ACM*, Vol. 29, No. 2 (1982), pp. 310–332.

Jaeschke, B., and Schek, H. J., (1982). "Remarks on the algebra of non first normal form relations," *Proceedings ACM SIGACT/SIGMOD Symposium on Principles of Database Systems*, Los Angeles.

Kobayashi, I., (1980). "An overview of database management technology," TR CS-4-1, Sanno College, Kanagawa 259-11, Japan.

Kuper, G. M., (1987). "Logic Programming with Sets," *Proceedings ACM SIGACT/SIGMOD Symposium on Principles of Database Systems*.

Naqvi, S. A., (1986). "A Logic for Negation in Database Systems," *Proceedings Workshop on Foundations of Deductive Databases and Logic Programming*, Minker J., (ed.).

Przymusinski, T. C., "On the Semantics of Stratified Deductive Databases and Logic Programs," to appear in *Journal of Logic Programming*.

Schek, H., and Scholl, M., (1986). "The Relational Model with relation-valued attributes," in *Information Systems*, Vol. 11, No. 2 (1986), pp. 137–147.

Shipman, D., (1981)., "The Functional Data Model and the Data Language Daplex," *ACM Transactions on Database Systems*.

Stonebraker, M., (1986). "Object Management in Postgres using Procedures," in the *Postgres Papers*, UCB report.

Van Gelder, A., (1986). "Negation as Failure Using Tight Derivations for General Logic Programs," *Proceedings of Workshop on Foundations of Deductive Database and Logic Programming*.

Verso, J., (pen name for the Verso team) (1986). "Verso: a Database Machine Based on non-1NF Relations," Inria Internal Report.

Appendix

In this appendix, Theorems 21.1 and 21.2 are proven.

To prove Theorem 21.1, we first show that each monostratum program is growing, X-finitary, and stable on X, for some X. To do that, we use the following technical lemma:

LEMMA A.1. Let J and K be two interpretations such that $J|_X = K|_X$ for a given set X of symbols, and θ_J and θ_K two valuations with $\theta_J X = \theta_K X$ for each variable X. If t is a term such that each function symbol occurring in t belongs to X, then $\theta_J t = \theta_K t$.

Proof. The result is obvious if t contains no function symbols. Now consider $t = F(t_1, \ldots, t_n)$ where F is in X and $t_1, \ldots, t_n$ contain no function symbol. Then

$$\theta_J F(t_1, \ldots, t_n) = \{x \mid [x \in F(\theta_J t_1, \ldots, \theta_J t_n)] \in J\}, \text{ by definition}$$

$$= \{x \mid [x \in F(\theta_J t_1, \ldots, \theta_J t_n)] \in J|_X\}, \text{ since } F \text{ is in } X$$

$$= \{x \mid [x \in F(\theta_J t_1, \ldots, \theta_J t_n)] \in K|_X\}, \text{ since } J|_X = K|_X$$

$$= \{x \mid [x \in F(\theta_K t_1, \ldots, \theta_K t_n)] \in K|_X\}, \text{ since } t_1, \ldots, t_n$$
$$\text{contain no function symbol}$$

$$= \{x \mid [x \in F(\theta_K t_1, \ldots, \theta_K t_n)] \in K\}, \text{ since } F \text{ is in } X$$

$$= \theta_K F(t_1, \ldots, t_n)$$

By induction of the imbrication of function symbols, $\theta_J t = \theta_K t$ for each term t containing only function symbols in X.

We now consider X-finitarity and stability.

LEMMA A.2.   Let P be a monostratum program, and X the set of symbols in P which are not defined in P. Then T_P is X-finitary and stable on X.

Proof.   Consider first stability on X. For each interpretation I of P, $T_P(I)$ contains only atoms that are built from a defined symbol. Thus $(T_P(I))|_X = \varnothing \subseteq I|_X$, so T_P is stable on X.

We next prove that T_P is X-finitary. Let (I_n) be a growing sequence of interpretations such that $I_n|_X = I_0|_X$ for all n. Let $J = \cup_{n=0}^{x} I_n$, and let $A \in T_P(J)$. To conclude the proof, it suffices to show that $A \in T_P(I_k)$ for some k. Since $A \in T_P(J)$, A is the result of applying a rule $r : A' \leftarrow L_1, \ldots, L_m$ in P with a valuation θ_J. For each k, let $\theta_{Ik}x = \theta_J x$ for each variable x. We shall prove that A is the result of applying r with θ_{Ik} for some k.

Let X be the set of symbols that are not defined in P. Clearly, $J|_X = I_k|_X$ for each k. Let $t_1 \in F(t_2, \ldots, t_n)$ or $P(t_1, \ldots, t_n)$ be an atom in rule r, and let $i \in [1..n]$. Each function symbol G appearing in t_i is a total determinant, and thus is not defined since P is monostratum. Since $J|_X = I_k|_X$, $\theta_{Ik} t_i = \theta_J t_i$ by Theorem 21.3. Thus $(+)\theta_{Ik} t_i = \theta_J t_i$, for each atom $t_1 \in F(t_2, \ldots, t_n)$ or $P(t_1, \ldots, t_n)$ in rule r, and each $i \in [1..n]$.

Let $j \in [1..m]$. Since A is the result of applying r with θ_J, $J \models \theta_J L_j$. We prove that for k large enough, $I_k \models \theta_{Ik} L_j$. We distinguish four cases:

1. $L_j = P(t_1, \ldots, t_n)$. Then, $\theta_J L_j \in J$. Thus there exists an integer $k(j)$ such that for all $k \geq k(j)$, $\theta_J L_j \in I_k$. By $(+)$, $\theta_J L_j = \theta_{Ik} L_j$ for all $k \geq k(j)$. Thus for all $k \geq k(j)$, $\theta_{Ik} L_j \in I_k$, that is, $I_k \models \theta_{Ik} L_j$.

2. $L_j = [t_1 \in F(t_2, \ldots, t_n)]$. Then $[\theta_J t_1 \in F(\theta_J t_2, \ldots, \theta_J t_n)] \in J$. Then there exists an integer $k(j)$, such that for all $k \geq k(j)$, $[\theta_J t_1 \in F(\theta_J t_2, \ldots, \theta_J t_n)] \in I_k$. By $(+)$, for all $k \geq k(j)$, $[\theta_{Ik} t_1 \in F(\theta_{Ik} t_2, \ldots, \theta_{Ik} t_n)] \in I_k$, that is, $I_k \models \theta_{Ik} L_j$.

3. $L_j = \neg P(t_1, \ldots, t_n)$. Then $\theta_J P(t_1, \ldots, t_n) \notin J$. Then there exists an integer $k(j)(k(j) = 0)$, such that for all $k \geq k(j)$, $\theta_J P(t_1, \ldots, t_n) \notin I_k$. By $(+)$, $\theta_J P(t_1, \ldots, t_n) = \theta_{Ik} P(t_1, \ldots, t_n)$, for all k. Thus for all $k \geq k(j)$, $\theta_{Ik} P(t_1, \ldots, t_n) \notin I_k$, that is $I_k \models \theta_{Ik} L_j$.

4. The last case is treated similarly.

For each j in $[1..m]$, and each $k \geq k(j)$, $I_k \models \theta_{Ik} L_j$. Let $K = \sup(k(j))$, then $I_k \models \theta_{Ik} L_1 \wedge \ldots \wedge \theta_{Ik} L_n$. Let A_k be the result of applying the rule r with θ_{Ik}. By $(+)$, $A = A_k$. Thus $A \in T_P(I_k)$.

We also have:

LEMMA A.3.   If P is monostratum, T_P is growing.

Proof.   Let P be a monostratum program. Let I, J, M be interpretations such that $I \subseteq J \subseteq M \subseteq T \uparrow \omega(I)$. We prove that if $A \in T_p(J)$, then $A \in T_p(M)$.

Suppose that $A \in T_p(J)$. then A is the result of applying the rule $r : A' \leftarrow L_1, \ldots, L_m$ in P with a valuation θ_J. Let θ_M be a valuation such that $\theta_M x = \theta_J x$ for all variables x.

Let X be the set of symbols that are not defined in P. Clearly, $I|_X \subseteq J|_X \subseteq M|_X \subseteq (T_P \uparrow \omega(I))|_X = I|_X$. Let $t_1 \in F(t_2, \ldots, t_n)$ or $P(T_1, \ldots, t_n)$ be an atom in rule r, and let $i \in [1..n]$. Each function symbol G appearing in t_i is a total determinant, and thus is not defined since P is monostratum. Since $J|_X = M_X$, $\theta_M t_i = \theta_J t_i$ by Lemma 21.3. Thus $(+) \theta_M t_i = \theta_J t_i$, for each atom $t_1 \in (t_2, \ldots, t_n)$ or $P(t_1, \ldots, t_n)$ in rule r, and each $i \in [1..n]$.

We prove that $M \vDash \theta_M L_i$ for each i. Like in the previous lemma, there are four cases. We consider here the last case only. The others are left to the reader.

4. Let $L_i = \neg [t_1 \in F(t_2, \ldots, t_n)]$. Since A is the result of applying the rule with θ_J, $J \vDash \theta_J L_i$. Thus $[\theta_J t_1 \in F(\theta_J t_2, \ldots, \theta_J t_n)] \notin J$. Thus, by $(+)$, $[\theta_M t_1 \in F(\theta_M t_2, \ldots, \theta_M t_n)] = [\theta_J t_1 \in F(\theta_J t_2, \ldots, \theta_J t_n)] \notin J$. Let $B = [\theta_M t_1 \in F(\theta_M t_2, \ldots, \theta_M t_n)]$. Since $B \notin J$, $B \notin J|_X = M|_X$. Since the literal is negative, F is a total determinant of P. Thus F is not a defined symbol of P (P is monostratum) that is, $F \in X$. Hence $B \notin M$. Therefore, $[\theta_M t_1 \in F(\theta_M t_2, \ldots, \theta_M t_n)] \notin M$, that is, $M \vDash L_i$.

In each case, $M \vDash \theta_M L_i$. Let A'' be the result of applying rule r with θ_M. By $(+)$, $A'' = A$. Thus $A \in T_p(M)$.

The following proposition will be essential in the proof of Theorem 21.1.

PROPOSITION A.1.   Let T be an X-finitary, stable on X, and growing operator. Then for all I,

a. $T(T \uparrow \omega(I)) \subseteq T \uparrow \omega(I)$
b. $T \uparrow \omega(I) \subseteq T(T \uparrow \omega(I)) \cup I$

Proof.   First consider (a). Since T is stable on X,

$$(T \uparrow (n + 1)(I))|_X = (T \uparrow n(I))|_X = (T \uparrow 0(I))|_X$$

Thus the sequence $(T \uparrow n(I))$ is growing and $(T \uparrow n(I))|_X = (T \uparrow 0(I))|_X$. By the X-finitarity of T,

$$(+) T(\cup_{n=0}^x T \uparrow n(I)) \subseteq \cup_{n=0}^x T(T \uparrow n(I))$$

Thus,

$$T(T \uparrow \omega(I)) = T(\cup_{n=0}^x T \uparrow n(I))$$
$$\subseteq \cup_{n=0}^x T(T \uparrow n(I)) \text{ by } (+)$$
$$\subseteq \cup_{n=1}^x T \uparrow n(I) = T \uparrow \omega(I)$$

Now consider (b). Let $A \in T \uparrow \omega(I)$. Then either $A \in I$, or there exists $n \geq 1$ such that $A \in T \uparrow n(I)$. Thus either $A \in I$, or there exists $n \geq 0$ such that $A \in T(T \uparrow n(I))$. Since $I \subseteq T \uparrow n(I) \subseteq T \uparrow \omega(I)$, and since T is growing, $T(T \uparrow n(I)) \subseteq T(T \uparrow \omega(I))$. Thus $A \in T(T \uparrow \omega(I)) \cup I$.

Theorem 21.1, which exhibits a minimal (pre-)fixpoint of T_P, is a straightforward consequence of Lemmas 21.4, 21.5, and Proposition 21.4.

THEOREM 21.1.   Let P be a monostratum program. Then for each I,

☐ $T_P \uparrow \omega(I)$ is a minimal pre-fixpoint of T_P containing I.
☐ $T_P \uparrow \omega(\varnothing)$ is a minimal fixpoint of T_P.

Proof.   By Lemmas 21.4 and 21.5, T_P is stable on X, X-finitary, and growing. By definition, $T_P \uparrow \omega(I)$ contains I. Thus, by Proposition 21.4 (a), $T_P \uparrow \omega(I)$ is a pre-fixpoint of T_P containing I. By Proposition 21.4 (b), $T_P \uparrow \omega(\varnothing)$ is therefore a fixpoint of T_P.

Now consider the minimality. Suppose that there exists an interpretation J which is a pre-fixpoint of T_p such that $I \subseteq J \subseteq T_p \uparrow \omega(I)$. To conclude the proof, it suffices to show that $T_P \uparrow \omega(I) \subseteq J$.

First, $T_P \uparrow 0(I) = I \subseteq J$. Suppose that $T_P \uparrow n(I) \subseteq J$ for some n. Then $I \subseteq T_P \uparrow n(I) \subseteq J \subseteq T_P \uparrow \omega(I)$. Since T_P is growing, $T_P(T_P \uparrow n(I)) \subseteq T_P(J) \subseteq J$. Thus $T_P \uparrow (n + 1)(I) = T_P(T_P \uparrow n(I)) \cup T_P \uparrow n(I) \subseteq J$. By induction, $T_P \uparrow \omega(I) = \cup_{n=0}^{\infty} T_P \uparrow n(I) \subseteq J$.

Arbitrary stratified programs are now considered. First recall the notion of iterative powers of a sequence of operators, and the locality property [Apt, et al., 1986].

DEFINITION A.1.   Let $T_1, \ldots, T_m$ be a sequence of operators. The **iterative powers** of that sequence **w.r.t.** an interpretation I are defined by

☐ $K_0 = I$
☐ $K_i = T_i \uparrow \omega(K_{i-1})$ for each $i \in [1..m]$

The sequence of operators $T_1, \ldots, T_m$ is **local**, if for each I and J such that $I \subseteq J \subseteq K_m$, $T_i(J) = T_i(J \cap K_i)$.

Let $P = P_1 \cup \ldots \cup P_m$ be a stratified program. With the first stratum, we associate an operator T_1; with the second one, an operator T_2; and so on. Then we have:

LEMMA A.4.   Let $T_1, \ldots, T_m$ be the sequence of operators corresponding to a statified program $P = P_1 \cup \ldots \cup P_m$. This sequence is local.

Proof. First suppose that $T_i(J) \not\subseteq T_i(J \cap K_i)$ for some i. Let A be in $T_i(J) -$ $T_i(J \cap K_i)$. Then A is the result of applying some rule r in P_i. Since $J \cap K_i \subseteq$ J, and $A \notin T_i(J \cap K_i)$, the application of the rule uses a fact B not in $J \cap K_i$. Suppose that $B = [b_1 \in F(b_2, \ldots, b_n)]$. (The case $B = P(b_1, \ldots, b_n)$ is similar). Since B is used in the application of r,

(*i*) F is a determinant of r in P_i.

Since B is in $K_m - K_i$, B is the result of the application of a rule r' in P_j for some $j > i$. Thus

(*ii*) F is the defined symbol of a rule r' in P_j for $j > i$.

Clearly, (*i*) and (*ii*) together contradict the stratification condition on $P_1 \cup \ldots \cup P_{i-1}$. Hence, $T_i(J) \subseteq T_i(J \cap K_i)$. The reverse inclusion is proved in a similar way.

Theorem 21.2 will be a straightforward consequence of the following proposition:

PROPOSITION A.2.   Let $T_1, \ldots, T_M$ be a local sequence of operators such that for each $i \in [1..m]$, T_i is growing, X_i-finitary and stable on X_i, for some X_i. For each instance I, let (K_i) be the iterative powers of $T_1, \ldots, T_n$ w.r.t. I. Then[2]

1. $(\cup_{i=1}^m T_i) K_m \subseteq K_m$
2. $K_m \subseteq (\cup_{i=1}^m T_i) K_m \cup I$

Proof. Let I be an interpretation. Recall the result of the Proposition 21.4: if T is growing, X-finitary, and X-stable for some X,

a. $T(T \uparrow \omega(I)) \subseteq T \uparrow \omega(I)$
b. $T \uparrow \omega(I) \subseteq T(T \uparrow \omega(I)) \cup I$

1. $(\cup_{i=1}^m T_i K_m) = \cup_{i=1}^m T_i K_m$, by definition,
   $\subseteq \cup_{i=1}^m T_i K_i$, by locality,
   $\subseteq \cup_{i=1}^m K_i$, by (a),
   $\subseteq K_m$.

2. Conversely,
   $K_m = T_m \uparrow \omega(K_{m-1})$, by definition,
   $\subseteq T_m K_m \cup K_{m-1}$, by (b),
   $\subseteq (\cup_{i=1}^m T_i K_i) \cup I$, by induction,
   $\subseteq (\cup_{i=1}^m T_i K_m) \cup I$, by locality,
   $= (\cup_{i=1}^m T_i) K_m \cup I$, by definition.

---

[2] By definition, $(\cup_{i=1}^m T_i) J = \cup_{i=1}^m (T_i J)$.

We now conclude:

THEOREM 21.2.   Let $P = P_1 \cup \ldots \cup P_m$ be a stratified program, and $T_1, \ldots, T_m$ be the corresponding operators,

☐ $K_0 = \varnothing$.

☐ $K_i = T_i \uparrow \omega(K_{i-1})$ for each $i \in [1..m]$.

Then K_m is a minimal fixpoint of $\cup_{i=0}^m T_i$. Thus K_m is a minimal causal model of P.

Proof.   By Proposition 21.3, it suffices to show that K_m is a minimal fixpoint of $\cup_{i=0}^m T_i$. By Lemma 21.7, the sequence of operators is local. Thus, by Proposition 21.5,

1. $(\cup_{i=1}^m T_i)K_m \subseteq K_m$
2. $K_m \subseteq (\cup_{i=1}^m T_i)K_m$

Therefore, K_m is a fixpoint of $\cup_{i=0}^m T_i$. It remains to show the minimality. Let J be a pre-fixpoint of $\cup_{i=1}^m T_i$. We prove by induction on k that (*) if $J \subseteq K_k$, then $K_k \subseteq J$. For $k = 0$, $K_0 = \varnothing \subseteq J$. Suppose (*) is true for a certain k (first induction hypothesis). We prove by induction that:

(**)$T_{k+1} \uparrow j(K_k) \subseteq J$

For $j = 0$, it is by hypothesis. Suppose it is true for a certain j (second induction hypothesis). By (**), $K_k \subseteq T_{k+1} \uparrow j(K_k) \subseteq J \cap K_{k+1} \subseteq T_{k+1} \uparrow \omega(K_k)$. Since T_{k+1} is growing, $(+)T_{k+1}(T_{k+1} \uparrow j(K_k)) \subseteq T_{k+1}(J \cap K_{k+1})$.
Hence

$T_{k+1} \uparrow (j + 1)(K_k) = T_{k+1}(T_{k+1} \uparrow j(K_k)) \cup T_{k+1} \uparrow j(K_k)$, by definition,

$\subseteq T_{k+1}(T_{k+1} \uparrow j(K_k)) \cup J$, by second induction hypothesis,

$\subseteq T_{k+1}(J \cap K_{k+1}) \cup J$, by (+),

$= {}_{k+1}(J) \cup J$, by locality,

$\subseteq J$, since J is a pre-fixpoint of T_{k+1}.

Thus (**) holds for all j. By induction, (*) holds for all k. In particular, for $K = m$, if J is a pre-fixpoint of $\cup_{i=1}^m T_i$ such that $J \subseteq K_m$, then $K_m \subseteq J$, which concludes the proof.

PART V

DATABASE PROGRAMMING LANGUAGES

CHAPTER 22

REPRESENTING DATABASE PROGRAMS AS OBJECTS

David Maier

22.1 INTRODUCTION

Programming languages, as we know them, will be gone in 20 years. What is the point in conceiving a highly structured entity, having to reduce it to a linear representation, push it through a byte-wide knothole, and then have a compiler guess what structure you meant? With the advent of object-oriented database system and persistent programming environments, it is feasible to program by directly creating structures that represent programs, without going through the middlemen of a scanner and a parser. We in the database field should be the last ones proposing new lexical languages. We should be inventing storage types for program objects. Once we are free of the strictures of linear syntax, we should discover a wealth of variations for control structures, scoping rules, and binding environments. Ultimately, the semantics of program objects should be describable as yet other objects, giving the ultimate in portablility: the semantics of a programming system is ported along with a program.

This paper explores some desiderata for database programming models, indicates the problems with current approaches to database programming, and looks at the conflict between encapsulation and efficient access in database programming. I then propose *abstract objects* as a building block for database programming models, and look at the ramifications of this approach. I suspect many of the ideas I am advocating are also arising in the Persistent Programming Research Group [Atkinson, et al., 1987; Morrison, et al., 1987], although we differ on whether a structural approach to typing is desirable. What I am proposing may be more of an intermediate code, suitable for communication with a storage server, with the expectation that a semantic layer is placed over it.

22.2 WHAT MAKES A DATABASE COMPUTATION MODEL POWERFUL?

I claim that the power of relational algebra as an abstraction of disk storage comes from its encapsulation of iteration. Seven or eight common forms of iteration over sets of records are identified, and queries are expressed in terms of them. Since there are a small number of forms, their interactions can be studied in detail, giving rise to transformations that can be used for optimizing queries. Effort can be directed at efficient implementation of this handful of iteration forms. Since the iteration is expressed at a high level, multiple orderings for accessing records are permissible, and the physical ordering or records and foreknowledge of access patterns can be used to great advantage. Further, use of auxiliary access structures can be embedded in the evaluation methods for the algebraic operators, making applications independent of the presence or absence of such structures, and simplifying that code. A query processor can delay choosing a particular evaluation plan for an algebraic expression until the sizes of the arguments are known, allowing even more efficiencies in execution. None of these advantages is available when database manipulations are expressed with explicit looping structures. Looping gives a particular implementation of the query, from which it is nearly impossible to infer the intent. Thus, the range of transformations and evaluation choices is severely limited. Moreover, the record-at-a-time nature of explicit iterations places high demands on the communication bandwidth between application programs and the database system.

I expect the next generation of database systems to reside on a network of workstations, with a central or distributed storage manager, shared by application programs over the network. Here, the importance of being able to express iterations and other data-intensive operations succinctly is even greater. Whatever the database programming model, it must allow complex, data-intensive operations to be picked out of programs for execution by the storage manager, rather than forcing a record or object-at-a-time interface. As mentioned in the introduction, the definition of a complex operation should be storable as a database object, so its invocation can be accomplished by merely passing a reference, rather than passing the entire expression of the operation from the application to the storage manager every time it is executed.

22.3 WHY PERSISTENT PROGRAMMING LANGUAGES DO NOT SOLVE IT ALL

The problem I see with taking a programming language, imbuing it with persistence, and calling the result a database language, is that the initial language likely does not encapsulate iteration [Atkinson et al., 1983; Kaehler & Krasnev, 1983]. The interface to the storage manager is not able to express operations at a high level of intent, because that level is not present in the language. The storage manager ends up with an object-at-a-time interface, thus forcing a lot of data and command traffic between the application program and the storage manager. The storage manager has no behavioral component, and so any data manipulation must be done by moving the data to the application process space and operating on it there. Some persistent languages do provide a limited kind of associative access to the store [Schaffert, et al., 1986; O'Brien, et al., 1986], but the support is typically only for set selection. Even if such a feature is present, it is hard to use unless the language has a construct for expressing associative access. Most programming languages do not provide the semantics for reasoning about data access at a high level, making transformations for optimizations hard to come by, and limiting the availability of alternative evaluation methods.

Starting from a declarative programming language, such as a logic or functional language, gives a better start at expressing access at a high level [Tsur & Zaniolo, 1986]. However, such languages are generally inadequate for expressing update and user I/O, as they are value based. Further, the logic languages do not traditionally provide much in the way of typing. The functional languages have sophisticated typing systems, but those typing systems are value based, and are only recently being extended to handle reference. Neither paradigm seems to deal with object identity well.

22.4 EMBEDDED DML

I doubt many of us believe that an embedded data manipulation language is the best strategy for database programming. The problems with this approach are manifest, the most serious being *impedance mismatch* at the interface of the application language and the DML. The programming paradigms of the two languages are frequently at odds, as are the data structures supported. Much information is reflected back at the junction of the two. There is no type system spanning the application code and the DML, so little checking can be done on type agreement across the junction. The persistent programming approach does have the advantage of a single type system. However, the type systems of most languages were not conceived with persistent data in mind, particularly the difficulties in modifying type definitions when instances of those types persist.

It is interesting to observe how 4GLs and application generators deal with this typing problem. They generate the application code working off the type definitions of the database (the scheme of an extension of it), trying to ensure agreement between the types of database objects and their uses in the application code. The code is generated to be type correct, but typing still can not be checked across the boundary.

22.5 EXTENDING THE APPLICATION LANGUAGE

Another approach to capturing the high-level operators on data in the application language is to extend an imperative language with associative access constructs [Maier, et al., 1986]. The problem with this approach is that the resulting language is quite complex, and probably lacks orthogonality and transparency. The language ends up with multiple ways to do the same thing (but with only one amenable to optimization) and there are limitations on embedding imperative statements in the declarative extension. Supporting such an extension also means having to modify the parser for the original language.

22.6 ENCAPSULATION VERSUS ASSOCIATIVE ACCESS

Being able to model behavior along with structure in a database, and encapsulate the two together to create new data types, gives more sharing of code, easier integrity enforcement, and aids code reuse and modification. The physical structure of a data object is hidden; it may only be accessed or updated through the object's operation protocol.

However, most of the technology for database query processing depends on knowledge of the structure of objects, rather than just their protocol. For example, consider maintaining an index on a collection of objects, say Rectangles. What is an index, expressed in terms of protocol? It is a cache of results from evaluating some expression on each element of the collection. The results are organized by value. Then when it is desired to find all the elements of the collection with a specific value (or in a certain range) for the expression, the cache is consulted, rather than actually evaluating the expression on each element. For example, we might want to index the rectangles by their origin points. The expression could be

R origin

for each rectangle R (using Smalltalk message notation). The problem with maintaining such an index is in knowing that the "origin" message returns the same result twice in a row (it has no side effects), and in knowing what other messages to a rectangle can change the state in a way to affect the result of the R origin expression. If the expression were instead R center, where the center is computed from the origin and corner, how do I know a change to either of those values changes the result of R center? The problem is further complicated if the expression reaches further down into the objects. Suppose R origin actually a Point object, and that object has x and y position. If I build an index on

R origin yCoord

there is even more difficultly in detecting state changes. A Rectangle may store a Point object as part of its state, but changes to that Point object can occur withour actually changing the immediate state of the Rectangle object. (It still references all the same subobjects.)

What I need to know for maintaining an index on rectangles is that there is some message pair, say getOrigin and setOrigin that have a certain specification on their interaction: two invocations of getOrigin return the same result, as long as there is no intervening setOrigin invocation. In essence, I want to say there is a "origin" field in the Rectangle. I more or less want to dispense with the encapsulation and know about the structure of Rectangle objects. Must encapsulation just go out the window?

Some data models get around this problem by saying that certain structural aspects of the object are visible externally, as *components* [Schaffert, et al., 1986] *properties* [Ontologic, Inc., 1986]. We all know that a jet have engines, so let us just admit it in the protocol. Indexing, if allowed only on these visible subobject, is supportalbe without violating encapsulation. An interesting kink arises in Trellis/OWL, however. The implementation of a component may be specified as "field," meaning represent the component as a field in the object's private state, and do get and set in the obvious way. However, the get and set operations can also be implemented with arbitrary code, in which case there are no guarantees they will exhibit behavior necessary for index maintenance.

22.7 ABSTRACT OBJECTS

I propose here the notion of an *abstract object* as a basic building block for database programming objects. My approach is colored by experience with object-oriented databases. In particular, I assume a data model with complex objects having identity and in which objects can be shared subparts of other objects. An abstract object acts much as a term or pattern in a logic language, and it can be used both for decomposing and building concrete objects, much as a logical term acts under unification. However, abstract objects are objects, so they can be created, stored, manipulated, and viewed just as concrete database objects can. They can be composed to create compound queries and manipulation, commands. These abstract objects are very structural in nature, but they do possess a formal semantic theory built on a logic that incorporates identity and type hierarchies [Maier, 1986; Zhu & Maier, 1988].

An abstract object is essentially a template for a class of concrete objects with a given structure. They resemble Ait-Kaci's ψ-terms [Ait-Kaci, 1984], although we expect to use them in an environment where there are distinct meta-and ground levels, not just a single "type level." Suppose a RectSelect object consists of a Rectangle and a cursor Point. A Rectangle consists of origin and corner Points, and each Point has and x and y coordinate. The following abstract object could be used to choode all RectSelect objects where the cursor is on the bottom edge, and an origin has x coordinate O.

> RectSelect : RS(rect $->$ Rectangle : R(
>   origin $->$ Point : P1(x $->$ 0),
>   corner $->$Point : P2(y $->$ Int : N))
>   cursor $->$ Point : P3(x $->$ Int : M, y $->$ Int : N))

This abstract object has six abstract subobjects (a Rectangle, 3 Points, and 2 Ints) and one concrete subobject (Int O). Matching this template against RectSelect objects, when it succeeds, yields a 7-tuple of concrete objects, one corresponding to each abstract object. Thus, and abstract object can be used for structural matching and decomposition. An abstract object can also be used for creating new objects, and composing or updating existing objects. Consider the template

> Rectangle : R1(origin $->$ Point : P1,
>   corner $->$ Point : P3)

Given a tuple of three concrete objects (a Rectangle and two Points), this abstract object indicated how to wire them together to make a new object. Combining a matching template and making template into a command, I get

> Rectangle : R1(origin $->$ Point : P1,
>   corner $->$ Point : P3) $<==$
> RectSelect : RS(rect $->$ Rectangle : R(
>   origin $->$ Point : P1(x $->$ 0),
>   corner $->$ Point : P2(y $->$ Int : N))
>   Cursor $->$ Point : P3(x $->$ Int : M, y $->$ Int : N)).

which specifies the creation of a Rectangle (in the form of the command head) using parts of a RectSelect object matching the body. (I emphasize that the preceding construct is just a textual approximation of the actual command object.) Abstract objects can also be used for updates. If I wanted to update and original Rectangle in the RectSelect, instead of making a new one, I would write

```
Rectangle : R(origin -> Point : P1,
        corner -> Point : P3) <==
    RectSelect : RS(rect -> Rectangle : R(
            origin -> Point : P1(x -> 0),
            corner -> Point : P2(y -> Int : N))
        cursor -> Point : P3(x -> Int : M, y -> Int : N)).
```

If I wanted to merely modify the corner point of :R, rather than replace it, I would use

```
Point : P2(x -> : M) <===
    RectSelect : RS(rect -> Rectangle : R(
            origin -> Point : P1(x -> 0),
            corner -> Point : P2(y -> Int : N))
        cursor -> Point : P3(x -> Int : M, y -> Int : N)).
```

Or, I could create a new point for the corner for :R with the same coordinates as :P3.

```
Rectangle:R(corner -> Point : P4(x -> :M, y -> :N)) <==
    RectSelect : RS(rect -> Rectangle : R(
            origin -> Point : P1(x -> 0),
            corner -> Point : P2(y -> Int : N))
        cursor -> Point : P3(x -> Int : M, y -> Int : N)).
```

I can also introduce computation into commands

```
Point : P2(x -> (L - :M)) <==
    RectSelect : RS(rect -> Rectangle : R(
            origin -> Point : P1(x -> 0),
            corner -> Point : P2(x -> Int :L , y -> Int : N))
        cursor -> Point : P3(x -> Int : M, Y -> Int : N)).
```

The important property of such a command is that its processing can be separated into structural matching and making phases, with an intervening computational "mapping" phase. Such simple commands can be grouped and named to create compound commands.

22.8 RAMIFICATIONS AND EXTENSIONS

Some advantages that accrue from using abstract objects as the building blocks of database commands are as follows:

1. Commands can be stored in the database, making them easy to catalog and accessible for multiple applications. Moreover, I now have the possibility that two commands could share the same abstract object as a subpart. (Perhaps the make template of one command could be the match template of another).

2. Queries can have arbitrary literals, not just those with lexical conventions for representation in a source language. I can write a query that looks for a *Rectangle* containing a certain *Point*, without having to describe the *Point* by its state.

3. Expressing cyclic query structures is possible.

4. Commands can be viewed and edited with whatever mechanism exist for manipulating regular database objects.

5. As an intermediate step toward a completely "objectified" language, a simple interface between a programming language and the database system allows construction and evaluation of command objects, without major modification to the programming language itself. Adding new query functionality—range selection, equality verses indentity comparisons, aggregates—involves creating new flavors of objects, but not changes the programming language parser. Ultimately, however, I want to do away with any "surface" language, and have entire programs represented as objects, such as in the Garden system [Reiss, 1987].

6. With commands as objects, I can consider interpretations of those objects other than just their execution value. Abstract interpretations can be defined for them to give valuations in domains such as execution time or result size. As Atkinson, et al. [1983] point out, the compilation or optimization of such an object is just a particular view on the object [Atkinson, et al., 1987].

There are also a number of extensions and refinements to explore:

1. Is it possible to develop an abstract notion based on protocol rather than structure? Such an object might be viewed as a computation graph to be evaluated via graph reduction techniques, with an added reduction rule for database matching. The result of a reduction sequence would be nondeterministic, because an abstract object can match the database in multiple ways.

2. For a command object, what are strategies for evaluating portions of it on different processors? for example, the structural access could be done on a central storage server, and the computational part on a local workstation.

3. I do not think abstract objects are quite equivalent to logical variables. (I do not see how to unify two abstract objects). I think objects with logical variables would be useful for expressing and constraining partially defined objects and for representing alternative configurations or versions of an object. Perhaps the ability to store a name form a binding environment is place of a value would give equivalent power [Atkinson & Morrison, 1985].

References

Ait-Kaci, H., (1984). "A Lattice-Theoretic Approach to Computation Based on a Calculus of Partially Ordered Type Structures," Ph.D. Thesis, University of Pennsylvania.

Atkinson M. P., and Morrison R., (1985). "Types, bindings and parameters in a persistent environment," *Proceedings of Data Types and Persistence Workshop*, Appin, August.

Atkinson M. P., and Morrison R., and Pratten G. D., (1987). "Persistent information architectures," Univ. of Glasgow/Univ. of St. Andrews, *Persistent Programming Research Report* 36, June.

Atkinson M. P., Bailey P. J., Chisholm K. J., Cockshott W. P., and Morrison R., (1983). "An approach to persistent programming," *The Computer Journal*, Vol. 26, No. 4.

Kaehler T., and Krasner G., (1983). "LOOM—large object-oriented memory for Smalltalk-80 systems," *In Smalltalk-80: Bits of History, Words of Advise*, Reading, Mass.: Addison-Wesley.

Maier, D., (1986). "A Logic for Objects," Oregon Graduate Center TR CS/E-86-012, November, presented at the *Workshop on Deductive Databases and Logic Programming*, Washington, D.C., August.

Maier D., Stein J., Otis A., and Purdy A., (1986). "Development of an object-oriented DBMS," *Proc. 1986 ACM Conference on Object-Oriented Programming Systems, Languages and Applications*, September–October.

Morrison R., Atkinson M. P., and Dearle A., (1986). "Flexible incremental bindings in a persistent object store," Univ. of Glasgow/Univ. of St. Andrews, *Persistent Programming Research Report*, 38, June.

O'Brien P., Bullis B., and Schaffert C., (1986). "Persistent and Shared Objects in Trellis/Owl," *Proc. 1986 IEEE International Workshop on Object-Oriented Database System*.

Ontologic, Inc., (1986). *Vbase object manager user manual*, Billerica, MSS., November.

Reiss S. P., (1987). "An object-oriented framework for conceptual programming," in *Research Directions in Object-Oriented Programming*, Shriver, B., and Wegner, P. (eds.), Cambridge, Mass: MIT Press.

Schaffert, C., Cooper, T., Bullis, B., Kilian, M., and Wilpolt, C., (1986). "An Introduction to Trellis/Owl." *Proc. 1986 ACM Conference on Object-Oriented Programming Systems, Languages and Applications*, September–October.

Tsur, S., and Zaniolo, C., (1988). "LDL: A logic-based data-language," *VLDB XII*, August.

Zhu, J., and Maier, D., (1988). "Abstract Objects in an Object-Oriented Data Model," *Proceedings of Second International Conference on Expert Database Systems*, April.

CHAPTER 23

Data and Knowledge Model: A Proposal

Maurice A. W. Houtsma
Peter M. G. Apers

23.1 DATA AND KNOWLEDGE REPRESENTATION MODEL

23.1.1 Requirements

In [Houtsma, 1987] we have formulated some basic requirements that a data and knowledge representation model should fulfill. We shall summarize them here:

- ☐ A model should capture the semantics of the world modeled at the right abstraction level.
- ☐ It should support modularity.
- ☐ It should provide a good way of communication between the database designer and the user.
- ☐ It should allow for dynamic components, like virtual attributes.
- ☐ Knowledge should be specified in a form that is clear to the designer and the user of the system, eases explanation, and is easily modifiable.
- ☐ The processing of queries should be handled efficiently.

In the development of our DK model we start from a database point of view. This has the advantage of a strong theoretical background, availability of well-founded semantic data models, and the availability of large, reliable, multiuser systems. Our model is able to treat data and knowledge in a uniform and powerful way.

We use the Entity-Relationship model [Chen, 1976] as a basis for our ideas about integrating data and knowledge in one model. The main reason is that it is a well-developed semantic data model that fulfills the first three requirements mentioned before. However, we would like to stress that we expect our ideas to hold for other semantic data models [Shipman, 1981] as well.

Besides normal attributes we allow virtual attributes in our model. These attributes are not associated with a value, but with a rule that describes how to compute a value for these attributes. However, queries addressing the attributes do not notice the difference between normal attributes and virtual attributes.

The rules that give definitions for virtual attributes are specified in the form of Datalog-like clauses. This declarative way of specifying knowledge rules eases the support of explanation facilities. Moreover, the optimization of the handling of knowledge is not visible to the user but remains a separate part of the system. By storing the knowledge rules with the associated entity the modularity of the system is ensured. Finally, the model we have in mind can be mapped onto the relational algebra extended with recursion [Apers, et al., 1986 a,b,c]. This will guarantee an efficient processing of queries.

23.1.2 Components of the DK Model

The DK model consists of entities, relationships, and IsA links. The latter are used to represent generalization. An entity consists of three parts: attributes, rules, and constraints. An attribute may be an ordinary attribute as in the ER model or it may be a virtual attribute defined in the rule part. Queries addressing attributes will not notice the difference. Attributes may be complex in the sense that they are structured or they may represent sets.

The rule part gives definitions of virtual attributes in the form of Datalog-like clauses. In this way knowledge concerning an entity is represented in the form of clauses in the rule part of the entity itself. So, knowledge is stored in a modular way. Clauses may refer to attributes of the same entity or of other entities somehow connected via relationships or IsA links to this entity.

Constraints are represented in Horn clauses to represent additional knowledge concerning the entity. So their representation is not used to enforce them because probably not all constraints can be captured in this way.

Relationships are used to interconnect one or more entities. Whether to use the same structure as for entities or to just let a relationship connect occurrences of several entities without additional information is still under investigation.

IsA links are used to represent generalizations. The idea of generalizations is that attributes are connected to entities as high up in the generalization structure as possible, so that they are represented only once and can be inherited by specializations. In the DK model this holds for both normal and virtual attributes. This means that inheritance as treated by [Cardelli, 1984] should be extended to allow for the inheritance of clauses in the rule part as well. So, queries visiting a specialization may also ask for virtual attributes of the generalization.

Besides the basic entities discussed previously, derived entities can be defined. In this case the attributes of this derived entity are defined in terms of other entities using Datalog-like clauses. So a recursive definition is allowed.

Our DK model will allow for two types of queries:

☐ Normal queries, which want attribute values as an answer.

☐ Questions that will get the description of the answer in terms of Datalog-like clauses.

We will not discuss the components of our DK model separately.

23.1.3 Entities

As described previously entities consist of three parts; attributes, rules, and constraints. Each will be described now.

Attributes. As said before, data by nature are structured. Data are the basic facts we know about real-world entities, or at least the basic facts we think important enough to model. For instance, the data of employees could be: employee number, name, address, job, department, salary. These basic facts are represented by attributes in a data model.

Relational database systems are concentrated around structured data: relations. With the introduction of the relational data model strategies were developed to structure these data. The process of normalization structures data in a way to avoid redundancy, and thereby ambiguity problems. Once these structures are defined, they are intended to be stable over a long period of time. The reason is that the universe of discourse, which is reflected in the data structures, does not change very often. But the contents of the database can change very frequently.

By the influence of new applications on database systems other demands are made toward a data model. From CAD/CAM there arises a need to have complex objects and sets as data type in modeling reality. Therefore attempts are made to extend existing models with these requirements [Schek & Scholl, 1986], or define new models that support them [Lorie & Plouffe, 1983; Lum, 1985].

Besides requirements that arise through new applications, some existing extensions have to be dropped. Especially, because of the influence of logic on databases, handling null values is not clearly understood. Besides that, at the moment there is no good semantics for null values. Of course, in, for example, SQL there is a way of dealing with null-valued attributes, but this seems to be rather ad hoc and there is certainly no clear semantics behind it.

Another restriction being made in present data models is that every attribute of a tuple should have a fixed value. We allow so-called virtual attributes in our model. This means that instead of a value being associated to an attribute, we also allow a rule to be associated with an attribute. This rule has to describe how to compute a value for the attribute. Such rules should be given among the other rules associated with an entity, in the rule part. This part will be described in the next section.

So, we have seen that the modeling of structured data is well developed and can be captured by the notion of attributes. Recently, sets [Schek, 1986; Tsur & Zaniolo, 1986] and complex objects [Lorie & Plouffe, 1983; Lum, 1985; Zaniolo, 1985] are considered as possible attribute types. We allow these in our model as well. We also deviate from other data models by allowing virtual attributes, that is, attributes that do not have a value but a rule describing how to compute their value. Moreover, we also allow these virtual attributes to be multivalued.

Knowledge Rules. An observation made before is the need to model unstructured data as well as structured data. This unstructured data part can supply knowledge during query processing. Another observation made is the need for declarative knowledge representation. We have chosen to use Horn clauses. This provides us with sufficient reasoning power while being computationally feasible. Of course we could provide more deductive power by using full first-order logic, but this can lead to an inconsistent model or undecidability.

Another thing about the use of Horn clauses is that it can easily be mapped onto the relational algebra plus recursion. This will allow for an efficient implementation on a normal relational database management system.

Now that we have explained why we use Horn clauses we have to explain the use of Horn clause rules, and the mapping from predicates and their arguments onto the other components of our model. This has to be clear when adding a rule to the system and when developing an efficient query processing strategy.

A rule can be used for two different purposes: (*i*) it can be used to compute the value of a virtual attribute and (*ii*) it can be used to supply extra information. In the first case the rule supplies a way to compute the value of the virtual attribute, from the (virtual) attributes of other entities or the entity itself. Note that when we talk about computing a value this does not have to be a single value, but can be a set of values. In the second case a rule simultaneously instantiates several attributes. This is an extension of rules for virtual attributes, which will not be discussed here.

Although we allow for sets as well as complex objects in our model, we will concentrate on the former here. This is because sets can easily be introduced and are very illustrating when describing some examples later on. There are several papers describing how to handle complex objects [Lorie & Plouffe,

1983; Lum, 1985; Schek, 1986; Zaniolo, 1985], and because they are just part of our model, without forming the basis for it, we will not deviate from our story here.

Now we will describe what rules look like in our model. We have already stated that rules are Horn clauses, we will now make this more explicit. A rule consists of a head and a body. The predicate name in the head of a rule is the name of the virtual attribute the rule describes. The first argument of this predicate is a variable denoting the key value of the entity under consideration. When the entity has a multiple key the first arguments of the predicate will correspond with the key. The last argument of the predicate in the head denotes the value assigned to the virtual attribute.

The body of a rule describes how to compute the value for a virtual attribute. It consists of predicates, comparison operations, and simple arithmetic. We will now describe the mapping of the body of a rule onto other components of our model.

Predicates in the body of a rule can map onto different types of components. They can map onto attributes, virtual attributes, and relationships. The mapping between a predicate and an attribute is equal to the mapping described previously. The predicate name denotes the attribute involved, the first argument(s) the key of the entity, and the last argument the value of the attribute. This is exactly the same for virtual attributes, because they behave just like normal attributes.

A predicate maps onto a relationship if their names correspond. For simplicity there is an order on the entities involved in a relationship. This means the first argument denotes the key of the first entity involved in the relationship. The last argument consequently denotes the second entity involved the relationship.

Now that we have defined the matching between predicates and the other components of the model we will describe how to form meaningful rules with them. In other words, we will describe the semantics of rules.

The main question is what predicates are allowed in the body of a rule. First of all an object can address its own attributes and virtual attributes in the body of a rule, as described before. But it can also address attributes and rules from elsewhere in the IsA hierarchy. It will be allowed to address components of objects higher in the hierarchy (more general objects), but also components lower in the hierarchy (more specialized objects). In this last case it is not guaranteed that a value will be found; an object can be specialized but this is not mandatory. Modeling will be very important: the careful placement of rules. Attributes and rules will be placed as high in the hierarchy as possible, at a most general place.

In addition to attributes and rules from elsewhere in the IsA hierarchy, predicates can also match with attributes and virtual attributes from anywhere in the system. However, it is mandatory that the objects that own this attribute or virtual attribute are in some way connected to the object that started the search for the predicate. This connection does not have to be a direct relationship, but can be an indirect one (involving intermediate entities). So it is possible to mention a relationship that involves a more general entity in the body of a rule associated with a specialized entity.

Let us sketch again the main points described in this section. Knowledge rules can be used to compute the value of virtual attributes or supply extra information. Both sets and complex objects can be used in knowledge rules. We have concentrated on the use of knowledge rules for virtual attributes and the use of sets. Knowledge rules are represented declaratively in Horn clause logic. In knowledge rules attributes and virtual attributes of other entities in the generalization/specialization hierarchy can be addressed. Also (virtual) attributes of entities that can be reached through, probably several, relationships can be addressed. It shall be clear that knowledge rules provide a powerful way of deducing new information from the model and specific data values.

Constraints. The third part of an entity is the constraints part. Because there is a lot of semantic value present in constraints they can be very useful when answering queries. The use of constraints can be in preventing a (possibly expensive) database search operation or in answering otherwise insolvable queries. An example of this last type of use is a constraint that states the age of employees is always under 65. It can be used to answer a question like: "Will there ever be any employees with an age in between 65 and 70?"

In their appearance constraints resemble rules; the difference is that they have no head. This is because they do not compute the value of a variable, but rather state a truth. Besides this syntactic difference with rules, there also is a semantic difference. In constraints it is only allowed to use (virtual) attributes of the entity itself, or (virtual) attributes of generalizations of this entity. This is perfectly logical because these are the only things that actually belong to this entity. If a constraint addresses (virtual) attributes in other entities it should be placed in an appropriate relationship. Let us stress once again, as in Section 23.1, that constraints are only used to help answering queries. They are not in any way enforced by the system as they are specified here, mainly because the form they appear in is not fit to express all constraints. For instance, dynamic constraints cannot be formulated in this rule form.

23.1.4 Relationships

Besides entities there also appear relationships in our model. The sole reason for their existence is to connect entities, and therefore they can be of a very simple nature. As soon as there is a need to let them have (virtual) attributes, they should be made into entities.

We only model binary relationships, as is done by most people. To simplify query processing we suppose an order imposed on the relationship. This makes role names spurious. We do take into account the number of times a particular entity can appear in a certain relationship. This models the type of relationship (one-to-one, one-to-many, many-to-many) and can help answering some queries. As already discussed when describing the rule part of entities, entities are represented by their key when appearing in a relationship.

As opposed to semantic networks we do not take into account different type of links. Relationships and IsA links (discussed in the next section), are the only type of links we consider. Of course, having different type of links can sometimes supply extra information, but it can also lead to confusion. When traversing long paths of various types of links the semantics can become very unclear. The inference process becomes more difficult also, having to take into account which links can be traversed when, and what is their exact meaning.

Constraints. Although relationships are not allowed to have associated (virtual) attributes, they are allowed to have associated constraints. The reason is that many constraints are inherently part of relationships and are not in the right place when put inside entities. Constraints associated with relationships are syntactically exactly the same as those associated with entities.

Again, let us stress the fact that constraints are not enforced by the system as they are specified here. They are only used to process queries, and can in fact be looked on as a kind of prededuced information about entities involved in the relationships.

23.1.5 IsA links

In our model, IsA links are used to model generalization/specialization. We believe, as many others, that it is a desirable concept. From a specification point of view it allows to concentrate on the right level of abstraction. And from an implementation point of view it avoids data redundancy.

Because virtual attributes are considered as normal attributes, they can also be inherited by specializations. Moreover, a specialization may add its own rule to a virtual attribute it inherits. The solution will then be a combination of the answers of the respective rules.

When processing queries, IsA links can be used to traverse to other entities to see if they can supply the necessary information. They can be used to inspect more general objects, as well as more specialized objects when applicable. In each visited generalization/specialization an inference process can be started to search for the requested information, making use of relationships and their constraints.

We allow not only for normal inheritance, but also for multiple inheritance. This places some restrictions on the modeling of entities. When modeling, one should be very careful not to create situations where it is not clear what attributes are meant inside a rule. So, all attributes reachable from a certain entity should have a unique name.

By introducing IsA links we have introduced the concepts of generalization and specialization in our data and knowledge model. They make it possible to choose the right abstraction level when processing queries. But they also have an implication for the modeling phase. The modeling should be done very carefully, attributes should be placed as high as possible in the generalization hierarchy, and no anomalies should be introduced. We believe this to be one of the main differences with artificial intelligence; there exists a well-developed modeling phase and all relevant situations can be foreseen. This means for example that we do not need exceptions and thereby avoid the problems that come with them.

23.1.6 Example

Now that we have introduced the concepts of our model, let us give an example of its possibilities. We will show an example here to illustrate the modeling power. In the next section we will use the same example to illustrate how queries are processed.

```
ENTITY Researcher
  KEY empnr:INTEGER;
  ATTRIBUTES
    names:STRING;
    salary:INT;
    field:STRING;
  RULES
    knows_of(ENR, {TOPIC}) ← visits (ENR, CNAME) ∧
        appears_in(CNAME,   TOPIC) ∧ field   (TOPIC,F) ∧ field(ENR,F)
END Researcher
```

The rule states that researchers know about all topics that have been presented at a conference they visited, where the topic is inside their own field. The curly brackets mean that all values of the variable TOPIC that are found are gathered in one set. When these brackets are not used, a set of (enr, topic_name)-tuples will be presented to the user. Now, the rule results in a set of (enr, {topic_name})-tuples.

```
ENTITY Associate ISA Researcher
  ATTRIBUTES
  date_of_hire:DATE;
  duration_of_contract:{2,4};
  RULES
    knows_of(ENR, TOPIC) ← manages(PROF_ENR, ENR) ∧
        knows_of(PROF_ENR, < TOPIC >).
END Associate
```

The rule states that an associate knows about all topics that the professor who manages him knows about. Here the brackets around TOPIC denote that it is a variable that denotes a set of values. Therefore, the result of this rule will also be a set.

```
ENTITY Professor ISA Researcher
  ATTRIBUTES
    status:STRING;
  RULES
    knows_of(ENR, {TOPIC}) ← prog_comm(ENR,CNAME) ∧
      appears_in(CNAME, TOPIC).
  CONSTRAINTS
    salary(ENR, X) ∧ X > 80,000
END Professor
```

This rule, which was mentioned in the body of the *knows_of* rule for Associate, states that a professor knows about all topics that appeared in a conference where he was member of the program committee. Again the curly brackets denote that all values of the variable topic are gathered in a set. The constraint states that the salary of a professor should exceed 80K.

```
ENTITY Conference
  KEY conference_name:STRING;
  ATTRIBUTES
    place:STRING;
    weather_conditions:{good, solongsogood, bad};
END Conference
```

```
ENTITY Topics
  KEY topic_name:STRING;
  ATTRIBUTES
    field:STRING;
END Topics
```

```
RELATIONSHIP Visits
  BETWEEN Researcher, min:0,max:n
  AND Conference, min:50,max:n
END
```

```
RELATIONSHIP Prog_comm
  BETWEEN Professor, min:0,max:n
  AND Conference, min:5,max:20
END
```

```
RELATIONSHIP Appears_in
   BETWEEN Conference, min:20,max:60
   AND Topics, min:1,max:n
END

RELATIONSHIP Manages
   BETWEEN Professor, min:3,max:20
   AND Associate, min:1,max:1;
   CONSTRAINTS
   manages(PNR, ANR) ∧ salary(ANR,X) ∧ salary(PNR,Y) ∧ X < Y.
END
```

Here we see an example of a constraint associated with a relationship. It states that the salary of a professor should exceed the salary of the associates he manages.

As can be seen from the preceding example the use of IsA links eases the modeling. All (virtual) attributes from generalizations are inherited by specializations. Therefore it is not necessary to, for example, give a key to professor; this key is already inherited from researcher. It can also be seen very clearly that attributes and virtual attributes can be used in the body of rules inside specializations. This can be seen, for example, in the rule part of associate, where a virtual attribute of professor is used to compute an answer to the question about what topics an associate knows. This example is visualized by means of the entity relationship diagram in Fig. 23.1.

So this example has shown some of the power of our data and knowledge model. The use of entities, relationships and IsA links helps to model things at the right abstraction level and it supports modularity. Inheritance of attributes allows us to concentrate on data relevant to an object. The use of dynamic components in the form of virtual attributes has been shown. Rules that describe how to compute values for virtual attributes are inherited by specializations, which are allowed to add their own definition to the rule. This increases modeling power considerably. In Section 23.3, the processing of queries in our model is discussed along the lines of this same example.

23.2 RECURSIVE VIEWS

In our model we also allow for views, in particular even recursive views. Views represent another way of looking at the modeled entities. Therefore they have no graphical representation in our model. In fact, they can best be looked on as rules describing how to look on the data.

Views can be expressed as normal queries like: "All associates that earn between 20K and 30K." They can also be expressed as rules. Take as an example the entity *person* and the relationship *parent_of* between two entities. A recursive *ancestor* view can now be defined by the rule:

FIGURE 23.1
ER-DIAGRAM OF EXAMPLE

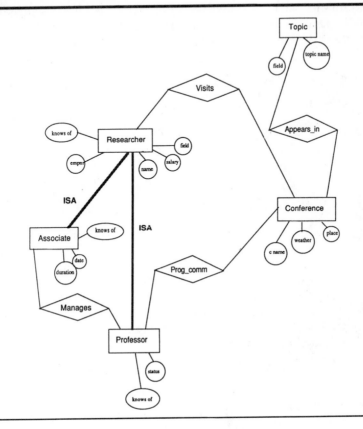

$$\text{anc\_view}(X, Y) \leftarrow \text{parent}(X,Y) \ \lor \ (\text{parent}(X, Z) \ \land \ \text{anc\_view}(Z, Y)).$$

The variables denote the keys used in the relationship parent. They are used to build an ancestor view that is presented to the user.

23.3 QUERIES AND THEIR PROCESSING IN THE DATA AND KNOWLEDGE MODEL

23.3.1 Introduction

Now that we have introduced our model in some detail and have shown an example of its modeling power, we will concentrate on the processing of queries. We will talk about the kind of queries that we foresee, and how we can make optimal use of the facilities our model provides to solve queries. An outline of a query processing algorithm will be sketched.

We will not describe a detailed query language at this moment. A query language should be the final step in providing a complete system, but to develop a full-fledged query language before the model has completely developed itself seems premature. Probably our query language will bear some resemblance with [Elmasri et al., 1985], for example.

23.3.2 Query Processing

In our system there are two main types of queries that can be posed.

☐ One can ask the actual value of (virtual) attributes of entities. This means that rules and constraints are used to compute values, and the database system is searched for values.

☐ One can ask how the answer to a query is obtained. This means that relevant rules and constraints are shown to the user.

These two types of queries will now be handled respectively.

Value-Oriented Queries. When the user asks for the value of one or more (virtual) attributes, it is the systems task to answer the query. It will therefore combine user-supplied information with knowledge provided by the model. By user-supplied information we mean that the user positions us somewhere in the model (e.g., by asking about a certain entity), and possibly restricts the value of some attributes. From there on, the system has to do the work.

The first important thing when processing queries is the kind of attribute the user asks for. If it is a real attribute, the generalization hierarchy will be traversed upward until an entity with this attribute is engaged. Because attributes in a generalization hierarchy have unique names, we do not have to look any further and can go directly to the database system to search for the value. If the requested attribute is a virtual one, we cannot stop when we engage with this virtual attribute. After all, on every level of the generalization/specialization hierarchy another rule for the same virtual attribute can appear. And because a virtual attribute only adds a definition to possibly inherited virtual attributes, the associated rules have to be applied on every level. This means that in the case of virtual attributes an inference process is started in every applicable entity along the generalization/specialization hierarchy.

An important optimization, which is independent of the type of attribute (virtual or not), is the use of constraints when processing queries. The constraints associated with entities as well as the constraints associated with relationships can be used here. They can be used to answer a query, for example, the query "Give all the professors that earn between 60K and 80K" can be answered with help of the constraint that all professors earn more than 80K. Constraints can also be used to restrict the set of entity instantiations under consideration, as a kind of extra selection criterion. When they are used for the first purpose, only constraints upward in the generalization hierarchy may be used. Constraints engaged when going downward in the generalization hierarchy (toward more specialized entities), may only be used for the second purpose.

With this in mind we will now sketch an outline of a query processing strategy.

```
Procedure search (E:Entity, A:Query): Answer
Begin
    search constraints in entity;
    search constraints in all relationships with E;
    If No answer yet and Q concerns attribute of E
    Then search database for value
    Else If Q concerns virtual attribute of E
        Then execute associated rule;
            ∀ X where ISA(E, X) Do search(X, Q);
            ∀ Y where ISA(Y, E) Do search(Y, Q);
        Else ∀ X where ISA(E, X) Do search(X, Q);
        Fi
    Fi
END
```

As can be seen from this algorithm, the inference process stops as soon as a real attribute is encountered. As long as nothing is encountered, the generalization hierarchy is traveled upward in search for the attribute. As soon as a virtual attribute is encountered the generalization hierarchy is traveled upward as well as downward. After all, for the instantiations that can be specialized a value may be found in a more specialized entity as well. Notice that the execution of rules can also lead to a separate inference process that uses the same search procedure.

Now let us take some example queries and show how they are solved. As a first query we take the following: "What is the salary of professor Persa?" The inference process starts in the entity type Professor, and because the answer cannot be found there it is moved to the entity type Researcher. Here it is noticed that *salary* is an attribute of Researcher, and the database can be searched for the value of the attribute *salary* that is inherited by professor Persa. The inference process is stopped now.

Another example is the query "About what topics does researcher Smith know?" It is noticed that *knows_of* is a virtual attribute of Researcher and therefore the corresponding rule has to be executed. This means looking at the conferences Smith has visited and selecting all the topics presented there that are associated with his field. These are then gathered into one set and give part of the solution. If Smith happens to be a professor as well, the rule that provides answers to *knows_of* for professors will also be executed. The answers are then combined and presented to the user.

Our last example will show even more clearly the power of the model and the use of inheritance of rules. Let us consider the question "About what topics does associate Wesson know?" The inference process starts by executing the rule for *knows_of* associated with Associate. This rule leads to two different inference processes: the *knows_of* rule for Professor is executed, and the *knows_of* rule for Researcher is executed *for the specific professor who manages Wesson*. These answers are combined and form part the total answer to the query. But besides the inference processes just described, there is another inference process started to compute answers to the query. Namely, the rule for Researcher is executed for the associate Wesson himself. The combination of all these answers will be the solution to the query.

We have thus seen that there are several ways of providing a solution to a query. Constraints, in entities as well as in relationships, can be used to answer a query or to focus on relevant data. Attributes, as well as virtual attributes, can be inherited along the generalization/specialization hierarchy. The involvement of virtual attributes can lead to several independent inference processes to compute the solution to a query.

Deduction-Oriented Queries.   The second type of query that is possible in our model is deduction oriented. The user has the possibility to ask how the answer to a query is derived. This means the system will show the deduction steps performed. Because the constraints and rules are in a declarative form, it is relatively easy to explain the reason for deduction steps without going into much technical detail. We imagine the user can ask to the how and why of deductions like in many expert systems.

Another thing that is eased by the use of Horn clause logic is a graphical explanation facility. Because of the direct mapping of predicates on entities, attributes, and relationships it becomes possible to show the user the relevant part of the data and knowledge model in the form of an ER diagram. It is then possible to visualize the deduction paths taken.

We will now come back to some of the previous examples. As we have described previously, the user can ask for the reason of an answer. For instance, the question can be "Why are there no professors with a salary between 60K and 80K?" The user is then shown the constraint that states that professors earn more than 80K. This same constraint is shown when the question is "Can there be employees who earn more than 70K?" When the user wants to know how the answer to the query "What topics does associate Wesson know about?" is deduced, the same kind of process takes place. The rule *knows_of* for Associate is shown, and it is shown that an associate can inherit values from Researcher. The user can then ask to be shown the *know_of* rule for Professor, or for Researcher.

So we have seen that a declarative way of specifying knowledge rules eases explanation facilities. The user is able to ask how a query is solved and why deductions are performed. We think it is an important step to be able to explain the reason for deductions to the user. However, there still is some more research to be done on this subject. We hope we can profit from expert system developments here.

23.4 MAPPING FROM THE DATA AND KNOWLEDGE MODEL ONTO THE DATABASE SYSTEM

Although our data and knowledge model provides considerable modeling power and query processing facilities, it is of a conceptually simple nature. Therefore the mapping of our data and knowledge model to an underlying relational database system is rather straightforward. The entities, with their attributes and relationships, can be mapped onto relations. Keys should be propagated down to specializations. Queries can then be translated into normal relational algebra operations like joins [Ullman, 1982]. Rules can be mapped onto relational algebra plus recursion [Houtsma, 1987]. Our work on this subject [Apers et al., 1986 a,b,c] can be very helpful in this respect.

Although an architecture for a system to support our data and knowledge model still has to be investigated, we have developed some ideas. The use of parallel systems like in [Kersten et al., 1987] seems to be especially promising.

23.5 CONCLUSION

In this paper we have presented a data and knowledge model that integrates the representation of data and knowledge. A declarative way of specifying knowledge, in the form of Horn clauses, is chosen. The main concepts of the DK model are modularity of modeling, generalization/specialization hierarchies, dynamic components in the form of virtual attributes, and inheritance of attributes and knowledge rules. Queries that are value-oriented and queries that ask for deductive steps performed are supported. Because of the straightforward way of mapping the DK model onto relational algebra plus recursion, efficient query processing is possible.

REFERENCES

Apers, P. M. G., Houtsma, M. A. W., and Brandse, F., (1986a). "Extending a Relational Interface with Recursion," *Proceedings of the 6th Advanced Database Symposium*, Tokyo, Japan, August 29–30.

Apers, P. M. G., Houtsma, M. A. W., and Brandse, F., (1986b). "Extending a Relational Interface with Recursion," Technical Report INF-86-10, Twente University of Technology, Enschede, the Netherlands.

Apers, P. M. G., Houtsma, M. A. W., and Brandse, F., (1986c). "Processing Recursive Queries in Relational Algebra," *Proc. IFIP TC2 working conference on Knowledge and Data (DS-2)*, Aldeia das Açoteias, Portugal, November 3–7.

Cardelli, L., (1984). "A semantics of multiple inheritance," in *Semantics of Data Types, Lecture Notes in Computer Science #173*, New York: Springer-Verlag, pp. 51–67.

Chen, P. P. S., (1976). "The entity-relationship model: toward a unified view of data," *ACM Transactions on Database Systems*, Vol. 1, March, pp. 9–36.

Elmasri, R., Weeldreyer, J., and Hevner, A., (1985). "The category concept: an extension to the entity-relationship model," *Data & Knowledge Engineering*, Vol. 1, June.

Houtsma, M. A. W., (1987). "The Data and Knowledge Model," Technical Report INF-87-35, University of Twente, Enschede, the Netherlands, December.

Houtsma, M. A. W. "Formalising the Data and Knowledge Model," Technical Report, in preparation, University of Twente.

Kersten, M. L., Apers, P. M. G., Houtsma, M. A. W., van Kuijk, H. J. A., and van de Weg, R. L. W., (1987). "A Distributed, Main-Memory Database Machine," *Proceedings 5th International Workshop on Database Machines*, Karuizawa, Japan, October 5–8.

Lorie, R. A., and Plouffe, W., (1983). "Complex objects and their use in design transactions," *Proceedings Annual Meeting-Database Week: Engineering Design Applications (IEEE)*, San José, Calif., May.

Lum, V., (1985). "Design of an integrated DBMS to support advanced applications," *Proceedings of the International Conference on Foundations of Data Organization*, Kyoto, Japan, May 21–24.

Schek, H. J., and Scholl, M. H., (1986). "The relational model with relation-valued attributes," *Information Systems*, Vol. 11, pp. 137–147.

Shipman, D. W., (1981). "The functional data model and the data language DAPLEX," *ACM Transactions on Database Systems*, Vol. 6, March, pp. 140–173.

Tsur, S., and Zaniolo, C., (1986). "LDL: a logic-based data-language," *Proceedings of the 12th International Conference on Very Large Data Bases*, Kyoto, Japan, August.

Ullman, J. D., (1982). *Principles of Database Systems*, Computer Science Press, Rockville, Md.

Zaniolo, C., (1985). "The representation and deductive retrieval of complex objects," *Proceedings of the 11th International Conference on Very Large Data Bases*, Stockholm, pp. 458–469.

CHAPTER 24

THE SEMANTICS OF UPDATE IN A FUNCTIONAL DATABASE PROGRAMMING LANGUAGE

Rishiyur S. Nikhil

24.1 INTRODUCTION

The dichotomy between databases and programming languages is one of expedience. Ideally, it should be possible for arbitrary objects created and manipulated by programs to be persistent. But today we know how to implement persistence efficiently only by restricting the structure of persistent objects and the operations that can be done on them.

For example, in current relational database systems, persistent objects must be flat, rectangular tables containing scalar values, and they must be manipulated only by a given set of relational operations. It is generally not easy to change the structure of the tables or to write arbitrary programs to manipulate them. Because of these restrictions, the database implementor can pre-plan disk layouts for the tables, can create indexes that use knowledge of these layouts, and compile queries so that they exploit this information thoroughly.

The limitations on structure and operations in current database systems are a serious hindrance in applications that must model complex data (e.g., in engineering design). In some applications, the limitations are so severe that implementors bypass database systems entirely—they store data in ordinary files, flattening objects before writing them out and reconstructing them after reading them in. Needless to say, the performance of persistent operations is not good. This approach also does not address issues of concurrency control and resilience.

Sometimes, implementors *encode* complex objects within, say, an existing relational system. For example, object containment in a programming language is normally implemented by pointers; in a relational system, pointers can be mimicked by foreign keys. But this layer of interpretation can again degrade performance, since the underlying relational system is unaware of the encoding. This approach also does not support data abstraction.

It is clear that persistence of complex objects must be supported directly (see also [Albano et al., 1983; Atkinson et al., 1981; Copeland & Maier, 1984]). But how to get adequate performance? One possibility is through parallelism. For this to become a reality, we need languages that do not obscure parallelism, and implementations that exploit the available parallelism. Functional languages have long been suggested as suitable for this purpose.

Our approach is based on the Tagged-token Dataflow parallel execution model [Arvind & Nikhil, 1987]. Here we begin with Id, a language designed for easy compilation into dataflow graphs, which constitute a parallel machine language. The core of Id is a functional programming language, including higher-order functions and nonstrictness in procedure calls and data structures.

But, in purely functional languages, incremental updates to large data structures can be difficult to express (see Section 24.5.4 for more on this topic), and are usually difficult to implement efficiently (see [Arvind et al., 1987] for more on this topic). "I-structures" in Id are an attempt to address these issues. I-structures are array-like data structures that can be incrementally defined (like updatable arrays), yet retain the determinacy and parallelism of functional languages.

In this paper, we present some ideas on how to extend Id to make it into a database programming language. First, we generalize the I-structure idea to a richer class of indexed structures supporting incremental definition. Then, we introduce the notion of databases and update transactions on databases. Along the way, we will find that the model can be extended naturally to express the retention and manipulation of historical data.

24.2 DATABASES AS ENVIRONMENTS

Consider an interactive programming system for a functional language. At any given time, there is a current *environment* of bindings associating names to values. The user engages in two kinds of activities:

☐ When a user enters a *definition*, he or she is specifying a new environment, usually in terms of the old. He or she is adding a new binding, or redefining an existing one. Viewing the environment as a database, this is an *update* transaction.

☐ When the user enters an *expression*, it is evaluated in the current environment, and an answer is printed. Viewing the environment as a database, this is a database *query*.

We model a database on exactly this idea. A database is an environment of bindings; update transactions specify new environments in terms of old; and queries are simply expressions evaluated in the latest environment. Thus, the operation of a single-user database system can be specified as a function from a list of transactions to a list of responses:[1]

```
Def dbsystem db (cons xact xacts) =
        {   resp, new_db = eval db xact
          In
            cons resp (dbsystem new_db xacts)  }   ;
```

The phrase (cons xact xacts) is a pattern that matches the input list, binding the name xact to the first transaction and xacts to the rest of the list of transactions. Xact is evaluated in the database environment to produce a response and a new database environment (of course, for query transactions, the new database will be the same as the old). Finally we construct and return the list of responses, beginning with this response and followed by the remaining list of responses obtained by running the remaining transactions against the new database.

The database system starts running when we invoke it with an empty database and the list of all transactions:

```
dbsystem empty_db xacts
```

A database shared among multiple users needs a little more packaging: we need a *manager* that nondeterministically receives transactions from individual users and merges them into a single list of transactions as input to dbsystem. The responses from dbsystem must then be dispatched to the appropriate

---

[1] We use Id notation here. As in most modern functional languages, application of a function f to argument a is written by juxtaposition: f a. Blocks (analogous to let or where expressions) are written

```
{   statement   ;
    . . .
    statement
 In
    expression  }
```

The left-hand sides of statements can be *patterns* that match the structure of the values returned by the right-hand sides.

users. The details are outside the scope of this paper; the interested reader is referred to [Henderson, 1982] or [Arvind & Brock, 1984] for suggested solutions.

Each binding in the database associates a name to a *database type* or to a *value* of arbitrary type. Each value v belongs to some type t, and we write this as v : t. The type structure is

☐ Primitive types: V (void), N (numbers), B (booleans), S (strings), SYM (symbols)

.
.
.

☐ Database types: Student, Course, Department,...

These can be viewed as abstract types and are introduced by the user explicitly. For each database type t, the system provides

☐ a constructor function make t which, when applied to a void argument, returns a new object of type t.
☐ a set all t containing all objects of type t.
☐ sets of objects of arbitrary, but uniform type: * t.
☐ finite tuples of objects of arbitrary type: (t1,...,tn).
☐ function types: t1 -> t2.

We will refer to such functions as *ordinary* functions, in contrast with indexed functions that follow.

☐ Indexed types: For every primitive and database type t1 and t2, there are indexed types:[2]

1.   t1   =>   t2
2.   t1   =>* t2
3.   t1   <=> t2
4.   t1   <=>* t2
5.   t1   *<=>* t2

The similarity to ordinary functions is deliberate—in queries, they are regarded as functions on finite domains. Like functions, they can be applied to arguments to produce results. For example, the object SStatus: Student => S can be applied to a Student object to produce a string. The indexed types represent one-to-one, one-to-many, and many-to-many relationships, with or without inverses. We will see examples as follows.

We will refer to objects with indexed types as *indexed* functions. For example, here is (the type of) a segment of a typical database:

---

[2] In [Nikhil, 1985], we used the notation - - ›, - - › *, etc., but - - › was easily confused with
- › in hand-written text.

```
Student      : TYPE
SName        : Student <=> S
SStatus      : Student  => S
STotalUnits  : Student  -> N
```

Student is a database type. SName is an invertible indexed function that maps Students to strings. There is a generic inverting function ∧, such that ∧ SName maps strings to Students. SStatus is a (noninvertible) indexed function that maps Students to strings, and STotalUnits is an ordinary function that maps Students to numbers. Another segment of the database is:

```
Course    : TYPE
CName     : Course <=> S
CUnits    : Course => N
CPrereq   : Course *<=>* Course
```

Course is another database type. CPrereq maps a Course into a set of Courses that are its prerequisites. ∧ CPrereq maps a Course into a set of Courses for which it is a prerequisite. The (type of the) rest of the database is:

```
Enrollment  : TYPE
EGrade      : Enrollment => S

S-Enroll    : Student <=>* Enrollment
C-Enroll    : Course  <=>* Enrollment
```

S-Enroll maps a Student into the set of his or her Enrollments, while ∧ S-Enroll maps an Enrollment into the corresponding Student.

The database type Enrollment (with associated functions) was introduced to model the occurrence of a student enrolling in a course, which allows associating various data with that event, such as grade, date of enrollment, name of supervisor who approved it, and so on. An alternative strategy would be to define the following functions directly on Student and Course:

```
Takes-Courses: Student *<=>* Course
Grade        : (Student,Course) -> S
```

In conventional database terminology, our database types correspond to distinct record types. => corresponds to an ordinary record field, whereas <=> corresponds to a record field that is also a key. The other indexed types correspond to one-to-many and many-to-many relationships, usually obtained by set owner/member links in CODASYL databases, and by joins in relational databases.

24.2.1 Queries

Queries are arbitrary applicative expressions evaluated in the database environment. A very powerful notation for expressions on collections is the "set comprehension" notation invented by Turner [1981]. This notation can be regarded as a significant generalization of relational calculus languages like SQL.

For example, here is a query to find the names of all special-status students taking 15-unit courses:

```
{ SName s | s <- all Student      ; SStatus s ==
                                      ''Special'' ;
            c <- all Course       ; CUnits c   == 15 ;
            e <- all Enrollment ; ^ S-Enroll e == s ;
                                   ^ C-Enroll e == c   }
```

In words: For all students s such that their status is special, for all courses c that have 15 units, for all enrollments corresponding to s and c, return the name of s.

Of course, the preceding expression may not be the most efficient way to compute the result. Here is a more efficient solution:

```
{ SName (^ S-Enroll e) | e <- all Enrollment ;
        CUnits (^ C-Enroll e) == 15 ;
        SStatus (^ S-Enroll e) == ''special'' }
```

In words: For all enrollments corresponding to 15-unit courses and special-status students, return the name of the corresponding student.

One of the strengths of a functional language is that its clean semantics makes programs amenable to very powerful transforms, resulting in significant optimizations. It is possible that such an optimizer could automatically produce the second query from the first.

The user can use a more algebraic notation that exploits a significant feature of functional languages: functions (both ordinary and indexed functions) are first-class values, that is, they can be arguments to and results from other functions, and components of data structures. This allows the use of high-level bulk operators to express common computations concisely. Examples of such operators are

- ☐ map f 1 returns a set containing the results of applying the function f to each member of the set 1.
- ☐ filter p 1 returns a set containing just those members of 1 that satisfy the predicate function p.
- ☐ compose f1 f2 is a function that takes an argument x and returns (f1 (f2 x)).

☐ fold op v 1 returns an accumulated value over the set 1, obtained by applying the binary function op pairwise to each element of 1, with initial value v. For example, fold (+) 0 1 sums up the set 1.

We use the standard curried notation of functional languages, so that fold (+) 0 is a function that takes a set of numbers as its argument and sums it up. The advantage of treating indexed functions like ordinary functions is uniformity—one can then extend all the power of these high-level operators to database structures.

Here is a more algebraic notation for the efficient version of the preceding query:

```
{ e_15_special e = (CUnits  (^ C-Enroll e) == 15)
                and (SStatus (^ S-Enroll e) == ''special'')
  In
    map (compose SName (^  S-Enroll))
       (filter e_15_special
              (all Enrollment)) }
```

e_15_special is a predicate that decides if the course related to enrollment e has 15 units and the student related to e has special status. Using it, we filter all enrollments, and map the composition of SName and ^ S-Enroll over the remaining enrollments to produce the desired set. This operator-based view of functional query languages and methods to implement them are explored at length in [Nikhil, 1984].

Because of our parallel model of computation, the enumeration of enrollments, the filtering, and the final mapping can all be overlapped in a pipelined manner (see [Nikhil, 1987]).

The function STotalUnits whose type was shown in the database environment is an ordinary function. Here is a possible definition for it:

```
Def STotalUnits s =
        fold (+) 0
        { CUnits (^ C-Enroll e) | e <- S-Enroll s }
```

that is, when applied to a Student, it computes that student's total units using other database functions. This is sometimes called a "derived function" in the database literature.

Here is a recursive query that checks if the course 6.001 is directly or indirectly a prerequisite for the course 6.004.

```
{ q c1 c2 = if (c1 == c2) then true
    else fold (or) false (map (q c1) (CPrereqs c2)) ;

  In
    q (^ CName ''6.001'') (^ CName ''6.004'') }
```

Note that one mixes indexed and ordinary functions freely. Definitions for ordinary functions may use recursion, conditionals, and so on. In short, the query language is a complete, high-level programming language.

24.3 OPERATIONS ON INDEXED FUNCTIONS

Indexed functions differ from ordinary functions in that they are defined incrementally with many statements, rather than in a single statement. An indexed function is first created using the `empty` construct, at which point it has an empty domain (undefined everywhere). It has zero information content, and is said to be "open." As the transaction progresses, incremental definitions *monotonically* (i.e., consistently) add more information to the object, defining it over a larger and larger domain. When the transaction completes, that is, the program terminates, the value of the indexed function is frozen, and it is said to be "closed." Incremental definitions can only be given for open indexed functions, that is, new indexed functions introduced in the current transaction.

The operations described as follows are inspired by I-structure operations in the dataflow language Id [Nikhil, 1987]. =›*, ‹=›*, and *‹=›*

24.3.1 Single-Valued Index Functions: =› and ‹=›

The expression:

```
empty (t1 => t2)
```

returns a new, empty, indexed function of type `t1 => t2`, that is, it initially maps all arguments to ⊥. For convenience, one can also say `empty e` where e is any expression of type `t1 => t2` (the value of e is irrelevant—the system only uses its type).

Given an indexed function `f: t1 => t2`, and expressions `e1: t1` and `e2: t2` that evaluate to `v` and `w`, respectively, the statement

```
f [e1] = e2
```

extends the definition of `f` so that it maps `v` to `w`. By executing many incremental definition statements, an initially empty `f` is gradually "filled in," defining it over a larger and larger domain.

Contrast this with statements for ordinary function definitions. For example,

```
g x = e
```

defines `g` at once for *all* arguments `x`. Each incremental definition statement, on the other hand, defines `f` only for one *specific* argument.

In our parallel model of computation, the order in which the incremental definitions are executed is unpredictable. Consequently, we allow a definition for f at each argument v *at most once*, that is, the value of (f v) can make at most one transition, from ⊥ to some w. Any attempt to redefine f at v so that it has some other value w' is treated as an *inconsistent* specification of f, and causes a run-time error. This rule is sometimes called the "single-assignment" rule in the dataflow literature.

If f is applied to an argument v within the same program, that part of the computation simply waits (if necessary) until f is defined at v by some other, concurrent part of the computation. The requirement that f can be given only a single definition at v ensures that each function application returns a unique, determinate result.

As we shall see later, in update transactions a new f :   t1 =>   t2 automatically inherits mappings from an old version unless specified otherwise. To inhibit this, for an expression e1 : t1 that evaluates to v, the statement

```
f  [e1]  =  undef
```

specifies that (f v) is always undefined. Any other attempt to define f at v is an error.

The treatment of <=> is similar. For an indexed function f :   t1 <=> t2 and expressions e1 : t1 and e2 : t2 that evaluate to v and w respectively, the statement:

```
f   [e1]   = e2
```

defines (f v) to be w and (∧ f w) to be v. It will succeed only if f was previously undefined at v *and* if (∧ f) was previously undefined at w.

For an indexed function f :   t1 <=> t2 and an expression e1 : t1 that evaluate to v, the statement

```
f  [e1]  =  undef
```

specifies that (f v) is always undefined. Any other attempt to define f at v is an error.

24.3.2 Multiple-Valued Index Functions: =›*, ‹=›*, and *‹=›*

Multiple-valued indexed functions initially map all arguments to $\perp_{set}$, the undefined set. As incremental definitions at some argument v are executed, the mapping improves to (insert w1 $\perp_{set}$), (insert w1 (insert w2 $\perp_{set}$)), and so on. If, at the end of the transaction, (f v) is

```
( insert w1 ( ... ( insert wn ⊥set ) ) )
```

then it becomes closed with those values, that is, (f v) is

```
(insert w1 (... (insert wn EmptySet)))
```

for subsequent transactions.

For an indexed function f : t1 =>* t2 and expressions e1 : t1 and e2 : t2 that evaluate to v and w respectively, the statement

```
f [e1] += e2
```

extends the definition of f so that (f v) includes w.

Again, as we shall see later, in update transactions a new f : t1 =>* t2 automatically inherits mappings from an old version unless specified otherwise. To inhibit this, for expressions e1 : t1 and e2 : t2 that evaluate to v and w respectively, the statement

```
f [e1] -= e2
```

specifies that (f v) always excludes w. Any other attempt to include w in (f v) is an error.

For an indexed function f : t1 <=>* t2 and expressions e1 : t1 and e2 : *t2 that evaluate to v and w respectively, the statement

```
f [e1] += e2
```

extends the definition of f so that (f v) includes w, and (∧ f w) returns v. It will succeed only if (∧ f) was previously undefined at w.

For an indexed function f : t1 <=>* t2 and expressions e1 : t1 and e2 : *t2 that evaluate to v and w respectively, the statement

```
f [e1] -= e2
```

specifies that (f v) always excludes w, and (∧ f w) never returns v. Any other attempt to define f to include this mapping is an error.

For an indexed function f : t1 *<=>* t2 and expressions e1 : t1 and e2 : t2 that evaluate to v and w respectively, the statement

```
f [e1] += e2
```

extends the definition of f so that (f v) includes w, and (∧ f w) includes v.

For an indexed function f : t1 *<=>* t2 and expressions e1 : t1 and e2 : t2 that evaluate to v and w respectively, the statement

```
f [e1] -= e2
```

specifies that (f v) always excludes w and that (∧ f w) always excludes v. Any other attempt to include this mapping in f is an error.

24.4 UPDATE TRANSACTIONS

Executing an update transaction against an environment (database) produces a new environment. The transaction itself is a specification of the new environment, based on the old. In principle, this involves specifying *all* the names in the new environment, together with their new bindings. In practice, however, most update transactions express only small changes to the environment. Thus, for convenience, we would like a notation by which we need to specify only the *difference* between the new and old environments.

The entire database can be regarded as a graph. Each internal node in the graph is either a set, a tuple, an ordinary function, or an indexed function. The leaves of the graphs are objects of the primitive types and database types. The root of the graph is the database environment itself, which, for uniformity, can be regarded as an indexed function of type SYM => object. The special symbol db in the database environment evaluates to the database environment object itself.

An update transaction is a program that specifies the new graph in terms of the old. At the beginning of the transaction, every node in the graph has a new "shadow" version. Nodes corresponding to indexed functions are open and empty, that is, with no outgoing edges in the graph. If e is an expression that refers to an object in the old graph, then new e refers to its new version (thus new db refers to the new database environment itself). The update transaction contains incremental definitions for the new versions of objects. At the end of the transaction, that is, when the program has terminated, the new version of each object inherits any old contents that were not incrementally redefined, after which it becomes closed.

The new extension of a type, for example, (new (all Student)) is $\perp_{set}$ until the end of the transaction, when it becomes closed, containing all objects of that type that are present in the new version of the database.

24.4.1 Examples

An update to increase the number of units for the course 6.006 by 3 units is

```
(new CUnits) [ ( ∧ CName ''6.006'' ) ] = (CUnits c) + 3
```

The update consists of a single statement that specifies an incremental definition of the new version of the indexed function bound to CUnits. The new version differs from the old in that the course referred to by ∧ CName ''6.006'' is now mapped to a number 3 units greater than before.

An update to change the name of student John Xiao to John Zhao is

```
(new SName) [^ SName ''John Xiao''] = ''John Zhao''
```

An update to increase the units of all courses by 3 is

```
{ f c = { (new CUnits) [c] = (CUnits c) + 3 } ;
  mapdo f (all Course) }
```

The first statement defines a temporary function f that increases the units of a course by 3. The second statement applies this to all courses (mapdo is like map in that it applies f to each course, but is different in that there are no results to be returned). In our parallel model of computation, all the applications of f can be performed in parallel.

An update to remove a grade erroneously recorded for John Zhao in the course 6.001 is

```
{ s = ^ SName ''John Zhao'' ;
  e = hd { e | e <- S-Enroll s;
               (^ C-Enroll e) == (^ CName ''6.001'') } ;
  (new EGrade) [ e ] = undef } ;
```

The first two statements locate the enrollment for John Zhao in 6.001. The last statement specifies that the new EGrade function will be undefined at that enrollment.

To drop an existing name (say SNationality: Student => S) from the top-level database environment use

```
(new db) ['SNationality] = undef
```

New db refers to the new database object. The binding indexed by the name SNationality is made undefined.

To introduce a new name into the top-level database environment, or to rebind an existing name to a completely new value, one simply supplies its definition. Examples are as follows:

```
{ f s = { c | c <- ^ C-Enroll (S-Enroll s) ;
              CUnits c > 12 } ;

  (new db) ['SHeavyCourses] = f ;

  (new db) ['CDescription] = empty (Course => S) }
```

This transaction defines two new database functions. SHeavyCourses is an ordinary function on Students that returns the set of courses the student takes with greater than 12 units. CDescription is an indexed function on Course objects that returns a string description. CDescription is still undefined on every course—other parts of this update transaction, or later update transactions, can fill it in incrementally.

Here is an update that introduces a generally useful function called theEnrollmentFor. Given a student name and a course name, it returns the enrollment corresponding to that student and course:

```
{ theEnrollmentFor sn cn =
      hd { e | e <- S-Enroll (^ SName sn) ;
               (CName (^C-Enroll e))  == cn } ;

  (new db) ['theEnrollmentFor] = theEnrollmentFor }
```

Update programs can themselves be stored in the database. For example, here is an update that introduces a function record_grades that can be used in subsequent transactions. It takes a course name and a set of student names and grades, and records the grades for that course.

```
{ record_grades Cn SnGs =
      {   f (Sn,G) = { e = theEnrollmentFor Sn Cn;
                       (new EGrade) [e] = G } ;
          mapdo f SnGs } ;

  (new db) ['record_grades] = record_grades } ;
```

The first statement defines the function value itself, and the second statement records it in the new database.

Another update introducing a function that can be used in subsequent transactions: given a student name and a course name, it adds that enrollment:

```
{ add sn cn =  { s = ^ SName sn ;
                 c = ^ CName cn ;
                 e = make Enrollment () ;
                 (new S-Enroll) [s] += e;
                 (new C-Enroll) [c] += e } ;

  (new db) ['add] = add }
```

Again, the first statement defines the function value itself, and the second statement records it in the new database.

An update introducing a function that, given a student name and a course name, deletes that enrollment, is

```
{  drop sn cn =  {  s = ^ SName sn ;
                    c = ^ CName cn ;
                    e = theEnrollmentFor sn cn ;
                    (new S-Enroll) [s] -= e ;
                    (new C-Enroll) [c] -= e ;
                    (new EGrade) [e] = undef }  ;

      (new db) ['drop] = drop }
```

Note that the way to remove an object from the database is to ensure that
there is no function defined on it. The object then disappears from the
database.

24.5 DISCUSSION

24.5.1 Parallelism

The major issues in designing a database programming language with parallelism are

- ☐ how to specify what can be done in parallel.
- ☐ determinacy, that is, guaranteeing that the result of the transaction
  does not depend on the run-time schedule for the parallel parts chosen by the system.

Inspired by the dataflow approach, especially I-structures in Id, our
model addresses both issues. Decomposition into parallel parts is implicit—
programs can be compiled into dataflow graphs, which constitute a parallel
machine language (for an outline of how this is done in Id, see [Arvind &
Nikhil, 1987] and [Nikhil, 1987]). The semantics of incremental definition, in
which the information content of a function increases monotonically during
an update transaction, ensures that the transactions are determinate.

24.5.2 Historical Data

The model of update just described can be extended to deal with historical
data. In Section 24.2 we modeled the database system as a function from a
database and list of transactions to a list of responses. Each transaction was
evaluated in the current database environment to produce a new database
environment. The old database was discarded.

Instead, we could retain the old database environments, modeling the
database system as a function from a *list* of database environments and a list
of transactions to the list of responses:

```
Def dbsystem dbs (cons xact xacts) =
        { resp, db' = eval dbs xact
        In
              cons rest (dbsystem (cons db' dbs) xacts) }

dbsystem (cons empty_db nil) xacts
```

Each transaction thus has the entire history of databases available to it. To make use of this, we need additional notation to specify that an expression (part of the transaction) must be evaluated in an arbitrary previous environment.

First, we need "environment expressions" that specify an environment by indexing into dbs, the history of database environments. There are various possibilities for specifying this indexing:

☐ By absolute position, where the initial, empty database supplied to dbsystem has position 0.

☐ By relative position, with the most recent database environment having position 0.

☐ By time, assuming that dbsystem records the creation time of each database environment.

☐ By name of creator, assuming that dbsystem records the name of the creator of each database environments.

☐ By arbitrary property, that is, the most recent database environment in which a given Boolean expression evaluates true.

☐ ...

Once we can specify particular environments, the phrase:

```
with environment-expression
     expression
```

can be used to evaluate an expression within that environment. Thus, we can write queries and updates that depend on any or all previous states of the database.

24.5.3 Concurrency Between Transactions

The parallelism that we have focused on so far is all within a single transaction. Referring to the database system model of Section 24.2, the parallelism is within the phrase: (eval db xact). Within dbsystem, the result database from one transaction is used as the environment in which to evaluate the next transaction.

This is not to imply that there cannot be any parallelism *between* transactions. First, since a closed database environment is never subsequently modified, a read-only transaction (query) can continue using an old database as long as necessary, without holding up subsequent update transactions. Second, even update transactions can be overlapped: the nonstrict semantics of our language allows (eval db xact) to return a value (the response and the new database) immediately, before the transaction has completed (this behavior is also exhibited by languages with lazy evaluation). This permits dbsystem to begin evaluating the next transaction immediately.

A problem arises due to aborted transactions, which can cascade through all subsequent transactions that have already begun executing. To avoid this, one will have to employ the usual solutions: either prevent multiple transactions from overlapping (pessimistic), or allow them to overlap, keeping track of which parts of the database they actually see, so that an abort does not cascade through noninterfering transactions (optimistic).

24.5.4 Comparison With Other Approaches

The top-level definition of the database system (dbsystem) that we presented in Section 24.2 is almost identical to other "functional" views ([Henderson, 1982; Argo et al., 1987]). The differences arise in the meaning of the phrase (eval db xact)—what is a database, what is a transaction, and what is the eval function?

One approach can be regarded as a "transaction-as-command" approach. For instance, the database is a bank balance—just a number. Transactions are commands of the form deposit x and withdraw x. The eval function interprets a transaction by examining whether it is a deposit or withdraw command, and constructs the response and new database appropriately:

```
Def eval db xact =
        {   command, x = xact ;
          In
            if command = 'withdraw then
              (''Here is'', x), (db − x)
            else if command = 'deposit then
              (''Deposited'', x), (db + x)
            else error  } ;
```

The problem with this approach is that even though the database system is modeled as functional program, the transaction language (deposit and withdraw commands) is a purely imperative language. Though we have not seen any more complicated examples in the literature, the natural generalization of such a language would be a conventional imperative language, with all the attendant sequentiality and difficult semantics.

The other approach may be suggested as a "transaction-as-function" approach. The database is a data structure, and a transaction is directly a function from a database to a response and new database. Thus, the eval function simply applies the transaction to database.

```
Def eval db xact = (xact db) ;
```

The user has the full generality of a functional language in which to specify queries and updates. Being functional, of course, there is plenty of parallelism available.

While this approach is very elegant if the database is a tree-like data structure, it becomes very awkward when the database is a general graph (with shared substructures). Consider a database that is a list of ten Course objects, five of which contain the same Classroom object, which in turn contains a number, its seating capacity. Now suppose the seating capacity is to be changed. The update transaction must of course rebuild the Classroom object with the new number. But unfortunately, we must also rebuild five Course objects to contain the new Classroom object, and then we must rebuild the top-level list to contain the five new Classroom objects in place of the old. In general, the transaction programmer must explicitly identify and rebuild *every path* from the root of the database down to the "updated" object.

In contrast, our approach can be viewed as an attempt to retain the expressive power, parallelism, and declarative nature of the transaction-as-function approach, while achieving the economy of expression of a more imperative approach.

24.6 FUTURE DIRECTIONS

The work described here is a preliminary attempt to design a declarative update language within the framework of a functional database system. There are many details to be completed, many issues still to be investigated. As a vehicle for this research, we are constructing a prototype of the system. This is initially implemented in Lisp to take advantage of Lisp's rich programming environment; later we expect to incorporate it into Id and to run it on our dataflow multiprocessor (emulated for now, a real one later). Until we have more experience with writing applications in our prototype, we cannot make an informed judgment as to whether it is easy or difficult to express updates in this model.

Despite the title of this paper, what we have presented is by no means a formal semantics, and until that event, we cannot possibly be precise in our claims about parallelism, determinacy, and so on. Once the language has reached a reasonably stable point, we expect to extend the formal semantics of Id, expressed as rewrite rules [Peyton Jones, 1987] to cover this database model.

There is a disturbing lack of type orthogonality in the indexed types—currently, the domain and range of an index type can only be database or primitive types. We are taking this position now for pragmatic reasons—it is not clear what it means to index on tuples, sets, nested structures, and so on.

In our model, an object is deleted automatically from the database when it no longer participates in any mappings (no query can be asked of it). The reason for this choice, rather than a command to delete an object directly, was that it is not clear what happens to the mappings in which the object participates. However, removing it from all mappings can be quite tedious to specify. This issue requires more investigation. A more difficult question: when can a *type* be deleted from the database, that is, what happens to existing objects of that type, mappings on those objects, et cetera?

The transaction language, like Id with I-structures, is not a purely functional language, though it does retain the parallelism and determinacy (and, we claim, declarative nature) of functional languages. The loss of referential transparency is not without cost: it can inhibit certain optimizations that are possible in functional languages. In Id, we have developed a programming methodology whereby we use I-structures only to define new, efficient functional array abstractions, after which the bulk of the program is written functionally [Arvind & Ekanadham, 1987]. Can such a methodology be extended to deal with our database extensions?

In a related project, we are looking at architectural and low-level programming issues, in implementing arbitrary object persistence in the tagged-token dataflow architecture, assuming explicit commands to store and retrieve objects. The gap between that implementation and the database model presented here is yet to be bridged.

References

Albano, A., Cardelli, L., and Orsini, R., (1983). "Galileo: A strongly typed interactive conceptual language," Bell Laboratories, Technical Report 83-11271-2.

Argo, G., Fairbairn, J., Hughes, J., Launchburh, J., and Trinder, P., (1987). "Implementing functional databases," *Proceedings of ALTAIR-CRAI Workshop on Database Programming Lanuages*, Roscoff, France.

Arvind, and Brock, J. Dean, (1984). "Resource managers in functional programming," *Journal of Parallel and Distributed Computing*, Vol. 1, No. 1, June.

Arvind, and Culler, D. E., (1985). "Managing resources in a parallel machine," *Proceedings of IFIP TC-10 Working Conference on Fifth Generation Computer Architecture*, July 15–18, Manchester, England.

Arvind, and Ekanadham, K., (1987). "Future scientific programming on parallel machines," *Proceedings of the International Conference on Supercoputing (ICS)*, June 8–12, Athens, Greece. New York: Springer-Verlag, LNCS 279.

Arvind, and Iannucci, R. A., (1987). "Two fundamental issues in multiprocessing," *Proceedings of DFVLR—1987 Conference on Parallel Processing in Science and Engineering*, June 25–29, Bonn-Bad Godesberg, W. Germany. New York: Springer-Verlag, LNCS 295.

Arvind, and Nikhil, R. S., (1987). "Executing a program on the MIT tagged-token dataflow architecture," *Proceedings of the PARLE Conference*, June 15–19, Eindhoven, The Netherlands, New York: Springer-Verlag, LNCS, Vol. 259.

Arvind, Nikhil, R. S., and Pingali, K. K., (1987). "I-structures: Data structures for parallel computing," *Proceedings of the Workshop on Graph Reduction*, September–October, Santa Fe, NM, pp. 336–369, Springer-Verlag, LNCS 279.

Atkinson, M. P., Chisholm, K. J., and Cockshott, W. P., (1981). "PS-Algol: An Algol with a persistent heap," *ACM SIGPLAN Notices*, Vol. 17, No. 7, July 24–31.

Copeland, G., and Maier, D., (1984). "Making Smalltalk a database system," *Proceedings of ACM SIGMOD*, p. 325.

Hecht, M. S., and Gabbe, J. D., (1983). "Shadowed management of free disk pages with a linked list," *ACM Transactions on Database Systems*, December pp. 503–514.

Henderson, P., (1982). "Purely functional operating systems," *Functional Programming and its Applications: An Advanced Course*, Cambridge, England: Cambridge University Press, pp. 177–192.

Nikhil, R. S., (1984). "An incremental, strongly-typed database query language," Ph.D. Thesis, Dept. of Computer and Information Science, University of Pennsylvania, August. Also technical report MS-CIS-85-02.

Nikhil, R. S., (1985). "Functional languages, functional databases," *Proceedings of the Workshop on Persistence and Data Types*, August, Appin, Scotland.

Nikhil, R. S., (1987). "Id Nouveau reference manual: Syntax and semantics," Computation Structure Group, MIT Laboratory for Computer Science, April.

Peyton Jones, S. L., (1987). *The Implementation of Functional Programming Languages*, Englewood Cliffs, N. J.: Prentice-Hall.

Turner, D. A., (1981). "The semantic elegance of applicative languages," *Proceedings of the ACM Conference on Functional Programming Languages and Computer Architecture*, October, Portsmouth, NH, pp. 85–92.

CHAPTER **25**

Toward a Formalism for Module Interconnection and Version Selection

Richard Hull
Dean Jacobs

25.1 INTRODUCTION

The use of modularization and information hiding is widely accepted as being central to managing the complexity of large software systems. The past decade has witnessed the development of several programming languages which provide features for modularization and separate compilation, for example, Ada [United States Department of Defense, 1983] and Modula2 [Wirth, 1982]. However, the capabilities of these languages are not sufficient to support the evolution of large and complex systems where many versions exist. Research has lead to the development of a variety of tools which support version control, software reuse, and system evolution, for example, Tichy [1985], Notkin [1985], Estublier [1985], Prieto-Diaz and Neighbors [1986], Bernard et al., [1987], Narayanaswamy and Scacchi [1987], Leblang and Chase [1987], and Winkler [1987].

This report introduces a simple yet formal model of module interconnection and version selection which incorporates and extends many current ideas in the area. The model provides a conceptual basis for the construction of modules from submodules, and for the selection of versions. Our current focus is to present an abstract model suitable for theoretical investigation. Ultimately the model is intended to provide a basis for program development tools, although the concepts may then be formulated in a different manner. In this report we do not address the important issue of "manufacturing" or "deriving" software objects, in the sense of MAKE [Feldman, 1979] and the models presented in Borison [1986] and Polak [1986]. We believe that our model can be integrated with one such as Borison [1986] to provide a comprehensive framework for configuration management.

The primary innovation of this report is a new formalism for specifying the structure of a system called a *module interconnection grammar* (MIG). A MIG is essentially a context-free grammar where the symbols are the names of module families, and the productions represent ways of constructing modules from submodules. A MIG tree, corresponding to a derivation tree, represents one possible way of constructing a system. A system instance consists of a set of module instances, one for each leaf in the tree. Internal nodes represent structural information, including the grouping of submodules and the flow of resources between them. (The use of internal nodes solely for structural information resembles the approach taken in Katz [1987] for VLSI design databases.) Different instances of a module family are distinguished by attributes that describe their characteristics. These attributes are used to specify system instances with desired characteristics.

In this report, we focus on the basic use of MIGs to describe how a system is constructed and how resources flow between modules. We show that much of the structural information contained in a MIG tree is unnecessary for execution and can be eliminated when the system is constructed. This leads to a notion of equivalence between MIG trees and a notion of equivalence between MIGs. In turn, this allows us to introduce equivalence-preserving transformations on MIGs which can be used during the evolution of a system to change the way it is viewed or to prepare it for subsequent transformations that do not preserve equivalence.

This report presents a preliminary stage of our research in this area. Two basic themes are pursued. First, we give a formal but somewhat simplified definition of the fundamental structures in our approach and study the properties of those structures. Second, we informally describe various generalizations that will be investigated in future work. In particular, we indicate how constraints on attributes may be imposed in order to specify which instances are appropriate in particular circumstances.

This report is organized as follows. In Section 25.2 we present an overview of the model and give an informal introduction to module interconnection grammars. In Section 25.3 we give a formal definition of the three primary structures in our scheme: system signatures, system specifications using module interconnection grammars, and system libraries. In Section 25.4 we show how MIG trees can be reduced to a minimal form that concisely describes the flow of resources between module instances. In Section 25.5 we introduce the notion of equivalence between MIGs and equivalence-preserving transformations on MIGs. Finally, in Section 25.6 we briefly discuss attributes and constraints.

25.2 OVERVIEW OF THE MODEL

It is generally accepted that large software systems should be decomposed into modules that share resources, such as procedures, functions, types, and variables, among themselves. While a variety of different module interconnection schemes have been proposed, no consensus among them has emerged. We adopt a scheme, based primarily on the module interconnection language Nu-MIL [Narayanaswamy and Scacchi, 1987], which is particularly suitable for programming in the large. There are two kinds of modules in this scheme; *atomic* modules and *compound* modules. Atomic modules are indivisible units in which resources originate and are used. Compound modules, which are composed of submodules, provide structure to the system. Every module must explicitly state which resources it imports and exports. A compound module provides a scope or namespace in which the imports and exports of its submodules can be matched.

It is instructive to compare this approach with the one taken in programming languages such as Ada. Consider the following skeleton of an Ada program unit.

```
package A is
   ...
end A;

with A ;
package P is
   ...
   package B is
      ...
   end B ;

end P ;
```

This program unit would be modeled in our approach by

```
MAIN ----> A P
P ----> P_DRIVER B
```

where → may be read "is constructed from." In this case, *MAIN* and *P* are compound modules and *A*, *P_DRIVER*, and *B* are atomic modules. The code associated with *P* in the Ada version is associated with *P_DRIVER* in our scheme. *P_DRIVER* and *B* may supply resources for each other. Similarly, *A* and *P* may supply resources for each other, although in this case resources flow only from *A* to *P*.

Our approach has several important advantages. First, *P* does not explicitly name the source (*A*) of its imports so it can be used easily in other contexts. Second, as detailed following, the names of all imported resources are explicitly stated, which facilitates intermodule consistency and compatibility checking. Third, internal Ada packages such as *B* appear inline, which interferes with separate compilation and module reuse. In general, this discourages nesting in the structure of a system. In contrast, our approach naturally supports the nesting of a module inside several different compound modules.

The manner in which compound modules are composed from submodules is specified using a *module interconnection grammar* (MIG). A MIG is essentially a context-free grammar where the symbols are the names of module families and the productions represent ways of constructing modules from submodules. The above example describes a MIG with two productions. In general, there may be many ways of constructing a module, for example,

```
MAIN ----> A P
MAIN ----> A Q
P ----> P_DRIVER B
Q ----> Q_DRIVER C
```

provides two ways of constructing *MAIN*.

A MIG is always interpreted with respect to a signature that describes the modules appearing in the system. In particular, a signature names the imports and exports of each module. For convenience, we often write the imports and exports of a module directly above and below its occurrence in a production. For example,

```
doit            foo          doit
MAIN ----->      A            P
helper          helper       foo


doit            doit          hoo
  P ----->     P_DRIVER        B
foo             hoo           foo
```

states that *MAIN* exports a resource *doit*, which originates in *P_DRIVER*, and imports a resource *helper*, which is used in *A*. There are various consistency conditions on productions which ensure that resources are introduced appropriately. For example, the production *MAIN → AP* is consistent because the export of *MAIN* and the imports of *A* and *P* are uniquely provided. It is possible to specify that resources be renamed within a scope, for example,

MAIN → *A[foo/goo]P* specifies that the resource *foo* in *A* is to be called *goo* within the scope.

A MIG tree, loosely analogous to a derivation tree, represents one possible way of constructing a system. For example, the following MIG tree represents one possible way of constructing *MAIN*.

```
        MAIN

A                    P


        P_DRIVER     B
```

A *system instance* consists of a set of module instances, one for each leaf in the tree. The structural information in the tree is necessary only to determine the manner in which resources flow between the module instances. A MIG tree can be reduced into a *resource flow graph* which directly specifies the flow of resources between the leaf nodes. For example, the preceding tree corresponds to the following resource flow graph.

```
          MAIN

helper                    doit

                    hoo
A          P_DRIVER                B
           foo
```

Two MIG trees are said to be equivalent if they reduce to the same resource flow graph. Two MIGs are said to be equivalent if they lead to equivalent MIG trees. This allows us to introduce the notion of equivalence-preserving transformations on MIGs which may be used during the evolution of a system.

The incorporation of attributes and constraints in this framework is discussed in Section 25.6

25.3 SYSTEM SIGNATURES, SPECIFICATIONS, AND LIBRARIES

In this section we give a formal definition of the three main structures in our scheme: system signatures, system specifications using module interconnection grammars, and system libraries. The formal definitions given here focus on the most basic components of our proposed framework. Several generalizations of the basic definitions are presented more informally in remarks.

DEFINITION 25.1.   A *(system) signature* is a four-tuple $S = <M, R, i, e>$ where

- ☐ M is a set of abstract names called *module names*, partitioned into two sets *atom(M)*, the *atomic* module names, and *comp(M)*, the *compound* module names.
- ☐ R is a set of abstract names called *resource names*.
- ☐ i and e are functions from M to the powerset of R, which satisfies the following condition.
- ☐ *Module consistency:* For all $m \in M, i(m) \cap e(m) = \{\}$.

M is the set of module names and R is the set of resource names permitted in the given system. The functions i and e specify the imports and exports respectively of each module. The module consistency condition states that no resource can be both imported and exported by the same module. Note that several modules may export the same resource—as a result, a given resource may be provided by a different module in different configurations.

DEFINITION 25.2.   A *module interconnection grammar* (MIG) is a triple $G = <S, P, C>$ where

- ☐ $S = <M, R, i, e>$ is a signature.
- ☐ P is a set of *productions* (or rules) of the form $p = A \rightarrow B_1 \ldots B_n$ where $n \geq 1$ and $A \in comp(M)$ and $B_1, \ldots, B_n \in M$.
- ☐ $C \in M$ is called the *root module*, which satisfies the following consistency conditions:
- ☐ *Non-recursiveness:* There is no sequence of rules $p_1, \ldots, p_n$ $(n \geq 1)$ where for each j, $1 \leq j \leq n$, the head of p_{j+1} occurs in the tail of p_j, and the head of p_1 occurs in the tail of p_n.
- ☐ *Resource completeness:* For each rule $A \rightarrow B_1 \ldots B_n \in P$, $\cup_{k=1}^{n} i(B_k) \cup e(A) \subseteq \cup_{k=1}^{n} e(B_k) \cup i(A)$.
- ☐ *Resource uniqueness:* For each rule $A \rightarrow B_1 \ldots B_n \in P$, the sets $i(A), e(B_1), \ldots, e(B_n)$ are pairwise disjoint.

The first condition rules out the possibility of a module appearing within itself. The second condition guarantees that each resource required in a scope is provided. (This resembles conditions on resources specified in Tichy [1985]. The third condition guarantees that every resource is uniquely provided, that is, that name conflicts do not occur. Note that atomic module names are analogous to terminal symbols and compound module names are analogous to nonterminal symbols.

A number of generalizations of this definition are possible. For example, the distinction between atomic and compound module names could be dropped. Two other generalizations are presented in the remarks that follow.

Remark 25.1

Modules developed independently may not be consistent in their naming of shared resources and some mechanism for renaming resources within a scope must be provided. We define a *name change function* on a set of resource names R to be a mapping from R to R. A name change function will generally be the identity on most of its domain except for some distinct names $x_1, \ldots, x_k$ which are mapped to (not necessarily distinct) names $y_1, \ldots, y_k$. We denote such a function by $[x_1/y_1, \ldots, x_k/y_k]$. It may be that $y_i = y_j$ above if, for example, the same resource is used for two different imports of a submodule. A name change function η is said to be *applicable* to a module $m \in M$ if the module consistency condition is not violated, that is, if $\eta(i(m)) \cap \eta(e(m)) = \{\}$. (Here we extend the domain of η from elements of R to subsets of R in the usual way). A (generalized) production can now be defined to be $A \rightarrow B_1[\eta_1] \ldots B_n[\eta_n]$ where η_i is applicable to B_i and the resource completeness and uniqueness conditions are not violated.

Remark 25.2

Another possible generalization is to allow different instances of a module to import and export different sets of resources. This may occur, for example, if the capabilities of a module are expanded as it evolves. To formalize this, we must arrange it so that functions e and i are associated with module *occurrences* in productions rather than being fixed over the entire system by the signature. Thus, a production would be defined as a triple $p = <A \rightarrow B_1 \ldots B_n, i_p, e_p>$ which satisfies resource completeness and uniqueness.

We now return to the formal development of the basic model. The structure of a particular version of a system is represented by a "MIG tree," which is closely related to a derivation tree of a context-free grammar.

DEFINITION 25.3. Let $G = <S, P, C>$ be a MIG over the signature $S = <M, R, i, e>$. A *MIG tree* of G is a labeled tree $T = <V, E, \lambda>$ where

☐ $<V, E>$ is a tree (i.e., a directed, rooted, strongly acyclic graph with vertices V and edges E contained in $V \times V$) and

☐ λ is a function from V to M, that is, a node labeling that satisfies

☐ for root w, $\lambda(w) = C$.

☐ if v is an internal node with children $v_1, \ldots, v_n$, then $\lambda(v) \rightarrow \lambda(v_1) \ldots \lambda(v_n) \in P$.

☐ if v is a leaf node, then $\lambda(v) \in atom(M)$.

Each node of a MIG tree corresponds to a module, and a node's children correspond to submodules of that module. The same module name may occur more than once in a system—λ need not be 1–1—and there may be distinct (nonisomorphic) subtrees below each occurrence.

Our next major step is to define "instances" of a MIG tree, that is, actual pieces of code structured according to the tree. To do this, we need the notion of a library of module instances.

DEFINITION 25.4.   A *library* is a four-tuple $L = <N,R,i,e>$ where

- $\square$ N is a set of abstract names called *module instance names*.
- $\square$ R is a set of resource names.
- $\square$ i and e are functions from N to the powerset of R, which satisfies the following condition:
- $\square$ *Module consistency:* For all $n \in N, i(n) \cap e(n) = \{\}$.

The module instance names should be viewed as unique identifiers for module instances. In this definition of a library, the only information about an instance which is maintained is its imports and exports. Considerably more information should be maintained, for example, the actual code associated with the instance, the name of the module the instance is intended to implement, and various attribute values as discussed in Section 25.6.

The connection between libraries and system specifications is given in the following two definitions. (The first resembles notions in Tichy [1985] and Narayanaswamy and Scacchi, [1987].)

DEFINITION 25.5.   Let $S = <M,R,i_s,e_s>$ be a signature and $L = <N,R,i_L,e_L>$ be a library. Then $n \in N$ *implements* (or is an implementation of) $m \in atom(M)$ if

- $\square$ $i_L(n) \subseteq i_s(m)$
- $\square$ $e_L(n) \supseteq e_S(m)$.

We now define a system instance.

DEFINITION 25.6.   Let $S = <M,R,i_S,e_S>$ be a signature,

- $\square$ $G = <S,P,C>$ be a MIG,
- $\square$ $T = <V,E,\lambda>$ be a MIG tree of G, and
- $\square$ $L = <N,R,i_L,e_L>$ be a library.

A *system instance* of T from L is a mapping I from the leaves of T to N such that for each leaf w of T, $I(w)$ is an implementation of $\lambda(w)$.

Intuitively, T implicitly describes the manner in which resources are interchanged among the instances given by I. The definition of implementation together with the consistency conditions on MIGs ensure that each resource needed by a module in I is uniquely provided. The definition of *implements* can be generalized to incorporate constraints based on attribute values. In that case, more of the integrity of the system given by I can be ensured. Additional possible constraints include typing information and pre/post conditions. If the members of a module family have little in common, then such constraints cannot be imposed. In this case, integrity checking must be performed after particular module instances have been selected.

25.4 REDUCING MIG TREES

Suppose that T is a MIG tree, and I is an instance of it. Intuitively, T describes the manner in which resources are interchanged among module instances given by I. In this section we introduce an abstraction called "resource flow graphs" for representing this linkage information directly, and describe how a MIG tree T can be "reduced" to a resource flow graph $red(T)$. Intuitively, T and $red(T)$ specify the same flow of resources—I can also be interpreted as an instance of $red(T)$—and differ only in the structural information they provide. This formalizes the notion that the compiled version of a large software system may contain less structural information than the representation maintained by the programming environment.

DEFINITION 25.7. Let $S = <M, R, i, e>$ be a signature. A *resource flow graph* (RFG) for S is a directed graph $H = <W, F, \mu, \rho>$ where

☐ $< W, F >$ is a directed graph (duplicate edges are permitted).
☐ μ is a mapping from W to M, that is, a node labeling,
☐ ρ is a mapping from F to R, that is, an edge labeling, which satisfies the following conditions:
☐ For all edges f from x to y, $\rho(f) \in e((x))$ and $\rho(f) \in i((y))$.
☐ For all edges f and g to y, $\rho(f) \neq \rho(g)$.

Intuitively, if x is a node of H, then x represents a module instance with name (x). If f is an edge from x to y, then f represents the fact that the module at x exports a resource named $\rho(f)$ to the module at y. The first preceding condition guarantees that (x) actually exports this resource and (y) actually imports it. The second condition guarantees that each resource is uniquely provided.

Note that if resource name changes are to be incorporated, then two edge label functions ϵ and ι are needed in place of ρ. In this context, if f goes from x to y, this means that x exports a resource with name $\epsilon(f)$, and that y imports that resource under the name $\iota(f)$.

We now give a nonconstructive definition of $red(T)$. An efficient algorithm for computing $red(T)$ will be presented in subsequent reports.

DEFINITION 25.8.   Let $S = <M, R, ie>$ be a signature, $G = <S, P, C>$ be a MIG, and $T = <V, E, \lambda>$ be a MIG tree of G. The *reduction* of T is the RFG $red(T) = <W, F, \mu, \rho>$ which satisfies the following conditions.

1. W is the set of leaves of T together with the node *root* where $\lambda(root) = C$.
2. μ is the restriction of λ to W.
3. An edge f from leaf x to leaf y is included in F with $\rho(f) = r$ "iff" there is
   a. A sequence of at least two nodes $x = z_1, \ldots, z_k$ in T such that for $1 < j \le k <z_j, z_{j+1}> \in E$ and $r \in e(\lambda(z_{j-1}))$.
   b. A sequence of at least two nodes $z_k, \ldots, z_n = y$ in T such that for $k \le j < n <z_j, z_{j+1}> \in E$ and $r \in i(\lambda(z_{j+1}))$.
4. An edge f from leaf x to *root* is included in F with $\rho(f) = r$ iff for all nodes z on the path from x up to *root* in T, $r \in e(\lambda(z))$.
5. An edge f from *root* to leaf y is included in F with $\rho(f) = r$ iff for all nodes z on the path from *root* down to y in T, $r \in i(\lambda(z))$.

Condition 3 states that a resource r flows from leaf x to leaf y if there is a path up the tree from x on which r is exported and a path back down to y on which r is imported. The node *root* is included to represent the imports and exports of the system as a whole, as described by conditions 5 and 4 respectively. The following is easily verified.

PROPOSITION 25.1.   For a MIG tree T, the graph $red(T)$ defined as before is an RFG.

Note that $red(T)$ cannot be constructed by matching imports and exports of the leaves of T directly, since the same resource name may be used several times in different contexts. Moreover, if resource name changes are incorporated, then renaming might occur at each edge of a witness path $z_1, \ldots, z_n$.

To simplify compilation in the programming language Ada, cycles are not permitted in the import/export relationships between modules. This motivates us to study those MIG trees T for which $red(T)$ is acyclic. We now give a sufficient condition for acyclicity.

DEFINITION 25.9.   A production $A \rightarrow B_1 \ldots B_n$ is *acyclic* if the import/export relationships between $B_1 \ldots B_n$ are acyclic.

PROPOSITION 25.2.   If all productions used in constructing T are acyclic then $red(T)$ is acyclic.

Proof Essence: If $red(T)$ is cyclic then the production used at the least common ancestor in T of all modules participating in the cycle must be cyclic.

The converse of this proposition is not true: it is possible to construct a T using a cyclic production for which $red(T)$ is acyclic, as the following example shows.

```
r , t                    q , r              p , t
MAIN        -->            A                  B
                          p                  q


q , r                     r                  q
  A         -->           W                  X
  p                       p


p , t                     p                  t
  B         -->           Y                  Z
  q                       q

                                                MAIN

             W              X              Y              Z
```

This system exhibits very poor structure; it is hard to imagine a circumstance where the atomic modules should be grouped in this way. In fact, a criterion of good design might be that if $red(T)$ is acyclic then all productions used in constructing T should be acyclic.

25.5 EQUIVALENCE OF MIG TREES AND MIGS

A fundamental research issue concerns the development of a general theory of system evolution. In this section we indicate one direction that can be pursued in this area. In particular, we introduce a notion of equivalence between MIG trees, based on the RFGs associated with them, and then extend this notion to equivalence between MIGs. This allows us to define several local structural transformations on MIGS which preserve equivalence. We expect that, in the context where resource renaming is permitted, a natural extension of these transformations can be defined which is complete in the sense that it allows a MIG to be transformed into any equivalent MIG.

We begin with the definition of equivalence between MIG trees.

DEFINITION 25.10. Let T_1 and T_2 be MIG trees over possibly different signatures and MIGs. T_1 and T_2 are *equivalent*, denoted $T_1 \equiv T_2$, if $red(T_1)$ and $red(T_2)$ are isomorphic by an isomorphism that respects the node and edge labelings.

In this definition, the focus is on MIG trees T_1 and T_2 more or less independent of their underlying signatures and MIGs. This seems appropriate in the context of system evolution where both the internal structure and the functionality of a system may be modified. Equivalence as defined here focuses on the case where internal structure is modified but functionality is preserved.

We now introduce notions of dominance and equivalence between MIGs. Let $trees(G)$ denote the set of all MIG trees of G.

DEFINITION 25.11. Let G_1 and G_2 be MIGs, potentially over different signatures. G_2 *dominates* G_1, denoted $G_1 \le G_2$, if for every MIG tree $T_1 \in trees(G_1)$ there is a MIG tree $T_2 \in trees(G_2)$ such that $T_1 \equiv T_2$. G_1 and G_2 are *equivalent*, denoted $G_1 \equiv G_2$, if $G_1 \le G_2$ and $G_2 \le G_1$.

Intuitively, if G_2 dominates G_1 then G_2 allows more ways of constructing the given system. During system evolution, extension of a grammar to a dominant grammar is guaranteed to maintain upward compatibility. As in equivalence between MIG trees, equivalence between MIGs focuses on the case where internal structure is modified but functionality is preserved.

We now describe several structural transformations that convert a MIG G into an equivalent MIG $\hat{G}$. It is not our intention to provide the most convenient set of transformations, rather, we provide a minimal set that is in some sense complete. We start with a basic transformation that allows the order of nonterminals within a production to be permuted. This transformation is of use primarily in conjunction with other transformations defined subsequently.

DEFINITION 25.12. Let G be a MIG and let $\hat{G}$ be a MIG that is identical to G except that the order of nonterminals within some production p has been permuted. Then $\hat{G}$ is the result of *reordering* G at p.

It is intuitively clear that reordering preserves equivalence.

We now introduce a transformation that allows a collection of modules to be encapsulated together into a single module.

DEFINITION 25.13. Let $S = <M, R, i, e>$ be a signature, $G = <S, P, C>$ be a MIG, and $p \in P$ have the form $A \to B_1 \ldots B_j B_{j+1} \ldots B_n$. Let $\hat{G} = <\hat{S}, \hat{P}, \hat{C}>$ be the MIG that is identical to G except that

1. A new module name X has been added to $\hat{S}$.
2. The production p in $\hat{P}$ has been replaced by $A \to B_1 \ldots B_j X$.
3. The production $X \to B_{j+1} \ldots B_n$ has been added to $\hat{P}$.
4. $\hat{i}(X) = \cup_{k=j+1}^{n} i(B_k) - \cup_{k=j+1}^{n} e(B_k)$; and $\hat{e}(M) = \cup_{k=j+1}^{n} e(B_k)$.

Then $\hat{G}$ is the result of *nesting* $B_{j+1}, \ldots, B_n$ at p.

PROPOSITION 25.3. Nesting preserves equivalence.

Proof sketch: Show $G \leq \hat{G}$ and $\hat{G} \leq G$. In both cases, show by construction that for any MIG tree generated by the dominated grammar, there is an equivalent MIG tree generated by the dominating grammar.

Note that an arbitrary collection of modules can be nested by first applying reordering.

We now define "unnesting," the inverse of nesting. A general definition of unnesting is possible only if renaming is permitted, since the exposure of hidden names may result in name conflicts. The following restricted definition, in which unnesting is permitted only if there are no name conflicts, indicates the general approach.

DEFINITION 25.14. Let $G = \langle S, P, C \rangle$ be a MIG, $p \in P$ have the form $A \to B_1 \ldots B_j \ldots B_n$, and $q_1, \ldots, q_k$ be the set of all rules in P with head B_j. Furthermore, suppose for each module M in the tail of any rule q_i and each module B_l, $l \neq j$, $e(M) \cap e(B_l) = \{\}$. Let $\hat{G} = \langle \hat{S}, \hat{P}, \hat{C} \rangle$ be the MIG that is identical to G except that the production p in $\hat{P}$ has been replaced by the k productions $A \to B_1 \ldots B_{j-1} tail_i B_{j+1} \ldots B_n$, where $tail_i$ is the tail of rule q_i. Then $\hat{G}$ is the result of *unnesting B_j at p.*

PROPOSITION 25.4.   Unnesting preserves equivalence.

Proof sketch: Similar to the proof for nesting.

The extra preceding condition that exports of modules M and B_l be disjoint is needed to ensure that $\hat{G}$ is in fact a MIG. In particular, if unnesting is applied when this condition does not hold then the resource uniqueness condition for MIGs will be violated. This restriction on the circumstances under which unnesting can be applied can be removed if renaming is permitted.

A variety of other useful equivalence-preserving transformations on MIGs can be defined, for example, addition and removal of "unreachable" productions and replacement of a module by an equivalent module. In subsequent work we will provide a set of transformations which is complete in the sense that it allows a MIG to be transformed into any equivalent MIG. If we restrict our attention to equivalence-preserving transformations on MIG trees, we can show that reordering, nesting, unnesting, and name-changing are complete. A generalization of this work may be useful for providing an analogous result for MIGs.

The preceding discussion provides only a brief introduction to the many possible research directions in this area. Of particular interest is the development of a complete and practically useful set of transformations for system evolution. Such transformations might include the capabilities of creating new modules, converting atomic modules to compound modules, adding new imported and exported resources to a module, and changing the source of a resource from one module to another.

25.6 ATTRIBUTES, EQUATIONS, AND CONSTRAINTS

In this section we briefly discuss adding attributes, equations, and constraints to our scheme. In this more general context, instances of a module family are distinguished by attributes that describe their characteristics. Attributes can be associated with modules and/or particular resources in modules. Attribute values may be given by the programmer, derived from the code, or computed using attribute equations. Equations can be associated with productions and, in some cases, with the resource attributes of atomic modules. If I is a system instance, the atomic attribute values and the equations together imply attribute values for the compound modules of I, and ultimately the root of I. It is possible to impose constraints on attribute values that limit which instances are appropriate in a particular circumstance. The process of constructing a system instance entails selecting module instances that satisfy these constraints.

We now present three examples which illustrate our general approach, and indicate the kinds of research problems we hope to address. For this discussion we focus on a simple MIG containing the one production

```
     join
    format                    sort       join         format
 QUERY_PROC   --->          SORTER      JOINER       FORMATTER
                                         sort
                                        format
```

which we abbreviate as $QP \rightarrow SJF$. This corresponds to a simple relational database query processor. We suppose further that we have a library containing module instances S_1 and S_2 which implement S; J_1, J_2, and J_3 which implement J; and F_1 and F_2 which implement F.

For the first example, let us suppose that there is an attribute tm which records the set of target machines on which instances can run. We assume that the library holds this information for its atomic module instances. For example, we suppose:

$S_1.tm = \{VAX, PDP, SUN\}$
$S_2.tm = \{VAX, IBM\}$

$J_1.tm = \{VAX\}$
$J_2.tm = \{PDP, SUN\}$
$J_3.tm = \{IBM\}$

$F_1.tm = F_2.tm = \{VAX, PDP, SUN, IBM\}.$

Suppose now that I_1 is the system instance where $I_1(S) = S_1$, $I_1(J) = J_2$, and $I_1(F) = F_2$. For this discussion we abbreviate this by saying that $I_1 =$

$< S_1, J_2, F_2 >$. Intuitively, to determine which machines I_1 runs on we intersect the three sets associated with the atomic module instances that form I_1, that is,

$$I_1(QP.tm) = S_1.tm \cap J_2.tm \cap F_2.tm$$

In general, we capture the preceding intuition by associating the *equation*

$$QP.tm = S.tm \cap J.tm \cap F.tm$$

with the production $QP \rightarrow SJF$. In the library here, each instance of F runs on all of the relevant machines. If it is known that this will always be true, then the preceding equation can be replaced with the simpler equation $QP.tm = S.tm \cap J.tm$.

Consider the instance $I_2 = < S_1, J_3, F_1 >$. If we apply the first preceding equation we find that $I_2(QP.tm) = \{\}$. Intuitively, I_2 is not valid. This is formalized by requiring that all system instances satisfy the *constraint* $QP.tm \neq \{\}$. It is clear that a bottom-up computation can be used to determine whether a given system instance satisfies this constraint.

In the present situation, it is also possible to use a top-down computation to infer constraints on submodules from constraints on the root module. To illustrate, suppose that we are interested in finding all system instances I that run on a VAX. This is expressed using the constraint $QP.tm \supseteq \{VAX\}$. From the equation we see that a system instance will satisfy this if and only if the following three constraints are satisfied:

$$S.tm \supseteq \{VAX\}$$
$$J.tm \supseteq \{VAX\}$$
$$F.tm \supseteq \{VAX\}$$

Using this characterization, we easily see that the set of system instances that run on the VAX contains precisely $< S_1, J_1, F_1 >$, $< S_1, J_{1,F2} >$, $< S_2, J_1, F_1 >$, and $< S_2, J_1, F_2 >$. We note that this top-down approach to finding system instances is closely related to that of Winkler [1987], although in the present context it is more restricted. It also suggests that in a practical implementation of a system library, efficient access to module instances via attribute values should be provided.

In the case of the attribute *tm*, satisfaction of the constraint $QP.tm \supseteq \{VAX\}$ is accomplished by the submodules in an essentially independent manner. In our next example, we present an equation that forces the attribute values to interact. Specifically, suppose that an attribute *mmu* for *main_memory_usage* is defined for the three atomic modules, and suppose that the equation

$$QP.mmu = J.mmu + max(S.mmu, F.mmu)$$

is associated with the production. The constraint $QP.mmu \leq 100K$ now restricts attention to system instances I such that $I(J.mmu + max(I(S.mmu), I(F.mmu)) \leq 100K$. One way to find such instances is to use a backtracking algorithm. A fundamental direction for our research is to explore other approaches to finding these instances.

Our third example concerns attributes associated with resources. The discussion here is admittedly informal and simplistic, but illustrates some of the fundamental issues and questions. We suppose that the attribute *speed* is associated to each of the resources sort, format, and join. In the interest of simplicity, we assume that the possible values of speed are functions from N (the natural numbers) to N which map the size of an input to the worst-case running time of the resource on inputs of that size. Suppose further that for module instances $S_1, S_2, F_1,$ and F_2 we have

$$S_1.sort^e.speed = 5nlogn$$
$$S_2.sort^e.speed = 2n^2$$

$$F_1.format^e.speed = 30n$$
$$F_2.format^e.speed = 50n$$

In the above we have included superscripts "e" as a reminder that the resources here are exported; superscripts "i" have analogous meaning.

We now consider how the speed of the join resource can be specified. In general, this will depend on the speed with which the sort and format resources are provided. To capture this, we associate equations with the module instances for J:

$$J_1.join^e.speed = 2(J_1.sort^i.speed) + J_1.format^i.speed + 4n^2$$
$$J_2.join^e.speed = 3(J_2.sort^i.speed) + J_2.format^i.speed + 2n^2$$

We also assume that the equation $QP.join^e.speed = J.join^e.speed$ is associated with the production. Under the preceding assumptions, the instance $I_3 = \langle S_1, J_2, F_2 \rangle$ satisfies:

$$
\begin{aligned}
I_3(QP.join^e.speed)mark &= J_2.join^e.speed \\
&= 3J_2.sort^i.speed + J_2.format^i.speed + 2n^2 \\
&= 3S_1.sort^e.speed + F_2.format^e.speed + 2n^2 \\
&= 3*5n \log n + 50n + 2n^2 \\
&= 2n^2 + 15n \log n + 50n.
\end{aligned}
$$

Thus, I_3 satisfies the constraint $QP.join^e.speed \leq 3n^2$. As with the constraint concerning main-memory usage, other system instances satisfying this constraint can be obtained using a backtracking approach.

The preceding discussion provides a bottom-up mechanism for checking whether constraints are satisfied. In some cases, a top-down approach can be used to infer constraints at the leaves which are implied by constraints at the root. Algorithms based on dynamic programming can also be used. In general, the problem of efficiently inferring constraints and selecting system instances which satisfy them is open for research.

REFERENCES

Bernard, Y., Lacroix, M., Lavency, P., and Vanhoedenaghe, M., (1987). "Configuration management in an open environment," *Proc. 1st European Software Engineering Conf.*, Strasbourg, France, September, pp. 37–45.

Borison, E., (1986). "A model of software manufacture," In *Proc. of the Intl. Workshop on Advanced Programming Environments*, IFIP WG 2.4, Trondheim, Norway, June, pp. 197–220.

Estublier, J., (1985). "A configuration manager: the Adele database of programs," *Workshop of Software Engineering Env. for Prog. in the Large*, Cape Cod, June, pp. 140–147.

Feldman, S. I., (1979). "MAKE—A program for maintaining computer programs," *Software—Practice and Experience*, Vol. 9, pp. 255–265.

Katz, R., (1987). "Managing change in a computer-aided design database," *Proc. Intl. Conf. on Very Large Data Bases*, Brighton, England, September, pp. 455–462.

Leblang, D. B., and Chase, R. P. Jr., (1987). "Parallel software configuration management in a network computing environment," *IEEE Software*, to appear.

Narayanaswamy, K., and Scacchi, W., (1987). "A database foundation to support software system evolution," *Journal of Systems and Software*, Vol. 7, pp. 37–49.

Notkin, D., (1985). "The GANDALF project," *Journal of Systems and Software*, Vol. 5, No. 2, pp. 91–105.

Polak, W., (1986). "Framework for a knowledge-based programming environment," In *Proceedings of the International Workshop on Advanced Programming Environments*, IFIP WG 2.4, Trondheim, Norway, June, pp. 566–575.

Prieto-Diaz, R., and Neighbors, J. M., (1986). "Module interconnection languages," *Journal of Systems and Software*, Vol. 6, pp. 307–334.

Tichy, W. F., (1985). "RCS—a system for version control," *Software Practice and Experience*, Vol. 15, No. 7, pp. 637–654.

Winkler, J. F. H., (1987). "Version control in families of large programs," *Proceedings of the 9th International Conference on Software Engineering*, Monterey, March, pp. 150–161.

Wirth, N., (1982). *Programming in Modula-2.*, New York: Springer-Verlag.

United States Department of Defense, (1983). *Reference Manual for the Ada Programming Language*, ANSI/MIL-STD 1815A, Washington, D.C., January.

CHAPTER 26

Manipulating complex objects

M. Lacroix
M. Vanhoedenaghe

26.1 INTRODUCTION

Engineering applications require database systems offering facilities other than those available in current commercial systems. A key requirement is the support of complex objects, that is, data structuring facilities richer than those offered by flat data models such as the relational and entity-relationship models. The data definition component of COMS (Complex Object Management System) is based on the ADDL data model [LaCroix & Pirotte, 1981], which features classical data constructors such as set, list, n-tuple, mapping, union, and recursive combination thereof. Although it is not a flat data model, it is nevertheless similar to the relational model in that it represents the objects as values in the database.

Another major requirement of engineering applications is the availability of the data manipulation operations at the application programming interface. Tools in software engineering and CAD applications are typically written in general-purpose programming languages, and can implement quite sophisticated algorithms accessing and manipulating complex objects. The application programming interface to database systems is generally difficult due to mismatches between the operations and objects of the DBMS and those of the host programming language [LaCroix & Pirotte, 1983]. The data manipulation operations of COMS, which are described in the present paper are designed to facilitate their integration in general-purpose languages. The same manipulation operations apply on database and program space objects. The integration with host programming languages described in the present paper has deliberately been chosen to be simple: the data manipulation operations have to be made available as library functions in existing languages. The expressions and control structures do not belong to the DML presented here; they belong to the host programming languages.

This paper is organized as follows. The data structures of the model are briefly presented in Section 26.2. Section 26.3 is centered on a description of the DML independently of the technicalities of its integration in programming languages: the retrieval and construction operations, the updates, the transactions, and finally the type conversions. The sharing of components objects is specifically discussed in Section 26.4. Section 26.5 is centered on the issues of integrating the data manipulation operations with host languages; the concrete choices made for C and Prolog are shown. Section 26.6 eventually mentions some open issues, and attempts at situating our work with respect to others.

26.2 OVERVIEW OF ADDL DATA STRUCTURES

An ADDL schema consists of a set of type definitions. A type definition associates a type name to a type expression. A type expression is a type name, a basic type, or the application of a type constructor on other type expressions. A basic type is exactly like a domain in the relational model. The available type constructors are: n-tuple (aggregation), set, list, mapping (function defined in extension), and disjoint union (generalization). For a further description of these constructs, see [LaCroix & Pirotte, 1981].

There is a distinguished type name `database` for which only one object will exist: the whole database.

The following is an example ADDL schema describing the structure of a simplified hierarchic file system. This file system has a users part and a system part. In the users part, each user name is associated to a home directory, a home directory is a directory, a directory associates names to the directories and files it contains, and a file consists of an owner and a contents. The system part is a directory containing the system files and directories.

```
(1) database       : <users : user_name --> home_directory,
                        system: directory >

(2) home_directory : directory
```

```
(3) directory      : name --> (directory OR file)

(4) file           : <owner: user_name, contents: bytes>
```

1. The database is a pair containing a users component and a system component. The users component is a mapping associating objects of type user_name to objects of type home_directory. User_name is not further refined in the schema; it is a basic type, that is, a user-defined atomic type. (A basic type is atomic in that its structure is not known by the DBMS. The basic types also have to be assigned a representation in terms of numbers, byte or character strings, etc; this representation is not shown here.) The system component is a directory.

2. A home_directory is a directory; in other words, a home_directory is a special kind of directory, or home_directory is a subtype of directory.

3. A directory maps objects of type name into objects of type directory or file.

4. An object of type file is a pair consisting of an object of type user_name and an object of type bytes; these two types are not further refined, and are basic types.

As in the relational model, the objects are represented by values, that is, is no notion of entity existing independently of the values of its attributes.

The naming for the objects is essentially supported by the mappings. As a first approximation, a mapping is similar to a relation in the relational model (with the domain of the mapping corresponding to the primary key attributes, and the range corresponding the nonprimary key attributes). The essential difference is that the types of the domain and range of a mapping are not limited to basic types. In practice, it appears that the form of the domain of mappings can reasonably be restricted to basic types or n-tuples defined on basic types. A similar restriction can be found in the data model discussed in [Bancilhon & Khoshafian, 1986]; it is adopted in the current prototype implementation of COMS.

The use of mappings in the range of mappings as in the preceding schema, where a directory maps names to objects which can again be of type directory, allows for a recursive naming structure. The mapping also nicely describes in which context a name of a particular type uniquely identifies an object. In the preceding example a name only uniquely identifies an object in a directory. This is to be contrasted with the fact that a user_name always uniquely identifies a directory, since there can only be one occurrence of this mapping in the database.

Objects of a union type only belong to one of the alternative types constituting the union. In the preceding schema, an object in the range of a

directory mapping is either of type directory or file, and never of
both types.

There is also a *reference* type constructor, which is described in Section
26.4. It is used for explicitly sharing component objects.

26.3 THE DATA MANIPULATION LANGUAGE

Engineering applications generally involve the creation and manipulation of
a lot of intermediate or temporary objects. The data structuring and manipulation facilities that are used for the database objects are also available for
the intermediate objects in the program space. The only difference between
the database objects and the intermediate objects is that the database objects
are components of a usually quite large object: the whole database.

The DML operators of COMS are strongly typed. The type of an operator must match with the type of its operands. If two types have the same
name or if they have the same textual description, then they match. As a
consequence, two types having the same structure but using different names
for component types do not match. This rule is further refined for subtypes
(Section 26.3.5.1), union types (Section 26.3.5.2), and generic types (Section
26.3.1).

The DML operations are described here with a neutral notation that is
independent from the language in which they are used. The actual notations
can vary with the host programming language in which they are used (see
Section 26.5). The expressions and the assignment statements which are used
in the present section are also those of a neutral and imaginary general-
purpose algorithmic language.

26.3.1 The Retrieval and Construction Operators

The operators for retrieving components of complex objects and for constructing new objects are functions; that is, they do not have any side effect.
The arguments and results of these operators are *paths* referring to objects.
However, the reader can for the time being safely make the simplifying
assumption that these arguments and results are objects: paths are always
dereferenced to objects when they are given as arguments to retrieval and
construction operators. The distinction is only significant for the update operator (Section 26.3.2), and for object sharing (Section 26.4).

Retrieval and construction operators are defined for each of the ADDL
type constructors. The retrieval operators allow to select a component of a
complex object. For example, for lists the *head* and *tail* operators have the
following generic types:

head: LIST OF type_i → type_i
tail: LIST OF type_i → LIST OF type_i

A generic type describes a class of possible types of a given form. It matches any type whose description is obtained by replacing the generic name (here *type_i*) by a type.

Get returns the range object associated to a given domain object in a mapping. *Select* retrieves components of an aggregate object. Their types are

> get: dom_type × (dom_type −− > ran_type) → ran_type
> select: sel_i × <sel_1: type_1, . . . , sel_n: type_n>→ type_i

The *root* operator returns the whole database value.

EXAMPLE 26.1.

Suppose that the example database contains the following facts. The user John has a home_directory. This directory contains a subdirectory named sources and this subdirectory contains the file named test1.c. For accessing the owner of this file and assigning it into the variable the_owner one could write:

```
the_owner := select(''owner'',
             get(''test1.c'',
                 get(''sources'',
                     get(''John'',
                         select(''users'',
                                root()))))))
```

The construction operators allow to build new complex objects. *Make* is a general operator for building a new complex object of a given type. The arguments of the make operator are a type expression defining the type of the resulting object, and the component objects. Thus, if the type expression denotes an aggregate, an aggregate containing the components (if they are of the appropriate type) is constructed.

EXAMPLE 26.2.

In the following code fragment a new file is constructed using the components the_owner (being the user_name defined in Example 26.1) and byte_x.

```
the_file := make(''file'',the_owner,byte_x)
```

The other construction operators are specific for each type constructor. For example, the types of the *add_to_set* and *del_from_set* operators are defined as

> add_to_set: type_i × SET OF type_i → SET OF type_i
> del_from_set: type_i × SET OF type_i → SET OF type_i

For mappings, the types of the *add_to_map* and *del_from_map* operators are

add_to_map: dom × ran × (dom → ran)   →   (dom → ran)
del_from_map: dom   × (dom −− > ran) →   dom −− > ran

The DML further includes higher-order operators (i.e., operators where one of the arguments is an operator). For example, the *apply_all* operator applies an operator on each component of a set (or list) and returns a set (or list) containing the resulting objects; the *select_if* operator selects in a set, list or mapping all the components satisfying a condition; the *exists* operator returns *true* if a predicate holds for at least one element of the argument set, list, or mapping, and so on.

26.3.2 The Update Operator

The operators defined in previous sections allow retrieval of components of complex objects and construction of new ones.

In principle, these operators allow the standard technique of applicative languages for "changing" an object, that is, the construction of a new object, generally with selected pieces of the old one. Since the whole database is just a complex object, an update of the database might be done by reconstructing it. However, besides being very impractical, the reconstruction of a new database also makes concurrent updates virtually impossible.

One thus clearly needs a way to perform updates by somehow modifying components of complex objects "in place."

The update operations that are offered in relational systems or in the functional data model [Kulkarni & Atkinson, 1986] essentially amount to inserting or deleting tuples (or domain-range pairs) into/from relations (or functions) whose names are given in the database schema. This approach is apparently not easily adaptable to the update of complex objects. Since complex objects correspond roughly to relations containing subrelations as domain elements, the particular instances of these subrelations obviously have no name in the database schema.

The style of update "in place" of many algorithmic languages, which consists of changing pointers and the contents of locations can not be adopted here. The ADDL data model used in COMS only makes use of values for representing the objects; it does not rely on notions such as pointers and locations for building complex structures.

The approach adopted in the design of the update operations consists in identifying an object with a retrieval expression and being able to replace the identified object with another one. The identification of the object to be updated has to play a role similar to the name of a relation in a relational schema, and should not expose internal names of the DBMS. *Paths* are used for identifying the object to be replaced. The retrieval and construction expressions introduced in the previous section return such *paths*. A path can—

as rough approximation—be compared to the programming language notion of pointer to a location. We will see that these paths are "pointers" only in terms of the structure and values of the complex objects, and that their fine semantics is different from that of pointers.

The update operation has the following form:

update(a_path, a_new_object)

where *a_path* denotes the object to be replaced by *a_new_object*. In fact, *a_path* and *a_new_object* are retrieval expressions, construction expressions, or program variables (i.e., *paths*). *Update* does not dereference its first argument, which somehow specifies where *a_new_object* must be stored. It does dereference its second argument.

The type of the *a_new_object* must match with the type defined in the database schema for the complex object being updated. *Update* returns its first argument.

EXAMPLE 26.3.

Suppose that we have the same database as in Example 26.1 and that we want to substitute the user ''Beth'' for the owner of the file test1.c. Using the variable the_owner defined in Example 26.1, the following update operation has to be issued:

```
update(the_owner,''Beth'')
```

Updates can be performed in the same way on the database as on program space objects. Note that up to this point, the automatic dereferencing of the second argument of *update* prevents the introduction of paths as component into objects. This is consistent with the automatic dereferencing of the arguments of the construction operations described in Section 26.3.1. Object sharing by storing paths as component objects is discussed in Section 26.4. The notion of path is discussed further below. Paths also play a central role in the locking machinery underlying the transaction mechanism (Sec. 26.3.4).

26.3.3 What Is in a Path

A path is a system representation of where an object is with respect to the objects of which it is a component; this representation is in terms of the (logical) structure and the value of the object. The paths have a nested structure that is parallel to the nested structure of the objects: A path denoting a component object of an object is the path denoting the object completed with a logical location of the component in the context of the object. If path P2 refers to a component of an object referred to by path P1, then P1 is called a *parent path* of P2, and P2 is called a *child path* of P1. The representation of a path is opaque to the user.

Given the example database whose schema is given in Section 26.2, the path assigned into p by

```
p := get(''John'', select(''users'', root()) )
```

contains information specifying a logical location that is reached from the root of the database, by accessing first the users component (of what can only be a database aggregate) and then the entry (in a directory mapping) whose domain element is ''John''.

The difference between a path and a traditional pointer to a machine location is illustrated in the following example update. Suppose one modifies the users mapping by constructing a whole new mapping and then replacing the old mapping by the newly created one:

```
update( select(''users'', root()),
    add_to_map( . . . , select(''users'', root()) ))
```

Since the add_to_map operation is purely a construction operation, it denotes a new object, which is likely to be made of different machine locations from the one existing in the database before the update operation. Traditional pointers to machine locations would, of course, become invalid in this case, whereas a path like the one assigned to p—being only in terms of logical information—remains valid. There are of course constraints; namely, in this case, the new mapping should still contain a ''John'' entry.

26.3.4 Transactions

Until now, DML operators have been discussed without taking into account consistency considerations when several users concurrently access and modify the database.

The operations *begin_transaction, end_transaction*, and *abort_transaction* delimit the transactions on the database. Access to database objects can be done only inside transactions.

The execution of retrieval operations automatically sets *read locks* on the returned objects; the execution of the update operation automatically sets *write locks* on the modified object. An operation fails if it does not succeed in setting the appropriate locks. Setting a read lock on an object means setting a read lock on the path referring to that object and on each parent path. A read lock can be set on a path if there is no other transaction holding a write lock on that path. Setting a write lock on an object means setting a write lock on the path referring to that object. A write lock can be set on a path if

1. No other transaction holds a read or write lock on that path.
2. No other transaction holds a write lock on a parent path of the path.
3. No other transaction holds a write lock on a child path of the path.

The above locking scheme is meant to ensure a good level of concurrency. It avoids one of the pitfalls when dealing with complex objects; Typically, when a transaction accesses a complex object, the object should not entirely become write-protected from other transactions. For example, if a transaction, say T1, holds a read lock on John's home directory, because it has just executed a retrieval operation such as

```
JohnDir:= get(''John'', select(''users'', root()) );
```

a concurrent transaction, say T2, can acquire a write lock for a component object of JohnDir, provided neither T1 nor any other transaction is seeing it, that is, holds a read (or write) lock on that component. T2 could thus concurrently execute

```
JohnDir:= get(''John'', select(''users'', root()) );
            update(get(''test.c'', JohnDir),
                    a_new_file_value);
```

One can exploit the path feature and the fact that the complex objects are represented in terms of values for further increasing the concurrency. The above basic locking scheme can be refined for coping with "bulk" updates, which are updates performed by reconstructing a whole object, rather than by directly identifying the fine components to be modified. Bulk or set-at-time operations are very natural in some applications, and are indeed encouraged by the very nature of the data model supported by COMS. However, the basic locking scheme restricts these bulk updates. For example, if a transaction has already obtained a read lock on an element of a mapping, another transaction will not be able to replace the whole mapping even if it does not modify the locked element.

The basic locking scheme can be extended in a way that can informally be described as follows. A transaction can acquire a write lock on a path on which another transaction already holds a lock, provided the update for which the write lock is requested does not invalidate paths for which locks already exist. In practice, this means that for the case of a mapping, the new mapping that would result from the update still has to contain the domain-range objects traversed by existing locked paths. A further extension to the basic locking scheme can be proposed for increasing the concurrency level when a whole mapping, list, or set is replaced by another one. It consists in not keeping a write lock on the whole mapping, set, or list; only the paths to component objects that have been modified, added, or removed by the update have to be locked.

Clearly, these extensions of the basic locking scheme are rather costly to support. They are considered an experimental feature. The authors believe that such mechanisms will prove useful in the context of engineering applications, where the ability for the system to deal gracefully with access conflicts in long transactions is precious, even if it comes at the expense of system resources.

26.3.5 Type Conversions

Subtypes

The subtype constructor offers the facilities necessary for representing hierarchical type structures. The general form of a subtype definition is

```
subtype : supertype
```

In the example of Section 26.2 the type home_directory is defined as a subtype of the type directory. Thus, the objects of type home_directory have the same structure as the objects of type directory. However, the type home_directory is more informative: An object of type home_directory is a special kind of a directory.

An operator defined on the type supertype can be applied on an operand of type subtype. This automatic type coercion can be repeated several levels down in a type-subtype hierarchy.

The type-subtype coercion ensures that an operator defined on a given type remains stable when subtypes of this type are introduced; that is, the operator can be applied on the objects of the subtype without having to be redefined.

In a structure, a part of type supertype can be updated with an object of type subtype, with the same automatic type coercion; the reverse is not true.

The make operator introduced in Section 26.3.1 can be used for enriching or specializing the type of an object. For example, if x is an object of type supertype, the expression make(subtype, x) returns an object of type subtype.

Union Types

Besides its importance for defining variant structures for the objects, type union is essential in the definition of objects with a recursive structure.

Given an expression whose type is a union of alternative types, the *discriminate* operator is applied on the expression operators that are different for each of the alternative types, thus allowing a return to static type checking (in the sense that one can statically ascertain that all the cases are treated, and that no run-time error due to type mismatch will occur). For example, if expr is of type (t1 OR t2), and expr_1 (resp. expr_2) is to be evaluated if expr is of the type t1 (resp. t2), then one will write

```
discriminate( expr,
              ''t1'', expr_1 ,
              ''t2'', expr_2 )
```

However, since use of *discriminate* proved in practice to become tedious for some applications, its mandatory use has been relaxed. An operator defined on an alternative type of a union type can be applied on an operand of the union type if it is of the appropriate alternative. In this case, type errors have to be detected at run-time. This automatic type coercion is very similar to the automatic type coercion defined for subtypes; that is, subtypes behave as "unary unions." For example, a closer look at Example 26.1 will reveal that this automatic type coercion is used for each of the operands of the *get* operator. The *get* operator is defined on mapping types; however, in the examples its operands, being of the union type (directory OR file), are coerced to the alternative mapping type directory.

The *discriminate* operator is difficult to integrate as such in languages that do not allow functions or procedures to control the evaluation of their arguments. For coping with such cases, a *type* operator, returning the type of its arguments, is provided; the if-then-else or case-like constructs of the host language can then be used instead of *discriminate*.

26.3.6 Basic Objects

The values of the host language are turned into basic COMS objects with the *make* operator. When there are no ambiguities due to type unions, the conversion is implicit. This conversion has implicitly been used in the examples given above. Example 26.3 without implicit conversion is

```
update(the_owner,
        make(''user_name'', ''Beth'') )
```

Paths to basic objects can be turned into host language values with the *val* operator.

26.4 SHARING COMPONENT OBJECTS

Since objects are represented by values, multiple occurrences of objects that were originally the same will evolve independently when they are updated. An object can for example be used as a component, say C, in different objects, say O1 and O2; updating C in O1 has no effect on the C component of O2. In order to have shared components, one must somehow support the storing of references to (shared) objects into objects.

A form of sharing, in the style of the relational model, can readily be achieved by using "key values" (i.e., objects that occur in the domain of some mapping) as components. The "shared" object is the corresponding range object in the mapping. However, the access to an object shared in this way remains the responsibility of the application program. For example, if there are different mappings with the same type of domain and range, the application program has to know in which one to look. This also means that the DBMS cannot guarantee any form of referential integrity for objects shared in this way.

To overcome these difficulties, object sharing is directly supported in the system in terms of *references*. The possibility (or necessity) for objects to contain *references* is declared in their type definition in the schema. For example, the type `directory` in the schema of Section 26.2 can be redefined as

```
directory : name --> (directory OR file OR REF file)
```

for indicating that a `directory` entry can also contain a reference to a `file`.

Only a simple form of referential integrity is supported: A referenced object cannot disappear. In other words, the reference to the shared object (a path) has to remain valid after any update operation. The shared object itself can, of course, be updated.

The paths, which are returned by retrieval and construction operations, can be turned into references with the *mkref* operator. References are typed, and the type checking rules mentioned in Section 26.3 apply to them as well.

EXAMPLE 26.4.

The following code fragment puts a reference to the `test.c` file found in John's home directory into Beth's home directory under the name `test.stat.c`:

```
users := select(''users'', root());
 file := get(''test.c'', get(''John'', users));
update( get(''Beth'', users),
        add_to_map(''test.stat.c'',
                   mkref(file),
                   get(''Beth'', users)) );
```

The retrieval operations applicable on an object of type *t* are also applicable on objects of type *REF t*; the dereferencing is automatic. When references are used in type unions as in the example definition of `directory`, it is possible to distinguish between a `file` and a `REF file` with the *discriminate* operator (Section 26.3.5).

References into database objects can be stored into program space objects and vice versa. For database objects, the appropriate address space conversions (internal to the DBMS) are done at the end of a transaction (see Section 26.3.4), when the updated objects are made visible to concurrent applications.

26.5 INTEGRATING THE DML OPERATIONS IN PROGRAMMING LANGUAGES

The basic principle on which the integration of the DML operations relies is to make them available in the host language as library functions. Of course, several concrete issues have to be resolved when doing so in different host languages. They include

1. The correspondence between the objects and the data of the host language, and more particularly the kind of data in the host language that is used for representing paths.
2. The strong typing of DML operations; this type system in general cannot be supported by the host language.
3. Adaptation of higher-order operations such as *apply_all* (Section 26.3.1), and *discriminate* (Section 26.3.5) to take into account specificities or limitations of the host language regarding the control of the evaluation of the parameters of functions.
4. The way run-time errors (type-checking errors, deadlocks, retrieval of nonexisting components, etc.) are handled.

We sketch the solution of these issues devised for the integration into two very different languages: Prolog and C.

In Prolog, the DML operations are represented as predicates, with an extra argument representing the result "returned" by the operation.

1. We impose the restriction that the COMS basic objects are atomic; they are Prolog atoms and numbers. The complex objects are always denoted by paths, which appear as Prolog compound terms. These compound terms are opaque in that they can only be "accessed" by the predicates that represent the DML operations.
2. There is no type checking in Prolog, so the type checking of the COMS operations, which is in essence static, has to be done dynamically by relying on type information contained in the internal representation of the complex objects.
3. The operations that are passed as arguments to predicates, such as *discriminate*, are predicate names.
4. In case of run-time errors, the predicates fail.

In Prolog the same predicates can be used for both retrieval and construction operators, depending on which argument is instantiated. For example:

```
make(Type_expr,Components,Object)
```

☐ denotes the construction operator if `Type_expr` and `Components` are instantiated, but

☐ denotes the retrieval operator returning the components of the given object if `Object` is instantiated.

In C, the DML operations are represented as library functions.

1. The C simple values correspond to COMS basic objects. The paths to complex objects are manipulated as pointers. The structures referred by these pointers are the system representation of paths; they are opaque to the user and are only to be accessed by the functions representing to the DML operations. These pointers can be passed as parameters to user-defined functions and can also be assigned in variables. The structured values of C, such as arrays and structures, could as well be used as "big" basic COMS values; they are atomic as far as COMS is concerned, and compound in C.

2. The type system of C is too weak to support the COMS type system. For instance, there is no way to define the type of a function such as *head* (Section 26.3.1) since this type is generic. Dynamic type checking of the operations similar to what is done at the Prolog interface is the simplest solution to implement. Apart from performance problems, it presents the drawback of not allowing the type checking of the user-defined functions to which COMS objects are passed. The feasibility of a static type checker for C programs embedding COMS operations has not been explored.

3. Pointers to functions can be passed as arguments to the functions implementing the higher-order operators.

4. The C library style of returning zero or negative values as error codes is used for the run-time errors. Errors propagate in nested expressions: Giving as argument an error code instead of a path produces an error.

26.6 CONCLUDING REMARKS

26.6.1 Call Interfaces and Integration

The style of the DML, whereby the objects returned by the operations can be directly used in other operations, makes the "integration" of the DML in host languages as functions calls look satisfactory. There are, however, drawbacks to this approach.

1. Complex DML expressions are always noted as function compositions, which look cumbersome to users accustomed to infix operators.

2. A lot of checks that are in essence static (e.g., type checking, use of database operations inside transactions) have to be performed dynamically.

These drawbacks would, of course, not exist if we had opted for the design of a new integrated language, or an extension of an existing one. The most important requirement fulfilled by the described DML operations is that they can easily be made available in different host languages. It should be stressed that this does not preclude the development of a fully integrated language. Such a development is particularly suited in contexts where a new dedicated language has to be designed anyway. Such a full integration is indeed currently examined for the command ("shell") language of a programming environment [Bernard et al., 1987].

26.6.2 Persistency

Our approach to persistency is very similar to PS-Algol [Atkinson et al., 1983]. The COMS persistent values are the components of the database value; in PS-Algol the persistent values are those that can be obtained from some kind of "Root object." If a distinction is made (as in [Buneman & Atkinson, 1986]) between a notion of persistency, which is a property of a type, and of particular values, the kind of persistency featured in COMS is the one associated with values. The same database types can be used for both persistent and nonpersistent values.

26.6.3 Transactions

The transaction mechanism defined in Section 26.3.4 shows how concurrent accesses to complex objects can be managed. It is, however, rather conventional in the sense that is does not take into account all the specificities of engineering transactions. As pointed out in [Haskin & Lorie, 1982], [Klahod et al., 1985], and [Kim et al., 1984], these engineering transactions have a long lifetime, touch a lot of data, are nested, and have to support teamwork. Further work includes the support of such engineering transactions in COMS (e.g., the addition of a *check-out* operator allowing one to explicitly put a write lock on an object, and the experimentation with a less restrictive locking mechanism permitting team members to see intermediate results).

26.6.4 Subtypes and Inheritance

Hierarchical type structures can be defined using subtypes. This structuring capability together with the automatic type coercion offers a facility similar to the one offered in object-oriented systems, where the methods defined on a class are inherited by all its subclasses. However, the modeling of the information specific to that subclass, by the addition of instance variables, is easier in object-oriented systems than in COMS.

26.6.5 References in Systems of the Relational Family

COMS supports an explicit reference mechanism, which coexists with the possibility to use "keys" of other objects as components of objects, in the very style of the Relational Model. The rationale for introducing the reference feature is that the relational style of dealing with references is not very practical for nested objects. In relational terms, a reference to an object typically has to be done with a varying number of "key attributes," depending on the depth at which the referenced object is nested. This difficulty is likely to be encountered in systems based on non-normal form relations that support the nesting of relations at arbitrary depths. The notion of reference proposed here is probably also usable for those systems.

A COMS reference might somehow be viewed as an internal representation of a query identifying the referenced object. This is another way of explaining the robustness of references against the reconstruction of objects into which they refer. Of course, the class of queries that correspond to references is limited. This view nevertheless suggests that systems allowing the storing of queries in the database as first class objects, like POSTGRES [Stonebraker & Rowe, 1986], implicitly have a reference mechanism at least as powerful as that of COMS. The use of a full-fledged query language for expressing references, however, poses new challenges for the maintenance of the referential integrity.

References

Atkinson, M. P., Bailey, P. J., Chisholm, K. J., Cockshott, P. W., and Morrison, R., (1983). "An Approach to Persistent Programming," *The Computer Journal*, Vol. 26, No. 4, pp. 360–365.

Bancilhon, F., and Khoshafian, F. S., (1986). "A Calculus for Complex Objects," *ACM SIGACT-SIGMOD Symposium on Principles of Database Systems*, Cambridge, Mass., pp. 53–59.

Bernard, Y., LaCroix, M., Lavency, P., and Vanhoedenaghe, M., (1987). "Configuration Management in an Open Environment," *Proceedings of the 1st European Software Engineering Conference*, Strasbourg, France, pp. 37–45.

Buneman, P., and Atkinson, M. P., (1986). "Inheritance and Persistence in Database Programming Languages," *Proceedings of the ACM-SIGMOD International Conference on Management of Data*, Washington, D.C., pp. 4–15.

Haskin, R. L., and Lorie, R. A., (1982). "On Extending the Functions of a Relational Database System," *Proceedings ACM-SIGMOD International Conference on Management of Data*, Orlando, Fla.

Kim, W., Lorie R., McNabb, D., and Plouffe, W., (1984). "A Transaction Mechanism for Engineering Design Databases," *Proceedings Tenth International Conference on Very Large Data Bases*, Singapore.

Klahold P., Schlageter, G., Unland, R., and Wilkes, W., (1985). "A Transaction Model Supporting Complex Applications in Integrated Information Systems," *Proceedings ACM-SIGMOD International Conference on Management of Data*, Austin, Texas.

Kulkarni, K. G., and Atkinson, M. P., (1986). "EFDM: Extended Functional Data Model," *The Computer Journal*, Vol. 29, No. 1, pp. 38–46.

LaCroix, M., and Pirotte, A., (1981). "Data Structures for CAD Object Description," *Proceedings 18th Design Automation Conference*, Nashville.

LaCroix, M., and Pirotte, A., (1983). "Comparison of Database Interfaces for Application Programming," *Information Systems*, Vol. 8, No. 3, pp. 217–229.

Stonebraker, M., and Rowe, L. A., (1986). "The Design of POSTGRES," *Proceedings ACM-SIGMOD International Conference on Management of Data*, Washington, D.C., pp. 340–355.